DRAMATIC VERSE 1973-1985

Also by Tony Harrison

POETRY

Earthworks (Northern House, 1964)
Newcastle in Peru (Eagle Press, 1969)
The Loiners (London Magazine Editions, 1970)
Palladas: Poems (Anvil Press Poetry, 1975)
From 'The School of Eloquence' and other poems
    (Rex Collings, 1978)
Continuous (Rex Collings, 1981)
A Kumquat for John Keats (Bloodaxe Books, 1981)
U.S. Martial (Bloodaxe Books, 1981)
Selected Poems (Penguin/Viking, 1984)
v. (Bloodaxe Books, 1985)
The Fire-Gap (Bloodaxe Books, 1985)

THEATRE

Aikin Mata [with James Simmons] (OUP, 1966)
The Misanthrope (Rex Collings, 1973)
Phaedra Britannica (Rex Collings, 1975)
Bow Down (Rex Collings, 1977)
The Passion (Rex Collings, 1977)
The Bartered Bride (G. Schirmer, 1978)
The Oresteia (Rex Collings, 1981)
The Mysteries (Faber, 1985)

DRAMATIC VERSE
1973-1985
TONY HARRISON

BLOODAXE BOOKS

First published 1985 by
Bloodaxe Books Ltd,
P.O. Box 1SN,
Newcastle upon Tyne NE99 1SN.

ISBN: 0 906427 81 9

Bloodaxe Books Ltd acknowledges
the financial assistance of Northern Arts.

Typesetting by True North, Newcastle upon Tyne.

Printed in Great Britain by
Tyneside Free Press Workshop Ltd, Newcastle upon Tyne.

I, *for instance, sometimes write*
Adaptations. Or some people prefer the phrase
'Based on', and this is how it is: I use
Old material to make a new play, then
Put under the title
The name of the dead writer who is extremely
Famous and quite unknown, and before
The name of the dead writer I put the little word 'After'
Then one group will write that I am
Very respectful and others that I am nothing of the sort and all
The dead writer's failures
Will be ascribed
To me and all my successes
To the dead writer who is extremely
Famous and quite unknown, and of whom
Nobody knows whether he himself
Was the writer or maybe the
Adaptor.

LION FEUCHTWANGER,
'Adaptations' (1924)
– written after collaborating with Brecht
on their version of 'Edward II' *after* Marlowe

Acknowledgements

These plays are fully covered by copyright and all applications for performing rights should be made to Fraser & Dunlop (Scripts) Ltd, 91 Regent Street, London W1R 8RU.

The Misanthrope (1973), *Phaedra Britannica* (1975), *Bow Down* (1977) and *The Oresteia* (1981) were first published by Rex Collings Ltd, to whom grateful acknowledgement is made. The text of *Bow Down* is the revised version used as the score of the libretto published by Universal Editions (London) Ltd in 1980. *The Bartered Bride* was first published by G. Schirmer, Inc., New York, in 1978. The other three plays are previously unpublished.

The jacket photographs show: *The Oresteia*, with the masked Barrie Rutter at Epidauros (main picture, Nobby Clark); *The Misanthrope*, with Diana Rigg and Alec McCowen (top inset, Zoe Dominic); *The Bartered Bride*, with Teresa Stratas and Jon Vickers (middle inset, Beth Bergman); *The Big H*, with Barrie Rutter (bottom inset, BBC copyright photograph); and Tony Harrison working with actors in a *Bow Down* rehearsal (back cover inset, Nobby Clark).

Contents

THE MISANTHROPE (1973)

THE MISANTHROPE

This version of Molière's *Le Misanthrope* was first produced by the National Theatre Company at the Old Vic on 22 February 1973 with the following cast:

ALCESTE	Alec McCowen
CELIMENE	Diana Rigg
ARSINOE	Gillian Barge
ACASTE	Nicholas Clay
CLITANDRE	Jeremy Clyde
ORONTE	Gawn Grainger
DUBOIS	James Hayes
PHILINTE	Alan MacNaughtan
ELIANTE	Jeanne Watts
SECRETARY OF THE ACADEMY	Clive Merrison
BASQUE	Paul Curran
PRODUCTION	John Dexter
SCENERY & COSTUMES	Tanya Moiseiwitsch
LIGHTING	Andy Phillips
MUSIC	Marc Wilkinson
STAGE MANAGER	Diana Boddington
DEPUTY STAGE MANAGER	Tony Walters
ASSISTANT STAGE MANAGERS	Elizabeth Markham
	Phil Robins
ASSISTANT TO PRODUCER	Harry Lomax

ACT ONE

ALCESTE *sits alone in darkness, listening to the music of Lully.*
PHILINTE *enters from the party in progress downstairs, switches on*
the light, sees ALCESTE, *and turns off the hi-fi.*

PHILINTE.
Now what is it? What's wrong?

ALCESTE.   O go away!

PHILINTE.
But what is it? What's wrong?

ALCESTE.   Please go away!

PHILINTE.
Alceste, please tell me what's got into you . . .

ALCESTE.
I said leave me alone. You spoil the view.

PHILINTE.
Don't start shouting and, please, hear people out.

ALCESTE.
No, why should I? And, if I like, I'll shout.

PHILINTE.
But why this typical 'splenetic fit'?
Though I'm your friend, I don't think friends permit . . .

ALCESTE.
Me, your friend? You can cross me off your list.
After what I've just clapped eyes on I insist
our friendship's finished. 'Friends' (so-called) who'll sell
their friendship everywhere can go to Hell.

PHILINTE.
Now that's not fair, Alceste. It's most unjust.

ALCESTE.
You should be mortified with self disgust.
There's no excuse for it. That sort of trick
revolts all decent men, and makes me sick.
Downstairs just now, what did I see you do?
You hoist your glass and hail, not hail, *halloo*
some person from a distance, and then zoom
into warm embraces from across the room,

drench the man with kisses, smile and swear
your lasting friendship, shout *mon cher, mon cher*
so many times you sounded quite inspired,
then when you sidled back and I inquired:
Who's that, the long-lost friend you rushed to hug?
all you do's look sheepish, and then shrug.
No sooner is his back turned than you start
picking him to pieces, pulling him apart,
all that 'friendship' faded from your heart.
It's foul and ignominious to betray
your own sincerity in this cheap way.
If, God forbid, it'd been me to blame,
I'd hang myself tomorrow out of shame.

PHILINTE.

O surely not! I think I'll just remit
your sentence this time, and not swing for it.

ALCESTE.

Don't think you'll soften me with that sweet smile.
Your humour's like your actions: infantile!

PHILINTE.

But seriously, what would you have me do?

ALCESTE.

Adopt behaviour both sincere and true.
Act like a decent man, and let words fall
only from the heart, or not at all.

PHILINTE.

But if a man shows friendship when you've met,
you should pay back the compliments you get,
and try as best you can to match his tone
and balance his good manners with your own.

ALCESTE.

Disgusting! Every modish socialite
bends over backwards to appear polite.
There's nothing I loathe more than empty grins
and cringing grimaces and wagging chins,
politeness mongers, charmers with two faces,
dabblers in nonsensical fine phrases,
outvying one another in their little game
of praise-me-I'll-praise-you. It's all the same
if you're idiot or hero. What's the good

of friendship and respect if it's bestowed
on any nincompoop and simpleton
your praiser-to-the-skies next happens on?
No! No! Not one right-thinking man, not one
'd want such ten-a-penny honours done.
Glittering praise can lose its brilliance
when we see it shared with half of France.
Esteem's based on a scale, it's not much worse
praising nothing than the universe.
You'll be no friend of mine if you comply
with these false manners of society.
From the bottom of my heart I must reject
that sort of indiscriminate respect.
If someone honours me I want it known
that it's an honour for myself alone.
Flinging love all over's *not* my line.
The 'buddy' of Mankind's no *friend* of mine.

PHILINTE.
But in society (if we belong that is)
we must conform to its civilities.

ALCESTE.
No, we must be merciless in our tirade
against this pseudo-civil masquerade.
Let real feelings shine out through our speech,
a deep sincerity where guile can't reach,
no pretty compliments, but true regard,
open, not hidden in some slick charade.

PHILINTE.
But there're times when speaking out one's mind
'd be ridiculous or plain unkind.
With all due deference to your strict code
there are occasions when restraint is good.
All kinds of social chaos would ensue
if everybody spoke his mind like you.
Supposing there's a man we can't abide,
do we say so, or keep our hate inside?

ALCESTE.
Say so, say so!

PHILINTE.   I see; and would you tell
Emilie (poor superannuated *belle*),

she's past all beauty, and a perfect scream
under the make-up and foundation cream?

ALCESTE.
Yes.

PHILINTE.
And Dorilas how much he bores us all
with how-I-won-back-France for Charles de Gaulle,
the Maquis mastermind who saved the war?
Would you say that to him?

ALCESTE.   I would, and more!

PHILINTE.
You're making fun of me.

ALCESTE.   *I don't make fun.*
In things like this I won't spare anyone.
The City, Politics, the Arts (so called!)
I've seen them all, Philinte, and I'm appalled.
Black rage comes over me, it makes me rave
seeing the dreadful way most men behave.
There's not a walk of life where you don't meet
flattery, injustice, selfishness, deceit.
I'm utterly exasperated and my mind
's made up, I'm finished, finished with mankind!

PHILINTE.
Your dark philosophy's too bleak by half.
Your moods of black despair just make me laugh.
I think by now I know you pretty well . . .
we're very like Ariste and Sganarelle,
the brothers in that thing by Molière,
you know, *The School of Husbands*, that one where . . .

ALCESTE.
For God's sake, spare us *Molière* quotations!

PHILINTE.
But, please, no more hell-fire denunciations!
The world's not going to change because of you.
You're fond of frankness . . . do you know it's true
that people snigger at this quirk of yours?
Everywhere you go, society guffaws.
Your fulminations on the age's lies
just make you seem comic in most men's eyes.

ALCESTE.
>So much the better! Comic in their sight?
>That only goes to prove that my way's right.
>Mankind's so low and loathsome in *my* eyes,
>I'd start to panic if it thought me wise.

PHILINTE.
>I think you'd write off all humanity!

ALCESTE.
>Because I hate them, all of them, that's why.

PHILINTE.
>We're living in bad times I know, that's true,
>but even so there *must* be just a few . . .

ALCESTE.
>A few? Not one! Not one a man can trust.
>The whole lot fill me with complete disgust.
>Some because they're vicious, all the rest
>because they nod at vice and aren't depressed
>or full of righteous anger at the thought
>of wickedness at large, as good men ought.
>It's taking tolerance to wild extremes
>to tolerate that swine and his low schemes,
>that awful, foul, objectionable swine –
>the one who's tried to grab this land of mine,
>whose trumped-up action's hauled me into court.
>*Cultivating* monsters of that sort!
>There's plainly a villain under that veneer.
>The truth of what he is is all too clear.
>Those sheepish humble looks, that sickly grin
>take only those who've never met him in.
>The guttersnipe! There's no one who can't guess
>the tricks he's stooped to for his quick success.
>The niche he's carved himself, in padded plush
>makes talent vomit and real virtue blush.
>Call him a bastard and everyone hoorays
>but he's still the blue-eyed boy of smart *soirées*.
>That grinning hypocrite, that nepotist's
>on all society reception lists.
>Despite his obvious and blatant flaws
>his smirk's his Sesame through *salon* doors.
>In rat-race intrigue he's a class apart
>straight to the post before his betters start.

When I see vice given its head I feel
the pity of it pierce me like cold steel.
In these moods what I want 's some wild retreat
where humanity and I need never meet.

PHILINTE.
A little understanding's what's required.
Humanity leaves much to be desired
I know that very well, but let's not rant
about its vices. Let's be tolerant.
Moderation's where true wisdom lies.
What we should be is *reasonably* wise.
You're living in the past. Diogenes
isn't quite the type for times like these.
All your harping on that ancient theme
strikes the modern age as too extreme.
Compromise; accommodate; don't force
your principles to run too stiff a course.
It's sheer, outrageous folly to pretend
you'll change things or imagine you'll amend
mankind's perversity one little jot.
You think your anger's wisdom, but it's not.
Like you I see a hundred things a day
that could be better, but I don't inveigh
against them angrily, and unlike you,
I've learnt to be tolerant of what men do,
I take them as they come, put up with them.
'Bile' 's no more philosophical than 'phlegm'.
In social intercourse the golden rule
's not curse, like you, but, like me 'keep one's cool'.

ALCESTE.
So, whatever vast disaster or mishap
you're philosophical and never flap?
If you were in my shoes and someone planned
to gain possession of your precious land;
betrayed you, slandered you, what then? What then?
Would you still show 'tolerance' for men?
Maligned, betrayed, and robbed! You'd be a fool
to watch all that occur and 'keep your cool'.

PHILINTE.
But when I see self-interest, graft, deceit,
when I see men swindle, steal, lie, cheat,

I feel about as much sense of dismay
as if I'd seen some beast devour its prey,
or if I'd watched, say, monkeys in the zoo
doing what monkeys are supposed to do.
All your diatribes are off the track.
It's basic human nature you attack.
That's your humanity. There's no escape.
These are the antics of the 'naked ape'.

ALCESTE.
So, I'm to see myself knocked down, laid low,
and torn to pieces, robbed and never . . . O
it's pointless talking and I'll say no more.

PHILINTE.
Calm down, Alceste. And turn your mind to law.
Your 'hypocrite', remember, and his suit.

ALCESTE.
But there's absolutely nothing to dispute.

PHILINTE.
But you've selected your solicitors?

ALCESTE.
Yes, reason and the justice of my cause.

PHILINTE.
And won't you pay the judge the usual visit?

ALCESTE.
No! I see, my case is doubtful is it?

PHILINTE.
Of course not, no, but if the man's in league
with others, then there's bound to be intrigue.

ALCESTE.
There's right and wrong. There's no two ways about it.

PHILINTE.
I wouldn't be too sure. I rather doubt it.

ALCESTE.
I won't budge an inch.

PHILINTE.   He will though; he'll plot
    your overthrow.

ALCESTE.   And if he does, so what?

PHILINTE.
    You'll find out you were wrong.

ALCESTE.   Let's see then, eh?

PHILINTE.
    But . . .

ALCESTE.   I'll gladly see the verdict go his way.

PHILINTE.
    You'll what! . . .

ALCESTE.   My adversary's success
    will only go to show man's wickedness.
    To prove men low enough to prostitute
    fair play, before the world, I'll lose my suit.

PHILINTE.
    What a man!

ALCESTE.   That satisfaction 'll be worth
    every penny, though it costs the earth.

PHILINTE.
    Alceste, people'll laugh and call you mad
    to hear you talk like that.

ALCESTE.   That's just too bad.

PHILINTE.
    Has the widow you're besotted by eschewed
    frivolity for your stern rectitude,
    this dug-out of ideals? Does Célimène
    share your strenuous moral regimen?
    I'm flabbergasted that, for one whose face
    seems to be turned against the human race,
    in spite of everything you say you hate,
    one member of it still can fascinate,
    and even more astonished by the one
    you've lavished this strange adoration on.
    Eliante, whose sincerity commands respect,
    who thinks of who most kindly, you reject.
    One most respectable Arsinoé,
    has feelings for you that are thrown away.
    And you love Célimène, whose acid skits

make her the reigning queen of bitchy wits,
a Jezebel, whose whole style typifies
those 'dreadful modern ways', that you despise.
Faults that in others you ruthlessly attack
in lovely Célimène don't seem so black.
Does beauty cancel them? Or don't you mind?
If you can't *see* her faults you must be blind.

ALCESTE.
Not blind! No, absolutely wide awake!
No standards lowered for the widow's sake.
Although I love her I'm the first to seize
on all her obvious infirmities.
But not withstanding those, in spite of all,
La Belle Dame sans Merci has me in thrall.
The rest is modishness, that's something I,
through my deep love for her, can purify.

PHILINTE.
That's no mean feat if you're successful. If!
And you're convinced she loves you?

ALCESTE   Positive!
I couldn't love her if she weren't sincere.

PHILINTE.
Then if her love for you 's so very clear.
why do your rivals cause you such distress?

ALCESTE.
True love desires uniquely to possess
its object, not go shares with other men.
That's what I've come to say to Célimène.

PHILINTE.
If I were you her cousin Eliante
'd be the sort of lover that I'd want;
she thinks a lot of you, that's very clear.
She's tender, frank, dependable, sincere.
Sincere, Alceste, which means she's so much more
the sort of person you've a weak spot for.

ALCESTE.
That's true, and reason tells me so each day.
But love won't function in a rational way.

PHILINTE.
I'm rather worried though that your affair's . . .

Enter ORONTE, *glass in hand, from the party downstairs.*

ORONTE.
Lovely party! Marvellous do downstairs!
(*To Alceste.*)
Heard you were up here, though, and thought what luck
to catch Alceste alone . . . I've read your book.
I know your essays backwards, read the lot!
We two should get acquainted better, what?
You really are a most distinguished man.
I love your work. Consider me your "fan".
Your talents draw my homage and applause.
I would so love to be a friend of yours.
Friendship with someone of my stamp and sort
's not to be sneezed at, really, I'd've thought.
Excuse me (*cough*) it's you I've been addressing,
(*Alceste looks surprised.*)
I'm sorry I can see that I'm distressing . . .

ALCESTE.
No, no, not in the least. It's just I'm dazed
to find myself so eloquently praised.

ORONTE.
It should be no surprise to hear your name
made much of; why, the whole world does the same!

ALCESTE.
Monsieur!

ORONTE.   Your reputation's nation-wide.
Not only I, all France is starry-eyed.

ALCESTE.
Monsieur!

ORONTE.   In my humble view, for what it's worth,
there's nobody quite like you on God's earth.

ALCESTE.
Monsieur!

ORONTE.   Let lightning flash and strike me dead
if there's the slightest lie in all I've said.
To show you let me demonstrate, like this,

Your hand, then, on our friendship, yours and mine!

ALCESTE.
Monsieur!

ORONTE.   Not interested? Do you decline?

ALCESTE.
The honour that you do me 's far too great.
Friendships develop at a slower rate.
It's the very name of friendship you profane
if you repeat the word like a refrain.
It's judgement, choice, consideration pave
the way to friendship and we can't behave
as if we're bosom friends until we've found
we actually share some common ground.
Our characters may prove so different.
We'd soon regret our rushed vows and repent.

ORONTE.
Excellently put! Your insight and good sense
just make my hero-worship more intense.
If time will make us friends I'll gladly wait,
but, in the meantime, please don't hesitate,
if there's anything at all that I can do,
Elyséewise, a place, an interview,
just say the word. Most people are aware
just what my standing is with those "up there".
There can't be many men much more *au fait*
with all that happens at the Elysée.
I'm "in" with those that matter, even HE
treats me like his own; yes, honestly!
So count on me to help you "oil the wheels".
Now, since you're an author, and a man who feels,
to inaugurate our friendship I'll recite
a little poem I've felt moved to write.
I'd welcome your reactions and some hint
on whether it seems good enough to print.
Perhaps you could suggest (I know it's cheek)
which editors you know are *sympathique*.

ALCESTE.
I'm afraid I'm not well-suited to the task.

ORONTE.
    O, not well-suited? Why's that may I ask?

ALCESTE.
    Frankness is my *forte*. I'm afraid you'd find
    I'm uncomfortably prone to speak my mind.

ORONTE.
    Frankness! Just what I ask. No, I insist.
    I'm not just looking for a eulogist.
    I've come expecting you to be quite straight.
    I'll feel resentful if you hesitate.
    I'm not afraid of, I demand sincerity.

ALCESTE.
    Since you insist, Monsieur, then yes, I'll try.

ORONTE.
    HOPE . . . it's about a girl, a little thing
    who's rather kept me dangling on a string.
    HOPE . . . just my inmost feelings, nothing planned.
    It's just as it came out you understand.

ALCESTE.
    Proceed!

ORONTE.   HOPE . . . what I'd really like to know 's
    if the intensity of feeling shows
    and if I've got the rhythm right, or wrong.

ALCESTE.
    Read it and we'll see.

ORONTE.   Didn't take me long.
    Not fifteen minutes. Came to me in bed.

ALCESTE.
    Time's immaterial. Please go ahead.

ORONTE.
    HOPE . . . that's the title, HOPE. Before I read . . .

ALCESTE.
    I think we've got the picture. Please proceed!

ORONTE. (*Reads.*)
    'Hope was assuaging:
    its glimmer
    cheered my gloomy pilgrimage

to the gold shrine of your love . . .

a mirage of water pool and palms
to a nomad lost in the Sahara . . .

but in the end it only makes thirst worse.'

PHILINTE.
That's rather touching. Yes. I like that bit.

ALCESTE. (*Aside.*)
How can you like that stuff, you hypocrite?

ORONTE. (*Reads.*)
'Darling, if this hot trek
to some phantasmal Mecca
of love's consummation
is some sort of Herculean labour
then I've fallen by the wayside.'

PHILINTE.
Intriguing, yes, I like your turn of phrase.

ALCESTE. (*Aside.*)
Flatterer! It's rubbish, not worth any praise.

ORONTE. (*Reads.*)
'A deeper, darker otherwhere
is unfulfilment . . .

we who have bathed in the lustrous light
of your charisma
now languish in miasmal black despair

and all we hopeless lovers share
the nightmare of the bathosphere.'

PHILINTE.
That 'dying fall!' It closes beautifully!

ALCESTE. (*Aside.*)
I wish *he'd* fall and break his neck and die
and cart his doggerel with him off to Hell.

PHILINTE.
I've never before heard verses . . . shaped . . . so well.

ALCESTE. (*Aside.*)
Good God!

ORONTE. (*To Philinte.*)
   It's just your kindness, I'm afraid.

PHILINTE.
 No, no!

ALCESTE. (*Aside.*)
   What is it then you . . . renegade!

ORONTE. (*To Alceste.*)
 What do *you* think? And don't forget your pact.
 Your frank opinion, mind. I don't want tact.

ALCESTE.
 It's very delicate. I think we'd all admit
 a need for flattery, at least a bit,
 when it's a question of our taste at stake.
 We must be careful just what line we take.
 I'll tell you something, though. One day I'd read
 a certain someone's verses and I said,
 'A man in your position *has* to know
 exactly to what lengths he ought to go
 and keep his itch to scribble well in hand.
 Poetry's a pastime, understand;
 one shouldn't go too far and let the thing
 get out of hand and think of publishing.
 The man who can't say no and who persists
 ends up a sitting duck for satirists.'

ORONTE.
 And just what is it that you're hinting at?
 That I waste my time?

ALCESTE.   No, I don't say that.
 What I told him was . . . I said, 'Now, look,
 nothing 's more humdrum than a boring book.
 It's the one thing people can't forgive.
 They'll always latch onto the negative.
 No matter what good qualities you've got,
 people'll judge you by your weakest spot.'

ORONTE.
 It *is* my poem that you're getting at!

ALCESTE.
 I wouldn't say that. No! I don't say that.
 I reminded him of men in our own times

who'd come to grief through turning out bad rhymes.

ORONTE.
   Do *I* write badly? Am I one of those men?

ALCESTE.
   I don't say that. This is what I hinted then.
   'Why write at all, unless the urge is bad,
   and if so, keep it to yourself, don't add
   more slim volumes to the mounds of verse.
   Writing's mad, but publishing's far worse.
   The only poets the public can forgive
   're those poor so-and-sos who write to live.
   Take my advice, resist the itch, resist
   the urge to star on some poor poetry list,
   to end up laughing stock and *salon* martyr,
   all for some private press's *imprimatur.*'
   That's the advice I tried to get across.

ORONTE.
   I take your point, but still I'm at a loss
   to know what 's in my poem . . .

ALCESTE.   Jesus wept!
   It's bloody rubbish, rhythmically inept,
   vacuous verbiage, wind, gas, guff.
   All lovestruck amateurs churn out that stuff.
   It's formless, slack, a nauseating sprawl,
   and riddled with stale clichés; that's not all.
   'Thirst worse' cacophonous, and those *'ek eks'*
   sound like a bullfrog in the throes of sex.
   Ah! terrible stuff gets written nowadays.
   Our ancestors, though crude in many ways,
   had better taste, and, honestly, I'd trade
   all modern verse for this old serenade!
      If Good King Harry said to me
      You may possess my gay Paree
      if you will send your love away,
      then this is what I'd say:
      Good King Harry, Sire, thankee
      for offering me your gay Paree,
      I'd liefer keep my love by far,
      yea, Sire, my love, tra-la!
   The rhyming's awkward, and the style's *passé.*
   but far better than the rubbish of today,

that pretentious gibberish you all admire.
Here speaks the true voice of desire:
  If Good King Harry said to me
  You may possess my gay Paree,
  if you will send your love away
  then this is what I'd say:
  Good King Harry, Sire, thankee
  for offering me your gay Paree.
  I'd liefer keep my love by far,
  yea, Sire, my love, tra-la!
There speaks the voice of true authentic passion
(*Oronte and Philinte laugh.*)
Mock on, mock on. In spite of current fashion.
I much prefer it to the flowery haze
and gaudy glitter all the critics praise.

ORONTE.
 And I maintain my poem's rather good.

ALCESTE.
 I suppose there's every reason why you should.
 You must excuse me if I can't agree.

ORONTE.
 That many others do 's enough for me.

ALCESTE.
 Yes, they can do what I can't, that's pretend.

ORONTE.
 Ah, so you're "an intellectual" my friend?

ALCESTE.
 You'd say so, if I praised your verse, no doubt.

ORONTE.
 Your praise is something I can do without.

ALCESTE.
 You'll have to, I'm afraid.

ORONTE.   I'd like to read
 a poem of your own dashed off at speed.

ALCESTE.
 Mine might be just as bad as yours, God knows,
 but I wouldn't shove the thing beneath your nose!

ORONTE.
> Such arrogance! I don't know how you dare . . .

ALCESTE.
> O, go and find your flattery elsewhere!

ORONTE.
> Now, little man, just watch your manners, please.

ALCESTE.
> Don't take that tone with me, you . . . Hercules!

PHILINTE.
> Gentlemen, enough. I beg you, please, no more.

ORONTE.
> Apologise for that behaviour, *or* . . .!

ALCESTE.
> You'll bring your famous 'influence' to bear?

ORONTE.
> And all I have to do is cross that square.

Exit ORONTE. PHILINTE *watches him go down the stairs and then pours two drinks. He begins to follow* ALCESTE *with them.*

PHILINTE.
> You see what your 'sincerity' can do?
> There's bound to be bad blood between you two.
> All the man wanted was a little pat.

ALCESTE.
> Don't talk to me.

PHILINTE.   But I . . .

ALCESTE.   Not after that!

PHILINTE.
> It's too . . .

ALCESTE.   Leave me alone.

PHILINTE.   If I . . .

ALCESTE.   No more, I say.

PHILINTE.
> But what . . .

ALCESTE.   *No more.*

PHILINTE.   But . . .

ALCESTE.   Still?

PHILINTE.   Is that the way . . .?

ALCESTE.
   O, stop following me about, you pest.

PHILINTE.
   I'd better keep my eye on you, Alceste.

PHILINTE *notices* CELIMENE *enter from downstairs.* He gives the 2
glasses of champagne to CELIMENE. Exit PHILINTE. CELIMENE
approaches the abstracted ALCESTE, *and clinks the glasses together.*
As ALCESTE *speaks* CELIMENE *drains first one glass, then the other.*

ALCESTE.
   I'll come straight to the point if you don't mind.
   There're things in your behaviour that I find
   quite reprehensible. In fact I'm so annoyed
   I honestly can't see how we'll avoid
   the inevitable break. I can't pretend –
   sooner or later this thing's bound to end.
   And if I swore my patience was unending
   reality'd soon prove I *was* pretending.

CELIMENE.
   So that's why you stormed off? I see. I see.
   Another moral lecture. (*Sigh.*) Poor me!

ALCESTE.
   It's not a moral lecture. (*Pause.*) Célimène
   you're rather too hospitable to men.
   Far too many swarm here round your door.
   I'm sorry, I can't stand it any more.

CELIMENE.
   Am I to blame if men can't keep away?
   I'm not the one who's leading them astray.
   They're sweet. They visit. What do you suggest?
   A mounted sentry, or an entrance test?

ALCESTE.
   No, not a sentry, but you might . . . well . . . mm
   temper the welcome you extend to them.
   I know that there's your beauty, and there's you,
   and that's one single entity, not two,

your beauty's something that you can't conceal,
a woman can't sequester sex-appeal –
one glance though from those eyes brings men to heel.
Then small attentions here, a favour there
keep all your hopefuls from complete despair.
The hopes you dangle out before them all
just help to keep them at your beck and call.
If, once or twice perhaps, you could say NO,
they'd take the hint alright, and they'd soon go.
But what I'd like to know 's what freak of luck's
helped to put Clitandre in your good books?
What amazing talents does the "thing" possess,
what sublimity of virtue? Let me guess.
I'm at a loss. Now let me see. *I know!*
It's his little finger like a *croissant*, so,
crooked at *Angelina's* where he sips his tea
among the titled queens of "gay" Paree!
What makes *him* captivate the social scene?
Second-skin gauchos in crêpe-de-chine?
Those golden blow-wave curls (that aren't his own)?
Those knickerbockers, or obsequious tone?
Or is it his giggle and his shrill falsett-
o hoity-toity voice makes him your pet?

CELIMENE.
You mustn't go on like this. It isn't fair.
Just why I lead him on you're well aware.
You know he's said he'd put in a good word
to get my lawsuit favourably heard.

ALCESTE.
Lose your lawsuit and have no cause to pander
to odious little pipsqueaks like Clitandre.

CELIMENE.
It grows and grows this jealousy of yours!

ALCESTE.
Those you let court you grow, so there's good cause.

CELIMENE.
Surely I'd've thought it wouldn't've mattered
to see my friendliness so widely scattered?
You'd really have much more to shout about
if there were only one I'd singled out.

ALCESTE.
> You blame me for my jealousy, but what,
> I ask you, sets *me* above that other lot?

CELIMENE.
> The joy of knowing that my love's for you.

ALCESTE.
> Yes, yes, but how can I be sure that's true?

CELIMENE.
> The simple fact I've told you that it's so
> should be enough, and all you need to know.

ALCESTE.
> But how can I be certain that you're not
> saying the same thing to that other lot?

CELIMENE.
> A pretty compliment that is, a fine way
> for a lover to be talking, I must say.
> To kill all your mad jealousies stone dead
> I take back everything that I just said.
> Now you won't need to worry any more.
> Satisfied?

ALCESTE.   God, what do I love you for?
> If I could only wriggle off the hook,
> I'd give thanks to the Lord and bless my luck.
> I've done everything I can to break this gaol
> and gain my freedom but to no avail.
> My efforts just don't get me anywhere.
> My love for you's a cross I've got to bear.

CELIMENE.
> It's certainly unique, I must admit.

ALCESTE.
> Nothing in the world compares with it.
> Imagination just can't plumb my heart.
> The love I bear for you 's a thing apart.

CELIMENE.
> It's the novel way you show it though, Alceste.
> All you seem to love for 's to protest.
> You can't tell crankiness and love apart.
> It's bloodymindedness that fires your heart.

ALCESTE.
Then give my 'bloodymindedness' some peace.
This wilful vacillation's got to cease.
Look, Célimène, there's just the two of us.
Let's use these precious moments to discuss . . .

Enter BASQUE.

BASQUE.
The marquis 's downstairs, Madame.

CELIMENE.   Which one?

BASQUE.   Acaste.

CELIMENE.
Then show the marquis up, please . . .

ALCESTE.   Damn and blast!

Exit BASQUE.

Can I never have two words with you alone
and must you be 'at home' to everyone?

CELIMENE.
I can't not see him. He'd be most upset.

ALCESTE.
I've never known you 'not see' people yet.

CELIMENE.
But he wouldn't come to see me any more
if he thought I thought he was a bore.

ALCESTE.
Would that matter so much, Célimène?

CELIMENE.
Alceste, we've *got* to cultivate such men.
They're influential people with a say
in big decisions at the Elysée.
Their tongues do nothing much by way of good
but their sharp edges can and do draw blood.
Whoever else you may have on your side
falling foul of that set 's suicide.

ALCESTE.
What you mean is, given half the chance,
you'd be at home to all the men in France,

    though all the arguments of reason show . . .

Enter BASQUE.

BASQUE.
    The *other* marquis, Ma'am.

ALCESTE. (*Making as if to leave.*)
                           Clitandre! O, no!

CELIMENE.
    And where're you going to?

ALCESTE.   I'm off.

CELIMENE.   No stay!

ALCESTE.
    Why?

CELIMENE. Please!

ALCESTE.   No!

CELIMENE.   For me?

ALCESTE.   No, I'm away!
    Unless you're really spoiling for a battle
    you'd want to spare me all their tittle-tattle.

CELIMENE.
    Please stay. I want you to.

ALCESTE.   I couldn't, no.

CELIMENE. O please do what you like, and, go, please, go!

ALCESTE *sits. Enter* ELIANTE *and* PHILINTE.

ELIANTE.
    They're coming up the stairs, the two marquis.
    Were you aware?

CELIMENE. (*Nodding, and to Basque.*)
               Champagne and glasses, please.
    (*To Alceste.*)
    Not gone yet?

ALCESTE.   No, not yet. I'm here to see
    you finally decide on them or me.

CELIMENE.
    Ssssshh!

ALCESTE.   Make up your mind. This very minute!

CELIMENE.
        Such madness!

ALCESTE.   Yes, but there's some method in it.

CELIMENE.
        Are you demanding I . . .

ALCESTE.   decide.

CELIMENE.   Decide?

ALCESTE.
        Decide. My patience has been more than tried.

Enter CLITANDRE *and* ACASTE.

CLITANDRE.   (*Still laughing and removing tie.*)
        We've been at a lateish evening 'over there'.
        Hilarious, (*kiss-kiss*) the whole affair!
        I was absolutely helpless. Who'd've thought
        Elysée functions could provide such sport?
        That old buffoon Cléonte convulsed 'the Court'
        until the table heaved with stifled laughs
        at his gauche manners and his social gaffes.
        Couldn't someone let him know that's *not* the way
        he'll get 'preferment' at the Elysée?

CELIMENE.
        That wine-stained tie he wears, those baggy breeches
        have everyone he meets at once in stitches.
        He never learns. He just gets more bizarre,
        adding new *faux pas* to his repertoire.

ACASTE.
        Talking of weird people, my head's sore
        after a session with the world's worst bore,
        blabbermouth Damon – on the street, my cab
        waiting at the kerbside; blab, blab, blab!

CELIMENE.
        When Damon's logorrhoea's in full spate
        he's like an LP played at 78,
        and all that comes across when Damon speaks
        is squeaking gibberish and high-pitched shrieks.

CLITANDRE *utters a high-pitched shriek.*

ELIANTE. (*To Philinte.*)
    What did I tell you. They're off to a good start,
    pulling their friends' characters apart.

ACASTE.
    And what about Timante? He's rather odd.

CELIMENE.
    Our cloak-and-dagger-ite! A grudging nod
    in passing 's all you get from that tin god,
    as though he'd got such urgent things to do
    he hadn't a second he could spare for you.
    It's all an act. If he's got news, it's *pssts*
    and sideways glances like stage anarchists.
    He'll halt a conversation in mid-word
    to whisper something hush-hush, and absurd.
    He looks around him, beckons you away,
    leans closer, cups his hands, and breathes: *Nice day!*

ACASTE.
    And Géralde?

CELIMENE.   Him? O, I've never been so bored!
    He'll only deign to mention a milord.
    Rank's his mania. His conversation runs
    on nothing else but horses, hounds and guns.
    The Almanach de Gotha, A to Z,
    he's learnt by heart and carries in his head.
    If anyone's got blood tinged slightly blue
    Géralde knows his first name and calls him *tu*.

CLITANDRE.
    He and Bélise are on good terms, I hear.

CELIMENE.
    Poor silly creature, and so dull. My dear,
    I suffer martyrdoms when she comes round.
    Getting conversations off the ground
    with her 's like slavery; one sweats and strains
    for subjects, honestly one racks one's brains
    but she's so unforthcoming, so half-dead,
    chat plummets to silence like a lump of lead.
    A little warmer? Turned out nice again!
    Chilly, don't you think? It looks like rain!
    gambits to break the ice with anyone
    but not Bélise; one sentence and she's done.

It's bad enough her visiting at all,
but dragged out half the day, intolerable.
Look at the clock, yawn, play the busy host,
she no more budges than a wooden post.

ACASTE.
Adraste?

CELIMENE.   An utter megalomaniac!
His conversation's just one long attack.
The 'foul Establishment' 's his constant theme
because it doesn't share his self-esteem.
How could the latest Government 've passed
him over, him, the great-I-am, Acaste?
The 'old-boy network', 'the incestuous set'
stops him starring in the Cabinet.
Something Machiavellian and underhand
prevents *his* being a power in the land.

CLITANDRE.
You've heard the trend? These days the rendezvous
for people who are "in" 's *chez* you-know-who.

CELIMENE.
But they only to to Cléon's for the food.

ELIANTE.
Cléon's cuisine though 's not to be pooh-poohed.

CELIMENE.
The dinner turns to sawdust on one's lips
when Cléon's served with everything, like chips.
He tells a boring story and you'd swear
the Château Mouton Rothschild 's *ordinaire*.

PHILINTE.
His uncle Damis though 's well spoken of.

CELIMENE.
Yes, we're friends.

PHILINTE.   He's sound and sensible enough.

CELIMENE.
Yeees! But exasperating nonetheless.
Those superior displays of cleverness!
He's like some sort of robot, stiff and slow,
and programmed only to repeat *bon mots*!

Since he's turned his mind to being a 'wit',
he's got 'good taste' and nothing pleases it.
He's supercilious about new plays.
The critic is the man who won't show praise;
only idiots laugh, and fools applaud;
the clever thing to be 's blasé and bored.
His weekly condescending book review
's never about the books but his I.Q.
Ordinary smalltalk too he quibbles at.
He's far too exalted for that sort of chat.

ACASTE.
Yes, dammit, yes, that's Damis to a tee.

CLITANDRE.
You're marvellous. I love your mimicry.

ALCESTE.
Go on, go on, and give the knife more twists.
You socialites are such brave satirists
behind men's backs. If one showed up, you'd rush
to greet the man effusively and crush
him to your bosom in a false embrace
and only say *enchanté* to his face.

CLITANDRE.
Why pick on us, Alceste? You should address
your disapproval to our kind hostess.

ALCESTE.
No, dammit, no! It's you two that I blame.
Your fawning makes her slander men's good name.
The lady's gifted with malicious wit,
but it's your flattery that fosters it.
Once she finds there's no one to applaud
her badinage she'll soon enough get bored.
Most infringement of the moral code's
the fault of sycophants and fawning toads.

PHILINTE.
Why take up their cause? You yourself condemn
the frailties we criticise in them.

CELIMENE.
His whole life-style depends on saying no.
Alceste, agree? He'd never stoop so low.

No! Mustn't he go on proving he was born
under the stars of dissidence and scorn?
He's not one of us, no, not Alceste;
not wanting to seem so makes him protest.
He's contradictory in every way;
when all the rest are AYES, he's always NAY,
so contradictory he's even peeved
once his own ideas 've been believed.
When someone else has held them he's been known
to demolish opinions that *were* his own.

Laughter.

ALCESTE.
They're on your side. You're safe. Go on, enjoy
the public torture of your whipping boy!

PHILINTE.
But isn't she half-right? It is your way
to contradict whatever people say.
No matter what *their* feelings, pro or con,
it's always the opposition that you're on.

ALCESTE.
Because they're always so far off the track,
I always have good grounds for my attack.
They sometimes flatter and they sometimes sneer,
either shameless and corrupt, or cavalier.

CELIMENE.
But . . .

ALCESTE.   But nothing, though it's the end of me,
I've got to say I hate your repartee.
These people only wrong you when they fawn
on flaws like yours which secretly they scorn.

CLITANDRE.
Speaking for myself, I really wouldn't know.
I've always found her perfectly just so.

ACASTE.
The most charming lady that I've ever met.
I haven't noticed any defects yet!

ALCESTE.
I've noticed plenty, *and* I'm not afraid

of saying so. I call a spade a spade.
If loving someone deeply means you creep,
if love means criticism 's put to sleep,
keep it. That may be love for such as you;
it's not the sort of love that I call true.
I'd banish those wet lovers who kow-towed
to every half-baked thought I spoke aloud,
who laughed at my bad jokes, who cheered my views,
who treated last year's gossip as hot news,
'worshipped the very ground on which I trod'
and grovelled to my whims, as if I'm God.

CELIMENE.
    And if you had your way, my dear Alceste,
    we'd say our keenest critics loved us best.
    Sweet-talk's finished, kindness is no use.
    The surest sign of love is foul abuse.

ELIANTE.
    How does that bit in old Lucretius go,
    that bit on blinkered lovers? O, you know;
    it's something like: 'whatever's negative's
    soon metamorphosed by new adjectives:
    the girl whose face is pinched and deathly white
    's not plain anaemic, she's "pre-Raphaelite".
    The loved one's figure's like Venus de Milo's –
    even the girl who weighs a hundred kilos!
    "Earth Mother" 's how some doting lover dubs
    his monstrous mistress with enormous bubs.
    "A touch of tarbrush?" No, that's healthy tan.
    The one called "Junoesque" 's more like a man.
    The slut's "Bohemian", the dwarf's virtue
    's *multum in parvo* like a good haiku.
    There's "self respect" for arrogant conceit.
    The windbag's extrovert, the dumb's "discreet";
    stupidity's "good nature", slyness "wit",'
    et cetera . . . it's not inapposite!

ALCESTE.
    But *I* . . .

CELIMENE.   I think we've heard enough from you.
    Come to the balcony and see my view.
    (*To Acaste and Clitandre.*)
    Going already, gentlemen?

ACASTE.   No!

CLITANDRE.   No!

ALCESTE. (*To Célimène.*)
    You seem to be worrying in case they go.
    (*To Acaste and Clitandre.*)
    Go when you like. But let me make this clear.
    When you decide to go, I'll still be here.

ACASTE.
    Unless our hostess thinks I'm in the way.
    I'm absolutely free.

CLITANDRE.   And *I* can stay.

CELIMENE.
    Is this your notion of a joke, Alceste.

ALCESTE.
    I want to see whose presence suits you best.

Enter BASQUE.

BASQUE. (*To Alceste.*)
    Sir, there's a man downstairs 'd like a word.
    Says it's important. Not to be deferred!

ALCESTE.
    There's nothing I'm aware of that can't wait.

BASQUE.
    Something about a 'feud' to arbitrate.
    Perhaps I should say, sir, the person *says*
    he's official, sir. *Académie Française.*
    I'd say myself he's *bona fide*, sir:
    the car's a black one with a tricolour.

Enter OFFICIAL *of the Académie Française.*

ALCESTE.
    They tell me that you're from the *Académ* –

OFFICIAL.
    – *ie Française*, indeed, sir, yes.

ALCESTE.   Well, here I am.

OFFICIAL.
    It's just a word or two, sir, in your ear.

ALCESTE.
>Then out with it, dear fellow, loud and clear.

OFFICIAL.
>The *Académie Française*, whose Members are . . .

ALCESTE.
>At midnight?

OFFICIAL.   . . . taking their brandy and cigar
>at *Maxim's*, sir, wondered if you've time to spare.
>There's a little matter that they'd like to air.

ALCESTE.
>So late?

OFFICIAL.   If you don't mind.

ALCESTE.   What can they want?

PHILINTE.
>It's that ridiculous business with Oronte.

CELIMENE. (*To Philinte.*)
>What's this?

PHILINTE.   O, he was his usual self about
>a poem of Oronte's and they fell out.
>The sort of private row they like to handle.
>They don't like media creating scandal.
>They simply want to stop it getting worse.

ALCESTE.
>No compromise. I refuse to praise his verse!

PHILINTE.
>Alceste! It is the *Academicians* though!
>I'll come with you. Come on. We'd better go.

ALCESTE.
>If they suppose they're going to persuade . . .
>to . . . somehow . . . change my mind, then I'm afraid,
>with all due deference to those gentlemen,
>the *Académie Française* can think again.
>Admire his poem? No, I'm adamant.
>His verse is vile. I can't and won't recant.

PHILINTE.
>But couldn't you try to be a little . . .

ALCESTE.   No!
It's dreadful and I'll go on saying so.

PHILINTE.
You ought to be a little more accommodating.
Let's go. We mustn't keep the Members waiting.

ALCESTE.
I'll go but nothing will induce me to . . .

PHILINTE.
We must go *now*, Alceste. But couldn't you . . .?

ALCESTE.
Listen, only a Special Powers Act
passed by the Elysée 'd make me retract,
but, otherwise, whatever Paris thinks,
I'll go on saying that his poem stinks.
The author of that poem should've been
beheaded for it on the Guillotine.
(*Laughter.*)
Dammit, I wasn't aware my words could cause
such wild amusement and inane guffaws.

CELIMENE.
Go, at once.

ALCESTE.   Yes, but I'll be back again
to finish off *our* business, Célimène.

Exit ALCESTE. CLITANDRE *and* ACASTE *continue laughing for some moments.*

CLITANDRE.
Mon cher Marquis, you positively beam
with untroubled *joie-de-vivre*, and self-esteem.
But, frankly, do you really have good cause
for this wide-eyed complacency of yours?

ACASTE.
Well, all things considered, I fail to see
the slightest cause at all for misery.
I'm young and healthy, rich, my blood's as blue
as any in all France can lay claim to.
Connections help, and when your family tree 's
as illustrious as mine it guarantees
an open *entrée* into most careers:

the Diplomatic Corps, the Grenadiers,
and, if I fancied, my family could fix
some cushy sinecure in politics.
My nonchalant panache, my poise, my flair
shine both in *salons* and the open air:
I've ridden, skied, played polo, fenced
better than any I've been matched against.
I've a lot of talents! And as for wit,
though I say so myself, I've heaps of it.
Impromptu apothegms and suave *bon goût*
got me my column in the right review.
First-night audiences at all new plays
hold back their condemnation or their praise
until they've read 'Acaste's piece', *then* they know
just what the reactions are they ought to show.
I'm the arbiter. If I'm bored, they're bored,
and if I write SEE THIS the sheep applaud.
Assured and polished and a handsome creature
(my teeth, I think my most outstanding feature)
my sportman's figure and my splendid gear
easily made me *Best Dressed Man* last year.
Where women are concerned I get my way.
I'm *persona grata* at the Elysée.
Comb Europe if you like. You'd be hard put
to find anyone at all so fortunate.
Honestly I couldn't, even if I tried
feel any other way but satisfied.

CLITANDRE.
The whole word's at your feet. I wonder you
waste time here as often as you do.

ACASTE.
I wouldn't dream of coming to pay court
in vain; I'm afraid I'm not that sort.
I leave all that for chappies less endowed –
'to burn for beauties pitiless and proud',
to languish at their feet, and to submit
to haughty treatment. I'll have none of it.
Your half-baked lovers in the end resort
to sighs and blubbing when they're paying court,
and hope to gain, by laying siege with tears,
what merit couldn't in a thousand years.
But pukka men like me, sir, don't fork out

their love on credit and then go without.
All women have their value, men as well
fetch market prices when they want to sell.
If a woman wants to boast she's made a kill
and bagged my heart. All right! She'll foot the bill.
One has to strike a bargain, and to make
the scale weigh even, give and *take.*

CLITANDRE.
You think you stand a chance the way things go?

ACASTE.
I've pretty good reasons for believing so.

CLITANDRE.
I wouldn't be too sure. You've got it wrong.
It's just been wishful thinking all along.

ACASTE.
That's right, wrong all along, Clitandre.
And to think it's only now the truth has dawned.

CLITANDRE.
You're sure?

ACASTE. No, I've been wrong!

CLITANDRE. But can you prove . . .

ACASTE.
Wrong, all along!

CLITANDRE. Has she confessed her love?

ACASTE.
No, she treats me badly . . .

CLITANDRE. No, really, please!

ACASTE.
Cold shoulder only.

CLITANDRE. Acaste, please don't tease.
What signs *has* she given? Or are there none?

ACASTE.
None. I'm rejected. You're the lucky one.
She really hates me. Yes, my only hope
's oblivion; poison or a length of rope.

CLITANDRE.
>   O balls! This quarrelling's no earthly use.
>   What I suggest we need 's to make a truce.
>   Then if, for example, I get some sure sign
>   that Célimène's decided she'll be mine,
>   or you, I suppose, that she'll be yours,
>   the one not chosen graciously withdraws,
>   and lets the favourite take a few lengths lead.

ACASTE.
>   Absolutely! A bargain! Yes, agreed!
>   But sshhh . . .

Enter CELIMENE.

CELIMENE.   Still here?

CLITANDRE.   Love roots us to the spot.

ACASTE.
>   Was that a car I heard downstairs, or not?

CELIMENE.
>   Yes, guess who's turned up now? Arsinoé!
>   I had been hoping that she'd stay away.
>   The darling's downstairs now with Eliante.
>   What's on her mind this time? What can she want?

ACASTE.
>   Prim and proper isn't she, Arsinoé?
>   Prudish and puritan, or so they say.

CELIMENE.
>   It's all hypocrisy. I'm not impressed.
>   At heart she's just as randy as the rest.
>   All that disdainful holier-than-thou
>   hides nothing more holy than a sacred cow.
>   She *longs* to get her hooks into a man,
>   but, however hard she tries, she never can.
>   The sight of others' lovers make her green
>   with jealousy and so '*the world's obscene*',
>   she says, '*the age is blind*' (that's to herself)
>   because she knows that she's left on the shelf.
>   Her role as puritan's transparent cover
>   for her frustrated life without a lover.
>   She brands all beauty sinful. She's afraid

it puts her feeble 'charms' into the shade.
She'd like a lover, that's what she'd like best,
even (can you imagine it?) Alceste!
If Alceste's nice to me, she's got the nerve
to think I'm trespassing on *her* preserve.
She's so envious, poor dear, she takes delight
in doing me down to others out of spite.
Prim and proper is she. O that's rich.
She's stupid, rude . . . in fact a perfect . . . Dar-

Enter ARSINOE.

-ling! I was worried for you. Here you are!
Nice to see you, Arsinoé, my dear!

ARSINOE.
It's something that I think you ought to hear.

CELIMENE.
It's good you've come.

Exeunt ACASTE *and* CLITANDRE *laughing.*

ARSINOE.   It's just as well they've gone.

CELIMENE.
A drink?

ARSINOE.   No, thank you! I've no need of one.
I've always thought true friendship shows up best
and puts sincerity to the surest test
in matters of most importance, such as things
touching on a friend's good name, which brings
me here in haste and genuine concern
to do you and your honour a good turn.
Yesterday I called on people known
for their principles and high moral tone
whose conversation soon came round to you;
your conduct and the scandals that ensue
were not thought proper I'm afraid to say:
the crowds that flock here almost every day
and you encourage, your flirtatiousness,
the goings on, found censure in excess
of what was just. Of course, you'll be aware
whose side I was on in this affair!
I did everything I could to justify
your good intentions and sincerity,

but, as you well know, even for a friend,
there are some things one simply can't defend,
and even I, reluctantly, confessed
your style of living wasn't of the best.
People imagine things (you know how it is).
They see so many "improprieties".
One does hear rumours, dear, but if you chose,
an effort at reform could soon scotch those.
Not that I believe you've gone too far,
God forbid! Well, you know what people are!
They think the slightest rumour's proof of blame.
One must be good in deed as well as name.
I know you'll take this warning as well-meant,
a token only of my good intent.
Think about the things I recommend.
Believe me, I speak only as a friend.

CELIMENE.

Honestly, I'm grateful for your kind concern,
so grateful, let me straightaway return
the favour done me, and, since you've been so nice,
let me offer *you* some good advice.
I'm very grateful, not at all upset.
Honestly, you've put me in your debt.
The friendship that you proved when you related
all this gossip, now must be reciprocated.
In distinguished company the other day
a discussion started on the proper way
for people to live lives of rectitude.
Your name came up at once: '*That prude,*'
said one, '*she's over-zealous, far too keen*
to be the sort of model that I mean.'
'*Pious fraud,*' said one, another '*pseud!*'
plus something unrepeatable and pretty lewd.
Nobody found it in him to excuse
the pompous shambles of your moral views,
that coy blush, that clearly put-on pout
whenever a few bad words get flung about,
that prissy, patently transparent, *moue*
even if the air's turned slightly blue,
that scornful high-horse manner you employ
in all your dealings with the *hoi polloi.*
Your bitter killjoy sermons that resent

everything that's pure and innocent.
One who professes such concern for God
doesn't go to Mass dressed *à la mode!*
(Their words, not mine) and one who seems so pure
shouldn't spend so much on *haute couture.*
And someone who devotes herself to prayer
reads a Bible, not *Elle* and *Marie Claire.*
She looks like Lady Pious when she prays
but not to the maids she beats and underpays.
She'd daub a fig leaf on a Rubens nude
but with a naked *man* she's not a prude.
I sprang to your defence as best I could,
naturally, but I couldn't do much good.
Denounced their talk as scandal, but no use,
just one good word against so much abuse.
They all ganged up against me. In the end
they came to this conclusion, my dear friend:
Best leave the sins of others well alone
until you've made some headway with your own.
Only a long self-searching can equip
someone to be the age's scourge and whip.
And even then reform's best left to them
ordained by God almighty to condemn.
'I know *you'll* take this warning as well-meant,
a token only of my good intent.
Think about the things I recommend.
Believe me I speak only as a friend.'

ARSINOE.
One lays oneself wide open when one tries,
however constructively, to criticise,
but if this is the reaction that I get,
I can see how deeply that you've been upset.

CELIMENE.
No, not at all. It might be a good thing
if everyone took up this 'counselling'.
Frankness may well open people's eyes
to those parts of themselves they fantasize,
their self-deceptions and their vanities.
We ought to make these little talks routine,
a, say, weekly survey of the social scene.
The latest tittle-tattle, all the chat,
the two of us swap gossip, tit for tat?

ARSINOE.
>Not much gossip about you comes to my ears.
>I'm the usual target for their sneers.

CELIMENE.
>We celebrate, we praise; we scorn, we scold,
>and all depending if we're young or old.
>When young, we love, then later we abide
>by decorum and act all dignified.
>And dignity, I gather, 's no bad ploy
>when you've got no more youth left to enjoy.
>I've heard it helps a woman sublimate
>her inability to snare a mate,
>and earns her pure frustration a good name.
>When I'm your age I may well do the same
>and cultivate your scorn of 'turpitude'.
>But twenty 's far too soon to be a prude.

ARSINOE.
>A trivial advantage! No cause to shout
>and nothing to get so uppity about.
>What difference there is gives you no cause
>to brag so rudely of this 'youth' of yours.
>But why this tizzy? I'm really at a loss
>to know why you flare up and get so cross.

CELIMENE.
>And I, my dear, have no idea why
>you should criticise me in society.
>It's not my fault, that I should bear the brunt
>of all your spinsterish impoverishment.
>There's nothing I can do to change the fact
>that lovers want me or my looks attract.
>I sympathise. But, look, Arsinoé,
>the field's wide open. No one's in your way.

ARSINOE.
>As if one cared about your lovers. Pooh!
>I don't care what great packs sniff after you.
>As if your lovers could make me upset.
>Lovers aren't so difficult to get.
>If a woman seeks attention, and success,
>one knows the price she pays, O, dear me, yes.
>Is men's "pure love" entirely what it seems?
>Is it your "character" what fills their dreams?

I doubt it very much. We're all aware
just what you're getting up to everywhere.
There're many women I know well endowed
with all a man could wish, but there's no crowd
of lovers yapping all hours at *their* door.
So what, we ask ourselves, are men here for?
The conclusion that we come to straightaway 's:
Those conquests? Elementary! *She pays.*
It's not for your sweet smile that men come here.
Your little victories must cost you dear.
Don't flaunt your petty triumphs out of spite,
or think your looks give you some sort of right
to sneer at others. God, if anyone
were envious of the victories you've won,
she could, by flinging caution to the wind
like you, get lovers, if she had the mind.

CELIMENE.
Then do! Then do! Ha! Ha! I do believe
you've got some secret weapon up your . . . sleeve.

ARSINOE.
I think we'd better leave things as they are,
or one of us I'm sure 'll go too far.
Believe me, if I hadn't had to wait,
I'd've gone much sooner, but my driver's late.

CELIMENE.
You know you're welcome, dear Arsinoé.
Please don't imagine you must dash away.
And, O how very timely, that Alceste's
come back again. I *must* attend my guests.
I'm sure you won't feel sorry if I go.

Enter ALCESTE.

I must see what they're doing down below.
Alceste, dear, entertain Arsinoé,
then she won't think me rude if I don't stay.

Exit CELIMENE.

ARSINOE.
So! We're left together for a little chat!
You know, I don't at all object to that.
She couldn't've done better if she'd tried.

I'm overjoyed our visits coincide.
You must realise, Alceste, a woman finds
a lot to love and honour in fine minds.
When I contemplate your gifts, I must confess
I feel immense concern for your success.
But you're neglected and the Powers-that-be
've passed you over, I think, shamefully.

ALCESTE.

I don't see why the State should condescend
to honour me. What for? I can't pretend
I've rendered any service; so why fret?
There's nothing that I've done they *can* forget.

ARSINOE.

Not everybody honoured by the State
's done something stirring to commemorate.
Know-how counts, the right time and right place.
That your talents 're passed over 's a disgrace.

ALCESTE.

My talents! Nothing there to shout about.
I'm very sure that France gets by without.
You can't expect the Powers-that-be to ferret
men's buried talents out and dig for merit.

ARSINOE.

Real talent doesn't need it. It's with good cause
that certain people set high store by yours.
Yesterday I heard your praises sung
in two high circles of the topmost rung.

ALCESTE.

There's so much sheer confusion nowadays,
everybody gets fair shares of praise.
It makes the greatest honours seem quite petty
when they're flung about like cheap confetti.
Anyone at all! the lowest of the low
get picture-profiles in *Le Figaro*.

ARSINOE.

If only Politics attracted you,
then your great talents 'd receive their due.
The slightest glimmerings of interest!
Just say the word and I could do the rest.
I've got good friends who'd easily ensure

you got promotion or a sinecure.

ALCESTE.

And what would I do, ME, among such sham.
I shun such places. It's the way I am.
Politics! I'm afraid I'm just not suited.
My lungs can't breathe an air that's so polluted.
I just don't have the qualities of guile
to cut a figure there or "make my pile".
The thing I'm best at 's saying what I mean
not double-talk and -think, and saccharine.
The man who can't tell lies won't last two ticks
in the suave chicanery of politics.
I'm well aware that people who aren't "in"
don't get their ribbons and their bits of tin.
What sort of title could 'the Court' confer
on perfect candour? Mm? *Légion d'Honneur?*
But there are advantages – one needn't grovel
or praise the Minister's most recent novel
or be some *grande dame*'s lap dog, or applaud
the so-called humour of some other fraud.

ARSINOE.

Well, if you wish, let's leave the matter there.
What worries me far more though 's your affair.
Quite frankly and sincerely I'd prefer
your heart bestowed on anyone but *her*.
You deserve far better, someone far above
the creature you've entrusted with your love.

ALCESTE.

Think of what you're saying. You pretend
to be the woman that you slander 's friend . . .

ARSINOE.

I know, but I feel affronted, hurt, and sad,
to see the sufferings your poor heart 's had.
I feel for you, my friend, but I'm afraid
I have to tell you that your trust's betrayed.

ALCESTE.

Thank you! I appreciate your kind concern.
It's things like that a lover wants to learn!

ARSINOE.

My friend she may be, but I've got say

a fine man like yourself 's just thrown away
on one like Célimène whose love's all show.

ALCESTE.
>You may be right. I really wouldn't know
>what goes on in people's hearts. But it's unkind
>to put suspicious thoughts into my mind.

ARSINOE.
>Of course, if you're quite happy to remain
>deceived, there's nothing simpler. I'll refrain.

ALCESTE.
>No, but innuendoes I can do without.
>There's nothing more tormenting than half-doubt.
>And I'd be far more grateful if you tried
>to tell me facts that could be verified.

ARSINOE.
>Very well, that's good enough for me!
>I'll give you evidence that you can *see*.
>Come with me to my house and there I'll give,
>once and for all, I hope, proof positive
>of the infidelities of Célimène.
>Then, if you ever feel like love again,
>if may be that Arsinoé can find
>some far gentler way of being kind.

Exeunt ALCESTE *and* ARSINOE.

ACT TWO

Enter ELIANTE *and* PHILINTE.

PHILINTE.
>   Never in my life, never have I met
>   a man so stubborn and so obstinate.
>   We thought we'd have all night to stand about
>   before this weird affair got sorted out.
>   Academicians can't have ever heard
>   another case so trivial and absurd;
>   tried everything they knew to budge Alceste,
>   but, at each attempt to shift him, he'd protest:
>   *No, gentlemen,* he says, *No, absolutely not!*
>   *I won't take back a thing. No, not one jot.*
>   *What is it that he wants my praises for?*
>   *Recommendation for the Prix Goncourt?*
>   *It's no dishonour that he can't write well.*
>   *One can be bad and still respectable.*
>   *A man of great distinction in his way,*
>   *brave and brilliant, but* not *Corneille!*
>   *His style of living's lavish, and, of course,*
>   *he looks magnificent astride a horse;*
>   *he's marvellous in many, many ways –*
>   *I'll praise his grand munificence, I'll praise*
>   *his expert fencing and his spry "gavotte"*
>   *but his poetry, no, absolutely not.*
>   *That sort of doggerel, slapdash and slipshod*
>   *'s best read aloud – before a firing squad!*
>   After fresh persuasions and more parley
>   the Members brought him to a grudged finale,
>   and almost had to go down on their knees!
>   This was his concession: *I'm hard to please.*
>   *I'm sorry I'm so grudging with my praise.*
>   (Collapse of stout Académie Française!)
>   *Believe me* (to Oronte), *how very sad*
>   *it makes me* here *to say your poem's bad!*
>   On that the two shook hands. M. Malraux
>   seemed heartily relieved to see him go.

ELIANTE.
>   He is a *bit* obsessive, I suppose,
>   but my admiration for him grows and grows.
>   It's heroic, even noble, how he clings

to his proud motto: *Frankness in all things.*
These days that sort of virtue 's very rare.
There should be people like him everywhere.

PHILINTE.
The more I know of him the more bizarre
it seems to me his slavish passions are.
Given the kind of star Alceste's born under,
the fact he loves at all 's an earthly wonder.
I'm utterly amazed, but far, far more
that it's your cousin he 's a weak spot for.

ELIANTE.
Clearly a case of 'Unlike poles attract'.
They haven't much in common, that's a fact.

PHILINTE.
From what you've seen, do you believe she cares?

ELIANTE.
It's so difficult to say in these affairs.
How *can* one tell, Philinte? I think you'd find
she was confused as well in her own mind.
Sometimes she loves and doesn't quite know why.
Sometimes she swears she does, but it's a lie.

PHILINTE.
I rather think our friend 's in for far more
from your dear cousin than he's bargained for.
If I were him I'd turn my thoughts elsewhere
and put my feelings in *your* tender care.

ELIANTE.
I can't disguise I care and wouldn't try.
It's things like this demand sincerity.
Although it's not to me his feelings turn
his welfare and not mine 's my one concern.
For his sake I'd be only too delighted
if, in the end, our two friends *were* united,
but if it comes about (and it might well,
love always being unpredictable)
things don't work out exactly as he's planned
and Célimène gives someone else her hand,
then I'll be waiting to accept Alceste
and not be bothered that I'm second best.

PHILINTE.
> And how could I object when I approve
> the focus of your interests and love?
> Alceste can bear me out on how I've tried
> to speak on your behalf and take your side.
> But if and when they marry, *if* and *when*
> Alceste at last succeeds with Célimène,
> and you must put your feelings on the shelf,
> I'll gladly, gladly offer you myself.
> I'd feel most honoured, absolutely blessed
> to offer you my love as second best.

ELIANTE.
> Ah, Philinte, you're making fun of me!

PHILINTE.
> No, I'm sincere. I mean it. Seriously.
> If this were the occasion, Eliante, I'd lay
> my heart wide open; and so I will; one day.

Enter ALCESTE *in a towering fury.*

ALCESTE. (*To Eliante.*)
> Help me punish her! This is the last straw.
> My constancy can't stand it any more.

ELIANTE.
> But what is it?

ALCESTE.   I just don't want to live.
> I'll kill myself. There's no alternative.
> The world could hurtle back to Nothingness
> and I'd be stoical. But this! But this!
> It's all . . . my love's . . . I can't speak even . . . I . . .

ELIANTE.
> Now come, Alceste. You must calm down. Please try.

ALCESTE.
> God in Heaven. How can one reconcile.
> something so beautiful and yet so vile.

ELIANTE.
> But what's happened?

ALCESTE.   Over! Done! Who'd' re believed . . .?
> She . . . it's Célimène . . . she's . . . *I've been deceived!*

ELIANTE.
  Are you sure?

PHILINTE.   Jealousy creates all kinds
  of fantastic monsters in suspicious minds.

ALCESTE.
  Go away, you! The letter I've got here
  in her own writing makes it all too clear.
  A letter to . . . Oronte! This envelope
  contains her blackened name, my blasted hope.
  Oronte! Of all the men *the* unlikeliest!
  He wasn't even *on* my rivals' list.

PHILINTE.
  Letters can be deceptive and the harm
  one imagines done a false alarm.

ALCESTE.
  I've told you once before. Leave me alone.
  Bother yourself with problems of your own.

ELIANTE.
  Now, now, you must keep calm and this disgrace . . .

ALCESTE.
  is something only you can help me face.
  It's to you now that I turn to set me free
  from this bitter, all-consuming agony.
  Avenge me on your cousin, who betrays
  a tenderness kept burning all these days.
  Avenge me, Eliante. I'm torn apart.

ELIANTE.
  Avenge you? How can I?

ALCESTE.   Accept my heart.
  Take it, instead of the one who tortures me.
  Yes, take it, please. It's simple, don't you see.
  By offering you my tenderest emotion,
  my care, attention and profound devotion,
  by laying all my feelings at your feet,
  I can get my own back on her foul deceit.

ELIANTE.
  As sorry as I am to see you suffer
  and not ungrateful for the love you offer,

I can't help wondering when you decide
that everything's been over-magnified
and you've found out you've made too big a fuss,
what happens to your vengeance? And to us?
Lovers' quarrels see-saw, we all know,
backwards and forwards, up/down, to and fro,
bad reports believed, then unbelieved,
sentenced one minute, and the next reprieved.
Even when it's clear, the case quite watertight,
guilt soon becomes innocence, wrong right.
All lovers' tiffs blow over pretty soon,
hated this morning, loved this afternoon.

ALCESTE.

No! The knife's been twisted too far in.
I'm absolutely through with Célimène!
Ab-so-lute-ly! No question of retreat.
I'd rather die than grovel at her feet.
Is that her now? It is. I feel my hate
go fizzing up its fuse to detonate!
I'll spring the charge on her. She'll be non-plussed.
Then when I've ground her down into the dust,
I'll bring to you a heart made whole again
and free of the treacherous charms of Célimène.

Enter CELIMENE.

God, help me master my emotion!

CELIMENE.

Ah!
(*To Alceste.*) Now, Alceste, what's all this new commotion?
What on earth's the meaning of those sighs,
those terrible black looks, those blazing eyes?

ALCESTE.

Of all foul things on Earth I know of few
whose damnable evil 's a patch on you.
If Heaven or Hell, or both combined
spawned worse demons, they'd be hard to find.

CELIMENE.

Charming! Thank you! Now that's what I call love.

ALCESTE.

It's no laughing matter. I've got proof

of your deceptions. Incontestable! Now
you should blush, not laugh, if you know how.
All my premonitions have proved right.
It wasn't for nothing that my love took fright.
You see. You see. Suspicion 's a good scout.
I followed in its trail and found you out.
In spite of your deceit my guiding star
's led me to discover what you are.
Love's something no one has much power over.
Its growth's spontaneous in every lover.
Force is quite useless. Hearts can't be coerced
except if they consent to submit first,
and if, at the very outset, Célimène,
you'd rejected my advances, there and then,
I'd've only had my luck not you to blame,
but to have been encouraged and had the flame
fanned into hopeful fire so shamelessly
's unforgiveable; sheer downright treachery!
And I've got every reason to complain
and every reason now to give full rein
to anger, yes, after such hard blows,
watch out, Célimène, be on your toes,
I'm not responsible for what I do.
My anger 's on the prowl because of you.

CELIMENE.
Such wild behaviour! (*To Philinte.*) Too much wine downstairs?

ALCESTE.
No, too much Célimène and her affairs.
The baited barb of beauty. Gobble that,
you're hooked, you're skinned, you're sizzling in the fat.
(*Pause.*)
Looks are so deceptive. I thought you *must*
've meant sincerity and truth and trust.

CELIMENE.
What is it then that's given you offence?

ALCESTE.
How very clever! You! all innocence!
Very well then. Straight down to the cause.
Look at this. (*Produces letter.*) This writing? Is it yours?
Of course! This letter damns you right enough.
There's no plea possible against such proof.

CELIMENE.
> And is it *this*, that all your upset 's for?

ALCESTE.
> Look at it, Célimène, and blush some more.

CELIMENE.
> Why should I blush?

ALCESTE.   Brazen as well as sly!
> There's no signature and so you'll lie.

CELIMENE.
> Why should I disown it when it's mine?

ALCESTE.
> Read it! You're condemned by every line.
> Look, and deny you're guilty if you can.

CELIMENE.
> Really, you're a foolish, foolish man.

ALCESTE.
> No shrugging off this letter, I'm afraid,
> and is it any wonder I'm dismayed
> that it's Oronte's love that you really want.

CELIMENE.
> Who told you that this letter 's to Oronte?

ALCESTE.
> Those who gave me it. Perhaps there's some mistake?
> And if there is, what difference does it make?
> Am I less inured, you less stained with shame?

CELIMENE.
> But if it's to a woman, where 's the blame?
> Can you interpret *that* as an affront?

ALCESTE.
> Ah, very clever! Absolutely brilliant!
> So that's the way you'll throw me off the scent?
> Oh, of course, that finishes the argument.
> How dare you try on such deceitful tricks?
> Or do you take us all for lunatics?
> So now let's see what deviousness you try
> to give support to such a blatant lie.
> A woman! How can you possibly pretend

this note's intended for a woman friend?
Please explain, to clear yourself, just what
does this mean here . . .

CELIMENE.   I certainly will not!
Your behaviour really puts me in a fury.
What right have you to play at judge and jury?
How dare you say such things? It's a disgrace
to fling such accusations in my face.

ALCESTE.
Now let's not lose our tempers or complain.
This expression here now. Please explain . . .

CELIMENE.
No! No! I'll do nothing of the kind.
I don't care anymore what's on your mind.

ALCESTE.
Please explain what proves this letter to be meant
for a woman friend, then I'll relent.

CELIMENE.
No, I'd rather you believed it's to Oronte.
It's *his* attentions that I really want.
His conversation, his 'person' pleases me.
So say anything you like and I'll agree.
Carry on your quarrel as you think best,
but don't, don't pester *me* again, Alceste.

ALCESTE.
God, could anything more cruel be invented,
and was ever any heart so much tormented?
I come to complain how cruelly I'm used
and in the end it's me who stands accused!
The woman does her damnedest to provoke
my jealousy then treats it as a joke,
lets me believe the worst, then crows, and cackles,
and I can't hack away these dreadful shackles,
the heavy ball and chain, the dangling noose,
I see them very well but can't break loose.
O what I need to steel me 's cold disdain
to scorn ingratitude and sneer at pain.
(*To Célimène.*)
You're diabolical! You take a man's weak spots
and tie the poor fool up in subtle knots.

Please clear yourself, it's more than I can bear
to leave the question hanging in the air.
Please don't make me think you love another man.
Show me this note's innocent, if you can.
Try to *pretend* you're faithful. Please, please, try.
And I'll try to pretend it's not a lie.

CELIMENE.

Jealousy 's turned your brain, my poor friend.
You don't deserve my love. Pretend? Pretend?
Why should I lower myself to be untrue
I'd like to be informed? To humour you?
Well, really! And if I had another *beau*,
wouldn't I be sincere and tell you so?
Are all my frank assurances in vain
against those fantasies you entertain?
Should they matter? You've had my guarantee.
Even to half-believe them insults me.
A woman who confesses love like this
breaks through great barriers of prejudice.
The so-called "honour of the sex" prevents
a frank expression of her sentiments.
If a woman's overcome that sense of shame
and the man's not satisfied, then *he's* to blame.
After all the woman's had to struggle through
surely the man could be assured it's true.
Ah! Your suspicions make me angry. You're . . .
you're absolutely not worth caring for.
It's too absurd. I'm really not quite sane
to go on being kind when you complain.
I should find someone else instead of you.
Then all your allegations *would* come true.

ALCESTE.

Ah, it never fails to take me by surprise,
my feebleness. Your sweet talk may be lies,
but I must learn to swallow it all whole.
I'm at your faithless mercy, heart and soul.
I'll hang on till the bitter end and see
just how far you'll go with perfidy.

CELIMENE.

No, you don't love me as you really ought.

ALCESTE.
>My love goes far beyond the common sort.
>So keen was I to show it that I wished
>you were unlovable, impoverished,
>a pauper and a beggar and low-born,
>an object of derision and of scorn
>and with one act of sudden transformation
>my love could raise you from your lowly station,
>in one fell swoop make up for that poor start,
>by making a public offer of my heart,
>so that the world could see and know and say:
>*He made her everything she is today.*

CELIMENE.
>O such benevolence deserves a plaque!
>Whatever could I do to pay you back . . .
>O here's Dubois. About to emigrate!

Enter DUBOIS *laden with luggage.*

ALCESTE.
>What's this?

DUBOIS.   Allow me, sir, to explicate.

ALCESTE.
>Please do.

DUBOIS.   It's something most bizarre. Mysterious.

ALCESTE.
>But what?

DUBOIS.   Yes, very strange, and *could* be serious.

ALCESTE.
>But how?

DUBOIS.   Have I your leave to . . .

ALCESTE.   speak, or shout
>for all I care, but, quickly, spit it out.

DUBOIS.
>In front of . . .

ALCESTE.   all the world if needs be, man.
>For God's sake tell me, clearly, *if* you can.
>And *now.*

DUBOIS.   The time, sir, 's come to expedite,
        to put it rather crudely, sir, our flight.

ALCESTE.
        Our what?

DUBOIS.   Our flight, sir, flight. We must proceed
        with all due caution, but at double speed.

ALCESTE.
        What for, man?

DUBOIS.   Sir, once more let me stress
        we must leave Paris by the next express.

ALCESTE.
        Leave Paris, why?

DUBOIS.   No time at all to lose.
        No time for long farewells or fond adieus.

ALCESTE.
        What does this mean?

DUBOIS.   It means (to specify,
        to be absolutely blunt) it means . . . Goodbye!

ALCESTE.
        I'm warning you, Dubois . . . Dubois, look here.
        Start again, at once, and make things clear.

DUBOIS.
        A person, sir; black looks, black coat, black hat,
        appeared, sir, in the kitchen, just like that,
        deposited a paper, and then went –
        a very legal-looking document.
        It looks to me a little like a writ
        with stamps and signatures all over it,
        some sort of summons, surely, but I'm blessed
        if I could make it out, Monsieur Alceste.

ALCESTE.
        And why, please, does this paper that you say
        the man delivered mean our getaway?

DUBOIS.
        Then after, sir, about an hour or so,
        another person called, and *him* you know,
        he calls quite often on you, seemed distressed

to find you out tonight, Monsieur Alceste.
Yes, most disturbed, but knowing he could send
dependable Dubois to help his friend,
he urged me, very gravely, to convey,
without procrastination or delay,
this urgent message to my master, sir . . .
his name was . . . just a minute . . . mm . . . mm . . . er . . .

ALCESTE.
O never mind his name. What did he say?

DUBOIS.
One of your friends, he was, sir, anyway.
He said, and I repeat, sir: *Tell Alceste*
he must leave Paris and escape arrest.

ALCESTE.
Escape arrest, and was that all he said?

DUBOIS.
Except it would be better if you fled.
He dashed a quick note off for me to bring.
He said the note would tell you everything.

ALCESTE.
Give it to me then.

CELIMENE.   What's all this about?

ALCESTE.
I'm not quite sure. I'm *trying* to find out.
(*To Dubois.*)
You, you great idiot, not found it yet?

DUBOIS. (*After a long search.*)
I must have left it somewhere . . . I forget . . .

ALCESTE.
I don't know what . . .

CELIMENE.   Alceste! You ought to sort
this nonsense out at once, you really ought!

ALCESTE.
No matter what I do, it seems that fate
's imposed its veto on our *tête-à-tête*.
I've still got many things to say to you.
When I come back, please, one more interview?

ACT THREE

On stage, ALCESTE *and* PHILINTE.

ALCESTE.
>No, my mind's made up I've got to go.

PHILINTE.
>Must you? Really? However hard the blow.

ALCESTE.
>Coax and wheedle to your heart's content.
>My mind's made up, and what I said I meant.
>This age is fastened in corruption's claws.
>I'm opting out of this foul world of yours.
>This world where wrong seems right, and right seems wrong
>can count me out of it. I don't belong.
>After what's happened in my lawsuit, how . . .
>how can I possibly remain here now?
>Everything that renders life worthwhile,
>everything that counters lies and guile –
>Justice, Honour, Goodness, Truth and Law
>should've crushed that swine, or else what's Justice for?
>All the papers said my cause was just
>and I'm the one who's trampled in the dust.
>Thanks to black perjury that ruthless sinner
>whose past's notorious comes off the winner.
>Truth drops a curtsey to the man's deceit,
>and Justice flops, and crawls to kiss his feet!
>He'd get away with anything; he'd quote
>some legal precedent, then cut my throat.
>His hypocritical grimace never fails –
>one quick smirk at the jury tips the scales.
>To crown it all the Court gives him a writ.
>Harried and hounded by that hypocrite!
>Not satisfied with that. Not satisfied,
>there's yet another trick the devil's tried.
>A pamphlet's just been published, and suppressed.
>All booksellers that stock it risk arrest.
>This obscene libel seeks to implicate
>some of the closest to the Head of State.
>Although he hasn't mentioned me by name,
>he's dropped hints to the Press that I'm to blame.
>And, look at this, this headline here, just look!

SEARCH FOR AUTHOR OF SUBVERSIVE BOOK:
EXPERT OPINION ANALYSES STYLE!
And a picture of Oronte (just *see* that smile!).
Which author does 'expert' Oronte suggest:
'There's only one it could be, that's Alceste.'
Oronte! Someone I tried my very best
to be quite fair with, yes, Oronte, the pest,
coming with his verses for a 'fair' critique,
and when I *am* fair, and, in all conscience, seek
to do justice to the truth and him as well,
he helps to brand me as a criminal.
All this irreconcilable bad blood
and all because his poem was no good!
And if that's human nature God forbid!
If that's what men are like then I'm well rid.
This is the sort of good faith, self respect,
concern for truth, and justice I expect.
Their persecution 's more than I can face.
Now I'm quitting this benighted place,
this terrible jungle where men eat men.
Traitors! You'll never see my face again.

PHILINTE.

I'm pretty sure the problem's not as great
as you make out. If I were you I'd wait.
Whatever charges they've trumped up, Alceste,
you've managed so far to avoid arrest.
Lies can boomerang and choke the liar.
All these tales and scandals could backfire.

ALCESTE.

He doesn't mind. He thrives on his disgrace.
His crimes seem licensed. Far from losing face
his stock 's sky-high; he's lionised in town,
and all because he's made me look a clown.

PHILINTE.

Up till now most people have ignored
the malicious gossip that he's spread abroad,
and so I wouldn't worry any more
if I were you; at least not on that score.
As for your lawsuit, where you rightly feel
hard done by, you could easily appeal.

ALCESTE.
> No second hearings! I accept the first.
> The last thing that I'd want is it reversed.
> Let it stand. Then posterity 'll know
> how far corruption and abuse can go,
> proof of all the mean and dirty tricks
> of Mankind circa 1966.
> If it costs 20,000 francs, I'll pay;
> I'll pay, and earn the right to have my say,
> denounce the age and hate man and dissever
> myself from all his wickedness for ever.

PHILINTE.
> But after all . . .

ALCESTE.   But after all! What, what
> do you propose to say about all that
> that 's not superfluous. You wouldn't dare
> try to excuse this sickening affair.

PHILINTE.
> No! No! Everything you say. Agreed! Agreed!
> The world *is* governed by intrigue and greed.
> Cunning and fraudulence *do* come off best,
> men *ought* to be different, yes, Alceste,
> but does man's lack of justice give you cause
> to flee society with all its flaws.
> It's through these very flaws we exercise
> the discipline of our philosophies.
> It's virtue's noblest enterprise, the aim
> of everything we do in virtue's name.
> Supposing probity *were* general,
> hearts were open, just and tractable,
> what use would all our virtues be, whose point,
> when all the world seems really out of joint,
> 's to bear with others' contumely and spite
> without annoyance, even though we're right.
> Virtue in a heart can counteract . . .

ALCESTE.
> Quite a performance that, yes, quite an act!
> You've always got so many things to say.
> Philinte, your fine talk's simply thrown away.
> What reason tells me I already know:
> it's for my good entirely if I go.

I can't control my tongue. It won't obey.
I'm not responsible for what I say.
Look at all the trouble I've incurred!
Trouble seems to stalk my every word.
Now, leave me to wait here. And no more fuss!
I've a little proposition to discuss
with Célimène and what I mean to do
's find out what her love is: false or true.

PHILINTE.
Let's go up to Eliante. We could wait there.

ALCESTE.
I've too much on my mind I must prepare.
You go. I'm better left to nurse this mood
of black resentment here in solitude.
This gloomy little corner suits me best.
(*Sits.*)
The perfect setting! O I'm so depressed.

PHILINTE.
You'll find yourself bad company in that state.
I'll fetch down Eliante to help you wait.

Exit PHILINTE. *Enter* CELIMENE *and* ORONTE.

ORONTE.
I need some proof. It goes against the books
to keep a lover years on tenterhooks.
If you welcome my attentions, as you say,
please stop wavering and name the day.
Some little gesture that would help to prove
that you reciprocate my ardent love.
And all I ask 's Alceste's head on a plate.
Banish him today and don't prevaricate.
Please say to him . . . today . . . please . . . Célimène,
say: *Never show your face round here again!*

CELIMENE.
What's happened between you two, I'd like to know?
You thought him marvellous not long ago.

ORONTE.
The whys and wherefores just don't signify.
More to the point though 's where your feelings lie.
Keep one of us and set the other free.

You really have to choose: Alceste or me.

ALCESTE. (*Emerging from his corner.*)
Choose, yes, choose. Your friend here's justified
in his demands which I endorse. Decide!
His impatience is my own, his anguish mine.
I too insist on having some sure sign.
Things can't go on like this indefinitely.
The time has come to choose: Oronte or me!

ORONTE.
I've no desire to prejudice your chances
by indiscreet, importunate advances.

ALCESTE.
Jealousy or not, I certainly don't want
to share her heart with you, Monsieur Oronte.

ORONTE.
And if she chooses your love and not mine . . .

ALCESTE.
If it's to *you* her sympathies incline . . .

ORONTE.
I'll give up all those hopes I had before . . .

ALCESTE.
I swear I'll never see her any more.

ORONTE.
Now, you can speak. No need to hum and hah.

ALCESTE.
Don't be afraid to tell us how things are.

ORONTE.
Only decide which one's the one for you.

ALCESTE.
To clinch the matter, choose between us two.

Pause.

ORONTE.
It can't be difficult to pick one out!

ALCESTE.
Can you hesitate at all, or be in doubt?

CELIMENE.
> This isn't the time and place and that's a fact.
> O such demands. Please, gentlemen, some tact!
> It's not that I've got anything to hide,
> my heart's not wavering from side to side,
> but what I *do* find difficult to do
> 's announce my choice in front of both of you.
> I think that anything at all unpleasant
> shouldn't be spoken with another present.
> It's possible to hint one's attitude
> without going to extremes and being rude.
> I think that gentle clues are quite enough
> to let a lover know he's lost his love.

ORONTE.
> No, not at all. It's frankness that we want.
> I've no objections.

ALCESTE.   And *I'm* adamant.
> *I* insist. Choose now between our loves.
> *I* surely don't need handling with kid-gloves.
> You try to keep the whole world on a string.
> It's got to end at once, this wavering.
> No more half-hints, no titillating clues,
> We want it cut and dried: accept/refuse.
> Silence itself 's a sort of answer though.
> I take it silence means quite simply: NO!

ORONTE.
> I'm grateful that you've been so down-to-earth.
> I second what you say for all I'm worth.

CELIMENE.
> I'm really quite fed up of this affair.
> Demanding this and that! It isn't fair.
> Haven't I told you why I hesitate?
> Here's Eliante. Ask her. She'll arbitrate.

Enter ELIANTE *and* PHILINTE.

> Eliante! Look, I'm the victim of a plot.
> They cooked it up together, like as not.
> They both go on and on to make me choose,
> which one of them I'll have, and which refuse.
> They want me to announce it just like that,
> one to be chosen, one to be squashed flat.

Please tell them, Eliante, it's just not done.

ELIANTE.
      If you want allies, sorry, *I'm* not one.
      I belong to the opposition. I'm inclined
      to side with people who can speak their mind.

ORONTE. (*To Célimène.*)
      It's pointless your protesting I'm afraid.

ALCESTE.
      You can't depend on Eliante for aid.

ORONTE.
      Please speak, and put an end to our suspense.

ALCESTE.
      Or don't. It doesn't make much difference.

ORONTE.
      One little word; then let the curtain fall.

ALCESTE.
      I'll understand if you don't speak at all.

Enter ARSINOE, ACASTE, CLITANDRE.

ACASTE. (*To Célimène.*)
      Have you got two minutes you can spare for us?
      We've got a 'little something' to discuss.

CLITANDRE. (*To Alceste and Oronte.*)
      A good thing you're here too. The reason why
      you'll discover to your horror by and by.

ARSINOE.
      Forgive me for intruding once again,
      but they requested it, these gentlemen,
      who turned up at my house in such a state
      of agitation to insinuate
      such dreadful things against you, dear, that . . . well . . .
      they seemed quite utterly incredible.
      Of course I couldn't believe that it was you,
      knowing how kind you are; and thoughtful too.
      I said: *No, it can't be!* The case they made
      did seem rather damning, I'm afraid.
      Forgetting, then, our little *contretemps*
      for 'auld lang syne', my dear, I've come along

with these two gentlemen to hear you clear
yourself at once from this new slander . . . dear.

ACASTE.

Yes, let's all be calm and civilised and see
just how you bluff this out and wriggle free.
This is a letter to Clitandre from you.

CLITANDRE.

And this is to Acaste, this *billet doux*.

ACASTE.

We won't need any expert to decypher
this all too well-known hand we've all an eye for.
I've had, and so, I know, have all of you,
sizeable amounts of *billet doux*,
so proof's superfluous. This little note
's a fine example, gentlemen, I quote:
(*Reads.*)
My dear Clitandre
'What a strange man you are to moan when I'm in high spirits
and to complain that I'm never so lively as when I'm not with
you. Nothing could be further from the truth. And if you don't
come very soon to beg my pardon for this insult, I'll never
forgive you as long as I live. That great hulk of a Viscount. (*He
ought to have been here!*) . . . That great hulk of a Viscount,
you complain of first, isn't my type at all. Ever since I watched
him spitting for at least three quarters of an hour into a well to
make circles in the water, I've not much cared for him. As for
the little Marquis (*that's me, gentlemen, though I shouldn't
boast*) . . . As for the little Marquis, who held my hand so
interminably yesterday, he's of no account at all, absolutely
insignificant, a tailor's dummy, that's all the little Marquis is.
As for that character in green velvet (*your turn, Alceste*) . . . As
for that character in green velvet well, he's occasionally
amusing with his blunt irascibility and forthright ways, but
there are a million other times when I find him the world's
worst bore. As for the would-be poet (*your bit this*) . . . as for
the would-be poet, who fancies himself one of the intel-
ligentsia, and tries desperately to pass himself off as an author,
in spite of what everybody tells him, I can't even be bothered
listening any more, and his prose is about as tedious as his
verse. So try to believe me when I say I don't enjoy myself, quite
as much as you imagine, and that I miss you more than I'd ever

like to say at all those 'entertainments' I'm forced to go to, and that there's nothing quite like the company of one who loves to add real zest to life.'

CLITANDRE.
And now for me!
(*Reads.*) My dear Acaste
'Your little hanger-on Clitandre, who plays the languishing lover all the time, is the very last man on earth I could feel real friendship for. He must be out of his mind if he's convinced himself that I feel anything at all for him; and you must be out of yours to believe that I don't love you. Be reasonable and take a leaf out of his book, and come and see me as often as you can. That would be some compensation for my having to be pestered by Clitandre.'
This does your character enormous credit.
You really are a . . . No, I haven't said it!
We're going now and everywhere we call
we'll show this likeness of you, warts and all.

Exit CLITANDRE.

ACASTE.
I could say much. It's not worth the attempt.
You're quite beneath all anger and contempt.
Your 'little marquis' certainly won't cry:
He's got far better fish than you to fry!

Exit ACASTE.

ORONTE.
So after all those letters that you wrote
you turn on me like this and cut my throat!
You little gadabout, you seem to swear
undying, false devotion everywhere.
I've been a fool, but now the truth has dawned.
I'm grateful for the favour. I've been warned.
I've got my heart back and I'm glad to get it.
My only satisfaction's *you'll* regret it.
(*To Alceste.*)
I'm thankful I've escaped this creature's claws.
I won't stand in your way. She's yours; all yours.

Exit ORONTE.

ARSINOE.
O never have I felt so much disgust.
I'm shocked, I must speak out. I really must.

This fine and worthy man, Monsieur Alceste
(I'm not so much concerned about the rest)
who worshipped you (to everyone's surprise)
Alceste, who thought the sun shone from eyes,
Alceste . . .

ALCESTE.   I'll handle this if you don't mind.
Please don't waste your time in being kind.
Crusading for my cause in this keen way
's not something I'd feel able to repay.
If, to avenge myself on Célimène,
you think that I'll choose you, please think again.

ARSINOE.
What gave you the idea that I did?
As if I'd try to snare you! God forbid!
Such vanity! There's something monstrous in it,
if you can think such things a single minute.
This Madam's surplus stock 's a merchandise
I'd be an idiot to overprize.
Come down off your high horse before you fall.
My class of person 's not your type at all!
Dance attendance on that creature there.
You and that woman make a perfect pair!

Exit ARSINOE.

ALCESTE.
I've waited in the wings all this long time
patiently watching this strange pantomime.
Have I proved my powers of self control
and may I now . . .

CELIMENE.   Unburden your whole soul.
Yes, go on. I deserve all your complaint.
You're free to criticise without restraint.
I'm wrong and I admit it. Enough, enough,
no more pretending, no more lies and bluff.
I could despise the anger of the rest,
but you I know I've wronged, my poor Alceste.
Your resentment's justified. I realise
how culpable I must seem in your eyes.
All the evidence you've been given leads
to conclusive proof of my misdeeds.
There's every reason why you should detest

me utterly. You have my leave, Alceste.

ALCESTE.
    Ah, you traitor, I only wish I could.
    If tenderness were crushable, I would.
    I want, I want to let myself give way
    to hate, but my heart just won't obey.
    (*To Eliante and Philinte.*)
    Just how degrading can a passion get?
    Now watch me grovel. You've seen nothing yet.
    There's more to come. Just stay and watch the show.
    You'll see my weakness reach an all-time low.
    Never call men wise. Look how they behave.
    There's no perfection this side of the grave.
    (*To Célimène.*)
    You've no idea what "being faithful" means . . .
    But I'm willing to forget these painful scenes.
    concoct excuses for your crimes and say
    the vicious times and youth led you astray,
    provided that, on your part, you consent
    to share my self-inflicted banishment,
    away in the country, where I want to find
    a life-long haven and avoid mankind.
    In this way only, in the public eye,
    can you do penance for the injury
    those letters caused, and only if you do,
    can I pick up the threads of loving you.

CELIMENE.
    Renounce the world before I'm old and grey?
    Go to your wilderness and pine away?

ALCESTE.
    But if your love were anything like mine,
    you'd forget the outside world and never pine.

CELIMENE.
    I'm only twenty! I'd be terrified!
    Just you and me, and all that countryside!
    I'm not sufficiently high-minded to agree
    to such a fate. It's simply just not me!
    But if my hand's enough and you're content
    to marry and stay in Paris, I consent,
    and marriage . . .

ALCESTE.   No, now I hate you, loathe, abhor.
    This beats anything you've done before.
    If you can't think of me as your whole life
    as I would you, you'll never be my wife.
    This last humiliation's set me free
    from love's degrading tyranny.
    (*To Eliante.*)
    To me you're beautiful, your virtue's clear,
    and you're the only one who seems sincere.
    I started to admire you long ago
    and hope you'll let me go on doing so,
    but, please, with all my troubles, understand
    if now I hesitate to seek your hand.
    I feel unworthy of it. It seems that Fate
    didn't intend me for the married state.
    Cast off by one not fit to lace your shoes,
    my love's beneath your notice. You'd refuse.

ELIANTE.
    Don't blame yourself, my friend. I understand.
    I'm sure there'll be no problem with my hand.
    I think a little pressure might persuade
    your good friend here to volunteer his aid.

PHILINTE.
    This makes my deepest wishes all come true.
    I'd shirk no sacrifice in serving you.

ALCESTE.
    I hope you'll always feel so, and both win
    a joy and happiness that's genuine.
    For me, betrayed on *all* sides and laid low
    by heaped injustices, it's time to go,
    and leave man floundering in this foul morass
    where vice goes swaggering as bold as brass,
    and go on looking for a safe retreat
    where honesty can stand on its own feet.

Exit ALCESTE.

PHILINTE.
    Let's go after him, and see if we can't find
    some way (*any* way!) to change his mind.

Exeunt PHILINTE *and* ELIANTE *together.* CELIMENE *remains seated, alone.*

PHAEDRA BRITANNICA (1975)

PHAEDRA BRITANNICA

Phaedra Britannica (after Racine) was first performed by the National Theatre Company at the Old Vic on 9 September 1975 with the following cast:

GOVERNOR	Michael Gough
MEMSAHIB, the Governor's Wife	Diana Rigg
THOMAS THEOPHILUS, the Governor's son by his first wife	David Yelland
BURLEIGH, his tutor	Robert Eddison
ADC to the Governor	Daniel Thorndike
LILAMANI	Diana Quick
TARA, her attendant	Illona Linthwaite
AYAH	Alaknanda Samarth
CHUPRASSIE	Ishaq Bux
SERVANTS	Talat Hussain
	Jagdish Kumar
	Albert Moses
DIRECTOR	John Dexter
DESIGNER	Tanya Moiseiwitsch
ASSISTANT TO DESIGNER	Timian Alsaker
LIGHTING	Andy Phillips
STAFF DIRECTOR	Harry Lomax
VOCAL COACH	Catherine Fleming
PRODUCTION MANAGER	Richard Bullimore
STAGE MANAGER	Diana Boddington
DEPUTY STAGE MANAGER	John Caulfield
ASSISTANT STAGE MANAGERS	Tim Spring
	Karen Stone
SOUND	Sylvia Carter

ACT ONE

The scene is the Durbar Hall of the Governor's Residency in British India, a few years bfore the Indian Mutiny. THOMAS THEOPHILUS *and* BURLEIGH *stand behind the classical colonnade inhaling what is left of the fresh night air, and listening to the bugle from the Fort off-stage playing reveille.*

THOMAS.
> No! No! I can't. *I can't.* How can I stay?
> I've got to go at once. At once. *Today!*
> The Governor's been gone now half a year,
> I can't stay loitering and loafing here
> frustrated and ashamed I'm not the one
> directing the search-parties, me, his son!
> It's almost up, the dawn. I must prepare.

BURLEIGH.
> And where will you start looking? Where?
> The Company's had sepoys scout as far
> as Jalalabad and Peshawar
> north to the very outposts where its *raj*
> is constantly beset by sabotage.
> Unpacified child-murdering marauders
> make it a certain death to cross our borders.
> You know the Governor! He might have strayed
> into those areas still unsurveyed.
> Thomas, you know as well as I that soon
> the search'll be called off for the monsoon.
> Could even come today, the first cloudburst.
> This damned hot weather's at its very worst.
> Who wouldn't give a coffer of rupees
> to lower the mercury a few degrees?
> Besides, perhaps for reasons of his own
> H.E. prefers his whereabouts unknown.
> One knows his nature, ready to pursue
> anything that's savage, strange, or new,
> his "curiosity" how wild tribes live,
> his "scholar" 's passion for the primitive.
> Frankly it would be no great surprise
> if he were living somewhere in disguise,
> and, cool as ever, 's ready to embark
> on some fresh enterprise that's best kept dark,
> absorbed, preoccupied both day, *and* night,

let's say "researching" some strange marriage rite!
Leading some new unfortunate astray!

THOMAS.
>   Show some respect. Be careful what you say!
>   Father's the Governor. He's good. He's great,
>   no loose romancer and gross reprobate.
>   My father's in some danger and not caught
>   in any trammels of that trivial sort.
>   When he was new out here and young, perhaps
>   there *was* the occasional moral lapse.
>   Not now, though, Burleigh. All that's of the past.
>   The Governor's heart is constant and steadfast.
>   No footloose fancy. No inconstant vow.
>   His life revolves round 'the Memsahib' now.
>   I'm going for two reasons: one, to find
>   my father; two, leave *this place* far behind.

BURLEIGH.
>   'This place!' 'This place?' O surely that's not how
>   your childhood paradise seems to you now?
>   If 'this place', as you call it, 's lost its savour
>   where else I wonder will you find to favour?
>   Not Britain. No! Completely unimpressed!
>   There all you felt was homesick and depressed.
>   What's the real reason why you want to go?
>   Fear? Of what? Surely you can let me know!

THOMAS.
>   Yes, Burleigh, paradise it may have been . . .
>   until 'the Memsahib' came on the scene.
>   The Judge's daughter's presence soon destroyed
>   that carefree, tranquil life we all enjoyed . . .
>   a judge so unimpeachable and just
>   to have a wife destroyed by bestial lust
>   and daughters . . .

BURLEIGH.   Yes. Indeed. Of course one knew
>   that things were far from well between you two.
>   The storybook stepson/stepmother thing!
>   She wasn't long in starting harassing.
>   No sooner had she seen you, you were sent
>   to school in Britain i.e. banishment!
>   That particular storm's blown over though.
>   The old obsession's gone, or doesn't show.

Besides it seems his Excellency's wife
has quite succumbed and lost all hold on life.
Her nerves seem whittled down to fraying strings.
She's given in and lost all grip on things.
What happened to the mother years before 's
enough to give alarm for much less cause.
The India, we'd all like to ignore
struck at the Judge's family twice before,
bestial India, that undermined
his own wife's body and first daughter's mind.
Now she won't eat, can't sleep, and seems in pain,
though what it is no one can ascertain.
As to its nature she's quite sealed her lips.
A very strange complaint her Ladyship's,
not common fever with its heat and chills
but one of India's obscurer ills.
How can an ailing woman cause your flight?

THOMAS.
It's not the Memsahib. Or her vain spite.
(*Pause.*)
Remember the revolt? Ranjit and six sons
so bloodily destroyed by redcoat guns?
The daughter of that line that raised the war
against the Company and rule of law
under the strict restraint of house arrest . . .
She's the reason . . .

BURLEIGH.   Come! Can you detest
poor Lilamani so much, you as well
as the Governor want her life made hell?
And she so innocent! Would she have known
about her father's plans to seize the throne?
I don't believe she knew about their plot
to overthrow the Sahibs. Surely not!
Politics! Rebellion! I don't suppose
she's even acquainted with words like those.
She seems so full of charm. At least to me.

THOMAS.
If it were hatred, would I need to flee?

BURLEIGH.
A little tentative analysis
from me, your oldest friend, can't come amiss.

I've watched you struggling, I know for you
the Governor's character's not one, but two.
As law-enforcer, hunter; fine! But pride
has hardened your nature to his 'darker' side.
How long for I wonder? Are you still
fighting off love's *raj* with iron will?
India's spirits stung by your disgust
will never rest until you've kissed the dust.
And blood will out! Have the dark gods won?
And are you, after all, your father's son?
I've watched you struggle with yourself. My guess
(now don't flare up) 's capitulation. Yes?

THOMAS.
If you're my oldest friend you ought to know
I'd never let myself descend so low.
Still at the breast I started to drink in
chaste principles and pride and discipline.
Think of my Rajput mother who would ride
fearless through danger at the Governor's side.
Think of her merits. She surpassed most men.
Then say 'capitulation'. Think again.
And you know very well you played your part
stamping the Governor's image on my heart.
Your schoolroom stories of my father stirred
my blood to emulate the things I heard,
a giant cannibal fought hand to hand,
the cripplers grappled with, mutilation banned,
dacoits encountered, and suppressed by law,
rebellions put down, and so much more.
Like hunting tigers! All the rest in trees
he goes on foot as coolly as you please,
waits till it's almost on him, doesn't shoot,
but drives a bayonet through the pouncing brute!
All the maneaters that he's bayonetted!
A pyramid of heads! A pyramid!
(*Pause.*)
As for that other self, so swift to swear
his plausible empty love-vows everywhere . . .
Oudh! Hyderabad! Kabul! Each of those
stands for some scandal the whole province knows,
scores of "incidents" throughout Bengal,
O far too many to recall them all —

the purdahs plundered, the zenanas sacked,
many an infamously flagrant act –
the young girl daubed with kohl and henna dye
snatched from a Parsee caravanserai.
The Judge's daughters! Both! The sister's mind,
after her heart was broken, soon declined.
Disowned. A drunkard. Died. And then the other
became the Memsahib and my stepmother!
But she was fortunate in that at least
she had the benefit of rites and priest.
How many times I wanted to cut short
the countless details of that sordid sort.
If only time's recorder could erase
those blots and leave untarnished praise!
Will the gods humiliate me and extort
submission from me of that loathsome sort?
The Governor has exploits he can set
against those foibles and make men forget.
In me, with no such honours, they'd despise
the deliquescence of a lover's sighs.
What trampled monsters give me right to stray
even a little from the narrow way?
And if my pride were, somehow, overcome,
it's not to Lilamani I'd succumb.
Could I be so distracted to dispute
the Governor's veto for forbidden fruit?
She's quite untouchable. A strict taboo
falls like a scimitar between us two.
Prohibited. The Governor rightly fears
heirs to that family of mutineers.
And so she lives life out, forever barred
from wedlock, and the like, and under guard.
Am I to brave his wrath, espouse her cause,
and show the natives I despise his laws?

BURLEIGH.

You may protest. I fear it makes no odds
once your fate's been settled by the gods.
And I could see it happening. The more
he tried to blinker you the more you saw.
Hostility fed love. Your father's spite
bathed its victim with an added light.
Love's sweet, so why resist it, so why shy

from feelings common to humanity?
Such stubborn scruple in the face of love
which even your great heroes aren't above!
Siva's avatars subdue sahibs. Few
escape love's clutches. Why should you?
Submit, poor Thomas, pay love your salaams,
yield to the Princess's delightful charms.
The Governor yielded to your mother too
and from their mutual warmth created you.
Without their union you would not be,
you who wrestle against love to struggle free.
So why keep up this pitiful pretence?
Everyone has seen the difference.
For days now, even weeks, you have become –
how should one put it – well, less "mettlesome".
Nobody has seen you on "the morning ride"
racing your ponies by the riverside.
You don't play polo, you no longer train
wild Arab horses to accept the rein.
Your weapons rust. No more the hue and cry
we made the jungle ring with, you and I.
Like someone drugged on *bhang*, all heavy-eyed,
sick of some passion that you seek to hide,
it seems so obvious. You're all ablaze,
dazed and bewildered in a lover's maze.
The little Princess is it? Lost your heart?

THOMAS.
  I'm going to find my father, and must start.

BURLEIGH.
  I rather think her ladyship expects
  before you go your "filial" respects!

THOMAS.
  Present 'the Memsahib' with my salaams.

Exit THOMAS THEOPHILUS. *Enter* AYAH.

BURLEIGH.
  Good morning, ayah! Well, no new alarms?

AYAH.
  The Memsahib! She seems to *want* to die.
  Her days and nights are spent in agony.
  There's nothing I can do. She never sleeps,

but stares all through the night and sighs and weeps.
First wants the jalousies wide open, then
almost at once they must be closed again.
She wants the punkah fast, the punkah slow,
too high, she says, to cool her, then too low.
For hours she gazes at the silver thread
that marks hot weather, wishing herself dead;
she points and says: *Ayah, when it reaches there
my lungs will have exhausted all the air.*
Now she wants to see the day. It seems
her brief siestas bring her dreadful dreams.
She asks, nay, sahib, she commands no eye
shall gaze upon her in her agony . . .

Exit BURLEIGH. *Enter* MEMSAHIB.

MEMSAHIB.
. . . no more . . . I can't. Must stop.
No strength! . . . Can't move another step.
Dazzled. My eyes. O ayah, I can't bear
the sudden brightness. Sun. Light. Glare.
Can't, ayah, can't bear the light. The heat.
I don't seem able to stay on my feet.
Aaaggghhh . . .
(*Sits.*)

AYAH.   Heaven hear our desperate prayer.

MEMSAHIB.
These stifling rags! . . . give me air!
My hair piled up? Wound round? and who did that?
Cumbered my reason with a lumpish plait?
It weighs like stone. What meddling little maid
burdened my leaden brain with this huge braid?
Aaah all things weary me, and make me vexed!

AYAH.
Your wishes change one minute to the next.
Tired of your boudoir, you it was who said:
The sunrise, ayah. Help me out of bed.
You wanted dressing, wanted your hair done
to be presentable to see the sun.
You said: *Let in the sun, I want to see.*
Now you shrink from it in agony.

MEMSAHIB.
>That's where it all started, that red fire.
>. . . blinding, consuming . . . Ayah
>its light sinks in, right in, to scrutinise
>the sordidness concealed behind my eyes.
>This is the last time that I'll have to gaze
>on those all-seeing, penetrating rays.

AYAH.
>O all you ever talk about is dying . . .

MEMSAHIB.
>The jungle clearing, watching dustclouds flying . . .
>horse and boy one animal, the hard sound
>of hoofbeats on the baked hot weather ground . . .
>nearer . . . nearer . . .

AYAH.   Memsahib?

MEMSAHIB.   Mad! Oh no . . .
>Wandering! Letting reason and desire go.
>Your gods, the gods of India possess
>my darkened mind and make it powerless.
>I can feel my whole face hot with shame
>blushing for dreadful things I daren't name.

AYAH.
>Blush, Memsahib, but blush that you stay mute
>and make your sufferings much more acute.
>Scorning pity, to all our pleas a stone,
>do Memsahibs die loveless and alone?
>You're letting yourself die. Three times the night
>has dropped its purdah and obscured the light
>without you tasting food. You pine away.
>In letting go, Memsahib, you betray
>your husband, children, and the source of life.
>The Governor Sahib needs his faithful wife!
>Think when the children come and you're not here,
>the Governor away, have you no fear
>of what the Rajput woman's son might do
>to helpless children out of hate for you.
>Your children in Belait, have you no thought
>for them being subject to the half-breed's sport?
>Thomas Theophilus . . .

MEMSAHIB.   God!

AYAH (*Triumphant.*)   Still feel then?

MEMSAHIB.
        Ayah, never refer to him again.

AYAH.
        If I thought that it would rouse you I'd recite
        Thomas Theophilus day and night.
        Live, Memsahib, live. Mother love demands.
        Live and save your children from his hands.
        To let that half-breed Rajput colt control
        those who survived you should affront your soul,
        that cruel, heartless half-breed who can't feel
        grind Sahib's pukka sons beneath his heel?
        No time to waste. Each moment of delay
        Memsahib's precious lifeblood ebbs away.
        While there's an ember left that still glows red,
        fan life into flame. Come back from the dead.

MEMSAHIB.
        My guilty life has dragged out far too long.

AYAH.
        Guilt! Guilt! Your guilty life! What guilt? What wrong?
        What blood of innocents have those hands spilt?
        How could Memsahib's hands be stained with guilt?

MEMSAHIB.
        They're not. My hands are clean enough. You're right.
        I would to God my heart were half so white.

AYAH.
        What horror did that heart of hers hatch out
        that Memsahib's so penitent about?

MEMSAHIB.
        Better to let my heart's dark secret go
        with my dead body to the earth below.

AYAH.
        Pray do, pray do! But if Memsahib dies
        she must find someone else to close her eyes.
        Memsahib's life fades fast. Before it fades
        her ayah goes down first to warn the shades.
        Doors to oblivion are all unbarred.
        One knocks and enters. It is never hard.

When all one's hopes and longings have been wrecked
despair can guide one to the most direct.
Has ayah's faithfulness once failed the test?
The Memsahib was nursed upon this breast.
I left my little children and my man
far, far behind me in Baluchistan
to care for you. I even held your hand
crossing black water to the Sahib's land.
Daughter of Judge Sahib, will you repay
love and devotion in this cruel way?

MEMSAHIB.

Don't ayah. Stop insisting. It's no good.
This unspeakable truth would chill your blood.

AYAH.

Is truth so terrible, Memsahib? *Wai*,
could anything be worse than watch you die?

MEMSAHIB.

I'll die in any case. With twice the shame
once guilt, that's better nameless, gets a name.

AYAH. (*On her knees.*)

Memsahib, by these tears that wet your dress
rid ayah of her anguish, and confess.

MEMSAHIB. (*After a pause.*)

You wish it? Then I will. Up, off your knees.
(*Pause.*)

AYAH.

Memsahib made her promise. Tell me. Please.

MEMSAHIB.

I don't know what to say. Or how to start.
(*Pause.*)

AYAH.

Tell me, Memsahib. You break my heart.

MEMSAHIB. (*Sudden vehemence.*)

Mother! Driven by the dark gods' spite
beyond the frontiers of appetite.
A *judge's* wife! Obscene! Bestialities
Hindoos might sculpture on a temple frieze!

AYAH.

> Forget! Forget! The great wheel we are on
> turns all that horror to oblivion.

MEMSAHIB.

> Sister! Abandoned . . . by him too . . . left behind. . .
> driven to drugs and drink . . . Out of her mind!

AYAH.

> Memsahib, no. Don't let black despair
> flail at your family. Forbear. Forbear.

MEMSAHIB.

> It's India! Your cruel gods athirst
> for victims. Me the last and most accursed!

AYAH. (*Truth dawning.*)
> Not love?

MEMSAHIB.   Love. Like fever.

AYAH.   Memsahib, whom?

MEMSAHIB.

> Witness once more in me my family's doom.
> I love . . . I love . . . I love . . . You know the one
> I seemed to hate so much . . . the Rajput's son . . .

AYAH.

> Thomas Theophilus? The half-breed! Shame!

MEMSAHIB.

> I couldn't bring myself to speak his name.

AYAH.

> *Wai*, Memsahib, all my blood congeals.
> Love's a running sore that never heals.
> Our India destroys white womankind,
> sapping the body, softening the mind . . .

MEMSAHIB.

> It's not a sudden thing. This black malaise
> struck at the very heart of hopeful days.
> My wedding day in fact. The very day
> I gave my solemn promise to obey
> the Governor Sahib, turning down the aisle,
> I glimpsed his son. That steely, distant smile!
> I saw him, blushed, then blenched. I couldn't speak.

Things swam before my eyes. My limbs felt weak.
My body froze, then blazed. I felt flesh scorch
as Siva smoked me out with flaming torch.
I sensed the gods of India were there
behind the throbbing heat and stifling air.
Heart beat like a tom-tom, punkah flapped
backwards and forwards and my strength was sapped.
I felt you mocking, India, you brewed
strange potions out of lust and lassitude,
dark gods mocking, knowing they can claim
another woman with the Judge's name,
picking off the family one by one
each destroyed by lust and Eastern sun.
I tried to ward them off. I tried to douse
my heart's fierce holocaust with useless vows.
Tried the *bazaar!* Besought a Hindoo priest
to placate his deities. But nothing ceased.
I saw that sacrifice was offered at the shrine
of every god you Hindoos hold divine –
Siva, Kali, Krishna . . . that shaped stone . . .!
essayed their names myself, but could intone
only young Thomas's. He was my Lord.
He was the deity my lips adored.
His shape pursued me through the shimmering air.
I tried to flee him. He was everywhere.
O most unspeakable – In Sahib's bed
the son's eyes staring from his father's head!
Against every natural impulse of my soul
I played the stepmother's embittered role,
and had him hounded, and got Thomas sent
back home to Britain into banishment,
forced from his father's arms, his father's heart.
My husband and his favourite prised apart.
At first, relief. I started breathing. With him gone
I put the mask of Governor's Lady on.
I led a wholesome and quite blameless life,
the model mother and submissive wife,
grand lady and efficient châtelaine
adopting public roles to stifle pain.
Useless distractions, purposeless pretence!
The pain, when he returned, was more intense.
The old foe face to face and no escape.
The scars of love's old wounds began to gape,

the old sores fester, the flesh weep blood.
Nothing staunches love or stems the flood.
No longer veins on fire beneath the skin,
ravenous India had her claws deep in.
Ayah, ayah, O I utterly detest
this cancerous passion that consumes my breast.
I was about to die, and hide away
this sordid secret from the light of day.
But your entreaties wouldn't let me rest.
I gave in to your tears and I confessed.
Save your tears for after. Please don't try
to stir me back to life. I want to die.

Enter GOVERNOR'S ADC.

ADC.

Your Ladyship, alas, no one would choose
to bring your Ladyship this bitter news,
but someone had to. It's already known
by almost everyone but you alone.
His Excellency, the Governor of Bengal
is dead. Or killed. His death deprives us all.

Silent agony from MEMSAHIB.

AYAH.
    Wai!

ADC.   I regret there's nothing we can do
to bring him, or his relics, back to you.
The 'son' already knows. The news was brought
by scouts returned from searching to the Fort.
(*More silent agony.*)
Your Ladyship, I fear that there is more.
Bazaar talk mentions riot, even war.
Down from the mountains a murderous horde
have put a frontier outpost to the sword.
And Ranjit's daughter under house arrest
may be the focal point for fresh unrest.
There's panic in the quarters. What we need
's your Ladyship herself to give a lead.
Most vital in such times a figurehead,
someone to look to in the Governor's stead,
an example to the others, brave and calm,
someone to salute to and salaam.

(*Pause.*)
The Governor's (mm) 'son' 's about to go . . .
Commands a following . . . could overthrow
the rule of law . . . ambition thwarted, rank
from both his strains, own future pretty blank . . .
nobility on one and on the other
Rajput royal blood from his wild mother.
With disaffection rife he might decide
to throw his lot in with his mother's side.
Some of us consider that it's right
not to let the boy out of our sight.

AYAH.

The Memsahib has noted your report.
Now allow her time for grief and thought.

Exit ADC.

To think I thought it all a waste of breath
trying to talk Memsahib back from death.
I'd almost given up, prepared to go
with Memsahib to the world below.
His Excellency Sahib is no more.
The bazaar is humming with these threats of war.
His widow must put on the bravest front
for all the sahibs in the cantonment.
Memsahib, live! Fling guilt and shame aside.
Forget this pact with death, this suicide.
The Governor Sahib journeying beyond
releases you from shame and breaks your bond.
Death has condescended to remove
all barriers. Your love's a normal love.
Memsahib need no longer veil
a love which Death has placed within the pale.
It's likely that the half-breed Rajput colt
will swing to the other side and will revolt,
unite with Lilamani and make war
against the Company and rule of law.
Try to persuade him loyalty is best.
Soften the stubbornness within his breast.

MEMSAHIB.

Very well! Your arguments prevail. I'll try,
if there are means to help me, not to die.
If duty to my kin in this dark hour

can give me back one spark of vital power.

Enter MEMSHAHIB *and* AYAH. *Enter* LILAMANI *with* TARA *her attendant.*

LILAMANI.

>In here? The Governor's son? I don't believe . . .
>To speak with *me*, you say? To take his leave?
>Can this be true? Is this happening to me?

TARA.

>The first of many blessings. You'll soon see.
>Those suitors that the cruel tyrant banned
>will soon flock unopposed to seek your hand.
>Soon, Rani Sahiba, soon your royal due,
>freedom and empire will devolve on you.

LILAMANI.

>I thought it all bazaar talk, but now, no.
>I see from your glad face it must be so.

TARA.

>The brute who loosed the redcoat cannonade
>on Rani's noble brothers joins them as a shade.

LILAMANI.

>So, the Governor is dead. How did he die?

TARA.

>The most fantastic stories multiply –
>much speculation, but one rumour's rife
>how, yet again unfaithful to his wife,
>he helped another Sahib violate
>the Maharani of a native state,
>cloaking the nature of his real pursuit,
>licentiousness called "law-enforcement". Brute!
>Some say beyond the frontier, beyond
>the forbidden river, Indus, into Khond.
>They disappeared (they say in the bazaar)
>into the place where ghosts and dead souls are,
>the two white sahibs standing without dread
>among dark multitudes of silent dead!

LILAMANI.

>It's not possible! A living man descend
>among the ghostly dead before his end.

He must have been bewitched. The evil eye!

TARA.

> You seem to doubt his death, your Highness, why?
> Everyone believes what I have said.
> The Governor is dead, your Highness, dead.
> The Memsahib, with sahibs from the Fort,
> anxious for their skins, are holding court,
> worriedly debating under swinging fans
> potential chaos and contingent plans.
> They must be organised before the rain.

LILAMANI.

> Do you suppose his son is more humane?
> Would he look on my plight with more regard?

TARA.

> I'm sure he would.

LILAMANI.   No. No. He's very hard.

> She'd be most foolish the woman who expects
> kind treatment from a man who hates our sex.
> Haven't you noticed how he'll never ride
> anywhere near us but reins aside?
> You know what people say about how stern
> he is, a piece of ice that will not burn.

TARA.

> Too much phlegmatic Britain in his veins
> dampens the Rajput warmth his blood contains.
> I know the *myth*: ascetic, cold, severe,
> but not, I've noticed, with your Highness near.
> The reputation made me scrutinise
> this paragon's cold face and flint-like eyes.
> I saw no coldness there. His inmost heart
> and what they say of him are poles apart.
> He was enslaved the first time both your eyes
> exchanged shy glances, and although he tries
> in your presence to turn his eyes away,
> his eyes stay riveted, and won't obey.
> To call him lover would offend his pride
> but looks tell everything that mere words hide.

LILAMANI.

> You've know me all my life, would you have thought
> this shadow puppet of harsh fortune brought

into a world of bitterness and tears
should ever feel such love and its wild fears?
I, last of Ranjit's noble household, forced
to watch my brothers face the holocaust.
My father bayonetted! The redcoat guns
killed my six brothers. All my father's sons.
The eldest, proud and strong, a bloody mess
blown from a cannon into nothingness.
Smoking smithereens! India's red mud
churned even redder with her children's blood.
A state with no new Rajah on the throne.
Only I survive, defenceless and alone,
and drag my life out under strict taboo,
constant surveillance, what I think, say, do,
everywhere I go the Sahib's spies
watch all my movements with their prying eyes.
What is he afraid of? That love's warm breath
might bring my angry brothers back from death.
As if weak love-pangs such as mine could fan
long burnt out cinders back into a man.
You also were aware I could despise
the wary Sahib and his watchful spies,
indeed, love meant so little to me then
I almost could have thanked the Governor's men
for taking so much trouble to provide
external aids for what I felt inside,
that scorn I had of love. Until my eyes
first saw his son, and I felt otherwise.
It's not the handsomeness and blazoned grace
that Nature's lavished on his form and face
(which he's unconscious of, or quite ignores)
it's not entirely those that are the cause,
but something rarer and more precious still:
his father's good's in him without the ill,
the strengths that earned the Governor his great name
but not those weaknesses that mar his fame.
And what I love the most, I must confess,
is his obdurate scorn, his stubbornness.
The Memsahib made Governor Sahib fall –
grabbing a heart available to all.
You can't call conquest waiting in the queue
until the "conquered" one gets round to you.
No sense of victory where many more

have planted standards in the field before.
No, but to triumph over and subdue
a heart subject to no one until you,
to captivate and make a man of steel
know the pangs of love and learn to feel,
to make a man half-gladdened, half-forlorn,
finding himself in chains he's never worn,
chafing the harness that he half wants on,
fretting for freedom, but half glad it's gone,
that's what I call triumph, that's the kind
of hard-won victory I have in mind,
the uphill struggle it's a thrill to win –
breaking the wild, unwilling stallion in.
Whatever am I thinking though.
He's obstinate. He'd sneer at me I know.
Then perhaps you'll hear my outraged cries
against that haughty pride I eulogise.
That rod of iron bend?

TARA.   You soon will know.
He's coming now.

Enter THOMAS THEOPHILUS *ready to travel.*

THOMAS.   Madam, before I go
I wanted a few words with you to say
your position might well alter from today.
My father's dead. My presentiment was strong
that fate, not folly kept him gone so long.
No, nothing less than death could overthrow
my noble father, no mere mortal foe.
Only some darker superhuman force
could quench the hero's meteoric course.
My father *was* a hero. Fate sees fit
to take his brilliance and extinguish it.
Acknowledge his great virtues, even you,
and give the good in him its proper due.
Learn from a son's deep love to moderate
your just resentment and your family's hate.
Were I the Governor I'd countermand
the law forbidding men to seek your hand.
If I were on this dais you'd dispose
of self and heart exactly as you chose.

>If I were my dead father I'd revoke
>his interdictions, lift that cruel yoke . . .

LILAMANI.

>And even that you think of doing so
>moves me more deeply than you'll ever know.
>The ties of generosity like yours
>bind me more strictly than your father's laws.

THOMAS.

>No, let me finish. If I had any say
>you'd be a *reigning* princess. Now. Today.
>Your country gagged on blood. Blood, so much blood
>even the sun-baked earth was turned to mud,
>your brother's bloody gobbets and splashed gore
>splattered like catsup from the cannon's jaw.
>Though I'm ambitious I can never rise
>because of my mixed blood, my dual ties.
>Though my ambition's balked I can aid yours,
>and, if I may, I'd gladly serve your cause,
>in the only way I can, behind the scenes –
>the mediator's role, the go-between's!

LILAMANI.

>Can I believe my ears? Is all this true?
>What friendly deity persuaded you?
>To put your future into jeopardy,
>your precarious existence! All for me!
>It's quite enough to see you moderate
>your hate for me and . . .

THOMAS.   Hate you, Madam? Hate!
>So self respect and pride can brand a man
>as some unpacified barbarian?
>Wasn't my mother human just like yours?
>Am I some jungle freak that snarls and roars?
>In any case, by standing at your side,
>the wildest savage would be pacified.
>If anything is magic then you are.

LILAMANI.

>Sir, I beg you . . .

THOMAS.   No, I've gone too far.
>Reason's unseated. Nobody can rein
>runaway passions into line again.

My confession is so pressing, once begun
I have no other course but going on.
Look at this object. Shed tears for its sake,
watch iron bend, and adamantine break,
this monument to pride with feet of clay,
this sun-baked stubbornness that's given way,
this is the victim, me, who used to scoff
at lovers bound in chains they can't throw off,
who saw love's storms sink thousands in the sea
and felt secure and said: *this can't touch me,*
now humbled by the lot that most men share
I find myself adrift, I don't know where.
One moment only killed a lifetime's pride.
I submitted to my fate and my will died.
I fled and thrashed about, tried to subdue
the pain that was inside me caused by you.
Shadow, sunlight, dense forest, open space –
it didn't matter where – I saw your face.
I was the hunter once, but now I feel
more like the beast that flinches from the steel.
This prisoner before you vainly tries
to find some shred of self to recognise.
My weapons are beginning to corrode.
I've quite forgotten that I ever rode.
My idle mounts relaxing in their stall
no longer recognise their master's call.
My crudeness must astound you. You'll regret
having this monster snarling in your net.
You should value even more your praises sung
by such a novice and unpractised tongue.

Enter BURLEIGH.

BURLEIGH.
    Her ladyship desires an interview.
    I'm really not sure why.

THOMAS.   With me?

BURLEIGH.   With you.
    I'm not sure of the reason. All I know
    's she wishes a few words before you go.

THOMAS.
    How can I face her now, or she face me?

LILAMANI.

> I beg you lay aside your enmity.
> She shares in your bereavement. Try to show
> a little sympathy before you go.

THOMAS.

> I need some too. From you. Give me some sign
> of your reactions to those words of mine.
> My offers? Heart? What *am* I to believe?

LILAMANI.

> That I am just as willing to receive
> as you to give. Your gift of love alone
> is worth all worldly powers or mere throne.

Exit LILAMANI *making the gesture of* namaste *to* THOMAS THEOPHILUS.

THOMAS. (*To Burleigh.*)

> Soon the sun'll be too high for us to start.
> Please tell the men we're ready to depart,
> then come back in a breathless hurry, say
> how the men are anxious to be on their way.
> I could dispense with farewells of this sort.
> Friend. I depend on you to cut it short.

Exit BURLEIGH. *Enter* MEMSAHIB *and* AYAH *who remains behind the colonnade.*

MEMSAHIB.

> I'm told, sir, that you're anxious to depart.
> I'd hoped to shed the grief that's in my heart
> and blend my tears with yours, and to declare
> that, with this sense of danger in the air,
> now that we know for sure your father's gone,
> I scarcely have the will to carry on.
> The spirit of unrest extends and grows . . .
> I'm expendable to you, though, I suppose.
> It wouldn't worry you, stepmother fed
> to vultures, dogs . . . I'm sure you wish me dead.

THOMAS.

> I've never wished you anything so bad.

MEMSAHIB.

> I could have understood it if you had.
> To all appearances I seemed hell-bent
> on causing you much suffering and torment,

stepmother on the warpath, out for blood,
wreaking devastation where she could.
To all appearances! How could you know
the sad reality that lay below?
My schemes and subtle hints had one design
to keep your person far away from mine.
Suffocated by proximity,
stifled by contact of the least degree,
I wanted space between us, and so much
not even the lands we lived in came in touch.
Only with you in Britain, only then
could I begin to live and breathe again.
If penalties are gauged to the offence
and your hostility's my recompense
for what seemed mine to you, were you aware,
you'd know that punishment was less than fair.
No other woman ever fitted less
the type of stepmother aggressiveness . . .

THOMAS.
A mother, Madam, as is too well known
rejects outsiders to protect her own.
It's said to be a not uncommon fate
of second marriages, this kind of hate.

MEMSAHIB.
O I must be the one exception then
that proves your rule. Or you must think again.
The feelings of your own stepmother are . . .
rather different . . . different by far . . .

THOMAS.
Madam, it's still too early to succumb.
It's still just possible that news may come.
Your grief, perhaps, is somewhat premature.
Somewhere your husband is alive, I'm sure.
My father will come back. His life seems charmed.
India's dark gods won't have him harmed.
I've often thought that Siva and his crew
favoured my father, somehow, haven't you?

MEMSAHIB.
There is no voyage home from where he's gone.
No gods that anyone can call upon.
Even the gods of India give way

once greedy Death has fastened on its prey.
What am I saying? Dead? How could he be
when I can see him now in front of me?
I feel my heart . . . Forgive me. My distress
makes me, I fear, too prone to foolishness.

THOMAS.

I see that through desire a loving wife
can bring the man she longs for back to life.
As if you see him when you gaze at me!

MEMSAHIB.

I pine, sir. Yes. And smoulder. Desperately.
I love your father, anxious to forget
the fickle social butterfly who'd set
his cap at almost anything in skirts.
That's one side of your father that still hurts.
I see the Governor's womanising ghost
ravish the consort of his present 'host'!
When I say I love him I don't mean
the womaniser and the libertine,
no, I remember the attentive him,
still diffident, one might say almost grim,
yet so attractive, fresh, he could disarm
everybody with his youthful charm,
whether they were sahibs or Hindoo.
In all his youthful pride he looked like you,
your bearings, eyes, the way you sometimes speak,
the same aloofness and the same . . . physique.
(*Pause.*)
Mother was 'ill', and outbreaks of bad crime
kept Father on the circuits all the time;
my sister and myself felt lonely, *then*
your famous father swam into our ken.
A wild maneater of prodigious size
began most dreadfully to terrorize
the province that we lived in, and it claimed . . .
O . . . scores of victims, eaten, mauled and maimed.
A hunter even then of great repute
your father was called in to kill the brute.
He'd taken on so many beasts like these
he seemed like Theseus or like Hercules.
With his adventurous, eccentric life,
his exploits, books, his loves, his Rajput wife,

all this, to us two sisters, made him seem
the complete answer to a young girl's dream.
We fell in love with him right from the start,
two sisters rivals for the same man's heart!
A pity you weren't there, that you weren't one
sent out to help. Too young to hold a gun!
The younger daughter might have been less slow,
less prone to stand back for her sister. No!
I would have taken the initiative.
Everything she gave, I too would give.
I would have led you to exactly where
the monstrous tiger had its tangled lair.
I would have shown you every little twist
to where the jungle's deep and gloomiest.
I sense your shots sink home with a soft thud!
The stillness of the beast! The smell of blood!
But for a few dim stars, the endless drone
of chirring insects we are quite alone.
Palpable jungle darkness all around.
Would I have cared if we were lost or found?
With you beside me and the night so black
who would ever want the daylight back?

THOMAS.
Madam . . . I don't think ever in my life . . .
Have you forgotten you're my father's wife?

MEMSAHIB.
Forgotten? I? What leads you to infer
that I no longer value honour, sir?

THOMAS.
Forgive me, Madam. I acknowledge to my shame
an unpardonable slander on your name.
I didn't understand . . . I couldn't tell . . .
I think . . . (*Turns.*)

MEMSAHIB.   You understood me very well!
I love you. Love! But when I spell out love
don't think that it's a passion I approve.
Do you suppose I wouldn't if I could
banish this fever throbbing in my blood?
I'm more hateful in my own than in your eyes.
India's chosen me to victimise.
I call on India to testify

how one by one she bled my family dry,
the gods of India whose savage glee
first gluts itself on them and now on me,
my mother and my sister, now my turn
to sizzle on love's spit until I burn.
You know very well how much I tried
to keep my distance, O I tried. I tried.
Keeping my distance led me to devise
a barrier of hate built up of lies –
I faked hard-heartedness, I cracked the whip,
filled you with hatred for her Ladyship,
was everything they say stepmothers are
until the Memsahib was your *bête noire*.
What use was that? I made you hate me more
only to love you fiercer than before.
I found you even harder to resist –
you were most beautiful when wretchedest.
You'd soon see if you looked at me! I said,
if for a second you could turn your head,
and, just for a moment, look into my eyes.
I think that even you would realise.
Aaggh! Revenge yourself. Go on, chastise
me for foul passions you despise.
There were many monsters that your father slew.
He missed the "maneater" in front of you.
How did he ever let this vile beast pass?
YOU give this animal the *coup de grâce!*
Yes, take the sword he gave you and destroy
the Governor's widow who dare love his boy.
Get your father's sword out. Thrust! Thrust! Thrust!
Kill the monster while it reeks of lust.
Or if you think that I'm too vile to kill,
and will not strike, give me the sword. I will.
(*Struggles with him.*)
Give me it!

Enter AYAH *emerging from colonnade and snatching the sword away.*

AYAH.   Stop, Memsahib. Come away.
        Think if you're noticed in such disarray.
        Someone's coming. Memsahib! The disgrace!

Exeunt MEMSAHIB *and* AYAH *still carrying the sword.*
Enter BURLEIGH.

BURLEIGH.
> Her Ladyship? Dragged off? My boy, your face!

THOMAS.
> We've got to get away from here. We must.
> I feel such nausea, and such disgust.
> I feel so utterly polluted . . . she . . .
> No. Consign the horror to eternity.

BURLEIGH.
> Thomas, the men are ready to depart.
> We'd best be off before the troubles start.
> Your father's death is felt as the first blow
> of widespread insurrection from below.
> Some rumours though insist he isn't dead.
> Seen somewhere near the frontier. So it's said.

THOMAS.
> Nothing must be ignored. Sift every clue.
> Anything we find we'll follow through,
> I don't care what the sources of it are –
> returning scouts, or spies, or the bazaar.

Exit BURLEIGH.

> But if he's dead, I'll help to bring this land
> under a cleaner, less corrupted hand.

Exit THOMAS THEOPHILUS.

ACT TWO

Bugle-calls off-stage. Enter CHUPRASSIE *and* SERVANTS. *Enter* ADC.
Enter MEMSAHIB *and* AYAH.

MEMSAHIB.

> Tell the Chuprassie, please, the answer's NO.
> The Memsahib's not fit to go on show.

Exit ADC *ushering* CHUPRASSIE *and* SERVANTS *out.*

> Hide me from the world's what they should do,
> conceal my raw desire from public view.
> Such thoughts which never ought to even reach
> the conscious mind I've put into plain speech.
> And how he heard it all, that block of wood,
> making as if he hadn't understood!
> I pour out my secret, inmost heart
> and all he wants to do is to depart!
> He pawed the ground, and had no other thought
> than how he could best cut my ravings short.
> The way he stood and shuffled with bowed head
> could only make my shame a deeper red.
> And even when I had his swordblade pressed
> all ready to be plunged into my breast,
> did he snatch it back? Made no attempt!
> Just stared at me! Such coldness! Such contempt!
> I touch it once, that's all, and in his sight
> it's been polluted by some dreadful blight.

AYAH.

> Self-pity, Memsahib, the way you brood
> nourish a passion that is best subdued.
> What would the Judge Sahib your father say
> if he were still alive and here today?
> He'd say: Find peace in duty, daughter, find
> some public service to assuage your mind.
> Duties a Governor's widow can perform
> to help the Sahibs ride the coming storm.

MEMSAHIB.

> The storm's already raging in my soul.
> The Memsahib's no touchstone of control!
> My reason's a torn punkah that can't move
> the airless atmosphere of febrile love.

O reason soon seems sapped and comatose
shut up in passions so stifling and close!

AYAH.
You could go home.

MEMSAHIB.   And leave him here? O no!

AYAH.
You had him sent away.

MEMSAHIB.   Yes, years ago.
It's too late now. He knows. He knows. I've crossed
the frontier of virtue and I'm lost.
Hope, for a moment, caught me unawares
and all my shame was bared to his cold stares.
When I was quite prepared for my demise
you dangled life and love before my eyes.
All your native guile and honied speech
put the unattainable within my reach.
I wanted, *wanted* O so much to die.
You had to come and stop me. Why? Why? Why?

AYAH.
Innocent or guilty, Memsahib, I'd do
even more than that if it's for you.
Spare your ayah though. Can you forget
that face of his, indifferent and hard-set?

MEMSAHIB.
Perhaps it's innocence and virgin youth
that makes his ways seem clumsy and uncouth.
Look at the stations where he's had to live
among the most far-flung and primitive.
Let's try to understand. Perhaps that's why.
It's the novelty of love that makes him shy.
So perhaps we shouldn't condemn him yet.

AYAH.
His Rajput blood, Memsahib, don't forget.
His mother was barbarian, half-wild.

MEMSAHIB.
Half-wild or not, she loved. She bore this child.

AYAH.
He hates all women and would never yield.

MEMSAHIB.
        Good, his hostility helps clear the field.
        If love is something that he'll never feel
        let's search elsewhere for his Achilles heel.
        Ambition! Dual parentage frustrates
        all hopes he might have had in both his states.
        (*Listens.*)
        Listen! Horses! Go make the boy believe
        in greatness I could help him to achieve.
        Say how my father's name would help provide
        some useful access on the legal side.
        O tell him now the Memsahib has schemes
        by which he'll realise his inmost dreams.
        Ayah, anything! Urge, implore him, cry.
        Say the Memsahib's about to die.
        And if it seems that you must grovel, do.
        Do anything. My life depends on you.
        Anything!

Exit AYAH.

                India, you see it all
        watching the haughty stoop, the mighty fall.
        Your gods possess dark powers no man can flout.
        How much more blood of mine can you squeeze out?
        How much further down can I be brought?
        If you want more, you'll find much better sport
        hunting a quarry harder to destroy,
        fleeter of foot, a virgin. Hunt the boy!
        O India! There's much more good pursuit
        chasing the suppler, more elusive brute.
        It's your sensual nature he ignores.
        Avenge yourslf. We have a common cause:
        to make him love . . .

Enter AYAH.

                        So soon? the answer's no.
        He wouldn't listen even. Let him go.

AYAH.
        Silence those feelings. Never let them stir.
        Remember your old self and who you were.
        Banish such thoughts for ever from your head.
        Your husband, Governor Sahib, isn't dead.

The people cheer, those few who recognise
the Governor Sahib in his new disguise.
Any moment now he will appear.

MEMSAHIB.
The Governor! Alive? And almost here!
If he's alive, all I can do is die.

AYAH.
Again you talk of death, Memsahib. Why?

MEMSAHIB.
And had I died this morning as I planned
and not let your persuasion stay my hand,
I might have earned some tears, and saved my face.
All I deserve's dishonour. Death. Disgrace.

AYAH.
Death! Death!

MEMSAHIB.   What have I done? What have I done?
The Governor will be here, and with his son.
The one who saw her grovel with cold eyes
will watch her Ladyship resort to lies,
tears of frustration just shed for the boy
turned so deceitfully to wifely joy,
the wife still burning for her husband's son
go through the motions of reunion,
the still flushed consort desperate to convince
the husband she betrayed not minutes since.
There's just a chance that he's so overcome,
so anxious for his father, he'll stay dumb.
Or maybe he'll tell all through sheer disgust
at seeing his father's wife display her lust.
And if he does keep quiet, I'm not one
to shirk the consequence of what I've done.
I can't forget things. I'm not one of those
frequenters of mess balls and evening shows,
who can commit their crimes and uncontrite
are never troubled by a sleepless night.
My conscience hurts me. Hurts. Each word I said
keeps echoing and booming through my head.
Those beastly heads his study's full of roar
as we enter *adulteress* and *whore*.
I see the hand of judgement start to scrawl

graffiti of my guilt on every wall.
Death's the only answer. Death. A swift release
from pain. For me and for my conscience, peace.
Is it so much to die? To one who's racked
by great torment it's a very simple act.
The only fear that lingers in my mind
is for my children. The shame I leave behind.
So many generations of blood-pride
obliterated by my suicide.
Think of the children, orphans, forced to face
those stories (all too true) of my disgrace.

AYAH.

I do. I weep for them. They'll suffer hell.
I fear those things will happen you foretell.
But why, Memsahib, why must you expose
your little children to such ills as those.
If you die, all that's likely to be said
's she couldn't face her husband, so she fled.
What greater sign of guilt could you provide
than plunging headlong into suicide.
Memsahib, think! This suicide of yours
does more than lawyers to defend his cause.
Your death saves him. Your tragedy becomes
a camp-fire story for his hunting chums.
Without you here, there's no more can be done.
I'm a poor ayah. He's the Governor's son.
My word against his son's! Huh, take my part
against a cherished favourite of his heart!
Then all India will hear and quite ignore
in all the din against the one voice for.
Memsahib I would rather die with you
than live to hear such stories, false or true.
Thomas Theophilus, Memsahib? How
do you feel about the half-breed now?

MEMSAHIB.

His head should be mounted along with all
the monsters on the Sahib's study wall.

AYAH.

Then don't give in submissively. Don't lose
without a struggle, Memsahib, accuse
the boy before the boy accuses you.

Who will contradict you if you do?
(*Takes up sword.*)
And this, Memsahib, look. Here's evidence:
the weapon in your hands, you, shaken, tense.

MEMSAHIB.
Purity put down? Innocence oppressed?

AYAH.
Only keep silent and I'll do the rest.
I suffer fear as well. I feel remorse.
I'd rather die but see no other course.
What are one poor ayah's scruples worth
with her Memsahib buried in the earth?
I'll speak, but making sure his anger goes
only to bitter words and not to blows.
And just supposing guiltless blood were spilt
to save your honour and to spare your guilt,
aren't these the measures that we have to take
when it's a question of your name at stake?
Honour must be saved at all expense
even the sacrifice of innocence.

Enter CHUPRASSIE *and* SERVANTS. *The* GOVERNOR *pushes through them and enters disguised as an Indian.*

GOVERNOR.
Fortune relenting has turned foul to fair
and returned me to your arms . . .

MEMSAHIB.   Sir, stay there!
Don't desecrate your joy. I've lost all right
to claim the eagerness of your delight.
You have been wronged. Fate brings you from the dead
but spits its venom at your wife instead.
No longer fit to bear the name of wife!

MEMSAHIB *hurries off closely followed by* AYAH.

GOVERNOR.
And this my welcome! The dead brought back to life.

THOMAS.
Your wife's the one to question. Only she
can help you clarify this mystery.
If desperation moves you, father, then
heed that of this most desperate of men,

and permit your shaken son to live his life
in some locality not near your wife.

GOVERNOR.
    What? Leave?

THOMAS.   As long as you, sir, were away,
    I'd no alternative except to stay,
    protecting those entrusted to my care,
    against my will: your wife; and Ranjit's heir.
    I did my best, but now with your return
    I need no longer stay, sir, and I yearn
    to prove myself your son and blood my spear
    on prey far grander than wild boar or deer.
    By my age, single-handed and alone,
    you'd toppled a cruel Sultan from his throne,
    shot scores of grim maneaters dead, and quelled
    banditry in savage districts, held
    the passes against unpacified Afghans
    and made the highroads safe for caravans.
    How many villagers you went to save
    from dacoits or maneaters came to wave
    and shout: *Jai! Sirkar ki jai!* around your tent
    Glory and victory to the Government!
    So many trophies on your walls by then
    to satisfy the lifetimes of most men.
    Old heroes could retire because they knew
    the rule of reason was secure with you.
    Obscurity! The undistinguished son
    of such a father, and with nothing done!
    Even my mother did more things than me.
    Father, I feel trapped in this obscurity.
    Let me have your weapons. I'll pursue
    the fiercest monsters as you used to do.
    I'll have the Residency walls and floors
    covered with trophies just as wild as yours.
    From private bedroom to official throne
    carpetted with beasts I've overthrown.
    Or make my going such a noble one
    the world would know at last that I'm your son.

GOVERNOR.
    What's this? What contagion of insanity
    makes my (so-called) loved ones flee from me?

Why did I ever come back from the dead
to find my family so filled with dread?
Of me? Myself the object to strike fear
into the ones I trusted and held dear!
(*Pause.*)
O India got into us somehow!
Absolute madness when I look back now,
part imbecility, part foolish prank
and probably the simpkin that we drank,
well anyhow, the upshot of it all
was a midnight entry, via the palace wall,
into a harem. My colleague, ADC
in charge of the suppression of Thuggee,
(he's more hot-blooded than you'd think, that man)
forced the favourite of the local Khan.
And, put it down to India, I'm afraid
that I 'assisted' in his escapade.
Taken by surprise, no time to draw
the tyrant had us seized and bound . . . I saw . . .
He kept . . . God knows what the monsters were.
I tell you even I was frightened, sir.
He kept . . . these somethings hungry in a pit.
I heard my friend thrown screaming into it.
My captor was a beast, obscene, perverse,
given to practices I won't rehearse,
to crude carnalties that overrode
every natural law and human code.
He'd draw the line at nothing. No taboo
would stop him doing what he wanted to.
I was shut up in a hole, a living tomb
so dark it seemed like Hell's own ante-room.
Chained naked like a beast – six months in there,
barely a spark of light or breath of air!
Then India relented, I suppose.
I broke the sentry's neck and stole his clothes
and made a quick escape, but not before
your father settled his outstanding score
with that black tyrant who'd devised all this.
I dropped him piecemeal down his own abyss,
that devilish despot and foul debauchee
chewed by his pet, flesh-starved monstrosity.
Disguised, I left that hell-hole far behind

restored to light and air, and my right mind.
Anxious to resume my shaken hold
on normal life I find the world turned cold.
This is my hearth and home and surely where
I have some right to breathe a cleaner air.
A season spent in hell, I've no desire
for whiffs of brimstone from the household fire.
I still smell prisons, yet I'm among
the very ones I yearned for for so long.
I see my dear ones with averted face
shunning the welcome of my warm embrace,
my presence striking terror in their soul
and wish I were still shut up in that hole.
I want the truth from you. I want it now.
What wrong has my wife suffered? When? Who? How?
Why isn't the culprit under lock and key?
You're in it too! Why don't you answer me?
Speak, why can't you? My flesh and blood! My son!
Is everyone against me? Everyone?
Ah India, I've given you my life.
Deliver up the man who's harmed my wife.
I'll get to know, by fair means or by foul,
what manner of strange monster's on the prowl.

Exit GOVERNOR.

THOMAS.
O this unventilated atmosphere!
Burleigh, my blood runs cold with sudden fear.
What if her Ladyship, while still a prey
to her strange frenzy, gives herself away?
Instead of a warm son and welcoming wife
my father finds a foul infection rife,
some plague that makes his hearth and home unclean;
like victims sickening in quarantine,
the wife and son to whom he's been restored,
shivering with symptoms in this fever ward.
As in the jungle when the beaters' ring
closes round the beast that's panicking,
I feel that sense of menace and my heart
thumps as the undergrowth is forced apart.

Enter AYAH *displaying the sword of Thomas Theophilus, and
followed by the* GOVERNOR.

GOVERNOR.
    ANIMAL! . . . Now it all comes out!
    The reversal everybody spoke about!
    The lower self comes creeping up from its lair
    out of the dismal swamps of God-knows-where.
    It lumbers leering from primeval slime
    where it's been lurking, biding it own time.
    How could his kind absorb our discipline,
    our laws of self-control, our claims of kin.
    I've expected far too much. It's in his blood.
    Control himself? I don't suppose he could.
    One should have known the worst. One ought to know
    that India once hooked in just won't let go.
    (*Takes the sword.*)
    And this the weapon! One he couldn't lift
    when I first gave it him. His father's gift!
    I don't suppose his sort acknowledge sin.
    Don't blood-ties count? To violate one's kin!
    And the Memsahib? Why did she allow
    this animal at liberty till now?
    Her silence makes his foulness almost fair.

AYAH.
    It was the Sahib's grief she wished to spare.
    The Memsahib, so sickened with sheer shame
    was she at kindling his lustful flame,
    her desperate feelings turned to suicide,
    and but for me, Sahib, she would have died.
    I saved her, Sahib. I preserved your wife
    in the very act of taking her own life.
    In pity for her sorrow and your fears
    I now explain the meaning of her tears.

The GOVERNOR *drives the sword into the dais on which throne stands.*

GOVERNOR.
    Barbarian! No wonder that in spite
    of all his efforts I could sense his fright.
    His chilly welcome took me by surprise,
    felt frozen by the scared look in his eyes.
    When did my son first show himself so foul?
    When did this animal first start to prowl?

AYAH.

> At the beginning of your married life
> the boy already had disturbed your wife.

GOVERNOR.

> And in my absence things came to a head?

AYAH.

> Everything occurred as I have said.
> We must not leave her on her own too long.
> Allow me to return where I belong.

Exit AYAH.

GOVERNOR. (*Seeing Thomas enter.*)

> Good God! Wouldn't anyone be taken in
> by looks so seemingly devoid of sin?
> No mark of his lascivious offence
> sullies that subtle mask of innocence.
> A beast in human shape! I'd like to brand
> ANIMAL on his flank with my my own hand!

THOMAS.

> May not a sympathetic son be told
> what makes his father's look seem hard and cold?

GOVERNOR.

> After dishonouring your father's name,
> still reeking of your lust and smirched with shame,
> the animal still has the brazen face
> to stand before his father in this place!
> Instead of running far away from me
> back to the jungle and its savagery,
> beyond our influence and rigid laws
> back to the world of bestial lusts like yours.
> Unless you want to share the fate of those
> whose lawlessness I crushed with iron blows,
> unless you want the Governor to show
> his famous skill in killing monsters, GO!
> India! Remember how I cleared
> your countryside of monsters that all feared.
> Now in return I ask your gods to take
> swift vengeance on this monster for my sake.
> If you cherish me in your dark heart,
> India, tear this animal apart!

THOMAS.
    Her Ladyship brands me with that foul sin?
    It's too revolting even to take in.

GOVERNOR.
    I think I can see through your little game.
    Your lust kept secret through the lady's shame.
    You loathsome animal, you put your trust
    in her reticence to conceal your lust,
    That's not enough. You should have had the sense
    not to have left behind this evidence,
    (*Taking sword and displaying it to Thomas Theophilus.*)
    or been more systematic, and instead
    of leaving her just speechless, left her dead.

THOMAS.
    Why do I stand and hear so black a lie
    and not speak truths I'd be acquitted by?
    Sir, there are dreadful things I could disclose
    nearer to yourself than you suppose.
    I could blurt secrets out. I could . . . but no,
    give me some credit for not doing so.
    I cannot wish more agony on you
    but please consider what I am and who.

THOMAS THEOPHILUS *takes sword from* GOVERNOR.

    A man first breaks small laws, then treads taboos
    basic to all men beneath his shoes.
    Like virtue vice develops. It takes time
    for petty to turn into heinous crime.
    Impossible! The twinkling of an eye
    turn innocence to bestiality!
    My mother's chastity was her renown.
    That and her courage. I've never let her down.
    I made restraint a virtue and subdued
    mutinous passions into servitude.
    My shibboleths were bridle, curb and bit.
    Lust! Bestiality! I mastered it!
    I'm the one who took restraint so far
    that I'm a laughing stock in the bazaar.
    You know the soubriquets they call me by,
    good-natured, and obscene, as well as I.
    I never thought of women, now I'm faced
    with charges of black lust. I'm chaste, sir. Chaste!

GOVERNOR.
>Your foul obsession must have taken hold
>from very early on to make you cold
>to every female influence but one.
>Wouldn't some black concubine have done?

THOMAS.
>Father! Sir! It's too much to conceal,
>I have to tell the truth. My heart *can* feel.
>It feels a chaste emotion, but for one
>you yourself placed interdictions on.
>It's Lilamani. Under house arrest.
>She's stormed my stubborn heart. There, I've confessed.
>Despite myself I contravened your law
>and this is what I need forgiveness for.

GOVERNOR.
>Very clever! You're ready to confess
>to that to hide the worse lasciviousness!

THOMAS.
>For six months now no matter how I've tried
>I've loved. I've loved her, and I'm terrified,
>and came to see you now to tell you so.
>Sir, how much further do I have to go.
>I swear by . . .

GOVERNOR.   O the guilty always flee
>as a desperate resort to perjury.
>Enough! Enough! No more tedious harangues,
>if it's on stuff like this your story hangs.

THOMAS.
>You think my story's false, and full of lies?
>Your wife, sir, in her heart knows otherwise.

GOVERNOR.
>Animal! How dare you. Don't say any more.

THOMAS.
>I'm to be sent away? Where? And how long for?

GOVERNOR.
>Across the Indus, the 'forbidden river',
>and beyond our frontiers. For ever!

THOMAS.
> Charged with such crimes, and your curse on my head,
> who will welcome me, or give me bread?

GOVERNOR.
> Peoples exist without *our* discipline,
> the lesser breeds, perhaps they'll take you in.
> Hospitality in the far North West
> means laying down your wife for any guest.
> You should feel welcome there. I'm sure you'll find
> depraved men, debauchees, of your own kind!

THOMAS.
> Debauchery! Compare my mother's, my own life
> with that of the woman who conceived your wife.
> Think of my parentage, then hers, and choose.
> Decide whose blood is coming out, sir. Whose?
> Think of my mother, Father! Think! At least
> she wasn't serviced by a slavering beast!

GOVERNOR.
> Go! Get out of my sight. Or else I'll shout
> for the sentries and have you frog-marched out.

Exit THOMAS THEOPHILUS.

> Like shivering and chill preceding fever
> I sense the presence of avenging Siva.
> My spine's an icicle, my inwards knot
> with pity for this monster I begot.
> God, I feel stifled by my wretchedness!
> How did I come to sire a beast like this?

Enter MEMSAHIB.

MEMSAHIB.
> Your shouting could be heard through all the doors.
> It made me terrified to hear those roars
> and bull-like bellowing. I feared far worse
> might follow on your homicidal curse.
> You still have time to call him back. You could.
> O do, I beg you. He's your flesh and blood.
> Spare some thought for me. How could I survive
> knowing that, but for me, he'd be alive.
> Could I live with the knowledge I'm the one
> who turned a father's hand against his son?

GOVERNOR.
>No, not a father's hand. A darker force
>than any man's ensures death takes it course.
>India owes me some destruction.

MEMSAHIB.   No!

GOVERNOR.
>Her gods are swift in paying what they owe.
>And now, in all its blackness, tell me all
>before the mercury of anger starts to fall.
>I want each little detail.

The GOVERNOR *turns and walks to the colonnade. A pause in which it seems the* MEMSAHIB *has the truth all ready to disclose.*

>You've not heard
>half of the guilt your stepson has incurred.
>He launched into a great frenzy against you.
>Implied that all you'd said just wasn't true!
>And in his own defence he swore that . . . Guess!
>He swore he loved the Indian princess!
>Lilamani . . .

MEMSAHIB.   Swore? What?

GOVERNOR.   Tried to confuse
>the issue. Lies all lies. A desperate ruse.
>(*Suddenly tense.*)
>I hope whatever happens happens soon.
>(*Leaving.*)
>Then everything washed clean by the monsoon!

Exit GOVERNOR.

MEMSAHIB.
>And just when I was coming to his aid!
>This thunderclap! This stunning cannonade!
>Stung by remorse and guilt I flung aside
>my ayah's arms and left her terrified.
>O God knows just how far I might have gone
>if I'd have let repentance drive me on.
>If he hadn't cut me short . . . God knows
>I had the truth all ready to disclose.
>And Lilamani (*Lilamani!*) stealing
>the little boy from me who has no feeling.
>The one who'd walled himself completely in

against invasions of the feminine!
Perhaps his heart's accessible to all,
and he has hundreds at his beck and call.
Women pawing him from every side
and I'm the only one he can't abide.
The charms of any native concubine
are no doubt more agreeable than mine.
The only one to whom he *can* say no!
Too old, too white for his seraglio!
Chastity? Surfeit! And I'd come to claim
his innocence, and ruin my own name!

Enter AYAH.

Ayah, have you heard the latest? Guess!

AYAH.
Memsahib, ayah comes to you in real distress.
I wondered why you'd torn yourself away.
I was very much afraid what you might say.

MEMSAHIB.
Ayah, there's competition. And, guess who?

AYAH.
Memsahi . . .

MEMSAHIB.   He loves another. Yes, it's true.
This fierce quarry no one could hunt down,
who countered blandishments with a cold frown,
this tiger frightening to standing beside,
gentle as a lamb, quite pacified.
That princess . . .

AYAH.   Her?

MEMSAHIB.   Yes *her*. Agh how much more
persecution has India in store?
As if being torn apart by two extremes,
first shivering despair, then fevered dreams,
as if the final insult of his cold rebuff
and all my sufferings were not enough.
Lovers? Them! What native sorcery has thrown
this smokescreen round them? When were they alone?
How? When? Where? You knew all along. You knew.
You could have told me sooner couldn't you?
Exchanging glances. Talking. Furtiveness.

Where did they hide, him? In the forest, yes.
To follow one's feelings through nature's course
without recriminations and remorse,
not to feel criminal, and meet as though
the sun shone on one's love and watched it grow!
Ah! Every day they must wake up and see
vistas with no black clouds, and feel so free!

AYAH.
They'll never meet again, Memsahib. Never!
Their love . . .

MEMSAHIB.   will survive for ever and ever.
Though they were twenty thousand miles apart
heart would heliograph to exiled heart,
across the Himalayas if need be.
Nothing can come between them. Even me!
Kisses! Promises! Touching one another!
scorning the fury of the mad step-mother.
Their happiness feeds off my jealousy.
That green-eyed monster is destroying me.
That mutinous family! No reason why
the Governor should show her leniency!
The father bayonetted, the brother shot
from a cannon. She should die too. Why not?
She's of their blood. They died. Why should she live?
Her crime is even harder to forgive.
How smoothly one progresses from the first
tentative transgressions to the worst.
My first steps taken, sick with vertigo,
I inched towards dishonour, now I go
with eyes wide open and with one bold stride
into the black abyss of homicide.
O, those white hands, remember? If I could
I'd plunge them elbow deep in guiltless blood.
How can I bear to have the sun's light pry
through every cranny at my misery?
There's nowhere, nowhere dark enough to hide.
No, everywhere the sun can get inside.
Close the shutters and black out the glare
you feel it then as heat, and everywhere:
the mercury a hundred in the shade,
the grass screens sprayed with water, and resprayed,
the hopeless, winnowing thermantidote –

heat like some animal that claws one's throat.
There's no escape from that all-seeing eye,
that presence everywhere except to die.
My Hell is India, always at high noon,
with no relief of night, and no monsoon,
and under that red sun's remorseless stare
mankind's grossest secrets are laid bare.
My Hell is such exposure, being brought
a guilty prisoner to my father's court.
I see the Judge's phantom with shocked face
jib at the details of his daughter's case,
hearing his once loved flesh and blood confess
to crimes of monumental loathsomeness.
Aghast but relentless he applies the Law
to horrors even he's not heard before.
His task is Judgement. Judges give no quarter,
and merciless he sentences his daughter.
Father, forgive me. Please forgive me. Try.
Harsh India's destroyed your family.
The same gods in your daughter. Recognise
the lust they kindled blazing in her eyes.
Repentence never lets up its pursuit.
I've broken laws, but never reaped the fruit!
Harried by ill luck till my last breath
all that seems left me is a dreadful death.

AYAH.

You are in love. And that's your destiny.
You're in the power of some evil eye.
Is love unheard of, even in these parts?
Memsahib, millions have human hearts.
Are you the first or last of us to fall.
Memsahib, love is common to us all.
Weakness is human, Memsahib, submit
to your humanity. Give way to it.
Even the gods, we Hindoos say, who fright
mere mortals sometimes, know delight.
Not only men, Memsahib, gods above
partake of pleasures and the joys of love.

MEMSAHIB.

You reptile! Spitting still! The snake still tries
to poison the Memsahib with black lies.
Your evil whispers drugged my sense of right.

The boy I shunned you urged into my sight.
Who gave you leave? Who gave you orders? Why
did you have to brand him? Now he'll die. He'll die.
His father mouths strange curses and implores
vengeance and justice from those gods of yours.
Let what agonies you've earned spell out the fate
of those low persons who corrupt the great.
You take our weaknesses and give them scope
and grease the incline of the downward slope.
Her Ladyship debased, demeaned, brought low,
down to the level of your blackness. Go!

Exit AYAH. MEMSAHIB *is left alone with the sense of India closing in.*
Exit MEMSAHIB.

Enter LILAMANI, *followed by* THOMAS THEOPHILUS.

LILAMANI.
    No! No! Your keeping silent's suicide!
This sacrifice you make to spare his pride
in normal circumstances would be one
that's most becoming in a loyal son,
but now with danger like a dangling sword
it's more a luxury you can't afford.
If, without much thought for me, you can consent
and so submissively to banishment,
then go; leave me to languish and to grieve.
But at least defend yourself before you leave,
defend your honour. There's still time yet
to persuade your father to retract his threat.
If you keep silent then the scales will tip
wholly in favour of her Ladyship.
Tell everything . . .

THOMAS.   Tell everything and show
my father his own shame, I couldn't, no.
Could I bear exposing his wife's lust
and watch his whole life crumble into dust?
The fullest horror's known to only you
and those who witness all we say and do.
If I didn't love you would I have revealed
obscenities to *you* I'd want concealed
even from myself! You gave your word
I never to pass on what you have heard.
And even if it proves at my expense

I have to make you swear to reticence.
That gesture of respect for him at least.
From every other tie I feel released.
Remember too that right is on our side.
Sooner or later I'll be justified.
Her Ladyship will surely not elude
the consequences of gross turpitude.
Leave this prison, and its poisoned air,
and follow me to exile, if you dare.
I can offer you the means you need to flee.
Even the guards on watch are all with me.
We could count on powerful allies in our fight
to win you back your throne, your lawful right.
My mother's tribe, the warlike Rajput clan
have sworn allegiance to us to a man.
Mountain chieftains and the Rajah's court
send secret guarantees of their support.
The Memsahib! Why should such as she
prosper by destroying you and me?
Now's the time. Everything is on our side.
And yet you look afraid and can't decide.

LILAMANI.

There's no dishonour in escape, indeed
I feel it only right I should be freed.
My family's heroes struggled to set free
our subdued people from white tyranny.
Your father is a tyrant and I owe
him no obedience. I'm free to go.
But I'm of royal blood, and many wait
for me to reassume the reins of state,
the last upholder of my father's name.
My followers permit no hint of shame . . .

THOMAS.

Nor I! My mother's gods are yours. Suppose
we swear our loyalty in front of those?
Near where my royal mother's buried, she
and all her ancient Rajput family,
there stands a shrine, a very holy place
where no perjurer dare show his face.
To stand in for our fathers we'll invoke
the gods, whose shrine it is, to join our yoke.

LILAMANI. (*Seeing Chuprassie enter with three servants.*)
>   The Governor's Chuprassie! Go, please, go.
>   I'll stay a while so nobody will know.
>   Send someone I can trust to be my guide
>   to lead me to the shrine to be your bride.

She makes the gesture of namaste *to* THOMAS THEOPHILUS *who, after a pause, returns the gesture and exits.*

Enter GOVERNOR *who first confers with* CHUPRASSIE.

GOVERNOR.
>   I'm told my son's been taking leave of you?

LILAMANI.
>   We said farewell. Your "intelligence" is true!

GOVERNOR.
>   Those lovely eyes! It's their work, then, all this?
>   First to hypnotise that stubbornness!

LILAMANI.
>   The truth is something that I can't deny.
>   He doesn't seem to share your enmity.
>   He's never treated me like a pariah.

GOVERNOR.
>   It doesn't operate like that, desire.
>   I suppose he swore his love 'for ever more'.
>   You're not the first. He's said it all before.

LILAMANI *remains silent.*

>   You should have kept him on a tighter rein.
>   Doesn't the competition cause you pain?

LILAMANI.
>   It should pain you to vilify your son,
>   especially so pure and chaste a one.
>   Have you so little knowledge of his heart?
>   Can't you tell innocence and guilt apart?
>   Don't listen to that snake, Memsahib's nurse.
>   Take back, Sahib, your rash assassin's curse.
>   Our gods may well give ear to your wild wish
>   because they find you brutish, devilish.
>   Sometimes it's anger makes the gods say yes
>   and gifts may be the gods' vindictiveness.

GOVERNOR.
>You're trying to throw dust into my eyes.
>Love's blinkered you to his depravities.

LILAMANI.
>Take care, Sahib. Your manly strength and skills
>have notched up many monsters in your kills.
>Their glazed eyes watch us talking, but not all
>have their heads hung on your study wall.
>Your great collection is still missing one . . .
>But I'm forbidden to go further by your son.
>Strangely enough his love for you 's not gone
>and his respect prevents my going on.
>Unless I leave your presence I'll forget
>myself and say things that we'll both regret.

Exit LILAMANI. *The sound of thunder.*

GOVERNOR.
>They're both in league to throw me off the track.
>A conspiracy to stretch me on the rack.
>In spite of my resolve some doubt still gnaws.
>A still small voice cries mercy, and I pause.
>Deep in my hardened heart to my surprise
>pity still sends out its feeble cries.
>(*Resolved again.*)
>I want it all made absolutely clear.
>(*Shouts.*)
>Chuprassie!

CHUPRASSIE.   Sir!

GOVERNOR.   Memsahib's ayah. Here.

Exit CHUPRASSIE. *Enter* ADC.

ADC.
>Sir! Her Ladyship! Something's very wrong.
>She's gripped by God knows what and can't last long.
>Whatever thoughts are passing through her head,
>she seems, your Excellency, almost dead.
>Her face is ghastly pale, her bloodless lips
>seem more a corpse's than her Ladyship's.
>The ayah's been sent packing by your wife.
>Fled to the forest careless of her life.
>Went to earth where none would give pursuit,

a region best relinquished to the brute.
No blacks and none of us (but you)'d give chase
into that swampy beast-infested place.
The jungle swallowed her. No search would find
much more than shreds of sari left behind.
What drove the woman there nobody knows.

GOVERNOR.
What's this?

ADC.   Her Ladyship finds no repose.
She hugs the children's likenesses, which seems
to calm her for a while, but then she screams
and pushes them away as if she could
no longer bear the thought of motherhood.
She walks or rather lurches to and fro,
not knowing where to sit or where to go.
She looks at one but seems to stare right through.
She knows there's someone there, she's not sure who.
She sat down at her desk three times and wrote
but each time changed her mind and burnt the note.
For pity's sake, sir, go and see your wife.

GOVERNOR.
The ayah dead! My dear one sick of life.
Someone fetch my son. I'll hear his case.
Let him defend himself before my face.

Exit ADC. *The* GOVERNOR *listens to the distant thunder of the coming monsoon.*

O God what if the thing's already done?

Thunder. Wind blows through the room. Enter BURLEIGH.

Ah! Burleigh, you. What's happened to my son?
You've been his tutor how long now? Well nigh . . .
But what's this, man? My God, you're weeping. Why?
My son! What's happened?

BURLEIGH.   *Now* you demonstrate
anxiety on his behalf. It's all too late.
He's dead.

GOVERNOR.   No!

BURLEIGH.   The gentlest boy I knew!
And, if I may say so, the most guiltless too.

GOVERNOR.
>My son dead? No! The moment I extend
>my arms to him, THEY hound him to his end.

BURLEIGH.
>We moved like a slow cortège out of the town.
>Even the horses jogged with heads hung down.
>He rode his finest white Arabian steed
>at little more than normal walking speed.
>The sepoy escort all looked just as grim
>and sullen out of sympathy for him.
>We're hated, but obeyed because we're feared.
>He was almost one of them; admired; revered.
>Then from the jungle came a dreadful cry.
>Birds and old dry leaves began to fly.
>And dust, like blood turned into powder, floats
>in huge spirals, blinds us, scours our throats.
>The wind got up, increased. The jungle trees
>first lent a little to a light stray breeze
>then began bending violently and then
>just as suddenly sprang straight again;
>then bent with force that made the palm leaves crack.
>Then all of a sudden all the sky went black,
>and from the deepest darkest part a cry
>like the first but lower rent the sky.
>Our hearts stand still. Blood freezes in our veins.
>Hair stiffens on our frightened horses' manes.
>The forest begins heaving like the sea,
>and seems to open up, and, suddenly,
>we see, festooned with seared lianas, IT
>some horrifying, monstrous, composite,
>like one of those concoctions that one sees
>in dark recesses on a temple frieze.
>An old woman told the sepoys it was Siva
>in his avatar of monster. They believe her.
>You know how sceptical I am, but there
>is the monster, and its bellows fill the air.
>The whole earth shudders as it moves its feet
>and shambles forward through the shimmering heat.
>An epidemic smell, the beast exhales
>a stink like cholera from its gold scales.
>Then everyone starts running, everyone
>except, that is, your son, your fearless son.

We all take shelter in a shrine nearby.
He reins in his horse and does not fly.
We see him all alone, without a fear,
grab that ordinary, native spear
he sometimes went hog-hunting with, and fling
the weapon with sure aim into the thing.
It gushes blood, breathes fire and smoky heat,
squirms and writhes before the horses' feet.
The thing with wide jaws like an open sluice
disgorges gore and vomits blackish juice.
The horses panic. A regular stampede!
He calls out to his own. They take no heed.
The one he's riding bolts and all in vain
he shouts *whoa, whoa,* and tugs hard on the rein.
He wastes his strength. From each champed bit
flies froth and slaver and blood-red spit.
The sepoys say that maddened Siva sank
a sharpened trident into each scorched flank.
They gallop, riderless but one, towards the rocks –
the snap of broken bones and cracked fetlocks,
as they collide and sprawl, and he
trails tangled in one stirrup helplessly.
Excuse my lack of self-control, these tears.
That cruel sight will haunt me all my years.
I saw him with my own eyes, sir, saw him towed
by the stallions he'd tamed himself and rode
in the cool of the morning, saw your son
dragged by the ponies he'd played polo on.
I hear him try to check them, *whoa there, whoa.*
It terrifies them more and still they go.
His body drags and twists, his clothes all tear.
He leaves a terrible trail of blood and hair.
That once fine handsome beauty with the look
of something dangling off a butcher's hook!
There was really nothing left to call a face.
At last the maddened horses slow their pace.
Staggering they slow down to a halt,
near where his princely forebears have their vault.
I follow, panting, sobbing. Sepoys wail.
Strewn flesh and bloodstains left an easy trail.
Rough rocks bearded with the boy's fine hair,
flesh on the sharp bamboo shoots! Everywhere!
Thomas, I say. He takes my hand. He tries

to open wide what once had been his eyes.
Dear friend, he gasps, *something has been sent
to snatch my life away. I'm innocent.
When I am gone, look after her for me,
little Lilamani, lovingly.
Perhaps one day when father's disabused
and pities the dead son he once accused
beg him treat her kindly and restore . . .*
With that his head fell back. He said no more.
The brave boy died, and left in my embrace
a lump of mangled flesh without a face.
Your 'gods' glut anger on the blameless one.
I doubt if you would recognise your son.
(*Thunder.*)

GOVERNOR.
Son, my son! All consolation in you gone.
I've murdered my own future. Thomas! Son!
India, you've served me all too well.
My life will be dragged out as one long hell.

Enter MEMSAHIB *unnoticed.*

BURLEIGH.
Then Lilamani came, afraid of you,
and what your enmity would make you do.
She stares, gripped by some suffocating dream
at blood-red undergrowth and sickly steam.
She sees (what an object for a lover's eyes)
that mess that was her loved one and denies
the evidence before her, clings to doubt.
She sees the pile of flesh but looks about
and asks for him. How could she face that grim,
raw, featureless heap, and think it him?
At last she's certain and pours out her hate
on all the gods the Hindoos venerate,
then cold and moaning, sickened, almost dead
she crumples by the corpse she should have wed.
Relaying his last wish fulfils my vow.
My joy in life's all gone. I loathe it now.
It's blighted at the root. It's meaningless.
Your son is dead and
(*Indicating the Memsahib.*)
                           there's his murderess!

GOVERNOR.
> Good evening, Madam. Well, it seems you've won.
> You've won your victory. I've lost my son.
> Now new suspicions and misgivings start
> sending tremors through my broken heart.
> But what's the use? No, take your spoil. Enjoy
> the harsh destruction of my gentle boy.
> Relish it, and gloat. Go on, lick your lips.
> The triumph (so far) 's all your Ladyship's.
> I'm willingly blinkered. Don't want to know.
> I'll think him a criminal if you say so.
> There's been more than enough to make me weep
> without my stirring up that murky·deep.
> Now I see it all. Given all my fame
> so that the world can better see my shame.
> This time there's no escape. No new disguise
> will ever shield me from their staring eyes.
> I want to cast off everything and run
> from you, from India, my mangled son,
> the very universe, and leave behind
> the frontiers marked out for humankind.

MEMSAHIB.
> No sir! Silence will no longer do!
> These accusations! They were all untrue.
> He's innocent . . .

GOVERNOR.   you were the very one
> whose testimony made me curse my son.
> You . . .!

MEMSAHIB.   Richard! Listen! I need to reassure
> a father that his son died chaste and pure.
> The guilt was mine. For which I now atone.
> The inordinate desire was mine alone.
> The ayah took advantage of my state
> of shock and faintness to incriminate
> your son to you, and of her own accord
> accused him. She's had her just reward.
> Like her, I wanted instant suicide
> but wished to clear his name before I died.
> I wanted, needed to confess, and so
> I chose another, slower way to go —

The MEMSAHIB *sinks to her knees.*

there's poison in my veins, and beat by beat
the heart that once was blazing loses heat.
It's all as if I saw you through dark gauze,
through rain beginning like a slow applause.
I hear it starting now, the rain, cool rain
giving the blood-red earth new life again.
Rain. Rain. Like purdah curtains. When I die
the dawn will bring you all a clearer sky.

MEMSAHIB *dies.*

ADC. She's dead!

GOVERNOR.   But her black actions, they won't die.
They'll blaze for ever in the memory.
Clearer than day it all comes home to me.
Now let me force myself to go and see
what's left of him, and try to expiate
my dabbling with strange gods I've come to hate.
He must be buried with all honours due
his mother's and my rank . . .

Enter LILAMANI.

                                            and as for you —
Your family were mutineers. I realise
I seem some savage brute to your young eyes.
Your family mutinied. They raised the war.
I had to administer the rule of law.
Your family, now mine, have borne the cost
of crossing certain bounds best left uncrossed.
Now try to ford, though times force us apart,
those frontiers of blood into my heart.

As the GOVERNOR *speaks the* CHUPRASSIE *and servants kneel and
begin a chant which gradually becomes dominant. The sound of rain
like slow applause.*

BOW DOWN (1977)

MUSIC: Harrison Birtwistle

BOW DOWN

Bow Down was devised by Tony Harrison with members of the National Theatre Company and first performed in the Cottesloe Theatre on 5 July 1977 with the following cast:

ACTORS	Brian Cox (Chorus 8)
	Morag Hood (Chorus 3)
	Anthony Milner (Chorus 2)
	Judith Paris (Chorus 7)
	Frederick Warder (Chorus 5)
MUSICIANS	Jonty Harrison (Chorus 2)
	Melinda Maxwell (Chorus 4)
	John Wesley-Barker (Chorus 9)
	Lorraine Wood (Chorus 6)
MUSIC DIRECTOR	Dominic Muldowney
DANCE	Judith Paris
COMPOSER	Harrison Birtwistle
DIRECTOR	Walter Donohue
DESIGNER	Jennifer Carey
PRODUCTION MANAGER	Jason Barnes
STAGE MANAGER	John Caulfield
DEPUTY STAGE MANAGER	Frank Nealon
ASST STAGE MANAGERS	Fiona Davie
	Sally Blake
	Jondon Gourkan

NOTE: *The source material of* Bow Down *was the ancient and traditional ballad of* The Two Sisters *which exists in numerous and varied versions throughout northern Britain, Scandinavia and America. No one version of the ballad can claim to be definitive, and each one possesses its characteristic detail, either topographical or linguistic. All the versions that we collected together from the various oral traditions and the sources gave us a basis of change in time and place for our exploration of what remained essentially the "same" story.* T.H./H.B.

Blackout. Silence. We begin to see a CHORUS *of nine people, of which* 2, 3, 5, 7, 8, *are actors and and* 1, 4, 6, 9, *are musicians. They are seated round a circle. Two drum beats initiate a choral pulse based on breathing. Out of the choral chant we see* CHORUS 7 *do a forward roll into the circle to become the* FAIR SISTER. *She is drowning in the sea. She cries out and her cries are cut off by the water. The* CHORUS *breathe in and propel* FAIR SISTER *to the surface on an expelled f sound.*

FAIR SISTER.
    O . . .
    O sister . . .
    O sis . . .
    O si . . .

At her final cry CHORUS 2 *becomes the* BLIND HARPER *who catches her cry and prolongs it with his own:*

BLIND HARPER.
    . . . . ster

Then he begins to walk round the outside of the choral circle composing a ballad. He is walking the sea-shore. He seems to have one foot in the water and one foot on the sand. As he feels the water deepen he evades it with a dexterity that has come from centuries of doing the same thing. His wavering "dance" follows the ebb and flow of the tides. He has been following the Northern coasts, searching, listening. His "dance" defines the contours of continents. He mutters fragments of a Ballad and as he passes each of the CHORUS *they take up a pitch from his mutter:*

BLIND HARPER.
    O min kaer søster! Du frelse mit liv;
    Så giver jeg dig min sølvslagne kniv.

    O synk, o synk, kom aldrig til land
    Så far jeg din sølvslagne kniv.

    O min kaer søster! Du hjaelpe mig på fod
    Så giver jeg dig mine sølvspaendte sko.

    O synk, o synk, kom aldrig på fod
    Så vel far jeg dine sølvspaendre sko.

    O min kaer søster! Du hjaelpe mig op;
    Så giver jeg dig min gule lok.

    O synk, o synk, kom aldrig op!
    Så vel far jeg din gule lok.

O min kaer søster. Du hjaelpe mig til land
Så giver jeg min faestemand.

O synk, o synk, kom aldrig til land
Så vel far din faestemand . . .

As the BLIND HARPER *passes round the* CHORUS *circle we see* CHORUS
3 *become the* DARK SISTER. *She goes into the circle behind the
drowned* FAIR SISTER *and we see her as if emerging from the* FAIR
SISTER. *We see the rigid arms of the* DARK SISTER *slowly open behind
the* FAIR SISTER. *They are the rigid arms of someone being racked and
tortured. As the* BLIND HARPER *obscures our view of the two sisters,
they sit and become two sisters in a bower. They sing a duet which is
a refrain from a ballad:*

I'll be true to my true love
if my love will be true to me.

During their duet the BLIND HARPER *returns to his place at* CHORUS 2,
muttering the ballad as he goes.

The SISTERS *dance together and as they dance the* CHORUS *interject
the following couplets from ballads:*

CHORUS 2.   There were two sisters in a bower,
            Their father was a baron of power.

CHORUS 8.   There were two sisters in a bower,
            The youngest was the fairest flower.

CHORUS 2.   There were two sisters who will die,
            One drowns wet and one drowns dry.

CHORUS 8.   There were two sisters by the firth,
            One sips salt and one chews earth.

CHORUS 2.   There were two sisters watching clouds,
            One saw swans and one saw shrouds.

CHORUS 8.   There were two sisters watching waves,
            One saw geese and one saw graves.

CHORUS 2 & 8.   There were two sisters in a bower,
CHORUS 5.   There came a knight to be their wooer.

During the dance and the couplets CHORUS 5 *has become the* SUITOR
*and mimes a journey on horseback around the circle. When he
returns to* CHORUS 5 *position, he enters the circle with the line:*

SUITOR.   There came a knight to be their wooer.

The two SISTERS *and the* SUITOR *then do a dance, for which the* CHORUS *play the music. As the dance proceeds* CHORUS 7, 8 & 2 *come to the narrative position and addresss different sections of the audience with the following couplets from ballads:*

CHORUS 7. He courted the eldest wi glove and ring,
CHORUS 8. But he loved the youngest above a'thing.

CHORUS 7. He courted the eldest wi brotch and knife,
CHORUS 2. But he loved the youngest as his wife.

CHORUS 7. He brought the eldest ring and glove,
CHORUS 8. But the youngest was his ain true-love.

CHORUS 7. He brought the eldest sheath and knife,
CHORUS 2. But the youngest was to be his wife.

CHORUS 7. He courted the eldest with jewels and rings,
CHORUS 8. But he loved the youngest best of all things.

CHORUS 7. He courted the eldest with a penknife.
CHORUS 2. And he vowed that he would take her life.

CHORUS 7. The eldest, she had a lover come,
CHORUS 8. And he fell in love with the youngest one.

CHORUS 7. He gave to the first a golden ring,
CHORUS 2 & 8. He gave to the second a far better thing.

During these couplets spoken by CHORUS 7, 8 & 2, *the* DARK SISTER *responds both to the spectacle of the dance between the* FAIR SISTER *and the* SUITOR *and to the couplets with the refrain:*

DARK SISTER.
        I'll be true to my true love
        if my love will be true to me

The DARK SISTER*'s refrain becomes increasingly jealous. As the* FAIR SISTER *and the* SUITOR *move out of the circle, we see the face of the* DARK SISTER *and see it set with dark resolution. The rhythm of the dance continues and* CHORUS 2 *enters the circle, silences the music and recites a ballad, with the* CHORUS *responding with refrains and half-lines:*

        There were two sisters in a bower,
                Bow down, bow down, bow down.
        There were two sisters in a bower,
        There came a knight to be their wooer.
                I'll be true to my love, and my love'll be true to me.

To the eldest he gave a beaver hat,
And the youngest she thought much of that.

To the youngest he gave a gay gold chain
And the eldest she thought much of the same.

These sisters were walking on the bryn,
And the elder pushed the younger in.

'O sister, oh sister, oh lend me your hand,
And I will give you both houses and land.'

'I'll neither give you my hand nor glove,
Unless you give me your true love.'

Away she sank, away she swam,
Until she came to a miller's dam.

The miller and daughter stood at the door,
And watched her floating down the shore.

'Oh father, oh father, I see a white swan,
Or else it is a fair woman.'

The miller he took up his long crook,
And the maiden up from the stream he took.

'I'll give to thee this gay gold chain,
If you'll take me back to my father again.'

The miller he took the gay gold chain,
And he pushed her into the water again.

The miller was hanged on his high gate
For drowning our poor sister Kate.

The cat's behind the butt . . .

On the final stanza after 'The cat's . . .' a drumbeat cuts off CHORUS 2
and he reverts instantly to the figure of the BLIND HARPER *and mut-*
tering his Scandinavian ballad returns to his position at CHORUS 2.

BLIND HARPER.
O min kaer søster! Du frelse mit liv;
Så giver jeg dig min sølvslagne kniv.

O synk, o synk, kom aldrig til land
Så far jeg din sølvslagne kniv.

O min kaer søster! Du hjaelpe mig på fod
Så giver jeg dig mine sølvspaendte sko.

O synk, o synk, kom aldrig på fod
Så vel far jeg dine sølvspaendre sko.

O min kaer søster! Du hjaelpe mig op;
Så giver jeg dig min gule lok.

O synk, o synk, kom aldrig op!
Så vel far jeg din gule lok.

O min kaer søster. Du hjaelpe mig til land
Så giver jeg min faestemand.

O synk, o synk, kom aldrig til land
Så vel far din faestemand . . .

CHORUS 2 *then initiates the new choral chant, out of which* CHORUS 3
as the DARK SISTER *and* CHORUS 7 *as the* FAIR SISTER *enter the circle
singing and pass one another diagonally:*

DARK SISTER. (*Sings.*)
      I'll be true to my true love
      if my love will be true to me.

FAIR SISTER. (*Sings.*)
      Down by the waters rolling

They recross and return to the positions of CHORUS 3 & 7, *and as they
do so* CHORUS 5 *in the mask of* DARK SISTER *and* CHORUS 8 *in the mask
of the* FAIR SISTER *enter the circle and become the two* SISTERS *in their
bower. The* DARK SISTER *puts rings on the fingers of the* FAIR SISTER.
Then the DARK SISTER *combs the long golden hair of the* FAIR SISTER.
During the combing CHORUS 2 *speaks:*

CHORUS 2.
      It fell oot upon a day
      the auldest ane to the youngest did say . . .

Then CHORUS 3 & 7 *as the voices of the* DARK SISTER *and* FAIR SISTER
speak to one another over the masked mime of combing hair:

DARK SISTER.
      Will you gae to the green and play?

FAIR SISTER.
      O sister, sister I daurna gang
      for fear I file my silver shoon

DARK SISTER.
>O sister, O sister will ye come to the stream,
>To see our father's ships come in?

FAIR SISTER.
>Sister, dear sister where shall we go play?
>Cold blows the wind, and the wind blows low.

DARK SISTER.
>O sister, O sister will ye go to the dams
>To hear the blackbird thrashin oer his songs?
>
>O sister, O sister, will ye go to the dams
>To see our father's fish-boats come safe to dry land?
>
>O sister, sister will ye go to the sea
>Our father's ships sail bonnilie?
>
>O sister, O sister gang down to yon strand
>And see our father's ships coming to dry land.
>
>O sister, O sister, will you go and take a walk
>And see our father's ships how they float?

During the DARK SISTER*'s attempts to persuade the* FAIR SISTER *to go down to the water, we hear the voice of the* FAIR SISTER *taunting the* DARK SISTER *in the tones of childhood:*

FAIR SISTER.
>Wash your hair in the salt sea brine
>it will never be as fair as mine.
>
>Even if your hair was gold
>you'll always live alone and cold.
>
>Wash yourself as white as you can
>you will never find a man.
>
>Wash yourself as white as bone
>but you'll always live alone.
>
>Wash yourself as white as flour
>you'll be one sister in a bower.

Then CHORUS 2 *from the* CHORUS 5 *position continues the narrative with:*

CHORUS 2.
>And as they walked by the linn
>
>As they were walking the salt sea brim

> When they came to the roaring linn
> The elder pushed . . .

CHORUS 3. (*Standing.*)   . . . dang . . .
CHORUS 7. (*Standing.*)   . . . shot . . .
CHORUS 2.   . . . the younger in.

The masked DARK SISTER *seizes the masked* FAIR SISTER *and they freeze in that position. We hear the voice of the* FAIR SISTER (CHORUS 7) *pleading with the* DARK SISTER (CHORUS 3) *to pull her out of the water:*

FAIR SISTER.
> O sister, sister, tak my middle
> And you shall have my golden girdle.

DARK SISTER.
> O sister, sister I'll not take your middle
> and I shall have your golden girdle.

FAIR SISTER.
> O sister, O sister reach your hand
> and ye shall be heir of half my land.

DARK SISTER.
> O sister, I'll not reach my hand
> and I'll be heir of *all* your land.

FAIR SISTER.
> O sister, reach me but your glove
> and sweet William shall be your love.

DARK SISTER.
> Sink on, nor hope for hand or glove
> and sweet William shall better be my love
>
> Your cherry cheeks and your yellow hair
> Garrd me gang maiden evermair.

On 'evermair' the masked DARK SISTER *pulls off the mask of the* FAIR SISTER *who as* CHORUS 8 *performs a version of the ballad:*

> There were two sisters, they went playing,
>> With a hie downe a downe-a
> To see their father's ships come sayling in.
>> With a hy downe a downe-a.
>
> And when they came unto the sea-brym,
>> The elder did push the younger in.

'O sister, O sister, take me by the gowne,
  And drawe me up upon the dry ground.'

'O sister, O sister, that may not bee,
  Till salt and oatmeale grow both of a tree.'

Sometymes she sanke, sometymes she swam,
  Until she came unto the mill-dam.

The miller runne hastily downe the cliffe,
And up he betook her withouten her life.

What did he doe with her brest-bone?
He made him a violl to play thereupon.

What did he doe with her fingers so small?
He made him peggs to his violl withall.

What did he doe with her nose-ridge?
Unto his violl he made him a bridge.

What did he doe with her veynes so blew?
He made him strings to his violl thereto.

What did he doe with her eyes so bright?
Upon his violl he played at first sight.

What did he doe with her tongue so rough?
Unto the violl it spake enough.

What did he doe with her two shinnes?
Unto the violl they danc'd Moll Syms.

Then bespake the treble string,
'O yonder is my father the king.'

Then bespake the second string,
'O yonder sitts my mother the queen.'

And then bespake the strings all three,
'O yonder is my sister that drownéd mee.

'Now pay the miller for his payne,
  With a hie downe a downe-a

And let him bee gone in the divel's name.'
  With a hy downe . . .

The ballad of CHORUS 8 *is ended abruptly by a scream of whistles,
and* CHORUS 8 *becomes the* BLIND HARPER. CHORUS 2 *also becomes*
BLIND HARPER *and returns from his position at* CHORUS 5 *back to*

CHORUS 2. *The whistles bring out* CHORUS 7 *who does a forward roll linto the circle, and is again the* FAIR SISTER *drowning. She cries out and her cries are cut off by the water:*

FAIR SISTER.
>O . . .
>O sister . . .
>O sis . . .
>O si . . .

BLIND HARPER (CHORUS 8) *picks up her cry and prolongs it with his own '. . . ster'. When the* FAIR SISTER *is under water and drowned she sings:*

FAIR SISTER. (*Singing and dancing her bridal.*)
>My golden shoes they drag me down
>to dance my bridal where I drown
>
>They drag me down my golden shoes
>to dance a dance I do not choose.
>
>My golden chains they drag me down
>to chain the chamber where I drown.
>
>They drag me down my golden chains
>where no one hears the harp's refrains.
>
>My golden rings they drag me down
>to seabed suitors where I drown
>
>They drag me down my golden rings
>. . . bowers of blackness . . . no one sings
>
>They drag me down, my golden veils
>the light's all tarnished, the sun's gold pales.

The FAIR SISTER *drowns. Her body becomes all fluidity, in the total possession of the sea. The body collapses front of stage.*

CHORUS *sing with flute:*
>I'll be true to my true love
>if my love will be true to me.

We see CHORUS 3 *in the mask of the* MILLER'S DAUGHTER *coming to fetch water with a golden bucket:*

MILLER'S DAUGHTER.
>Water, water, water, water
>life for the miller and his daughter . . .

Water drives the great millwheel
that grinds the wheat-ears into meal

Water's wedding with ground wheat
gives us golden bread to eat

Water, water, water, water
life for the miller and his daughter . . .

Watching for the dawn to break
water to fetch and bread to bake

Fetching, baking, hands all raw
though loving's what my hands are for –

These coarse hands caressed Sir Hugh
who got no pleasure from those two

Those two sisters in their bower
with skin as white as father's flour

Don't fetch water, can't bake bread
Can't please lovers in their bed.

MILLER'S DAUGHTER *goes to the water with her bucket and discovers
the body of the* FAIR SISTER.

MILLER'S DAUGHTER.
      Father, dear father, in our mill-dam
      it's either a fair maid or a milk-white swan.

The MILLER (CHORUS 8) *and the* MILLER'S SERVANT (CHORUS 2) *(in
masks) come out to view the body of the* FAIR SISTER. *The* MILLER'S
SERVANT *sees a sexual reverie. The* MILLER *sees riches.*

MILLER'S SERVANT.
      A vision! Never have I been
      so close before to such a queen.
      All I've had's the briefest peep
      through casements in the castle keep.
      I saw both sisters, dark and fair,
      the dark one combed the fair one's hair.
      One dusk I caught another glance
      and saw the sisters dance a dance.
      I heard the sighing of their frocks
      and glimpsed the glint of those gold locks.
      Then darkness fell, and all I saw
      were white hands touching, then no more.

Though battered by the boisterous brine
this lady's body is most fine.
The soggy garments hug her form –
(I wonder if her breasts are warm?)

If this grand lady were not dead
I would have had her maidenhead.

A miller's lackey with full power
over a lassie from yon bower!
Those well-groomed girls in gold and gauds
reared in bowers to love Lords,
pampered, spoon-fed bower brats
with plaited hair and powdered twats,
cooped and cosseted in a pen,
patted and poked by noblemen.
Neither of 'em fetch and carry
marking time until they marry.

A lady of such high degree
helpless and so close to me!
I've seen no lady close as this . . .

Would the dead grudge me one kiss?

He bends down a little as if to kiss the body of the FAIR SISTER *who rises and becomes the* GHOST, *behind the* MILLER *and* SERVANT *but unseen by them. As she rises she sings a long sustained note. The* MILLER *and* SERVANT *still react as though the body were lying on the floor before them.*

SERVANT. (*Bending down to kiss the lips of the Fair Sister.*)
   Pardon, my lady, if I'm so bold

SERVANT *mimes kissing the body on the ground. The* GHOST *behind them touches her lips. The* SERVANT *recoils.*

   Uggghh! She stinks, and her lips are cold!

MILLER.
   I've had scores of well-born girls,
   the women of kings and barons and earls.
   Into their castles the miller did go –
   hey with a gay and a grinding O!

   I have tell you too, my lad,
   it's not a maiden you'd've had.
   If songs speak truth this girl's been whored

by Knight, by Squire, King's son, and Lord,
Northumbrian nobles just passing through,
one called Sir John, the other Sir Hugh,
by a shadowy suitor who rode on a horse
by Willy the Scot, and Svenke who's Norse,
all sorts of riff-raff have been in
Pole, Estonian, Swede and Finn,
Faeroe farmer, drunken Dane
all had Ellen . . . Jean . . . Kate . . . Jane
And even (though that's another story)
the bonnie miller-lad o'Binnorie.
He's the one got in before 'em
by the bonnie mill-dams o'Norham.

SERVANT.
   I'd fancy it now, a little screw,
   if only her body weren't swollen and blue.

MILLER & SERVANT *study body, and the* GHOST *sings:*
   I'll be true . . .

MILLER.
   My lusts now tend another way –
   diamonds and gold, they don't decay.
   Amethyst, cornelian, jasper, jade's
   the sort of flesh that never fades.
   No good to you that corpse, it's cold
   but look at all that good red gold.

MILLER *removes one ring from the hand of the body and throws it into the bucket. Ping! Another. Another. Another. Eight in all, one ring from each finger. The* GHOST *sings 'prove true, my love prove true to me' each of the eight rings pinging on each word.*

Then they remove the body's upper garments and they both stare at the breasts.

SERVANT.
   O I'd love to knead them breasts like dough
   (*Moves to do so, then recoils.*)
   Can't bear the coldness of 'em though.

MILLER. (*Staring at breasts.*)
   Rubies! Take the shears and snip
   them nipples off her ladyship.

SERVANT *snips off one nipple, which the* MILLER *catches and throws*

into the bucket. Ping. Then another. Ping! The GHOST *behind them touches each of her breasts in turn and sings:*
>I'll be true to my true love

MILLER. (*Pointing to the body's navel.*)
>Look at that navel, see it shine!
>I saw it first, so that stone's mine.
>Quick scoop it out. I'll sell this hoard
>and live forever like a Lord.

SERVANT *scoops out the navel and throws it into the bucket. Ping! The* GHOST *touches her navel and sings:*
>Down by the waters rolling

SERVANT *stares at the body still dreaming erotic dreams.*

SERVANT. (*Dreamily.*)
>The loveliest lady I've ever seen.

MILLER.
>Ay, but her flesh is turning green.
>Best get off the rest of her clothes
>before she starts to decompose.
>Take her legs. Up with her bum.

They lift up the legs and pull off the drawers.

SERVANT. I . . . I . . . I . . . I'm going to come . . .

SERVANT *has an orgasm during which the* GHOST *sings:*
>Sing I die, sing I day.

MILLER.
>Fish your hand into your drawers.
>Anything you find there's yours.

SERVANT *fishes his hand into his drawers, and pulls out a very long string of pearls.*

MILLER. (*Pointing to between the body's legs.*)
>The jewel hidden in that hair,
>those tangled harpstrings, is most rare.
>Nestled in the thick of them's
>the gemmiest of gemmy gems, –
>crystal clitoris! Have a feel
>for what those golden wires conceal.

SERVANT *feels and reveals clitoris.*

MILLER.
>Think of what that stone'll fetch.
>Cut it off . . .

SERVANT *begins to cut off the clitoris. The* GHOST *touches her groin and sings:*
>I'll be true to my true love
>if my love'll be true to me

SERVANT.   I'm going to retch.

SERVANT *vomits into the bucket. When he has finished* MILLER *picks up the bucket and tosses the contents out into the auditorium. There is a huge shower of cellophane confetti like a slow-motion shower of precious stones.*

MILLER. (*To audience.*)
>Showers of jewels in his vomit.
>He'll make a mint of money from it.
>There's gems in every greasy gobbet.
>When his back is turned I'll rob it.

The GHOST *sings behind them:*
>Water is all my arms embrace
>Water is all that kisses my face.

MILLER & SERVANT *stare at the body and at one another.*

SERVANT.
>Don't do that. It's not a joke.

MILLER.
>I heard it too. The corpse. It spoke.

They are about to run when the GHOST *sings again and they are transfixed staring at the body.* GHOST *sings:*
>My lover is water I cannot hold
>and the taste of his kisses is salt and cold.

The GHOST *touches* MILLER & SERVANT *and they* SEE *her for the first time. Terrified they run back to their places in the* CHORUS. *There is a loud instrumental scream. The* GHOST *stands on the spot where the body lay and speaks to the audience.*

GHOST.
>For fishing a lady out of his dyke
>they blinded the miller with a golden spike.

GHOST *collapses to former position as drowned* FAIR SISTER. *There is another instrumental scream which brings up* CHORUS 2, 5, 7, *each as the* BLIND HARPER *at different stages of his journey.* BLIND HARPER 1 (CHORUS 2) *makes his journey around the outer circle behind the* CHORUS. BLIND HARPER 2 (CHORUS 8) *makes his journey around the inner circle, and* BLIND HARPER 3 (CHORUS 5) *describes a smaller circle around the body of the drowned* FAIR SISTER. *The three* BLIND HARPERS *speak the Danish version of the ballad, first heard at the beginning of the piece, when* CHORUS 2 *became the* BLIND HARPER *taking the pitch of the drowning* FAIR SISTER's *cries. The three* BLIND HARPERS *complete each other's phrases, going louder or less distinct, as they come into and go out of focus:*

1. 'Odense by der boede en mand
   To dejlige døtre havde han.
   O Herre, o Herre, o Herre Gud!

2. Den yngste var så klar som sol;
   den aeldste var så sort som jord.

3. Så kom der to bejlere gangende frem;
   Ja, de bejled til den yngste af dem.

4. Og alle vilde de den yngste ha';
   Ja, alle vilde de den aeldste forsmå.

5. Og lad os gå til stranden at to;
   Og lad os to os hvide.

6. O lad os to os hvide;
   At vi blive søstere lige.

7. Den yngste gik foran med udslagne hår;
   Den aeldste gik bagefter med onde råd.

8. Den yngste satte sig nee at to;
   Den aeldste skød hende ud med sin fod.

9. O min kaer søster! Du frelse mit liv
   Så giver jeg dig min sølvslagne kniv.

10. O synk, o synk, kom aldrig til land!
    Så får jeg din sølvslagne kniv.

11. O min kaer søster! Du hjaelpe mig på fod;
    Så giver jeg dig mine sølvspaendte sko.

12. O synk, o synk, kom aldrig på fod!
    Så vel får jeg dine sølvspaendte sko.

13.   O min kaer søster! Du hjaelpe mig op;
      Så giver jeg dig min gule lok.

14.   O synk, o synk, kom aldrig op!
      Så vel far jeg din gule lok.

15.   O min kaer søster! Du hjaelpe mig til land;
      Så giver jeg dig min faestemand.

16.   O synk, o synk, om aldrig til land
      Så vel far jeg din faestemand.

17.   Så kom der to spillemaend gangende frem;
      Ja, de skar af hende fingrene fem.

18.   Ja, da skar af hende fingrene sma;
      Ja, de gjorde til skruer.

19.   Så skar af hendes gule lok;
      Ja, det gjorde de til strenge.

20.   Og lad os ga hen til den by,
      Hvor det store bryllup er udi.

21.   Så spilled de for det forste:
      Og det var om bruden, der havde drukned sin søster.

22.   Så spilled de for det andet:
      Og det var om brudens søster, var flydt til lande.

23.   Så spilled for det tredje;
      Ja, der begyndte bruden at graede.

24.   Om søndagen sad jun på brudebaenk;
      Om mandagen lå hun, i jern var spaendt.

25.   Om tirsdagen lå hun på retterbank;
      Om onsdagen lå hun på bålet, var braendt.

      O Herre, o Herre, o Herre Gud!

During the speaking of this ballad, at various stages, by the three
BLIND HARPERS, *the* CHORUS *set up a choral rhythm with bamboo
pipes.*

BLIND HARPER 3 *finds the body of the* FAIR SISTER. *He makes it into a*
HARP. *He uses the gold from the* MILLER's *bucket to gild the* HARP. *He
places a gold mask on the face of the* FAIR SISTER. *Then he picks up the*
HARP, *and places it in position for its later performance in the court
of the* KING, *then the* BLIND HARPER *returns to his place in the*

CHORUS *and the* HARP *removes the gold mask and as* CHORUS 7 *performs her ballad:*

> There was twa sisters livd in a bouir,
>   Binnorie, O Binnorie
> Their father was a baron of pouir.
>   By the bonnie milldams of Binnorie.
>
> The youngest was meek, and fair as the may
> Whan she springs in the east wi the gowden day.
>
> The eldest austerne as the winter cauld,
> Ferce was her saul, and her seiming was bauld.
>
> A gallant squire cam sweet Isabel·to woo;
> Her sister had naething to love I trow.
>
> But filld was she wi dolour and ire,
> To see that to her the comlie squire
>
> Preferd the debonair Isabel:
> They hevin of love and spyte was her hell.
>
> Till ae ein she to her sister can say,
> 'Sweit sister, cum let us wauk and play.'
>
> They wauked up, and they wauked down,
> Sweit sang the birdis in the vallie loun.
>
> Whan they cam to the roaring lin,
> She drave unweiting Isabel in.
>
> 'O sister, sister, tak my hand,
> And ye shall hae my silver fan.'
>
> 'O sister, sister, tak my middle,
> And ye shall hae my gowden girdle.'
>
> Sumtimes she sank, sumtimes she swam,
> Till she cam to the miller's dam.
>
> The miller's dochter was out that ein,
> And saw her rowing down the streim.
>
> 'O father deir, in your mil-dam
> There is either a lady or a milk-white swan!'
>
> Twa days were gane, whan to her deir
> Her wraith at deid of nicht cold appeir.

'My luve, my deir, how can ye sleip,
Whan your Isabel lyes in the deip!

'My deir, how can ye sleip bot pain
Whan she by her cruel sister is slain!'

Up raise he sune, in frichfu mude:
'Busk ye, my meiny, and seik the flude.'

They socht her up and they socht her doun,
And spyd at last her glisterin gown.

They raised her wi richt meikle care;
Pale was her cheik and grein was her hair.

This ballad (CHORUS 7) *with the refrains from the* CHORUS *becomes the music of the Court where the wedding of the* DARK SISTER *is taking place.* CHORUS 8 *becomes the* KING. CHORUS 5 *the* SUITOR, *and* CHORUS 3 *is the* DARK SISTER *who is the bride. As the previous ballad ended they presented crowns and placed them on their heads to drumbeats. The* KING *brings the* SUITOR *and the* DARK SISTER *into the circle and brings them together. Then the* SUITOR (CHORUS 5) *and the* DARK SISTER (CHORUS 3) *do their wedding dance together. They are kneeling and are about to touch hands when the* HARP *begins to play:*

HARP. (*With Chorus.*)
        O true love who gave me your ring . . .

The SUITOR *recognises the voice of the* FAIR SISTER, *and takes up the note of 'ring' like a resonance.*

HARP. (*With Chorus.*)
        O Father, Father, Father the King.

The KING *recognises the voice of his daughter.*

HARP.
        O Alison, Ellen, Jane, Anne, Jean
        O sister, O sister you dang me in.

The KING *begins backing away from the kneeling* DARK SISTER *until he reaches the edge of the circle at the position of* CHORUS 3. *As he backs away he repeats the names the* DARK SISTER *is called in the ballads:*

THE KING.
        Alison, Ellen, Jean, Anne, Jane,

HARP.
> You must be put to cruel pain

The SUITOR, *also backing away to the edge of the circle at the position of* CHORUS 7.
> Anne, Ellen, Jane, Jean, Alison,

HARP.
> Confess, confess, what you have done
> (*Singing.*) O sister Alison, Jane, Anne, Jean . . .

The KING *and the* SUITOR *turn, and when they turn they have inverted their crowns so that now they look like visors, and they have the look of sinister inquisitors.*

KING.
> You must be stretched upon the rack
> until your bones they go *crack crack!*

SUITOR.
> Stretch her out upon the rack
> because her hair and soul are black.

The DARK SISTER *is stretched out on the rack by unseen torturers. She screams. The* INQUISITORS *repeat the first line of one version of the ballad. The* DARK SISTER *refuses to continue. The rack is tightened.*

INQUISITORS.
> There were two sisters in a bower,
> There came a knight to be their wooer.

DARK SISTER.
> Sing I die, sing I day.
> Sing I die, sing (*the boughs were bent to me*) I day.
> Sing I die (*the vows he made to me*), sing I day.

The DARK SISTER *confesses. During her confession the two* INQUISITORS *return to their places in the* CHORUS.

DARK SISTER.
> There were two sisters in a bower,
> There came a knight to be their wooer.

The ballad is spoken quickly, starting quietly and becoming louder. Behind it, the DARK SISTER *sings quietly.*

DARK SISTER. Bow down.

CHORUS 2. He courted the eldest with a penknife,
And vowed that he would take her life.

CHORUS 5. He courted the youngest with a glove,
And said that he'd be her true love.

CHORUS 3. 'O sister, O sister, will you go and take a walk,
And see our father's ships how they float?

CHORUS 8. 'O lean your foot upon the stone,
And wash your hands in that sea-foam.'

CHORUS 3. She leaned her foot upon the stone,
But her elder sister has tumbled her down.

CHORUS 2. 'O sister, O sister, give me your hand,
And I'll make you lady of all my land.'

CHORUS 5. 'O I'll not lend to you my hand,
But I'll be lady of all your land.'

CHORUS 2. 'O sister, O sister, give my your glove,
And I'll make you lady of my true love.'

CHORUS 8. 'It's I'll not lend to you my glove,
But I'll be lady of your true love.'

CHORUS 3. Sometimes she sank, and sometimes she swam,
Until she came to a miller's dam.

CHORUS 5. The miller's daughter was coming out wi speed,
For water for to bake some bread.

CHORUS 8. 'O father, father, stop the dam,
For it's either a lady or a milk-white swan.'

CHORUS 5. He dragged her out unto the shore,
And strippéd her of all she wore.

CHORUS 2. By cam a fiddler, and he was fair,
And he buskit his bow in her bonnie yellow hair.

CHORUS 5. By cam her father's harper, and he was fine,
And he made a harp o' her bonnie breast-bone.

CHORUS 2. When they came to her father's court,
The harp (and fiddle these words) spoke:

CHORUS 8. 'O God bless my father the king,
And I wish the same to my mother the queen.'

CHORUS 3. 'My sister Jane, she tumbled me in.'

The DARK SISTER *is taken from the rack and put into a deep pit on the sea-shore where her sister was drowned. As the earth is tossed in she pleads with her father, the* KING, *the* SUITOR *and the* BLIND HARPER. *There is no reaction from* CHORUS 2, 5 *and* 8, *seen previously as the* BLIND HARPER. CHORUS 3 *becomes the* HARP *again. Then she is the* FAIR SISTER *once more. She walks towards her sister with her arms outstretched. She embraces the* DARK SISTER *in an embrace of death.* CHORUS 2, 5 *and* 8 *are the* KING, *the* SUITOR *and the* BLIND HARPER, *but they are also all three the* BLIND HARPER *and the men of the* CHORUS.

THE HARP.   Drag her down to where I drowned,
              Bury her alive in the deep dark ground.

As THREE BLIND HARPERS:
CHORUS 5.   Bury her alive in the deep dark ground.
CHORUS.   Bury her alive in the deep dark ground.
CHORUS 2.   Bury her alive in the deep dark ground.

THE HARP.   Pile on the earth and choke her cry,
              I drowned wet and you'll drown dry.

DARK SISTER. O Father, Father, reach me your hand.

CHORUS 8 & 5. Black your hair
CHORUS 5 & 2.   and black your soul,
CHORUS 2 & 8. And black,

DARK SISTER. O true love, reach me your hand.

CHORUS 8 & 5.   black,
CHORUS 5 & 2.   black
CHORUS 2 & 8.   the deep dark hole.

DARK SISTER. O Harper, Harper, reach me your hand.

CHORUS 8 & 5. Drag her down to where I drowned,

CHORUS 5 & 2. Bu-ry her a-live in the deep dark ground.

ALL CHORUS.   Bu-ry her a-live in the deep dark ground.

FAIR SISTER. O sister, sister, I'll reach you my hand.

The three BLIND HARPERS *walk towards the pit where the* DARK SISTER *is buried. They speak in succession, but as if as one voice. Then they raise their feet high as if to stamp down the loose earth of the* DARK SISTER's *pit, and as they freeze with feet raised to stamp down, the* TWO SISTERS *rise and become as ghosts of the* FAIR SISTER *and* DARK SISTER. *The men continue their suspended motion of stamping down the earth. Their feet make no sound. The* FAIR SISTER *walks the perimeter and, as the men alternate a slow stamping on the grave, the*

DARK SISTER *sings her song. As the* DARK SISTER *speaks her final couplet, the* FAIR SISTER *has described the circle and they face each other, reaching towards each other. Before they are able to touch, the* FAIR SISTER *turns her head to the audience and as* CHORUS 3 *delivers her last lines.*

CHORUS 8   I'll make no
CHORUS 5.   strings
CHORUS 2.   of your dark
CHORUS 8.   hair,
CHORUS 5.   The tune
CHORUS 2.   would make
CHORUS 8.   the world
CHORUS 5.   despair.

CHORUS 5.   Lullabies
CHORUS 2.   with such black
CHORUS 8.   notes
CHORUS 5.   Choke cries
CHORUS 2.   of joy
CHORUS 8.   in children's
CHORUS 5.   throats.

CHORUS 2.   Ballads set
CHORUS 8.   to such dark
CHORUS 5.   lays,
CHORUS 2.   Make one
CHORUS 8.   night of
CHORUS 5.   all our
CHORUS 2.   days.

DARK SISTER. Under dark earth and up above,
                      dance the Miller, my Father and my love.

                      I feel them stamping, and their tread
                      packs the blackness round my head.

                      I feel the thud of dancing feet
                      pound my skull with steady beat.

                      The thump of men's boots on the ground
                      judders my grave, but makes no sound.

CHORUS 7.   And reaching through the sand to me,
                      My sister's hand out of the sea.

CHORUS 3.   The cat's behind the buttery shelf,
                      If you want any more you can sing it yourself.

Blackout.

THE BARTERED BRIDE (1978)
A Comic Opera

MUSIC: Bedřich Smetana

THE BARTERED BRIDE

This version of *The Bartered Bride* was first performed by the New York Metropolitan Opera on 25 November 1978 with the following cast:

KRUSINA, a farmer (baritone)	Derek Hammond-Stroud
LUDMILA, his wife (soprano)	Elizabeth Coss
MARENKA, their daughter (soprano)	Teresa Stratas
TOBIAS MICHA, a landowner (bass)	John Cheek
HATA, his wife (mezzo-soprano)	Jean Kraft
VASEK, their son (tenor)	Jon Vickers
JENIK, a farmhand (tenor)	Nicolai Gedda
KECAL, a village marriage broker (bass)	Martti Talvela
CIRCUS BARKER/MANAGER (tenor)	Alan Crowfoot
ESMERALDA, a gypsy girl (soprano)	Colette Boky
ORIGINAL CZECH LIBRETTO	Karel Sabina
CONDUCTOR	James Levine
PRODUCTION	John Dexter
SET & PROJECTION DESIGNER	Josef Svoboda
COSTUME DESIGNER	Jan Skalicky
LIGHTING DESIGNER	Gil Wechsler
CHOREOGRAPHER	Pavel Šmok

NOTE ON PRONUNCIATION:

š in Krušina, Tobiaš, Vašek = English *sh* as in *sh*ip.
ř in Mařenka has no English equivalent, occurs only in Czech, and is extremely difficult for non-Czech speakers to pronounce. The solution is probably to use the English sound [ʒ] as in mea*s*ure.
ch in Micha = Scottish *ch* as in lo*ch*, or German *ch* as in a*ch*.
c in Kecal = English *ts* as in i*ts*.
j in Jenik = English *y* as in *y*ou.
Some typical Czech diminutives have been retained as terms of endearment, and the č in Jeničku and Vašičku = English *ch* as in *ch*ur*ch*.

ACT ONE

A village in Bohemia. The spring feast day.

CHORUS.
> Still got strength to face the worst with,
> well-brewed beer to beat a thirst with,
> we've all earned this holiday!
> Make the most of all your chances,
> death means no more beer and dances,
> we've all earned this holiday!
> Wives and mothers, always losers,
> women workers, husbands boozers.
> Women's work is never-ending,
> men's main work is . . . elbow-bending!
> *(To Mařenka and Jenik.)*
> Think twice! Think twice!
> Women all cheat you!
> Husbands all beat you!
> Women badly treat you!
> Husbands badly treat you!
> Think twice! Think twice!
> Still got strength to face the worst with,
> well-brewed beer to beat a thirst with,
> we've all earned this holiday!
> We don't want this feast day spoiling,
> so you kill-joys keep away!

JENIK. *(To Mařenka.)*
> Don't I get my kiss today? It's you who's the kill-joy.

MARENKA. Don't tease me like that! Only now my mother broke the
> news that today they'll bring the boy my father's forced on me.
> Jenik! I won't have him!

JENIK.
> Don't then!
> Tell them that the one boy you'll ever love is me.
> Stubborn girls like you could go
> ten years only saying no!

CHORUS.
> Feast day's feast day, don't forget it,
> don't let gloomy thoughts upset it.
> Gloom wins only when you let it.

Still got strength to face the worst with,
well-brewed beer to beat a thirst with,
we've all earned this holiday!

We don't want this feast day spoiling,
so you kill-joys keep away!
Time for drinking! Time for dancing!
Not the time to be downhearted,
not now when the feast day's started.
The band goes oom-pa-pah, drink 'n dance, drink 'n dance.

MARENKA. You won't be getting me to dance today. Don't expect
me to.

JENIK. Marenka, still in a bad mood are you? What's the matter?

MARENKA. I've already told you! Farmer Micha arrives today with
Vašek to get the contract signed. Sometime this evening.

JENIK. And us? We've a contract too.

MARENKA. Doesn't seem to count! Papa puts debts before his
daughter. Years ago he got himself into debt and it's me who's
his mortgage. It's a family debt. Micha's hold on Papa.

JENIK. All I am's a farmhand!

MARENKA. Yes, but it's you I love, not money. Money's not the
point. But there's something else on your mind. Something
nags at you. When you believe I'm not around, your face gets so
mournful thinking of something else. O don't say that it's
someone somewhere else, another woman left behind at home.

JENIK. Never! Never!

MARENKA.
If there were another woman, and you'd led a double life,
all my love 'd turn to hatred and I'd never be your wife.
So I want the truth, Jeničku, why you left your home behind.
Do you think I've never noticed that there's someone on your
mind?
Tell the truth! Tell the truth! Tell the truth!
Tell the truth, Jeničku, why you left your home behind.

All the village keeps on saying nothing's known about your
early life as a child. And that's another reason Papa won't even
hear of your claim.

JENIK. I started life in a prosperous farming family. Father ran his
   fields and cattle wisely. But the mother I loved took ill and died.
   Things got worse when my father married a second wife, who
   didn't rest until she got her stepson thrown out. Into the world I
   had to go, a homeless farmhand sleeping above the stables.

JENIK & MARENKA.
   Home's Moravia, farm and family,
   but here I sleep in the straw.
   All that meant home's so far away,
   even home's a bolted door.

JENIK.
   But that's past and done with!
   All I want's a new life
   with a house, a piece of land, and you, my new wife!

JENIK & MARENKA.
   All I want's a new life
   with a house, a piece of land, and you, my new wife.
   Proper bed not straw to sleep on,
   land to graze our own few sheep on,
   we'll be married one day,
   with our own farm, one day we will.

They are about to kiss when MARENKA *sees* KECAL, KRUSINA *and*
LUDMILA *approaching.*

MARENKA. Oh, they're here! Papa's here with the broker! To talk
   with me!

JENIK.
   Then it's best I disappear.
   One day,
   we won't need to part.
   Only keep that in mind.
   One day.

MARENKA.
   One day!

Exeunt MARENKA *and* JENIK. *Enter* KECAL *with* KRUSINA *and*
LUDMILA.

KECAL.
   Get this straight, you've got no option!

Don't you try deny it.
Don't forget your written promise.
It's down in black and white!
She must agree to all we say.
When girls say no I'm quick.
I'm the only marriage broker
who's never missed a trick.
Your daughter may prove a problem.
Stubborn girl I've heard say.
But watch me, I'll persuade her fast
how to see things our way.
Get this straight, you've got an option, *etc.*

KRUSINA.
Well, what do you think, mother?
Me, I'm quite satisfied.

LUDMILA.
We should take more time before we all decide.
Things like this require some thinking
and thought by more than us three.
Maybe Mařenka's got objections why she can't agree.

KECAL.
Got objections?
Has the day come when children do as they please?
A grateful daughter's duty
is simply saying she agrees.

LUDMILA.
All depends on *who* is the bridegroom.

KECAL.
Who's the bridegroom? Who's the bridegroom?
(*To Krušina.*)
Typical of a woman!
Could you doubt the bridegroom's value
when his guarantor is me?
He's the son of Tobiaš Micha,
and worth a bit,
be sure of it,
and I vow,
that he's good for maybe forty, even fifty thou.
Get this straight, you've got no option, *etc.*

KRUSINA. Micha? Him I've met through business, never his children.

All I know is Micha's been married twice and each wife bore him one son. Our deal was made before the two boys were even born!

KECAL. Deals are deals, though! No avoiding the fact the village came to witness when you mortgaged off Mařenka. You mortgaged off your daughter as bond for debt.

LUDMILA. But may I ask which of Micha's sons you're speaking for?

KECAL. No harm asking, but there's only one around: Vašek! The first left after Hata, his stepmother, threw him out. God knows where he's gone to!

KRUSINA. Well, what sort of a fellow's Vašek? We'd like to know a bit about the boy.

KECAL.
Perfect manners, he's praised to the skies for,
no word or deed he ever need apologise for.
Such bargain husbands are rare today.
Never been a boy for causing trouble,
mothers pray for babies Vašek's double
simple, and ideal in every way.
All he drinks is milk and water,
doesn't booze, won't beat your daughter.
Strong enough, but not a Samson,
p'raps his looks aren't over-handsome,
but his cash'll soon enhance 'em!
Heir to many thriving acres
grazing juicy bacon makers,
fit as one-two-three-*four* fleas.
So then, down to business, *please!*

KRUSINA & LUDMILA.
If he's stamped with your approval,
we'd be fools to turn him down.

KECAL.
All he drinks is milk and water, *etc.*

KRUSINA & LUDMILA. (*Seeing Mařenka.*)
Here's Mařenka! This is where he earns his money.

KECAL.
Here's Marenka! This is where I earn my money.

Enter MARENKA *pretending to be busy.*

MARENKA.
>   Must get finished! Must get finished!
>   Must run, must get dressed soon.

KECAL.
>   When you know you'll want to look your best soon.
>   Since there's no one on the scene,
>   no one, you know what I mean,
>   I've a boy above the crowd,
>   a bridegroom who'd do you proud.

MARENKA.
>   A bridegroom who'd do *me* proud?

KRUSINA.
>   He's the one we choose,
>   never mind your views.

LUDMILA.
>   If the lad's not to your fancy
>   you can just refuse!

MARENKA.
>   He's the one they choose,
>   never mind my views,
>   but the lad's not to my fancy,
>   so I'll just refuse.

LUDMILA.
>   He's the one they choose,
>   never mind your views,
>   if the lad's not to your fancy,
>   you can just refuse!

KRUSINA & KECAL.
>   He's the one we choose,
>   never mind your views,
>   if the lad's not to your fancy,
>   don't you dare refuse.

KECAL.
>   Can't she make her mind up,
>   get the contract signed up?
>   There's no debating about it.
>   She'd better not start to doubt it.

MARENKA.

>Just ask if *she's* willing,
>since that *she* meant me,
>what if there are reasons,
>reasons prevent me?

KECAL.

>Reasons con, reasons pro,
>whatever you say, mine are better.
>You were promised years ago
>when your father was a debtor.

MARENKA.

>I love another!
>We love each other!

KRUSINA & LUDMILA.

>She loves another!
>They love each other!

KECAL.

>Well, your sweetheart's due for sacking.
>Better go and send him packing!

MARENKA.

>Vows of love just can't be repealed.

KECAL.

>Vows of love don't make a wedding.

MARENKA.

>But there's a contract signed and sealed!

KECAL.

>Worthless paper fit for shredding!

MARENKA.

>Just you try! Just you try!

KECAL.

>Wait and see what I can do
>once I get to work on you . . .
>I've an eagle eye. I'm quick.
>Cash and cunning do the trick.
>Snags, obstacles and what not,
>nous and know-how leap the lot.

ALL.
>   Snags, obstacles and what not,
>   nous and know-how leap the lot.

MARENKA. Jenik won't let me go! And just before you came he said
>   he'd marry me.

KRUSINA. I'm afraid that he has no choice now it's all down in black
>   and white. Don't forget my promise to Micha, which the
>   village witnessed.

LUDMILA. What on earth got into you, promising her to him?

KECAL. (*Producing the contract.*)
>   Got it here! All down in writing!
>   Duly signed by Micha and Krušina and witnesses.

MARENKA. Doesn't mean a thing. We weren't even born. Times have
>   changed now. We can live our own lives. No, we'll never give
>   in.

KECAL. God! The world's turned upside down!

KRUSINA. And when can we expect this Micha, along with Vašek?
>   Where's this 'bargain bridegroom' you told us 'd do her proud?
>   He doesn't do her proud at all, not coming here himself.

KECAL. Absolutely! He's bashful and backward, that's in addressing
>   ladies. Sometimes gets a little bit lost for words.

KRUSINA. That doesn't make the courting easy!

KECAL. Here's what my plan is: I think it's better just bumping into
>   Micha accidentally at the inn across the way. Here'll be like
>   Bedlam once they start their dancing. Don't think that other
>   boy's a problem. He'll give way to cash.

Exeunt KECAL, KRUSINA *and* LUDMILA. *The* CHORUS *begins to dance
the polka.*

CHORUS.
>   Grab a partner, form a couple,
>   time to get those stiff limbs supple.
>   Polka, polka, don't forget
>   life tomorrow's work and debt.
>   Brasses blaring, cymbals clashing,
>   petticoats and lace frills flashing.
>   Feel the ground beneath our feet
>   jumping to the music's beat.

ACT TWO

The inn.

CHORUS.
>Good beer's a friend to man, when life's both up and down,
>both joys to be drunk to and sorrows to drown.
>At wakes and at weddings there's boozing!
>*Alcohol!*
>Good beer gives us strength to bear the worst in life,
>bad harvests and winters and words with the wife,
>they're all borne the better for boozing!
>*Alcohol!*

JENIK.
>No, listen! You boozers! Your views are too crude.
>True love gives men more than any booze that's brewed.
>No beer or wine compares with true love,
>love that's returned by the girl you love.

CHORUS.
>Ah, true love's a fantasy, pie in the sky,
>and Kecal behind you 'll soon tell you why.

KECAL.
>Well, he'd do himself some good,
>if he followed what I told him:
>ready cash and ready cunning,
>all you need to make life pay.
>One with cash and crafty reason,
>he's the one who gets his way.

CHORUS.
>Good beer's a friend to man, when life's both up and down,
>both joys to be drunk to and sorrows to drown.
>At wakes and at weddings there's boozing!
>*Alcohol!*

JENIK.
>No love's the stay and staff of life.

KECAL.
>What about cash?

Furiant. Enter VASEK *dressed like a prospective bridegroom.*

VASEK. (*Stammering.*)
> M- m- m- m- mama th- th- th- thinks it's time
> Vašek h- h- h- heard ch- ch- ch- church bells chime.
> If I weren't so t- t- tongue-tied,
> I'd have already wooed a bride.
> Girls won't stay to hear
> w- w- what I've to say.
> All they d- d- do is l- l- laugh and jeer.

Enter MARENKA.

MARENKA. Bet you're the feast-day bridegroom who's to marry Mařenka.

VASEK.
> Y- y- yes, b- b- but h- h- how did you know?

MARENKA. All you've got to do is use your eyes. It's the way you're dressed. All the village talks of you, and pities you.

VASEK. P- p- pities me, but why?

MARENKA. It's because Mařenka's planning to cheat you. She's already in love.

VASEK. H- h- how can she love another? Sh- she's got me!

MARENKA. You? (ha ha ha!) You've never met, have you now?

VASEK. N- n- n- n- no! B- but she knows it's m- m- m- me she's to marry.

MARENKA. Of course she does. But knowing her, it wouldn't surprise a soul to hear that, once you're married, she plans to have you murdered.

VASEK. *M- m- m- m- murdered!* B- b- b- but it's m- m- mama who insists I've got to g- g- g- g- g- g- get married now.

MARENKA. Married! Well, why not? Easy as pie! Girls are falling over backwards. You're just what they want.

VASEK. I am!

MARENKA.
> Girls are going mad for you,
> you've only got to choose.
> So in love is one with you,
> she'll die if you refuse.

VASEK.
>O! O! O! Won't refuse
>O what good news!
>Are you sure it's me?
>Won't refuse her.
>O what good news!
>B- b- but Marenka, she'll be suing.

MARENKA. No! Aren't you forgetting how she plans to do you in?

VASEK. But m- m- mama's . . . bound to shriek at me!

MARENKA. But she'll stop it once she's seen your pretty bride-to-be.

VASEK. (*Making curves with his hands.*)
>Does that mean she's sorta . . .

MARENKA. 'Sorta' like Marenka!

VASEK. Is she tall, or shorter?

MARENKA.
>Same as your Marenka!
>Girls are going mad for you,
>you've only got to choose.
>So in love with you is one,
>she'll die if you refuse.

VASEK.
>O won't refuse. O what good news!
>You're sure it's me? Are you joking?

MARENKA.
>No, the matter's far too grave.
>She'll turn to suicide,
>kill herself with cyanide,
>rush down to the riverside
>where the water's deep and wide.
>Everyone will know she died
>rejected as your bride.

She pretends to weep.

VASEK.
>W- w- why do you cry?

MARENKA.
>It's because you'll let her die.

VASEK.

> I'd come to her aid,
> b- but I'm afraid.

MARENKA.

> You're scared of mama's frowning,
> when she who loves you so much
> this minute may be drowning.

VASEK.

> S- s- s- s- save her life!
> Let her b- be my wife.
> And if she looked like you.
> I'd do it now.

MARENKA.

> Could you manage me as well?

VASEK.

> V- v- very well!

MARENKA.

> Could you see me as your wife?

VASEK.

> B- b- bet your life!

MARENKA.

> Each night I'd kiss your tired eyes,
> sing you lilting lullabies.
> Could you manage me as well?

VASEK.

> V- v- very well!

MARENKA.

> Could you see me as your wife?

VASEK.

> B- b- bet your life!

MARENKA.

> Strike a bond between us both now.
> Swear an oath now:
> that Mařenka's bond is void,
> all the obligations forced on her
> are here and now destroyed.
> Swear an oath now!

VASEK.
> D- don't like to swear.
> W- w- w- wouldn't dare!

MARENKA.
> Once Mařenka's made your wife,
> you can say goodbye to life!
> Now I see you'd rather die.
> But what's the point in going on.
> I won't weep when you're gone.

VASEK.
> I'll s- swear the oath!

MARENKA. (*Raising her hand in a swearing gesture.*)
> She and I will never wed.

VASEK. (*Raising hand.*)
> N- n- never wed!

MARENKA.
> Cut my throat and strike me dead!

VASEK. (*Cutting his throat with hand.*)
> S- strike me dead!

MARENKA.
> Cross my heart and hope to die.

VASEK. (*Crossing his heart.*)
> H- hope to die!

MARENKA.
> And strike me dead!

VASEK. (*Cutting his throat.*)
> S- strike me dead!

MARENKA.
> And hope to die!

VASEK. (*Crossing heart.*)
> H- hope to die!

MARENKA.
> All claim to her I here deny.

VASEK.
> All claim I here deny.

MARENKA.
> Girls are going mad for you,
> you've only got to choose.
> So in love is one with you,
> she'll die if you refuse.

VASEK.
> O won't refuse!
> O what good news!

Exeunt MARENKA *and* VASEK.
The inn again. KECAL *and* JENIK *are in conversation.*

KECAL. There's no doubt she's your type, honest, good at work, and worth a pretty penny.

JENIK. Really? Are you sure that I'm the type for her?

KECAL. I'll take care of that. You merely say that Marenka's not your girl . . .

JENIK. No, I couldn't. Rather die than break my promise!

KECAL. God, these lovers! They're so stupid! All that really counts is money.

JENIK. So, this girl that you say is just my type comes with a dowry?

KECAL.
> *Big* one!

JENIK *makes to leave.*

KECAL.
> When I'm talking business talk,
> then you might at least stay.

JENIK.
> Business stops for beer today,
> it's the village feast day.

KECAL.
> Got no notion who I am?

JENIK.
> Not the faintest notion, no.
> Do you know about me, though?

KECAL.
> Not a bad lad, as lads go.
> Your work's quite up to scratch.

But you're crazy, crazy if
you hope to make a match.
Have you got cash to marry?

JENIK.

Don't imagine that it's cash
is every maiden's prayer.
Girl's prefer a lad with dash
to any millionaire.

KECAL.

Listen! Better get this straight
what love without cash *is*.
With no cash your married life's
one long round of clashes.
(*Kecal takes out his ledger of "eligibles".*)
If I knew more of you,
parents, birthplace, so on,
I'd have more to go on.

JENIK.

Far away! I was born far away,
near Moravia's farmlands.

KECAL.

Best get back there! Hereabouts
the girls are after men with cash, not farmhands!

JENIK.

Maybe most are like that here,
but they're not Marenka,
who is far above them all,
far, far above them all.

KECAL. (*To old men.*)
Same old lovers' song,
girls can do no wrong.
That's what all the boys say,
they're all blind.
(*To Jenik.*)
Once you're bamboozled
you'll soon change your mind.
Then you'll squeak and squeal,
beef how bruised you feel,
but your goose is cooked,
wriggle like an eel,

useless now that you're
well and truly hooked!
Someone smart like me, with bags of brains,
weighs his gains up first, weighs his cash gains,
thinks before, not after, will it pay?
If it won't, he smartly steals away.

JENIK.

Didn't quite get your meaning.
Don't think I understood.

KECAL.

I've got someone for you,
and this someone's twice as good:
Dowry from daddy starts you a new life.

JENIK.

Dowry from daddy starts me a new life.

KECAL.

Cows and cottage thrown in with a new wife.

JENIK.

Cows and cottage thrown in with a new wife.

KECAL.

Plenty besides that, plenty more pickings,
goose and a pig and twenty-one chickens.
She's bought a bed, a double, almost new.

KECAL & JENIK.

Plenty besides that, plenty more pickings, *etc.*

KECAL.

Now that's a chance I'd jump at, why not you?

JENIK.

Now that's a chance you'd jump at, I'm not you.

KECAL.

Dowry from daddy starts you a new life.
Now that's a chance I'd jump at, why not you?

JENIK.

Dowry from daddy starts me a new life.
That's a chance you'd jump at, I'm not you!

KECAL. Once you've given up Mařenka, there's some cash to ease the
heartache! Well then, shall we call it settled? There's a hundred

cash once you step aside.

JENIK. A measly hundred! That's not much to offer. Think how much I love her. She'd be a bargain twice the price.

KECAL. Well than, make it twice as much.

JENIK. Even that's too little.

KECAL. All right, three then! That's more than is normal, but I can't be bothered with bartering. I've decided I like you! Turn it down, and life 'll be unpleasant. The village could be made to hound a vagrant out. Back to your Moravia both unmarried and minus money.

JENIK. Who . . . who . . . who's the person who's paying the cash to me?

KECAL. (*Indicating himself.*) Who else?

JENIK. You! Did I hear you right? Not even millions would induce me to sell her to you.

KECAL. Don't be stupid! Got no time for women. One wife's enough for me. She's murder! Don't you know the one I'm representing is Vašek, the son of Tobias̆ Micha? After the matter's in the bag, the three hundred's yours. Once you're paid (*Whistles.*) quick make yourself scarce!

JENIK. All right, shake on it! Who can sneeze at cash? Cash on the nail and then the deal is settled. But on one condition: that Mar̆enka is to marry only one person, that's the son, son of Tobias̆ Micha, or our settled contract will be null and void.

KECAL. Down in writing. Down in writing. Down in black and white! That the only person she's to marry's Micha's son.

JENIK. And add: Jenik cedes her only to Tobias̆ Micha's son, and to no one other than him. Put it all down in the contract.

KECAL.
All down to the very letter.
(*Aside.*)
Why should he care who'll get her?

JENIK. One more condition!

KECAL. What?

JENIK. Put this in writing too: The moment that Mařenka and
    Micha's son are joined as man and wife, as soon as they're one,
    then Tobiaš Micha must agree that the debts that Mařenka's
    father owes are all cancelled. All that he owes cancelled
    outright.

KECAL. Yes, of course, it all goes down in black and white!

KECAL *moves over to the old men, and* JENIK *sits down among the*
young men.

JENIK.
        Black and white! Thinks he's
        brought off his barter.
        Soon he'll know just who
        will turn out smarter!
        What man who's known love
        ever gave a moment's thought to money?
        For love's the true prize
        above all on earth.
        All men who've known true love
        know love's true worth.
        Old men forget their lives once turned on love.
        Life stops with no love, wagons with no wheels.
        We who are young men know how strong love feels.

KECAL.
        Need some witnesses!
        Get some quickly.
        Down to business,
        all that's wanted now's
        a witnessed bond.

CHORUS.
        It's a contract,
        a marriage contract!

KECAL.
        Thanks to my know-how,
        my famous foresight,
        all I need's a bond
        in black and white.

CHORUS.
        It's nearly over!
        Now he needs a bond
        in black and white.

KECAL. (*Sitting at a table and writing.*)
 'Cede I forthwith while of sound mind
 my betrothed bride, the undersigned.'

CHORUS.
 Look at Jenik, calm and dry-eyed,
 puts no fight up to keep his bride.

JENIK.
 First this must be agreed to:
 the one person I'll cede to
 is the son of Tobiaš Micha.

KECAL. (*Writing.*)
 '. . . is the son of Tobiaš Micha.'

JENIK.
 If he swears his love is true,
 and in front of all of you
 proves he's freely chosen his bride,
 then I'll gladly step to one side.

KECAL.
 Down in writing!
 It goes right in.

CHORUS.
 Young men these days
 seem to have
 so little heart.

KRUSINA. (*To Jenik.*)
 Putting ours before your own sake
 shows you've got a lot of tact.
 So let me give your hand a shake.
 We appreciate your act.

KECAL.
 Hold your horses! I've not finished yet!
 'Noble sacrifices'
 don't need handshakes, just handouts.
 Better hear
 before you shake my hands
 what his price is.
 Three hundred cash,
 that's what we pay,
 to make him give her away.

CHORUS.
>God, the monster! Shameless monster!
>Making money out of love!

KRUSINA. (*To Jenik.*)
>Love is something set apart,
>you can't buy love, you can't sell love.
>Courtship's not a cattle mart.

KECAL.
>*Punctum satis!* Please sign your names.
>Jenik's first to sign,
>then there's Krušina next,
>(*Turning to Chorus.*)
>then you make your marks.

JENIK. (*Signing coolly.*)
>Glad to do it . . . Jenik Horák!

KRUSINA. (*Signing.*)
>Tramps like you can't love or care,
>someone come from God-knows-where!

CHORUS.
>God knows where he's from!
>Run him out.
>Sold Mařenka for three hundred!
>Out, out! Out, out!

JENIK *is chased out of the village by the Chorus.*

ACT THREE

The village.

VASEK. (*Alone.*)

S- scared to death, you h- heard her,
p- prophesy my m- murder!
W- worrisome this w- wooing,
m- means a lad's un- d- d- doing!
S- scared to death, you h- heard her,
p- prophesy my m- murder.
M- my beloved's h- h- hate'll
m- make the marriage f- f- fatal.
S- scared to death, you h- heard her,
p- prophesy my m- murder.

Offstage sound of a drum. Enter CIRCUS BARKER, ESMERALDA *and* CIRCUS TROUPE.

CIRCUS BARKERS. Celebrated sirs, ladies and gentlemen, may I advise you on this festive occasion of our sensational, splendiferous, especially assembled for your satisfaction, spectacles of skills and strength by circus stars, not to mention gypsy Esmeralda Salamanca who will titillate attention by tarantellas on the tightrope, and, in addition, caught on Coney Island, a savage Red Indian, swallowing swords and scissors and scimitars, something else beginning with S . . . er . . . sauerkraut and sausage! And the grand finale, top of the sensations is . . . (*Fanfare.*) . . . a real live American mountain grizzly, brought here at great expense and after being exhibited over the world before the dazzled public, performing with frisky Miss Salamanca frolicsome, freakishly flabbergasting fandangoes. With the greatest respect I urge you not to miss our show, seen in all the major towns of the world. So as to whet your appetite here's a little foretaste. For free! You there! Off we go!

The CIRCUS TROUPE *performs.*

VASEK. G- g- g- great! Can't wait to see it! Th- th- that g- g- g- g- gypsy's got g- g- gorgeous legs on her.

ESMERALDA. (*Curtseying to Vašek.*) Will the young gent come to watch our show?

VASEK. Try to stop me! I'd l- love to watch you do tightrope walking.

ESMERALDA *takes him behind the circus wagon. Enter* RED INDIAN *in great haste.*

RED INDIAN. Where's the manager? Where's the manager?
  (*Sees Circus Barker.*) Franta's been on the booze again, met with some locals, drank himself under the table, and nothing but nothing's going to get him sober. He's lying there saying I've to tell you to stuff the bear!

BARKER. Jesus! Jesus! But Franta's bear's the best! Must have a bear in the show. Dancing bears have always featured in my shows. No! No! Impossible! We must have a bear. Got to get hold of a substitute, a lad from round here, willing to dance.

RED INDIAN. Do we want people knowing that it's only a bearskin and avoiding the circus? And he must be Franta's size, otherwise the public 'll spot the trick at once. They're already waiting inside. No more than a minute left to look for a substitute.

BARKER. Where the hell is Esmeralda?

ESMERALDA *approaches and whispers with the* BARKER.

VASEK. Ah, what a beauty she is! W- wouldn't say no to her. That w-w- would get the gossip going. W- wouldn't it c- c- cause a p- p- proper stir?

ESMERALDA. (*Returning to Vašek.*) More I look at you, more I'd like you to kiss me.

VASEK. K- k- k- k- k- k- kiss you!

RED INDIAN. (*To Barker.*) There's a likely lad for the bearskin over there. Franta's skin 'd fit him to a T.

BARKER.
  You go and drum up lots of business there.
  I'll go and try to snare a new bear.

RED INDIAN *and the rest of the* CIRCUS TROUPE *file off in procession to the sound of the drum.*

BARKER. (*Approaching Vašek.*) Well, my good friend. Getting our Esmeralda's clothes off could be more than just a dream. Join our circus. You could be the star turn. With Esmeralda yours and just for the asking.

VASEK. B- be the star turn? I'd never kn- know what to do.

ESMERALDA. O, don't be shy. I can show you how.

VASEK. You can? Lucky me then!

BARKER. Life with us comedians means the best life: fame and . . . er . . . fortune everywhere you travel, food and drink in liberal helpings and women at your feet! Your fantasies brought fulfilment like a rich Sultan's. You'll be off you mother's apron strings and do all you've wanted. '*Kumstus kumstorum*' (as the Germans say in Latin!) What does William Shakespeare say: 'something . . . something . . . all the world's a stage.' But when pleasure's handed out, it's all we circus people get the plummy parts, bet your life, bet your life!

ESMERALDA. (*Coaxing.*) Go on, say you will. Be one of us, and you can do anything you want to me.

BARKER. What about a tryout, with no obligations? Only one day. Just today.

ESMERALDA. Just today, just today, and then, when the show's done, late at night, I'm yours. I'm yours for the taking!

VASEK. B- but what do I do?

ESMERALDA. Bear dance!

VASEK. D- d- dance bare! W- w- won't!

ESMERALDA. A dance together, can-can or a fandango.

VASEK. M- m- m- m- mama . . .!

ESMERALDA.
　She won't know it's you.

ESMERALDA & BARKER.
　Even your own mama
　won't know who you are,
　safe inside your bearskin,
　our new circus star.
　Furry friendly features
　cover over yours.
　Loud applause will greet your
　dance on your hind paws.
　You'll be cute and cuddly.
　Girls 'll queue to stroke your fur.
　Children cheer us, when we
　do our *pas de deux*.

Exeunt ESMERALDA *and* BARKER.

VASEK. O, I don't know what to do. F- f- first the girls w- w- want to
l- l- love me, then kill me.

Enter HATA, MICHA *and* KECAL.

HATA. Well, now's not the time for looking sad. Be cheerful,
Vašíčku! You're forgetting first it's a feast day and second the
day you start courting.

VASEK. But I'm f- f- frightened!

HATA. What are you frightened of, silly? Women aren't dangerous
creatures to run from. Marriage is marvellous. Ask any man in
the place to tell you.

KECAL. Exactly! All you've to do is sign the contract and you'll be
able to find out.

VASEK. W- w- what m- m- m- must I s- s- sign?

MICHA. That you'll marry Krušina's only daughter, Mařenka.

VASEK. W- w- w- w- w- w- w- won't!

HATA, MICHA, KECAL.
Won't! What's this? What's this? Says he won't!
He's taken leave of all his senses.
Who, Vašek, who? You've got to tell us who's
been making you refuse.

VASEK.
B- been told once w- wed s- soon be dead.
Once w- wed s- soon be dead's w- what she said.

HATA, MICHA, KECAL.
You're madder than a March hare, you!
Who tried to scare you?

VASEK. (*Mysteriously.*)
S- s- somebody! S- some . . . body.

HATA, MICHA, KECAL.
And who was this somebody?

VASEK.
A girl who promised me all sorts of things.

HATA, MICHA, KECAL.
And what did she say to you?

VASEK.
>Said she loved me, and I love her.

HATA.
>But *who* is she?

VASEK.
>D- don't know!

VASEK *runs off.*

HATA, MICHA, KECAL.
>I've got a strong suspicion.
>Someone somewhere's been up to something.
>They've got at Vašek's brain.

KECAL.
>I'll make him sane again.

HATA & MICHA.
>He'll make him sane again.

MARENKA *rushes in with a group of girls in feast-day costumes. They are followed by* KRUSINA, LUDMILA *and more villagers.*

MARENKA.
>No! I don't believe it!
>I couldn't bear the pain.
>I know he loves me
>much more than mere cash,
>much more than mere gain.

KRUSINA.
>But we all know it's true.

KECAL. (*Fishing for the contract.*)
>Must I prove it to you?

KRUSINA.
>Still won't believe we're right.

KECAL. (*Producing contract and thrusting it at Mařenka.*)
>Here, down in black and white!
>Usually costs me lots more.
>He sold quick, and cheap what's more!

MARENKA.
>No, love like his is not for sale!
>No, still I won't believe it.

There's some mistake. We're so in love.
I know Jenik's heart, I know.

KRUSINA.
Face the facts now, Mařenka,
though life seems far from fair.
The gossip says he's a rake
with lots of girls elsewhere.

KECAL.
Now sign right here, young lady.
Go get Vašek! Where's he?

LUDMILA. (*Seeing Vašek with the children.*)
He'd rather play with children than claim his bride-to-be.

MARENKA.
And now I'll never marry,
not Vašek anyhow.
I'd rather have to live alone.
My life's all finished now.

LUDMILA, HATA, KRUSINA, MICHA, KECAL.
No matter now what you feel,
what must be, must be, and time will heal.

KECAL. (*Calling after Vašek.*)
Hey, Vašek! Hey, don't go hide!
Come here quick and claim yor bride!

VASEK. (*Approaches reluctantly.*)
W- w- w- was it me you wanted
(*Recognising Mařenka.*)
Th- th- that's the g- g- girl who . . .

LUDMILA, HATA, KRUSINA, MICHA, KECAL.
She's the one who'll murder you?

VASEK.
Th-th-that's the very g-g-girl who'll . . .

LUDMILA, HATA, KRUSINA, MICHA, KECAL.
She's your bride, you silly fool!

VASEK.
I- if she's the one, she'll do.

LUDMILA, HATA, KRUSINA, MICHA, KECAL.
Well, she's your intended,

your bride, you lucky lad.

VASEK.
> Sh- she's not all that bad!

KECAL.
> Let's drop this if-and-butting,
> and stop this pussy-footing,
> and get the pen and ink.

MARENKA.
> Let me be alone now. Give me time to think.

LUDMILA, HATA, KRUSINA, MICHA, KECAL.
> Think it over, Marenka, don't say no.
> It's your last hope, if you let him go.
> Good men don't grow on trees to pick and choose.
> Think how much saying no will make you lose.
> Think it over, Marenka, don't say no.
> It's your last hope, if you let him go.

MARENKA.
> Leave me alone,
> all I want's to be alone.

Exeunt BOTH FAMILIES *and* KECAL.

MARENKA.
> O let me be! Just let me be.
> I don't need you to tell me.
> There, sealed and signed in his own hand,
> a contract made to sell me!
> He sold me after all we'd planned?
> Yet saw it with my own eyes.
> O how I yearn for Jenik now
> to deny all this as lies.
> How dark the day that dawned so bright!
> A dawn that promised new life.
> I thrilled to hear those words he spoke:
> 'my house, my land, my new wife.'
> And with his words the day seemed bright
> I *saw* our house, our own land,
> but now that house is crumbled stone,
> that farm is overgrown land.
>
> No! Bait to snare me all for gain.

All turned to dark that dawn now.
The day holds nothing more for me.
Its brightness has all gone now.
How dark the day that dawned so bright!
I thrilled to hear those words he spoke:
'my house, my land, my new wife.'
How dark the day that dawned so bright!

Enter JENIK.

JENIK.
Give me my kiss! Give me my kiss!
Got money for our farm now.
Whatever they all try to do,
our plans can't come to harm now!

MARENKA.
Damn you! What do you want from me?
Kecal will pay you your fee.
Collect the money that you've made
selling me off like cattle.
Well, let me hear it Tell me now.
Did you or not? Say yes or no.

JENIK.
Mařenka, only let me speak . . .

MARENKA.
All you need say is yes or no.
Truth! About the contract.

JENIK.
So be it! Sold you! Sold you! Sold you!

MARENKA
Then go away and don't come back.
There's no one here will miss you.

JENIK. (*Moving closer to Mařenka.*)
Then let me take my leave of you,
and just once let me kiss you.

MARENKA.
Don't come another inch near me!
I'm glad, glad to marry Vašek!

JENIK. (*Laughing.*)
Ha, ha, ha, ha!

Ha, ha, ha, ha!
O what a good match,
just your type, Vašek!

MARENKA.

So! All you do is laugh and jeer?

JENIK.

Soon you'll join the laughter.
Marenka, only let me *speak*!

MARENKA.

It's only cash you're after!

JENIK.

If you weren't such a stubborn mule,
you'd try, my dear, to hear me.
Just let me speak a word or two,
you'll see the truth can clear me.
If you weren't such a stubborn mule,
you'd try, my dear, to hear me.

MARENKA.

A liar's all that I can see,
and don't you dare my-dear me.
I never want you near again,
no, never, never near me.
A liar's all that I can see,
and don't you dare my-dear me.

KECAL *bustles in.*

KECAL. Ah, ah! Still waiting for me to fork the cash out? Only a moment longer now. Once it's all settled and written down, then you'll get your filthy lucre.

MARENKA. (*Turning on Jenik.*) So! It's true you sold me!

KECAL. Well, and you, Marenka? All set to marry Micha's son?

JENIK. Not a moment's doubt Marenka's ready to marry Micha's son and not another. That I'm certain of.

KECAL. Smart after all! Decided to help me.

MARENKA. You cheating, lying beast! No! I don't agree, not at any price. I'd sooner die than be married.

JENIK. (*To Kecal.*) What's your offer, if I change her mind, making her want to marry Micha's son?

MARENKA. What's this! After making more of your filthy lucre? No,
I can't believe it's happening. O Jenik, is this you? It can't be
true.

MARENKA *weeps*.

JENIK.
Please trust me, please trust me.
Trust in what I say.
You once did, so why not try trusting now.
Please believe no bride will ever have so fine a wedding day.
He loves you, Tobiaš Micha's son,
you'll both soon start your new life,
and soon you'll be so happy
when first you hear him call you wife.
So trust me, trust in what I say.
You once did, so why not try trusting now?

MARENKA.
I once did, I once did, but not now,
because your heart's turned to ice.

KECAL.
His sentiments are just like mine
and what he says is marvellous advice . . .
So, better let the parents know.
The contract needs approving.
It's all been going far too slow.
It's time we all got moving.

MARENKA.
Yes, better let the parents know.
The contract needs approving.
I don't see how I can say no.
It's time we all got moving.

JENIK.
So, better let the parents know.
The contract needs approving.
It should have finished long ago.
It's time we all got moving.

JENIK. (*To Marenka.*)
Don't you believe me any more?

MARENKA.
>Tramp! All you own is straw!

JENIK *moves out of sight.*

CHORUS.
>So well then, Marenka, what's it to be?
>Isn't it time you said you'll agree?

MARENKA. (*To herself.*)
>I'll pay him back! He'll rue the day!
>Jenik, your grin will fade soon.
>You liar, liar, Jenik, you,
>your joke 'll get repaid soon.
>(*To the others.*)
>I'll pay him back! He'll rue the day!

CHORUS.
>You show him, Marenka!
>The wisest way's as you decide.
>So bring the beer and toast the bride!

JENIK. (*Emerging.*)
>Yes, bring the beer and drink a toast,
>and I for one 'll drink the most.

HATA & MICHA (*In astonishment.*)
>Ah! Jenik! Come back from the dead!

JENIK. (*Ignoring Hata.*)
>No, father! Tired of stable straw,
>no proper home, no proper bed,
>I want my rights as son and heir,
>house, farmland as my rightful share.

KECAL.
>Can I believe my eyes or not?
>This good-for-nothing, God-knows-what
>is *Jenik*, Micha's elder lad.
>(*To Micha.*)
>He's gone to war. You said he had.

JENIK.
>Yes, indeed, this is Micha's son
>you see here now, the elder one.
>The only war I've had to fight 's
>against those fakes who claim my rights.

HATA.
> We've shed no tears on your behalf.
> You're nothing but a tramp, you!

JENIK.
> The *tramp's* come to claim his due,
> his bride, and father's 'fatted calf'.
> The bride-to-be belongs to me.
> I'm here to claim the bride I've won,
> the bride marked down for Micha's son.

HATA.
> A man like you, who sleeps in straw!

JENIK.
> No more though! What's mine's mine by law.
> A contract is . . . . a contract!
> Now we are two, she's got a choice.
> Give one or the other her voice.
> Him or me? Then it's over!

MARENKA.
> Ah, at last I see it clearly,
> Jeničku, dear, I'm yours! I'm yours!

KECAL.
> A man with brains! Admit defeat!
> They'll live to rue their laughter.
> He'll start to beat her soon; she'll cheat.
> They're living out an old deceit.
> No love is 'happy ever after'!

MICHA. (*To Kecal.*)
> Like all of us, your brains
> have taken this feast day off!

HATA.
> You've let us down, sir, let us down,
> so don't expect your payoff.

MARENKA, JENIK, HATA, LUDMILA, KRUSINA, MICHA.
> Like all of us, your brains
> have taken this feast day off.
> You've let us down, sir, let us down,
> so don't expect your payoff.

KECAL.

> A man with brains! Admit defeat!
> They'll live to rue their laughter.
> He'll start to beat her soon; she'll cheat.
> They're living out an old deceit.
> No love is 'happy ever after'!

CHORUS.

> Ha, ha, ha, ha!
> You've let them down,
> so don't expect your pay.

Exit KECAL.

Offstage uproar and alarm. BOYS *run on shouting.*

FIRST BOY. Run for your lives! The bear's broken loose!

SECOND BOY. The bear's gone berserk! He's coming this way.

Enter VASEK *in the bearskin. General alarm.* VASEK *removes the head.*

VASEK. (*Shouting.*) D- d- don't be scared! Look, it's a bearskin. It's
V- V- V- Vašek!

Everybody bursts out laughing.

HATA. (*Disgusted.*) How childish! Playing games again! It's too
disgraceful! Just wait till I get you home. I'll teach you to play at
bears.

Exit VASEK, *pursued by* HATA.

KRUSINA. (*To Micha.*)

> Well, now, farmer Micha, you'll agree that it's useless.
> Vašek's not ready to marry. Jenik's the one to have her.
> Remember, Micha, Jenik is your son, and you're his father.

LUDMILA.

> Give him his farm, let him start out
> his married life with new pride.
> First bless yor long-lost son and heir,
> and then bless your son's new bride.

MICHA.

> (*To Jenik, embracing him.*)
> I prayed to find you! Prayed for this!
> (*To Marenka.*)
> Now my son and you must kiss.

ALL.
> Happy endings happen sometimes,
> making up for all the glum times.
> Wives and husbands, side by side,
> make their peace and toast the bride,
> *the bartered bride!*

JENIK *and* MARENKA *kiss.*

THE ORESTEIA (1981)

MUSIC: Harrison Birtwistle

THE ORESTEIA

This version of *The Oresteia* of Aeschylus was first produced by the National Theatre Company of Great Britain in the Olivier Theatre on 28 November 1981 and at the ancient theatre of Epidauros in July 1982 with the following company:

Sean Baker
David Bamber
James Carter
Timothy Davies
Peter Dawson
Philip Donaghy
Roger Gartland
James Hayes

Greg Hicks
Kenny Ireland
Alfred Lynch
John Normington
Tony Robinson
David Roper
Barrie Rutter
Michael Thomas

DIRECTOR	Peter Hall
MUSIC	Harrison Birtwistle
DESIGNER	Jocelyn Herbert
ASSISTANT DESIGNER	Sue Jenkinson
LIGHTING	John Bury
MOVEMENT	Stuart Hopps
MOVEMENT ASSISTANT	Lyn Hockney
STAFF DIRECTOR	Kenneth Mackintosh
ASSISTANT DIRECTOR	Charlie Hanson
MUSIC DIRECTOR	Malcolm Bennett
MUSIC ASSISTANT	Ben Mason
VOICE	Jane Manning
PRODUCTION MANAGER	Michael Cass Jones
STAGE MANAGER	Rosemary Beattie
DEPUTY STAGE MANAGERS	Courtney Bryant
	Brewyeen Rowland
ASSISTANT STAGE MANAGERS	Jill Macfarlane
	Rebecca Peek
	Tim Speechley
	Lesley Walmsley
SOUND	Ric Green
ASSISTANT DESIGNER (MASKS)	Jenny West
ASSISTANT PRODUCTION MANAGER	Mark Taylor
ASSISTANT TO LIGHTING DESIGNER	Paul McLeish

| MUSICIANS | Malcolm Bennett, Simon Limbrick, Ben Mason (percussion); Helen Tunstall (harp); Rory Allam, John Harle, Jim Rae (wind). |
| INSTRUMENT DESIGN | Arthur Soothill, Brian Ackerman. |

NOTE: *This text is written to be performed, a rhythmic libretto for masks, music, and an all-male company.*   T.H.

ONE
AGAMEMNON

WATCHMAN.
No end to it all, though all year I've muttered
my pleas to the gods for a long groped for end.
Wish it were over, this waiting, this watching,
twelve weary months, night in and night out,
crouching and peering, head down like a bloodhound,
paws propping muzzle, up here on the palace,
the palace belonging the bloodclan of Atreus –
Agamemnon, Menelaus, bloodkin, our clanchiefs.

I've been so long staring I know the stars backwards,
the chiefs of the star-clans, king-stars, controllers,
those that dispense us the coldsnaps and dogdays.
I've had a whole year's worth so I ought to know.
A whole year of it! Still no sign of the signal
I'm supposed to catch sight of, the beacons,
the torch-blaze that means Troy's finally taken . . .

The woman says watch, so here I am watching.
That woman's not one who's all wan and woeful.
That woman's a man the way she gets moving.

Put down your palliasse. Dew-drenched by daybreak.
Not the soft bed you'd dream anything good in –
Fear stays all night. Sleep gives me short time.

Daren't drop off though. Might miss it. The beacon.
And if I missed it . . . life's not worth the living!
Sometimes, to stop nodding, I sing or try singing
but songs stick in my gullet. I feel more like weeping
when I think of the change that's come over this household,
good once and well ordered . . . but all that seems over . . .

Maybe tonight it'll finish, this watching, this waiting,
an end to the torment we've yearned for ten years.

Come on, blasted beacon, blaze out of the blackness!

Sees beacon.

It's there! An oasis like daylight in deserts of dark!
It's there! No mistaking!
                              Agamemnon's woman –
best let her know the beacon's been sighted.
Time all the women were wailing their welcome!

Troy's taken! Troy's down and Troy's flattened.
There'll be dancing in Argos and I'll lead the dance.
My master's struck lucky. So've I, I reckon.
Sighting the beacon's a dice-throw all sixes.

Soon I'll be grasping his hand, Agamemnon's . . .
Let him come home to us, whole and unharmed!

As for the rest . . . I'm not saying. Better not said.
Say that an ox ground my gob into silence.

They'd tell such a story, these walls, if they could.

Those who know what I know, know what I'm saying.
Those who don't know, won't know. Not from me.

Exit WATCHMAN.

Enter CHORUS.

CHORUS.
Ten years since clanchief Menelaus
and his bloodkin Agamemnon
(the twin-yoked rule from clan-chief Atreus –
double thronestones, double chief-staves)
pursued the war-suit against Priam,
launched the 1000 ship armada
off from Argos to smash Troy.

Mewing warcries   preybirds   shrilling
nest-theft   childloss   wild frustration
nestling snaffled   preybirds soaring
wildly sculling   swirling airstreams
using broad birdwings like oars
birthpangs   nothing   nestcare   nothing
nothing   fostered nestlings   nothing
crying   mewing   preybirds   shrilling

But one of the god powers up above them –
Apollo   Pan   or Zeus high he-god
hearing the birds' shrill desolation,
birds, guest-strangers in god-spaces
sends down the slow but certain Fury
to appease the grudge the grieved birds feel

So Zeus protector of man's guestright
sends the avenging sons of Atreus
down on Paris son of Priam

because of Helen, lust-lode, man-hive,
Helen the she manned by too many hes.

Bedbond   no   not bedbond   spearclash
swordhafts shattered   hacked bones smashed
sparring   skirmish   dustclouds   bloodstorm
Trojans   Greeks   not bedbond   bloodbath

The war in Troy's still in a stalemate
marking time at where it's got to
till the fulfilment that's been fated.
Once the Fury's after victims
no sacrifices   no libations
stop the headlong grudge's onrush.

But as for us   recruiter's refuse,
too old to join the expedition,
shrivelled leafage left to wither,
we go doddering about on sticks.
Neither the nurseling nor the senile
have juice enough to serve the Wargod.
Wargod-fodder's prime manhood.

Argos geezers, back to bairnhood,
ghosts still walking after cockcrow,
old men, dreams abroad in daylight.

She-child of Tyndareos, Clytemnestra,
what news have you had, what fresh reports?
You've given orders for sacrifice. Why?

All the godstones of this bloodclan
earthgods   skygods   threshold   market
look   they're all alight   all blazing

Look here   and there   the flaring firebrands
coaxed into flame by smooth-tongued torch-oils
brought out of store for great occasions

If you can tell us give us some comfort
soothe all that grief that's chewed into our guts.
Hope glimmers a little in these lit godstones,
blunts the sharp chops of gnashing despair.

Gab's the last god-gift of the flabby and feeble –
singing the omens that mobilised Argos:

Two preybirds came as prophecy
blackwing and silverhue
came for our twin kings to see
out of the blue   the blue

The right side was the side they flew
spear side   luck side   War
one blackwing   one silverhue
and everybody saw

and everybody saw them tear
with talon and with claw
the belly of a pregnant hare
and everybody saw

and everybody saw the brood
from their mauled mother torn
wallowing in warm lifeblood
and dead as soon as born

blackwing and silverhue
prophesying War
the twin preybirds that cry and mew
hungering for more . . .

Batter, batter the doom-drum, but believe there'll be better!

Calchas the clanseer cunning in seercraft
when he saw before him the armed sons of Atreus
knew what menfolk were meant by the preybirds –
Agamemnon   Menelaus   battle-hungry hare-devourers . . .

'Hosts commanded by twin birds
soldiers who leave these shores
first Fate will waste Troy's crops and herds
then make the inner city yours

The moment when the iron bit
's between the jaws of Troy
may no skycurse glower down on it
and no godgrudge destroy

Artemis   pure she-god   stung
with pity for the hare
all mothers and their unborn young
come under her kind care

her father's hounds with silent wings
swoop down on that scared beast
Artemis   she loves wee things
and loathes the preybirds' feast.'

blackwing and silverhue
prophesying War
the twin preybirds that cry and mew
hungering for more . . .

Batter, batter the doom-drum, but believe there'll be better!

Artemis pure she-god   stung
with pity for the hare
all mothers and their unborn young
come under her kind care

Kind even to the lion-pup
you're the one we cry to, you!
Kind to wild beasts at the pap
stop bad signs coming true.

Apollo   he-god   healer   your she-kin
Artemis   intervene   prevent her
sending winds on the fleet from the wrong direction
keeping the armada too long at anchor,

making a blood-debt sacrifice certain,
a sacrifice no one wants to eat meat from,
a sacrifice no one wants to sing songs to,
whetting the grudge in the clanchief's household,
weakening the bond between woman and manlord,
a grudge wanting blood for the spilling of childblood,
a grudge brooding only on seizing its blood-dues.

These omens both fair and foreboding
Calchas the clanseer saw in the birdsigns –

Batter, batter the doom-drum, but believe there'll be better!

So Agamemnon first clanchief of Argos
found no fault in the clanseer's foretelling
and went where the winds of his life-lot were listing,
the Achaian armada still anchored off Aulis.

Wind-force and wave-swell   keep the ships shorebound
men sapped of spirit   supplies running short
foodpots and grain jars   crapping their contents

ship planks gape open   frayed cables and rigging
time dragging   each day seeming two days
the flower of Argos   bedraggled and drooping

Calchas the clanseer   saw into the storm-cause –
Artemis   she-god   goaded to godgrudge

The clans and the clanchiefs   clamour for sea-calm
The god-sop that gets it   makes their guts sicken
The cure for the stormblast   makes strong men craven

The clanchiefs of Argos   drummed their staves on the earth
and wept and wept   and couldn't stop weeping

Then the first he-child of Atreus   Agamemnon
choked back his crying   and finally spoke:

hard   hard for a general   not to obey
hard   hard for a father   to kill his girl
his jewel   his joy   kill his own she-child
virgin-blood   father-guilt   griming the godstone

Can I choose either   without doing evil
leave the fleet in the lurch   shirker   deserter
let down the Allies   we've all sworn allegiance

They're asking for blood   it's right what they're asking

a virgin's blood only will calm the wind's bluster

So be it then   daughter!   there's no other way

Necessity   he kneels to it   neck into the yokestrap
the General   harnessed to what he can't change
and once into harness his whole life-lot lurches
towards the unspeakable horror   the crime

so men get gulled   get hauled into evil
recklessness starts it   then there's no stopping

so a Father can take his own she-child   take her
and kill her   his she-child   his own flesh and blood

The war-effort wants it   the war-effort gets it
the war for one woman   the whore-war   the whore-war

a virgin's blood launches the ships off to Troy

Her shrillings   beseechings   her cries   Papa   Papa
Iphigeneia   a virgin   a virgin

what's a virgin to hawks and to war-lords?

He says a god-plea   her father   her *father*   then orders
attendants to hoist her   up   on to the godstone

she bends herself double   beseeching Papa   Papa
wraps her clothes round her   making it harder
up   up   she gets hoisted   like a goat to the godstone

a gag in her mouth   her lovely mouth   curbed like a horse's
so that this bloodclan's not blasted by curses

her garments stream groundwards   the looseflow of saffron
cloth drifting   cloth trailing   she darts them all glances
that go through their hearts   deep into them   wounding

a painting   a sculpture   that seems to be speaking
seeking to say things   but locked in its stone

they know what her eyes say   that gang round the godstone

often they'd seen her   at meals with her father
in the place beside his   when they sat at his table
the welcoming table of King Agamemnon

she sat beside him   his innocent she-child
singing the lyresong after libations
the melodious gracethanks   to Zeus   the Preserver

What came next   didn't see   so can't tell you

What Calchas foretold all came to fulfilment

Suffering comes first   then after awareness

The future's the future   you'll know when it's here
foreseeing the future's to weep in advance

The present's enough   and what's going to happen
let it be what we've hoped for   us   the poor remnants
so long the sole bulwark of monarchless Argos

Enter CLYTEMNESTRA.

Clytemnestra, we come to you as we would to our clanchief
for it's right that we honour the wife of the clanchief
when the manlord himself's not here on the thronestone.
Is it good news and firm news or mere wishful thinking
that makes you sacrifice now on the godstones?

CLYTEMNESTRA.
  Like mother, like daughter . . . May last night's good news
  give birth this dawnlight to a day like her mother.
  What I've got to tell you's beyond all you've hoped for.
  The Greek armies have taken the city of Priam.

1. CH. Taken Troy? Did my ears hear you right?   ]
  CLYT. Wasn't I clear? Troy was taken last night.   ]

2. CH. My eyes fill with tears, tears of sheer joy.   ]
  CLYT. Then your eyes know it's true our taking of Troy.]

3. CH. Can you be certain with no news that's concrete?]
  CLYT. Yes, unless the whole thing's some he-god's deceit.]

4. CH. Or some dream of Troy taken which *seems* to you true.]
  CLYT. I put trust in seeming no more than you.   ]

5. CH. Some rumour has reached you the war's at andend?]
  CLYT. I'm no simple childwit! Don't condescend!   ]

6. CH. So Troy has been taken *when* did you say?   ]
  CLYT. Last night, she who just gave birth to today.
  CH. The news came so fast over such a long way!   ]

CLYTEMNESTRA.
  Firegod Hephaistos flashed out from Mount Ida
  flame after flame bore the beacon's despatches,
  jaded flame to fresh flame bearing the firenews.
  Ida to Crag Hermes on the island of Lemnos.
  From there its third stretch to the top of Mount Athos,
  the peak that Zeus favours, then further upwards
  and over the ocean dazzling and flaring
  luring up fish-shoals to see what the flash is,
  a fire-tailed comet transmitting its message
  to the watchtowers scanning the sky on Macistos.
  They weren't caught napping. They flung the flame onwards
  and it hurtled over Euripus and watchmen
  marked it from their Messapion outpost.
  They kindle heaped brushwood and speed the flame further.
  It gathers momentum. It doesn't diminish.
  It streaks like a meteor over Asopus
  and lands on Cithaeron and sparks off the next one.
  Again not neglected. So eager the watchmen
  they get up a blaze that doubles the last one.

From the bog of Gorgopis to Mount Aegiplanctus
the bright chain of firelinks remaining unbroken.
they spare no effort and heap on the kindling,
the flamehair streaming out over the headland
that faces gulf Saron and then dropping southwards
to the crag of Arachne that borders on Argos
and straight to the palace of Atreus,
the flame that was fathered in Troy's conflagration.

My torchbearers bore all the batons of blazes

That's the sign, the proof you've been wanting
all the way from Troy, from my manlord to me.

CHORUS.

The gods will get all our thanks for their bounty.
But your tale's such a marvel we'd like it repeated.
We'd like all the details. You said first that Hephaistos . . .

CLYTEMNESTRA.

Troy's held by the Greeks is the truth you're not grasping.
Pour oil on to vinegar in the same foodpot
they'll never blend in brotherly bloodbond.
So life-lots in conflict cause cries that conflict:
the Trojans all tearful, their arms round their fallen
embracing cold corpses, the widows, the orphans,
knowing their own lives mean only bond-chains,
keen for their bloodkin, their nearest, their dearest;
the Greeks, their whole night spent in harsh skirmish,
famished for breakfast swoop down onto Troy,
no billets allotted, all discipline broken,
each màn for himself, the luck of the straw-lot,
they bed themselves down in the houses they've captured,
free of the nightfrost, rough beds in the open,
sleep, for once without sentries, and wake up refreshed.
So provided they don't give Troy's gods provocation
and leave unmolested their sacrosanct seats
there's a chance that the victors will never be victims.
I hope our platoons aren't driven by lootlust
to bring what's tabooed back home here as booty.
They still need some safety on the last lap back home.
And even if the Greeks give grudge to no godheads
the dead that they've slaughtered can't sleep for ever.
Let disaster stop at the place it's reached so far,

the cycle be broken, and hope start to happen.
Let a life-lot that's lucky get crowned with the laurels.

You've heard all my feelings, those of a woman.

Exit CLYTEMNESTRA.

CHORUS.
You feel like a woman but talk like a man talks.
Now I've heard all your proofs now I can offer
the gratitude due to the gods who guard Argos.
The joy we feel now seems worth all we've suffered.

Zeus the high he-god with Night as his helper
cast a vast trammel over Troy's towers –
men get meshed in it   women   children
all dragged ashore and beached in harsh bondage.
Zeus cast it   Zeus   protector of guestright.
Zeus got the bullseye when he shot Paris
an arrow that took ten years to its target.

The Zeus-shot they call it   no doubting it either.

Zeus says it   it happens   his plans get accomplished.

So if somebody tells you gods take no notice
when the sacrosanct's trampled on   trod underfoot
point to what's happened   and call him a cretin
point to what's happened   ruin for recklessness
men over-ambitious   treasure-stuffed mansions
measureless riches that can't buy the best things

sufficiency's ample   real wealth is awareness

surfeit   satiety   gold tons are no bulwark
if the godstone of justice gets booted to blackness
true bloodright shattered to atoms of nothing.

Wordpower   temptations   techniques of inducement
soften the wretch up for their master   Destruction

Guilt can't be curtained   it glows through the nightdark

Base battle-bronze battered gets blackened and mottled
so a man's baseness gets clotted with bloodguilt.

The chased culprit's got as much chance of escaping
as a boy has of catching a blackbird bare-handed.

Time spatters the guilty   the blood a man sheds
smears his whole people   his touch clarts his clan.

Now he starts praying   the gods make their ears stone
the deaf gods trample him mid-supplication.

It was like that with Paris   guest-stranger and welcome
at the hospitable table of the bloodclan of Atreus –

his gratitude   guest-thanks   grabbing of Helen

and what did Helen bequeath to her people
spearclash and shieldclang   the massive armada

the dowry she went with to Troy was   destruction.

'A bad day for this house   a bad day for the master
look at the bedclothes   still rumpled with passion'

Menelaus apart   he's brooding his loveloss
stunned into silence   a shadow   a ghostman

statues mean nothing   stone's eyeless and lifeless

his sleep's full of dreamwives   Helen-shaped shadows
that bring ease a moment then vanish away

he tries to grasp her   she slips through his fingers
shadowing off down the flyways of sleep . . .

This is the anguish of the country's chief household

It doesn't stop there though   grief goes all over
each house in Argos sent someone to battle

and gets back for menfolk   jars full of cinders
a plectrum of sorrows plucks women's griefstrings:

'Geldshark Ares god of War
broker of men's bodies
usurer of living flesh
corpse-trafficker that god is –

give to WAR your men's fleshgold
and what are your returns?
kilos of cold clinker packed
in army-issue urns

wives   mothers   sisters   each one scans
the dogtags on the amphorae

which grey ashes are my man's?
they sift the jumbled names and cry:

my husband sacrificed his life

my brother's a battle-martyr

aye, for someone else's wife –

Helen, whore of Sparta!

whisper   mutter   belly-aching
the people's beef and bile: *this war's*
been Agamemnon's our clanchief's making,
the sons of Atreus and their "cause".

Where's my father   husband   boy?
where do all our loved ones lie?
six feet under near the Troy
they died to occupy.'

The people's rancour's a terrible burden
the whole clan can curse with one venomous voice.

Night's got something under its dark cloth

listen   dangers hum under its cover
gods see carnage   get the massacre marked –

Furies   the trackers   fulfilling the bloodgrudge
trip the transgressor   tread him into the ground
blown up and bloated   rubbed out into nothing
no one can save you among blurs and shadows.

Rising too high's a danger   it's risky
the pinnacles get the thunder's first flameclap
the cragpeaks feel the first storm-flash

Enough is enough when unmarred by mean mangrudge
Conqueror   captive   don't want to be either
I want to wear neither laurels nor bondchains.

1.   Those fires make the rumours fly through the street.
      Is it all true, or some he-god's deceit?

2.   Who's such a childwit to believe the flame first
      then feel despondent when the bubble's been burst

3.   Women! Women are always ready to act
      before they know if a rumour's true fact.

4.   Women are gullible. Minds like dry straw –
      one whoosh of belief and then nothing more.

We'll know soon enough what that blaze was about,
those beacons and bonfires, the new fangled flamegraphs,
whether there's anything in it or whether
it's just the wishful thinking women indulge in.

Look, there's a herald coming up from the seashore,
the mud of the trenches caked dry on his tunic.
He's wearing the olive-wreath, and there, look, behind him,
look at that dustcloud. That means that it's real news
not feminine flame-a-phores kindled on mountains,
but words spoken, man to man, and spoken directly.
He'll say rejoice or . . . that mustn't happen . . .
So far, so good. And let it continue . . .
and if there's anyone wants anything else for this bloodclan
I hope that he gets what his malice deserves.

Enter HERALD.

HERALD.
      Homesoil! Argos ground! Clanland! Home!
      A ten year absence ends in this bright dawn.
      Most hopes were shipwrecked. One scraped back safe,
      the hope that I'd make it back home here to die,
      die, and find rest in the earth I most cherish.
      Earth   Earth   Sun   Sun!
      Zeus   godchief   highest of he-gods
      Apollo   godseer   Pythian prophet
      those arrowshafts shot at us, hold back the volleys,
      god-aggro enough on the banks of Scamander.
      Now be the cure-all, the soul-salve Apollo.
      Hermes, he-god, and herald to godclans,
      guardian of heralds to men down below,
      and heroes under whose gaze we were drafted,
      welcome us back, those few spared the spearthrust.
      House of our clanchiefs, homes of my bloodkin,
      thronestones and godstones facing the sun's glare,
      if ever you once did, welcome your king back,
      look on him with kind eyes after his absence.
      Like a bright firebrand blazing through darkness
      to stop us all stumbling, King Agamemnon.
      Welcome him warmly. He's earned your warm welcome.

He swung the god-axe, Zeus the Avenger's,
tore Troy's roots up, dug her earth over,
her god-shrines shattered, her altars all gutted,
fruitful earth scorched into futureless dustbowls,
an empire gone putrid and tossed on time's midden.
Troy's neck got his yoke on, your clanchief's,
first he-child of Atreus, most lucky of life-lot,
worthier than any of the honours he's taken.
I doubt raper Paris thought it was worth it.
The town he brought doom on won't boast of his bridesnatch.
Branded for wife-theft he lost what he'd plundered,
his ancestral bloodclan razed root and branch.
Priam's sons paid for it. An eye for an eye,
or more like ten thousand eyes for each one.

1. CH. Welcome Herald! You're home. They war's far behind.
    HE. I kept alive for this. Now death I don't mind.

2. CH. Did you long for your home here back at the war?
    HE. What else do you think my weeping is for?

3. CH. You could say it was sweet, in a way, your disease.
    HE. Sweet? A disease! What riddles are these?

4. CH. That longing you had. We caught it here too.
    HE. You longed for us as we longed for you?

5. CH. So much that our gloom made us groan with despair.
    HE. What made you so gloomy? Our being out there?

6. CH. It's best for our safety if no more is said.
    HE. With the clanchiefs away what caused you this dread?
    CH. Like you we too wouldn't mind being dead.

HERALD.
Suffering. Suffering only the gods escape it entirely.
If you'd known firsthand our louse-ridden billets,
cramped berths on board, claustrophobic, foul bedding,
what didn't we have to complain of you tell me.
Ashore was no better. Worse. We bivouaced
under the walls with the enemy firing.
Drenched either by drizzle or dew from the ground.
Clothes mouldy with mildew. Locks crawling with lice.

First unbearable cold, snow blowing off Ida,
blizzards killing birdflocks frozen in flight.
Then heat! and even the ocean seemed stifled,

slumped, zephyrless, in unruffled siestas,
slack billows lolling in the deadest of doldrums.

But why go on? What's the point? The pain's over,
and for the dead so over and done with,
they'll never lust after a life-lot again.
The dead are dead. Who wants a head-count?
Why should the living scratch open old scabs.
We've left it behind us. Goodbye to all that!
We're what's left. There's some good for the living.
The pain and the losses don't quite overbalance.
We can shout out to the universe proudly:

The bloodclans of Argos in battle alliance
having mashed into ashes Asia's town Troy
now nail up these god-spoils to Hellas's he-gods.

For all that we'll get the credit and praises
and Zeus the god's whale's share. He made it happen.

That's all. That's all there is for the telling.

CHORUS.
Your news shows me that I was mistaken.
But you're never too old to learn a new lesson.
Clytemnestra, she should be first to hear the whole story.
The leftovers and scraps of it satisfy me.

Enter CLYTEMNESTRA.

CLYTEMNESTRA.
I started my triumph cry some time ago
when the first flame-messenger arrived in the darkness
proclaiming the capture and downfall of Troy.
And what did the men say? 'Just like a woman!
One beacon, that's all, and she thinks Troy's been captured'
Mutterings like that made me feel stupid.
I went on with the sacrifice in spite of their moaning,
then the whole city began 'behaving like women'
raising the triumph cry 'shouting and bawling'
feeding the thankfires almost to bursting.
And why should you tell me anything further?
I'll have the whole tale from the mouth of my manlord.
And it's his welcome now that must be fully prepared.
No day in the life of woman's sweeter than that one
when she flings the door open to welcome her manlord,

her manlord brought safely back from the war.
Go. Tell him come quickly. He's loved by his people.
Tell him he'll find his wife faithful and bond-true
as when he first left her, and, like a good bloodhound,
his loyal servant, and his enemies' foe.
He'll find all his treasures still with his seal on.
Tell him I've accepted no man's attentions.
I'm no more a breaker of bedbond,
than, as a woman, I wield a man's weapon.

Exit CLYTEMNESTRA.

CHORUS.
All the words of the woman are clear enough
if those who are listening give all their ears.
(*To Herald.*)
Herald, what about Menelaus our other clanchief?
You haven't said he's home safe as well.

1.   HE.   Falsehood is something fair lies never hide.
            The mask of glad messenger just wasn't mine.
     CH.   Skins can be fair and the fruit bad inside.
            Can't good news and truth ever share the same vine?

2.   HE.   Menelaus, he's missing that clan-chief of yours.
            He's gone, his ship's gone. And *this* is all true.
     CH.   He set sail with you though when the force left Troy's shore:
            Did a sudden storm blow up and snatch him from view?

3.   HE.   Storm! Yes, you've hit the bull's eye!
            'Storm' 's a small word that encompasses hell.
     CH.   Is he still living, or did the chief die?
            Is there anyone there in the fleet who can tell?

4.   HE.   No one knows anything, at least not us men,
            only the sun that looks down from the sky.
     CH.   How did the storm start? Why did it? When?
            Was it some godgrudge, and if a grudge, why?

HERALD.
A godgrudge! A godgrudge! Don't drag in *those* she-gods!
Some gods preside over pleasures, some pain.
Those she-gods go with the most galling godgrudge.
This day's a homecoming meant to be happy.
When a clan messenger's arrived shedding tears
to announce to his bloodclan what they've been dreading,

the rout of their armies, a mountainous death-toll,
with anguish for all in the rolls of the fallen,
the best lads in their tonloads tangled and landed
and gashed by the flesh-hook, the fish-gaff of Ares,
gaff-flukes and grapnel barbs gory with fleshbits –
if he comes so overbalanced with trouble
then that's the time to start hymning the Furies.
But if the news is good that he's bringing
and the city's wild with relief and success
who wants to be first to get the good curdled
and blurt it all out: 'Shipwreck. Shrewgrudge!
the grudges of she-gods shattered the Greek ships.'

Flame and saltwater are scarcely a bloodbond.
This time they were though, elements merging,
and their bond-proof – smashing our ships into splinters.

Blackness. Waveforce. Sea heaving and swelling.
Fierce thrashing galesqualls whistling from Thrace,
hurricanes blasting, rain lashing and pelting,
ship-prow smashing ship-prow, horned beast goring beast,
beasts with their horns locked butting each other.
You know when a collie not used to its charges
scatters the daft sheep every direction,
colliding, collapsing, that kind of chaos . . .
well that's how the waves were. Next morning
the Aegean had mushroomed with corpses and shipwreck.
Our ship though, amazing, still whole and undamaged.
Some god interceded, got our ship a pardon.
Our helm had been guided by the hand of some he-god.
Our ship was one that didn't get shattered.
Couldn't believe it, escaping that wave-grave,
couldn't believe our life-lot so lucky.
We were shocked in the clear light of morning,
chewing the cud of the nightmare we'd lived through.
If any of the others survived they'll be thinking
we're finished, finished, as we still do of them.
May everything still turn out for the better.
Menelaus, let's suppose that he's made it,
let's hope he's still somewhere under the sunlight.
Zeus can't want the whole bloodclan blasted.
That's the truth you wanted.   You've got it all now.

CHORUS.
> HELEN   wrecker   HELEN   Hell
> the one who first named her knew what was fated –
> HEL- a god guided his tongue right -EN
> HEL- spear-bride   gore-bride   war-whore   -EN
> HEL- ship-wrecker   man-breaker   Troy-knacker   -EN
>
> From silken bowers scented and flowing with curtains
> to seas that are breathed on and ruffled by zephyrs,
> and after her warhosts bristling with metal,
> trail-hounds snuffling the vanishing oar-spoor,
> tracking the beached ships up leafy Simois,
> trail-hounds scenting the seatracks and bloodslicks.
>
> Godgrudge and mangrudge ganging together
> shepherded the blood-bride surely to Troy,
> delayed counterblow to the sullied table,
> the wrong done to Zeus protector of guestright.
> They paid the blood-price, the bridegroom's bloodkin
> chanting the bride-hymn, hymning the bedbond.
> The new hymn they've learnt in the city of Priam's
> not about bedbond but a loud bawl at death
> calling Paris the doomgroom, the doomgroom.
> War-whore Helen brought suffering, slaughter,
> bloodgrudge, futility, childloss and bloodflow.
>
> 'Story: Man & Lion. This is it –
>
> Lion-cub brought in from the wild
> still whimpering for the tit
> Man treats it like a child
>
> They dandle it   they fondle   stroke
> they sit it in their laps
> delight of children and old folk
> sits up and begs for scraps
>
> Time passes and the man's cub grows
> no more a wean to rock to sleep
> suddenly its nature shows
> cub savages your sheep
>
> its thankyou for its bed and board
> its gratitude for care
> your whole flock torn   clawed   gnawed
> and bloodflow everywhere

Blood everywhere   blood everywhere
the whole house smirched   defiled
anguish   carnage   and despair
for fostering that child

That harmless orphaned furry beast
greeting for its nurse
was nothing but a fury-priest
a grudge-sent slaughter curse.

Helen to Troy   first windless calm   windless
a priceless treasure   yielding with soft feel
delicate eyeglints   rare orchid with heart-thorns
then abracadabra the nuptials turn nasty,
jinxwoman Helen   wormwood   lovegall
bringing the children of Priam disaster
spurred on by Zeus as protector of guestright,
blood-price   spoil-spouse   connubial Fury.

Wealth-pride never dies childless   never
but always breeds children that go the bad –
that's half of the story but what I say's this:

Wealth coupled with Hubris   that's the dark pedigree
that sends its black seeds from infant to infant

When bloodright gives birth the children are blotless –

Hubris I breeds Hubris II
O dark ancestral tree
Old arrogance will soon breed new
gory genealogy

Wealth-pride is the furious son
of a fiendish blood-dark mother
Violence is the other one
and dead spit of his brother

Justice shines through hovel smoke
she loves the man who's straight
Justice eats off plates of oak
scorns dainties off gold plate

Hands bespattered with shed blood
raise gilded rafters to the skies
Justice searching for the good
leaves with averted eyes

Justice doesn't kneel to fame
kiss affluence's feet
isn't dazzled by a name
gold-coined but counterfeit

Justice isn't put out of her stride
Justice can't be turned aside

Enter AGAMEMNON *with* CASSANDRA *and Trojan spoils.*

CHORUS.
Bloodshoot of Atreus, destroyer of Troy
what's the best title to give you   what honour
that isn't too high for you or too hackneyed?
What name does you justice   gives you your due?

The world's mostly mummery   sham and not gut-truth.
Someone's wretched and people start sighing;
the griefshow stops a lot short of the heart.
Someone's happy, they act the same hollowly
glum visages forced into grins that are joyless.
But a good judge of livestock knows his own cattle –
their eyes say one thing   he knows the other
their cow eyes may water   he knows it's not love.

I can hide nothing   now I can tell you
when you first marshalled the armies for Helen
your image was evil   I thought you misguided
to wage a long war for one lustful woman
so many cold grave urns for one gadding girl . . .

now though my heart's full   and I greet you
your victory makes everything worth it
the omens I loathed then seem justified now.

And while you were fighting   those who remained here
some have been faithful   and others . . .
but you'll soon sort out the sheepmen and goatmen.

AGAMEMNON.
First I greet Argos and the gods of this bloodclan.
They gave me safe passage and helped me smash Priam.
They stopped their ears to Troy's pleas and entreaties.
They cast their votes and pitched all the pebbles
into the bloodpot. Nothing went into the pot for acquittal
Hope hovered round it but hope's got no franchise.
Troy! you can almost see it smoking from Argos!

The rubble and debris still breathe out destruction,
the ashes of surfeited Asia still sighing,
the sickly cachou breath of soft living and riches.
The thanks owed our gods for their bounty's boundless.
Remember them, everyone, now in our triumph,
now that we've got Troy caught in our sweepnet.
They raped one woman. We razed the whole city.
Ground it to powder. Made mincemeat of Troy.
The monster of Argos, the horse-monster did it,
chock full of shock-troops, clearing Troy's bulwarks
just when the Pleiades were starting to wane,
leaping the battlements the ravening lion
glutted its bloodlust on Troy's royal children.

What you said about praising and joy I agree with.
Not many can look on success without mangrudge.
Grudge gangrenes the gut. The suffering's twofold:
one's own lack of luck, another's good life-lot.
I know what I'm saying, knew only too well
how men can dissemble, make friendship a sham.
Most of my comrades were shadow men, shadows.
Only Odysseus, first reluctant and cussèd,
once into harness pulled his weight beside me.
And whether he's dead or alive isn't certain . . .

As for the matters of bloodclan, clan-rite and clan gods
we'll call the clan council to meet in full conclave.
Emergencies needing immediate attention –
drastic surgery. Cauterise. Cut out the canker . . .

Now into the palace, my household hearthstone,
to give the thanks due to all my great godkin.
They sent me out. They brought me back safely.
I've won this once but I have to keep winning.

Enter CLYTEMNESTRA.

CLYTEMNESTRA.
Kinsmen, old men of Argos gathered before us
I'm not ashamed to confess in your presence
my love for my manlord. Time removes shyness.
I don't need to hear stories, I suffered firsthand.
I suffered greatly with my man at the warfront.
For a woman to sit alone at home waiting
with her man at the war's a terrible burden.

There's no end to the rumours she has to keep hearing.
News-runners arriving in rapid succession
bawling the worsening news to the bloodclan.
If my manlord received the wounds rumour gave him
he'd gape open now like a sea-fisher's grabnet.
I was driven distracted . . . rope round the rafters . . .
neck in the noose . . . getting tighter . . . half-throttled . . .

(*To Agamemnon.*)
that's why our child isn't here now in Argos,
our child, our bed-bond's first bloodshoot,
our *he*-child, Orestes.   No need for suspicion.
He's in Phocis with Strophius, our ally and friend.
Strophius warned me of possible troubles,
the threat to your life in the perils of warfare,
the likelihood here of popular rising.
When people are down they get trampled further.
My words have no wiles, and no guile to gull you.
Now my eyes are pumped dry. No more tears to squeeze out.
Eyes bleary with weeping and sleepless night-vigils
hoping the beacons from you would get kindled.
If I slept, *if*, a mere gnat-whine would wake me,
loud as a bugle bray, wake me from dreaming.
And what did I dream of? Your danger. Your deathwounds.
Ten years of tight corners crammed into a catnap!
All that I suffered but no longer feel fettered,
I'm free to say welcome, my lord, to your house,
welcome as the watchdog is in the sheepfold,
mainmast of our vessel, chief central rooftree.
Like an only child to its father you're welcome,
welcome as land is to those on the ocean,
welcome as dawn is after long nightsqualls,
as a spring is to travellers thirsting for water.

The release! Yanking necessity's yokestrap off!

Now, my great manlord, come down from your warcar.
But don't let those feet that have trampled Troy under
step on mere earth.

(*To Slaves.*)
                                        Why are you waiting?
Carry out my commands for strewing the pavestones,
drag the dark dye-flow right down from the doorway.
Let bloodright, true bloodright be the king's escort.

No sleeping for me till the gods get their pleasure.
The she-gods of life-lot, I'll be their she-kin,
the female enforcer of all they have fated.

AGAMEMNON.
She-child of Leda, my household's best bloodhound,
your words, like my absence, lasted too long.
Our praise-singers spout out such paeans for payment.
We are a warhawk, no woman wanting such welcomes.
Such prostrations, such purples suit pashas from Persia.
Don't come the Khan's courtiers, kowtow or cosset.
Don't grovel, suck up, salaam, and stop gawping!
Such gaudy displays goad gods into godgrudge.
Give honours to humans more meant for mankind
than such stuffs even skygods won't scorn to be swathed in.
The mortal who blackens such silks with his bootsoles
best beware of bad trouble, best look to his life-lot.
My fame's managed so far without fancy footmats.
The greatest of godgifts is canniness, caution.
Luck has to last the whole length of a lifetime.
If happiness fails in the last lap it's futile.
Fortune can only be first. All after it's failure.
Good luck gets the champion's laurels or nothing.
Runners up in the race are degrees of disaster.
My stride's strong and steady till disaster's left standing.

1.   CLYT.   Then stride 'strong and steady' on what we have strewn.
     AG.   No, it smells baleful. No blessing or boon!

2.   CLYT.   Is 'great' Agamemnon godstruck, afraid?
     AG.   No, but I stand by the statement I made.

3.   CLYT.   And potentate Priam? Would *he* tread it or not?
     AG.   That Trojan satrap? Traipse over the lot!

4.   CLYT.   Are you afraid of what the people might say?
     AG.   The voice of the people exerts its own sway.

5.   CLYT.   Mangrudge is proof that a man's reached great heights.
     AG.   And only he-women go looking for fights.

6.   CLYT.   Give way from the grace of your great victory.
     AG.   Would that give you joy, that gesture from me?
     CLYT.   Let me win a little, great manlord. Agree!

AGAMEMNON.
If it means so much . . .

(*To Slaves.*)
                              here, help get these boots off.
Campaign comrades, loyal old leathers.

Keep godgrudge off me as I tread on this sea-red.
I'll feel that I'm walking the women who wove it.
Mounds of rich silver went into its making.
So much for me . . .

(*Indicates Cassandra.*)
                              This stranger needs looking after.
The gods like some kindness from those who have triumphed.
Be kind. Nobody wants to end up in bondage.
Pick of the booty, the Trojan spoil loot-pearl,
this girl's the men's gift to grace their commander.

Well since I've yielded, I'll do what you ask me,
and tread on your red path into my palace.

AGAMEMNON *begins walking on the cloth towards the palace doors.*

CLYTEMNESTRA.
The sea's there for ever. No one can drain it.
And it oozes for ever the dyes of dark sea-red
to stain all the garments this house has a wealth of.
The gods have made sure that we've never been lacking.
And if gods had prescribed it as a rite for his safety
I would have trampled each inch of rich raiment.
If the treeroot's living the house gets new leafage
spreading cool shade at the time of the dogstar.
Your return's like a rare spell of sunshine in winter,
like Zeus when he ripens the sour grapes for the vintage.
A master's presence then 's the finishing stroke.

O Zeus, Zeus who brings all things to fulfilment
my fulfilment lies in serving your purpose.

Exit CLYTEMNESTRA.

CHORUS.
Fear whirs its wings round my heart
my soul flies into the future
the songnotes darken with prophecy.

Certainty's thronestone's deserted
nothing says go to my panic
Can't spit out the gobbets of nightmare

Sand's silted over the marks of the hawsers
Time's covered up the chainchafe of anchors
where the dogships strained at their leashes for Troy
and they've returned   my own eyes can see them
and still I'm uneasy   terrified   why?

Listen   a dirgesong nobody's strumming
Listen   the Furies' monotonous humming
Listen   strings tuned to the terror that's coming.

Enter CLYTEMNESTRA.

CLYTEMNESTRA.
You too, Cassandra. Cassandra, come in!
Zeus can't be angry. He wants you to join us
to share in the household's ritual washing
taking your place among all the slave-girls
at the godstone to one who keeps this house wealthy.

Come down from the warcar. Why be so haughty?

If it has to happen, enslavement,
they're lucky to fall to hereditary masters.
The ones who suddenly come into a fortune,
get rich by a windfall, they're brutal to slaves.
We'll treat you kindly according to custom.

CHORUS.
It's you she's addressing, Cassandra, no savvy?
You're fast in the fate-net, the shackles of life-lot.
You can't scramble out. Best do as you're bidden.

CLYTEMNESTRA.
Sparrowbrain! What does she jabber in, ba-ba gibberish?
I'll try her again. Go inside! Go inside!

CHORUS.
Go. It's best. And you haven't much choice.
Do as you're bidden. Come down from the car.

CLYTEMNESTRA.
I don't have time to stand about waiting.
The sacrifice. It's standing now at the godstone.
The victim's prepared. My dreams reach fulfilment.

If you want to partake in our worship, then come.

(*To Chorus.*)
Nothing gets through. Try her in dumbshow.

CHORUS.
>   An interpreter's needed. Somebody clever.
>   She's like a wild animal caught in a net.

CLYTEMNESTRA.
>   Maniac, more like, listening to voices.
>   Her father's city's caught fast in the net.
>   She'll go champing her chops on the chainbit
>   until her mettle and madness froth off as blood.
>   I'm not staying here to be sneered at by slavegirls.

Exit CLYTEMNESTRA.

CHORUS.
>   I pity the creature. She needs understanding.
>   Come down, poor woman, down from the warcar.
>   Necessity. Neck into the yokestrap!

CASSANDRA.
>   *otototoi popoi da!*
>   Apollo   Apollo!

CHORUS.
>   Apollo? Then that *otototoi*'s all wrong!
>   Apollo hates death-notes and dark sorts of song.

CASSANDRA.
>   *otototoi popoi da!*
>   Apollo   Apollo!

CHORUS.
>   Listen! Again. Apollo hates the sort of note
>   that comes strangled and anguished out of her throat.

CASSANDRA.
>   Apollo Apollo   waygod   destroyer
>   Again you're Cassandra's appalling destroyer!

CHORUS.
>   She's in a trance, about to prophesy.
>   Even in bondage her gift doesn't die.

CASSANDRA.
>   Apollo   Apollo   waygod   destroyer
>   where have you brought me   what house is this?

CHORUS.
> The house of Atreus. That much *I* know.
> It's a poor prophetess asks me questions though!

CASSANDRA.
> ah   ah   ah
> god-shunners   kin-killers
> child-charnel   man-shambles
> babe-spattered abattoir

CHORUS.
> She's like a bloodhound nose to the ground
> tracking the kill that's got to be found.

CASSANDRA.
> I track down the witnesses
> children   babes   shrieking butcher
> barbecued childflesh wolfed down by the father

CHORUS.
> Your prophetic powers none of us doubt.
> But that kind of vision we can well do without.

CASSANDRA.
> I see   somebody   evil   something
> agony   agony   more   more   more
> no one can bear it   no one can stop it
> help's far away over the ocean

CHORUS.
> Now I'm lost, though till now the tale was clear.
> We breathe *that* story in our atmosphere.

CASSANDRA.
> husband   bed-mate
> body washed in your bath-trough
>
> hand over hand   hauling the catch in

CHORUS.
> Now it's got worse. I can make no sense
> of these dense riddles that grow more dense.

CASSANDRA.
> net   hell-net
> she-snare   bed-mate   blood-mate

the deathpack howls over its victim
the fiendswarm surrounds it for stoning

CHORUS.

Don't rouse the Furies. Don't start them humming
you make me feel hopeless. Don't drag them in.

The heart loses blood as cloths lose dyestuff
and the sun oozes light at its setting.

Death moves in fast. I can feel his shadow.

CASSANDRA.

Look there   there   look
bull   cow   bull   cow   don't let them grapple
he's caught in the robe-net   she gores him and gores him
butting and butting   with blood-crusted horn
slumps into bathblood   bloodsplash

CHORUS.

I'm no good at oracles telling the future
but I recognise evil in what she keeps saying.
Evil's all men get out of oracles.
Her words spell out terror, and smell of the truth.

CASSANDRA.

him   me   him   me   him   me
woecups   mine slops over the brim
what have you brought me here for?
to die beside you   what else?

CHORUS.

Sing your own deathdirge, nightingale.
You're like the brown bird shrilling your grieftrills
warbling insatiably Itys O Itys!

CASSANDRA.

Wings   wings   no weeping   no wailing
Cassandra   bloodblade and hackblock

CHORUS.

This nightmare, this maelstrom, where does it come from?
Strange cries, shrill shriekings! Where will they end?

CASSANDRA.

Paris   blood bridals   kin-doom
Scamander   Scamander   Cassandra's Scamander

I was a youngster on your riverside once

Griefstreams of Acheron   I'll sing beside you.

CHORUS.
That's clear enough. A child couldn't miss it.
Your death songs pang me and pain me like snakefangs
Your anguish tears me in two just to listen.

CASSANDRA.
Troytowers tottering   Troytowers destroyed
sacrifice   sacrifice   beast after beast
all father's cattle   utterly useless
the Troy of my father   ashes   all ash

I'm on fire too   come crashing to earth.

CHORUS.
What is it wringing these cries from your body?
These painpangs and griefsongs? Don't understand.

CASSANDRA.
Off with the brideveil then. Look into truth's pupils
The truthgust. It's rising. Blowing fresh headwinds
sweeping sea-ripples into dawn's molten cauldron,
then building a woe-wave as big as a mountain.
Riddles are over. Keep close on my track now
as I scent out the spoor of ancient transgression.
Listen. The rooftops. Monotonous humming
that drones on forever and means only terror.
The blood-bolstered fiend-swarm holds its debauches,
cacophonous squatters that can't be evicted,
chant over and over the crime where it started
cursing a bedbond a bloodkin defiled
trampling all over the flowing bed-linen.

Have I shot wide or am I on target.
Swear I know all the curse of this bloodclan.

CHORUS.
And if I did swear, what good would it do,
what would it alter? But it's a wonder
a stranger like you knows the truth of our story.
It's as if you'd witnessed all you're describing.

1. CASS. Apollo the seergod put this power in my head.]
    CH.   A god, and so lovesick he'd bribe you to bed?

2. CASS. I've always thought it too shameful to tell.]
    CH.   Shame's a luxury for when life goes well.

3. CASS. He got me flat on my back. I felt his breath. Hot.]
    CH.   And did the he-god get what he wanted, or not?

4. CASS. I told him he could then later said no.]
    CH.   You've already been given the god-vision though?

5. CASS. I foretold Troy's downfall, the Trojans' defeat.]
 . CH.   And didn't Apollo make you pay for your cheat?

6. CASS. Yes, no one ever believed me, not one single word.]
    CH.   But we have believed all we have heard.

CASSANDRA.
      ah   ah   ah   ah

      truthpangs   truthpain   tornado and maelstrom
      doomfever   doom-ague shakes my body again

      look on the rooftops   dream-shadows   children
      killed by their bloodkin, their hands full of *ugh*
      offal and giblets   their very own innards
      held out to their father as succulent morsels.

      The lion plots vengeance   the lion that's gutless,
      the lion that lolls in my master's own chamber
      waiting to welcome my homecoming master
      (master, that's what as his slave I must call him)
      Commander of triremes, crusher of Priam,
      but blind to cabal, the insatiable hell-bitch,
      licking his hand   ears pricked in welcome.
      furry and cur-like concealing a Fury
      red-blooded, intrepid, the man-slaying woman
      what name of monster's best to describe her?
      Blood-sucker   basilisk   two-headed shark-hag,
      rock-trog skulking for sailors to wreck them,
      hell-dam fire-breathing war   war   at her husband,
      boundless in brazenness, hear her hosannas
      like battle-cries raised when the victory seems certain.
      But how well she dissembles that so wifely welcome.

      Whether I'm believed or not doesn't matter
      Whatever you do the future will happen.

Through pity and tears you'll know the true prophet.

CHORUS.
Thyestes eating his children, that I got, yes.
I sicken and tremble at truths so unfeigning.
The rest I can't fathom. I'm lost I'm afraid.

1. CASS.   Agamemnon. He's the one you'll see dead!   ⎤
    CH.   Ssshh! Such things shouldn't even be said.   ⎦

2. CASS.   Even unspoken this sore won't heal.   ⎤
    CH.   It will if the he-gods hear our appeal.   ⎦

3. CASS.   And while you're appealing your king's being hacked. ⎤
    CH.   I don't know the man who'd commit such an act!   ⎦

4. CASS.   If you say *man* then you don't understand.   ⎤
    CH.   I don't know the man, nor how it's been planned.   ⎦

5. CASS.   And yet it's your language you're hearing me speak. ⎤
    CH.   No oracle's clear, though they all speak in Greek. ⎦

CASSANDRA.
    ah   ah   fire in me   Apollo's

Two-legged lioness tupped by the wolfman
when the great lion's gone she'll kill Cassandra

brewing the witchbane   her bubbling grudge-broth
into the cauldron   death-dose for Cassandra

She sharpens the swordblade to hack down her husband
a hacking he earned by bringing me with him.

Why do I wear these garments that mock me,
the trappings of prophetess, rod, garb and raiment.

CASSANDRA *tears off the regalia of prophetess.*

I'm going to die but you'll go before me.
It's some satisfaction to trample these trappings.
Go and bestow these "gifts" on another.

ah   Apollo   Apollo   clawing my clothes off.
He grabs the prophetess garb off my body.
He mocked me, Apollo, though dressed as his prophet.
He wanted me scorned and derided by bloodkin,
called vagabond, mountebank, gypsy and starveling.
The god-seer casts his prophetess to disaster.

My father's own priestess now mere beast oblation
lifeblood flowing hot off the hackblock.

We won't die forgotten. Gods always notice.

He'll come our avenger, our bloodgrudge-fulfiller,
he'll come, motherkiller, wanderer, exile,
setting the copestone on this bloodclan's corruption,
the father's corpse drawing the son back to Argos.

Why these tears? These eyes saw Troy levelled.
And those who destroyed her doomed also to die.
Now it's for me to die . . .

CASSANDRA *approaches the palace.*

                                    the doorway to death
I pray for a clean blow, no painful convulsions,
my blood ebbing gently, closing my eyes.

CHORUS.
Such suffering, child, such pain in your wisdom.
If you can foresee death then why do you go to it
so meekly like a god-destined goat to the godstone?

1. CASS.   There's no escape now. No more delay.
    CH.   'While there's life there's . . .' you know what they say.

2. CASS.   No hope for me though. It's pointless all flight.
    CH.   How bravely you seem to face up to your plight.

3. CASS.   Yes only the doomed are ever called brave.
    CH.   But isn't it noble to face up to the grave?

4. CASS.   You mean like my father and brothers all died.

CASSANDRA *moves towards the palace and recoils.*

    CH.   What is it? Fear? Was that why you shied?

CASSANDRA.
    Ugh! Ugh!

5. CH.   What was that cry for? What sickens your brain?
    CASS.   The palace! It stinks like an abattoir drain!

6. CH.   It's the sacrifice made for our clanchief's return.
    CASS.   It stinks like the gas from a burial urn.
    CH.   It's only the incense the priests always burn.

CASSANDRA.
    I'll go inside, wailing our deaths, mine, Agamemnon's.
    Enough of life! Friends, I'm no frightened fledgling
    flinching with fear when the bushes get shaken.
    From you what I beg 's the bearing of witness,
    when woman for woman my killer's killed also
    and the man mated to doom gets killed for your clanchief.
    I beg this favour as a stranger going to die now.

CHORUS.
    I pity you, so open-eyed about dying.

CASSANDRA.
    A few last words, a requiem dirgesong
    I ask the sun whose last rays I'm addressing
    that when the avengers cut down the assassins
    one stroke's for the slavegirl butchered defenceless.
    Man's life! Luck's blotted out by the slenderest shadow.
    Trouble – a wet sponge wipes the slate empty.
    That pain's also nothing makes life a heartbreak.

CASSANDRA *enters palace.*

CHORUS.
    Human beings in their pride
    restless and dissatisfied

    No palace dweller bars his door
    to opulence and cries: *No more!*

    the gods let our great king destroy
    the topless towers of Priam's Troy

    vanquisher conquistador
    crowned with all the spoils of war

    now the blood that Atreus shed
    falls on Agamemnon's head

    he's to die but what's the good
    his death too cries out for blood

AGAMEMNON. (*Within.*)
    ah!

CHORUS.
    Whose was that voice screaming in terror?

AGAMEMNON. (*Within.*)
    ah!

CHORUS.
    That was the king unless I'm in error.
    Now we should take council and every man
    should say what he thinks is the safest plan.

1.   In my opinion we ought to bring
      the whole city here to help the king.

2.   And I say rush in, break down the door
      catch them with swords still dripping with gore.

3.   I'm also for action. I'll second that.
      any action at all 's better than chat.

4.   It's quite clear, I mean quite clear to me
      their action 's a prelude to tyranny!

5.   They don't discuss, they do, and while we prate
      they stamp their boots on all debate.

6.   But I haven't a plan and no one can
      go into action without a plan.

7.   Agreed! Hear, hear! There's no way talk
      can make a dead man get up and walk.

8.   Just to save our skins shall we stand by
      let murderers rule us, our clanchief die?

9.   No. Never! As for me I'd sooner die
      than live two seconds under tyranny.

10.   But can we, from the cries we heard,
      infer that murder *has* occurred?

11.   We should have proof before we act.
      Guesswork's not the same as fact.

12.   I think the meeting as a whole's agreed –
      conclusive evidence is what we need.

The palace doors swing open and reveal CLYTEMNESTRA *standing
over the bodies of* AGAMEMNON *and* CASSANDRA.

CLYTEMNESTRA.
    I've spoken many words to serve the moment
    which I've no compunction now to contradict.

How else but by lying and seeming so loving
could I have plotted my enemy's downfall?
How rig the net so it can't be leapt out of?
This is the bloodgrudge, the grudge's fruition
something I've brooded on quite a long time.
I've done what I meant to. I wouldn't deny it.
Over his head I cast a vast trammel
the sort that hauls in whole shoals at each casting.
He couldn't get out of his rich, flowing doom-robe.
Twice I struck him. He screamed twice, then crumpled.
Once he'd fallen I struck him a third blow,
one struck for Zeus in his role as corpse-keeper.
He lay there gasping and splurting his blood out
spraying me with dark blood-dew, dew I delight in
as much as the graincrop in the fresh gloss of rainfall
when the wheatbud's in labour and swells into birthpang.

So that's how it is, old men of Argos.
Cheer if you want to. I revel in glory.
He's had his libation, spurts from his bloodvein.
He poured woe and bitterness into our winebowl.
He's got the last goblet and laps up the leas!

CHORUS.
Your words revolt me. How can you trumpet,
so unlike a woman, over your manlord?

CLYTEMNESTRA.
Still you can treat me like a woman who's witless?
My heart's made of steel, and as I have stated,
whether you like it or not, there's Agamemnon.
This is the swordhand that brought him to bloodright.
I hacked down my husband. That's how it is.

CHORUS.
Woman! Some earthbane's driving you crazy.
To brave the damning voice of the people!
You've sown and you'll reap. Banishment. Exile.
Driven out of the country. Cursed at and spat at.

CLYTEMNESTRA.
O *now* you're ready with banishment, exile,
the people's hatred and public damnation.
And how did you punish this murderer here?
Meant as little to him as slaughtering cattle.

His sheepfolds were bursting, he butchered his she-child,
the she-child I laboured to launch on her life-lot,
as some specious god-sop to settle the stormsquall.
You should have banished *him* for pollution,
but it's now that you start to play at stern judges.
Banishment! *If* you can make me. *If* you enforce it.
If I prove the stronger I'll teach you some wisdom.
You'll go back to school and learn some hard lessons.

CHORUS.
You're maddened by powerlust, raving.
Your brain's beweeviled with blood-deeds.
Your eyes have red bloodflecks for pupils.
Your doom's to be honourless, friendless, defenceless
and stabwound for stabwound you'll reap retribution.

CLYTEMNESTRA.
Then listen to this, the oath that I'll swear by.
By bloodright exacted on behalf of my she-child,
by Iphigeneia whose bloodgrudge has roosted,
by the Fury for whom Agamemnon's the booty,
I swear I'll never let fear to my fireside
as long as the hearth's kept alight by Aegisthus,
loyal friend always, my shield, my protector.

Look at him, Shaggermemnon, shameless, shaft-happy,
ogler and grinder of Troy's golden girlhood.
Look at her, spearprize, prophetess, princess,
whore of his wartent, his bash back on shipboard.
They've got their deserts the two of them now.
There he lies. She's sung her swansong and lies
as she should do stretched out alongside him,
his 'dear' 's death a side-dish to the banquet of his.

CHORUS.
Please send me my end now, but not too painful,
let me lurch gently out of my life-lot
now that our king's been dragged under the death-yoke.

Two women made him suffer then die:

Wild Helen causing the death-throes of thousands
now you've won your garland of glory,
a blood-wreath whose redness can't be rubbed off.

CLYTEMNESTRA.
Don't call on death or surrender to torment.
Don't turn your hatred on Helen my she-kin.
Don't think she alone brought the Greeks to their ruin
as though only she were the cause of their anguish.

CHORUS.
As far back as Tantalus the grudge-demon started,
harried this bloodclan from those days to these days,
harries it now in the shapes of these she-kin,
Clytemnestra   Helen   those carrion crows
cawing discordantly over our gables
maws crammed with corpseflesh and carrion gobbets

CLYTEMNESTRA.
Better to blame the blood-guzzling grudge-hound
battening on us for three gorgings of gore.

He kindles the gore-lust in the guts of our bloodkin.
As one sore scars over new pus starts spurting.

CHORUS.
Insatiable bloodgrudge, gore-ogre, flesh-glutton
goes on and on plagueing and galling
but what isn't godsent?   Zeus is behind it.
Nothing occurs but the gods make it happen.

King Agamemnon, how can we mourn you,
how give a voice to bereavement and loveloss,
there in the spider's web spewing your life out
the impious weapon swung by the spousefiend?

CLYTEMNESTRA.
Spouse? No! Wife? No! What swung the swordblade's
the semblance, the shape of this corpse's spouse only.
Wielding the weapon was no wife and no woman
but his family's phantom, Atreus the flesh-chef
offering flayed these fully fledged victims
one for each butchered and barbecued babe.

CHORUS.
You guiltless? You guiltless? and who'll be your witness
though some god must have helped you fulfil the bloodgrudge.
Black Ares amok, wading deep in the blood-bog –
the bloodgrudge that goads him the cold joints of children.

King Agamemnon, how can we mourn you,
how give a voice to bereavement and loveloss,
there in the spider's web spewing your life out,
the impious weapon swung by the spousefiend?

CLYTEMNESTRA.
His death's no worse than the one he inflicted
when he forged his own link in this house's doom-chain.
He suffered the fate he made others suffer –
Iphigeneia still wept for, sweet flower, his she-child.

Don't go boasting in Hades, steel-slinger, sword-brute,
you got back your stabwounds, all you inflicted.

CHORUS.
My mind's off its moorings. Its foundations are shaking.
No longer a drizzle, a hammering bloodstorm,
Fate strops its blade for more and more blood-bouts.
Earth   Earth   Earth   why didn't you take me
rather than let me live to see the king humbled
sprawled out in his blood in a bathtub of silver.
Who'll bury the body? Who'll sing the gravedirge?

(*To Clytemnestra.*)
You wouldn't surely, first kill our clanchief
then pour specious tributes over his tombcairn?

Who'll mourn him with real grief and not a mask only?

CLYTEMNESTRA.
That's not your business. I hacked him down and the sword hand
strong enough to strike him can dig him a ditch.
No mourning. From no one. All that's forbidden.
Iphigeneia   she'll greet him by the waters of sorrow
flinging her arms round her father to kiss him.

CHORUS.
Choler for choler, bloodgrudge for bloodgrudge,
while Zeus the high he-god is still the gods' clanchief
the law for the living is killers get killed.
Blight's in the bloodstream, curse in the corpuscles,
the feet of this clan bogged down in the bloodquag.

CLYTEMNESTRA.
The future, the truth, you're beginning to see them.
I'll make a bond with this palace's bloodfiend.

What's happened so far I'll accept and fall in with,
hard though that is, I'll do it, provided
the fiend leaves this house and finds other quarters
to ravage the people and goad them to murder.
Riches mean nothing. A little suffices
if only this frenzy of kin-killing ceases.

Enter AEGISTHUS *from a side entrance with a silent bodyguard, an
"anti-chorus", the same number as the chorus.*

AEGISTHUS.
A great day when bloodright comes into its own.
This proves there are gods who see crimes and punish.
I'm happy, so happy to see this man tangled
in robes of dark red the Furies have woven,
fulfilling the bloodgrudge caused by his father.
This man's father, Atreus, once king of Argos,
there being some dispute as to who should be clanchief,
drove my father (his brother) Thyestes away.
Thyestes came back as a suppliant begging
at least his life sparing, the minimum mercy,
no son's blood staining his father's own threshold.
But this man's father, Atreus, Atreus the godless,
whose mask of warm welcome kept hatred hidden
threw a great banquet as if for Thyestes
and dished up his children as the daintiest titbits.
The fingers and toes he chopped off to disguise it
and my father alone of the guests got this childstew.
Not being aware what it was he was eating
he bolted the banquet that blasted this bloodclan.
When he knew what he chewed, he choked on the childstew,
shrieked, reeled backwards, spewed out the offal,
turned over the tables and cursed the whole bloodclan
grinding the meat into mush with his boot-heel.

And that's why your clanchief's lying there murdered.
And I wove the net we got him ensnared in.
Third son of Thyestes, I plotted for bloodright.
Driven out with my father while only a baby
as a man I've returned escorted by bloodright.
In exile I had all the threads twisted ready
biding my time for the trap to be fashioned.
Now I'd die happy, happy now bloodright's
got Agamemnon caught fast in fate's trammel.

CHORUS.

> Aegisthus, gloating on carnage. Revolting!
> You did it, plotted it, *you*, single-handed?
> The people will stone you. You don't stand a chance.

AEGISTHUS.

> Pretty grand talk to come out of the galleys!
> We've got the tiller. Get on with the rowing.
> Old as you are, you still can learn lessons
> though you'll find wisdom a tough course to take in.
> Prison. Starvation. They motivate scholars,
> make even dodderers like you get good totals.
> Don't push on the horse-goad. You'll get yourselves hurt.

CHORUS.

> Woman! Waiting at home for the menfolk
> wallowing , befouling a warrior's bedbond!
> How could *you* bring down a great soldier.

AEGISTHUS.

> Whinny like that again and you'll rue it.
> The songs of Orpheus may have tamed creatures,
> yours work on me in the other direction.
> A dose of the strongarm will soon get you docile.

CHORUS.

> You, rule Argos? You, who let a mere woman
> murder the king when you hadn't courage.

AEGISTHUS.

> Deception, that was the work for the woman.
> I, with my bloodgrudge, was under suspicion.
> Agamemnon's gold will buy off his people.
> And those who won't be bought will be broken.
> No colts without collars. Hunger and darkness
> they teach the mettlesome quieter manners.

CHORUS.

> Couldn't kill the king with your own hands could you?
> Let a woman get her clan and her clangods corrupted,
> the gods of Argos. But I tell you . . . Orestes . . .
> if he's alive (and luck guide his life-lot)
> he'll kill this couple, our bloodgrudge-fulfiller.

1. AEG.   You want your first lessons already, I see.]
    CH.   Comrades, you're needed. Stand firm with me.]

2. AEG.   Draw your swords out. Ready. Stand by.   ]
    CH.   Stand by. Not one of us here's afraid to die.]
    AEG.   I'm glad that you told me   So go ahead, die!]

CLYTEMNESTRA.
      (*Interrupting.*)
      No! No, my dear, no more blood-letting.
      There's been enough. Enough. Old men of Argos,
      go home now quietly before you regret it.
      We did what we had to. Let it rest there.
      The fiend's hooves have galloped over our spirits.
      Let it rest there. Take advice from a woman.

AEGISTHUS.
      But they, they gibe at me, mock me.
      You're pushing your luck you old foulmouths.
      I'm your new ruler. Don't you forget it.

1. CH.   Argives don't grovel to your evil sort.   ]
    AEG.   Then Argives like you will have to be taught.]

2. CH.   Not if Orestes comes back to his own.   ]
    AEG.   Exiles eat hope, all gristle and bone.   ]

3. CH.   Grow fat on injustice. Shit on the state!   ]
    AEG.   I'm warning you, old fool, before it's too late . . .]

4. CH.   Cock-a-doodle-doo, the dungheap lord,   ]
           crow a bit louder, your hen will applaud!   ]

CLYTEMNESTRA.
      Let the terriers yap, all bark and no bite!
      You and I, we'll rule this house, and set it right.

Exit CLYTEMNESTRA *with* AEGISTHUS, *into the house of Atreus.*
CHORUS *disperses silently.*

END OF PART 1

TWO
CHOEPHORI

ORESTES *and* PYLADES *at the grave of Agamemnon.*

ORESTES.

Hermes, he-god, who can go in and out of the ground,
he-god still wary to keep power with the fathers,
now I have need of you, back home from long exile.
This is the gravemound of Agamemnon, my father.
Help my cries through the ground to his ghost.
(*Cuts off two locks of hair.*)
I lop off one lock and so move into manhood.

And this one for your mound as a mark of my mourning.

Your son and heir wasn't here to salute you
no final farewell as the earth was flung over.

Look! There! What's that? That procession of women,
wending this way, all dressed in drab dirge-clothes.
What's it in aid of? More doom? More disaster?
They're carrying jars, jars full of libations.
I suppose that they're sops for my father's sore spirit.
It must be! There, among all the mourners
is my she-kin Electra, wasted by weeping.

Zeus! High he-god! Help it to happen,
the vengeance I want to take for my father.
(*To Pylades.*)
Pylades, you and I stand aside, keep out of eye shot
till we're sure of the meaning of the rites we're to witness.

CHORUS.

Coerced into keening by Queen Clytemnestra
for King Agamemnon as if for our bloodkin
we carry these ghost-sops out to his gravemound.
Lashed out to lament the lost lord of Argos
we Trojans trench flesh ruts into our faces.
There's no need to coerce us, we cry anyway.

Our lives have been one long meal of mourning,
one life-long banquet, one blow-out of bale.
We claw our clothes open, mad in our mourning.
Our ripped pap-wraps shriek as we shred them.

This bloodclan's doom-demon disguised as a dream
crashed through into Clytemnestra's calm midnight
and squeezed from the queen's throat a throttling shriek,
a cry that re-echoed through each recess and corner

and pounded for entry to the coops that we're penned in.
The whole household heard it. Our hair stood on end.
Then spoke a clanseer whose knowledge was nightmares:

'The bitter dead below bellow for blood-dues.'

So godsops she sends, empty gifts and libations
meant to ward off what gnaws her at night-time,
sends me out here as soon as the dawn breaks
that woman hated and loathed by the he-gods.
The grave-charms she wants get choked in my gullet.
What godsop or bribe makes spilt blood unspilt?
Shed blood's shed for ever. The dead stay dead.
This bloodclan, this house, what hasn't it suffered?
Murk, man-shunned and sunless smothers the bloodclan
when the clanchief, its light, is stifled by death,
death-doused, mouldering under his gravemound . . .
He counted for something, the king of this bloodclan,
battle-proof power, both strife-proof and plot-proof.
The lips of his people respected that power,
their hearts honoured their hero and helmsman.
Now all honour's usurped by terror the tyrant.
Success gets sucked up to. The god is good life-lot.
All grovel to that as to godhead or greater.
But to those who loll in the luck of their life-lot
the justice of bloodright's the bolt from the black –
some netted at noontide, others at night-time,
daylight or darkness, both nourish their doom.
When the earth's gullet's choked on the gore it has gulped
the bloodglut clots rock-like and can't reach earth's gut.
Guilt in the guilty likewise stays clotted
the cankers of guilt craze the culprit and kill him.
The blood of the killed, the bed blood of virgins
(both dooms we endured in the downfall of Troy)
is worn by the guilty like gauntlets of gore.
All the world's waters forced through one funnel
and sprayed at the bloodspot as much good as spittle!
Necessity! That brought us to where we are now,
hauled from our homeland, dragged here as drudges,
lugged into a life-lot, unloving and loathly,
brought into bondage, doom's dragnet round Troy,
we bite hard on the horsebit, gulp down our gall,
and go through these griefshows as she commanded.
But our grief is no shamming, the tears shed are true,

mourning our helplessness under harsh masters,
our massacred menfolk, the mass-graves of Troy.

ELECTRA.
Women, Troy's warspoils, now palace work-slaves
whose work gives the palace its appearance of order,
since you've been sent to attend me, give me advice.
What graveside grace goes best with these griefcups?
What address would my father find even decent?
'To the man from the woman, to the loved from the loving'!
Call Clytemnestra, my mother, a woman who loves!
I don't have the nerve, the effrontery for that.
What to say as I pour honey, then milk, wine and then water? –
What's usually intoned here 's useless, insulting.
'To those who send grave-gifts, send the good they deserve.'
The good they deserve 's the same fate as my father's.
No words, but a silence the way he was slaughtered
pouring the griefcups as if they were slop-pails.
Friends! Serfwomen, freeborn, both fettered to fate,
shackled to shame we share the same hatreds.
Between us there need be no sort of secret.

CHORUS.   I swear by the cairn that keeps the king's dust
          I speak all my secrets, and you have my trust . . .

1. EL.   Speak then. I swear the same oath you all swore.
    CH.   For those you can trust pray as you pour.

2. EL.   Those I can trust. Who near me 's still true?
    CH.   Yourself! Those who hate Aegisthus are too.

3. EL.   Then myself! And you? Do you count on my side?
    CH.   Judge only my words, then you can decide.

4. EL.   Who else can be counted? Consider and say . . .
    CH.   Orestes! *Orestes!* Though still far away.

5. EL.   Orestes! Orestes! The best thing to say!
    CH.   For those you can't trust, the killers, pray . . .

6. EL.   Pray what? Tell me, I'm eager to learn . . .
    CH.   Pray that a man or a god will return.

7. EL.   Return to reckon the guilt of those two?
    CH.   No! Kill them. That's all. *Blood for blood.* That will do.

8. EL.   Demand gods to deal death! Is that right or good?
    CH.   Right and good! Right and good! Blood demands blood.

ELECTRA.
 God-guide and ground-god, god-go-between, herald,
 linking upper and nether, the dead and the living,
 Hermes, he-god, help me and get them to hear me,
 the spirits I pray to, that prosper this palace,
 and get her to hear me, the greatest of she-gods,
 EARTH who pushes all beings out of her belly,
 suckles her creatures, and swells with their corpses.
 Get her to listen. I pour the libation
 and pray to my father:
        'Pity! For me! For Orestes!'
 This bloodclan's benighted and he's its bright beacon.
 We're both dispossessed, deprived of our bloodright.
 She bartered her bairns and bought as her bed-mate
 Aegisthus who shares in the guilt of your killing.
 Electra's a bondslave, and Orestes an exile.
 Clytemnestra and Aegisthus, basking and idle,
 loll in the luxury made by your labours.
 I pray Orestes returns with luck in his life-lot
 and my life-lot unsullied, not marred like my mother's,
 heart and hands blameless, unblemished by blood.

 These prayers on our part. And for them we oppose
 I pray the bloodgrudge-fulfiller will soon be appearing,
 the butchers be butchered, and pay blood for blood.

 Agamemnon, come up at the head of the ground-gods.
 Agamemnon, come up with Earth the great she-god,
 bring blessings and bloodright blazoned with laurels.
 These are my prayers, and I pour your libations.
 (To Chorus.)
 You water the seed of my prayer with your wailing.
 As I pour deliver the dead a due grave-dirge.

CHORUS.
 Tears drop on your dark head
 drop by drop the way you bled

 Your grave holds both bad and good
 what we beg is 'blood for blood'.

 Agamemnon, mind in murk,
 hear our words, make them work –

 Bloodgrudge-fulfiller
 come kill the killer

big bow bent back
sword in slash hack.

ELECTRA.

Gulped by Gaia the drinks have got through
through to my father . . .

(Sees lock of hair.)

                        . . . but here's something new!

1.   CH.   Fear makes my heart jig. What have you found?   ]
     EL.   A lock of hair has been laid on the mound.

2.   CH.   A man's or a woman's? Who put it there?   ]
     EL.   It looks like a bloodkin's, this lock of fine hair.

3.   CH.   A bloodkin's? I don't understand. Don't leave me to guess.]
     EL.   It's mine or it's no one's this mystery tress.

4.   CH.   Your mother, the murderer, she wouldn't dare . . .]
     EL.   Yet I've a feeling I know it, this hair.

5.   CH.   Whose is it then, if you say it seems known?   ]
     EL.   Whose I don't know, but it's so like my own.

6.   CH.   Orestes! Orestes has sent us this secret sign.   ]
     EL.   It can only be his hair, if it's not mine.

7.   CH.   Orestes in Argos? Too risky if that's what you meant.]
     EL.   No, for the sake of his father he had the lock sent.

     CH.   Only sent! The more cause to weep for him then.   ]
           Orestes will never see Argos again . . .

ELECTRA.

A surge of choler and grudge sweeps over my spirit,
spitted on pain like a stabwound or spearthrust.
Drops like the spindrift spat off a seaswell
break from my eyes at the sight of this curl.
Who else from Argos would this lock belong to?
Never hers, the murderess, my mother. My *mother*!
She's stifled and smothered all motherly feelings.
How can I know it's Orestes for certain.
Only hope makes us so foolish and stupid.

If this hair had a voice and was sent as a herald
then I wouldn't waver or be so distracted
and I'd know by its clear spoken message
that either it came from a head I detested

or was the bloodkin's I longed to believe it,
a grace to my grief, a grace to this gravemound.

The gods I've invoked are wise to what seaswells
we're whirled on, like sailors in shipwreck.
If we were meant to, then scrape home we will.
A great oak can sprout from the tiniest acorn.

I call on these gods for my prayers to be answered.

Enter ORESTES *and* PYLADES.

ORESTES.
> They're answered, those prayers. The gods favour you.
> Now pray that our future is fortunate too.

1.   EL.   *Our* future? Prayers answered? What do you mean? ⎤
     OR.   You prayed to see something. Now you have seen.   ⎦

2.   EL.   How do you know what it was that I prayed?   ⎤
     OR.   For your much-loved Orestes to come to your aid.   ⎦

3.   EL.   Then how can you say that the gods favour me?   ⎤
     OR.   You've got what you prayed for. Look! I am he!   ⎦

4.   EL.   Stranger you're weaving some net or some snare.   ⎤
     OR.   If you are entangled, I'm also trapped there.   ⎦

5.   EL.   You mock my misfortune, make it a game.   ⎤
     OR.   I mock my own then, my misfortune's the same. |
     EL.   Orestes! Orestes! Is that really your name?   ⎦

ORESTES.
> You look at me and still can't recognise
> your bloodkin, your brother before your eyes.
> Yet when you looked at the lock I had laid
> you gasped as if gazing straight into my face.
>
> (*Indicates lock of hair.*)
> Look that's where I lopped it from. Match it with mine.
> Look how alike, how akin the two locks are
>
> (*Produces a piece of weaving.*)
> Look at this weaving your fingers once fashioned,
> the stroke of your batten, the patterns of beasts.
>
> (*Electra excited.*)
> Easy! Still! Keep all emotion masked within.
> Our "nearest and dearest" would like us destroyed.

ELECTRA.
    Beloved, beacon of this blacked-out bloodclan,
    the seed of deliverance watered by weeping.
    The love of four bloodkin belongs to you only –
    loathed mother, lost father, sacrificed sister
    and brother, the bloodkin I truly believe in.

    Brute force and bloodright and Zeus the high he-god
    be your protectors in pursuing our bloodgrudge.

ORESTES.
    ZEUS, high he-god, steel us to the struggle,
    fledglings left fatherless when the great eagle
    got snarled in the shuffling coils of the she-snake,
    fatherless fledglings, famished orphans too feeble
    to carry the quarry off back to the eyrie,
    fledglings and fatherless, Orestes, Electra,
    both outcasts alike and blocked from their bloodright.
    Eagle Agamemnon gave the he-gods a gift glut.
    The godstones of Argos bubbled with bloodflow.
    Cut down his egrets, your guts will go goatless.
    With the bole of the bloodclan blasted no bull's gore
    will gurgle down godstones on sacrifice days.
    So nourish the nestlings, build up the bloodclan
    though now it looks much too low to be lifted.

CHORUS.
    Quiet, if you want your bloodclan rebuilding.
    The whole space of Argos whispers with spies.
    It only needs one to report to our rulers.
    One day very soon I hope we'll be watching
    their flesh spit through flames and bubbling pitch.

ORESTES.
    Apollo stays close till all gets accomplished.
    His oracle told me to push through our bloodgrudge.
    And if I flinched from fulfilling the bloodgrudge
    by killing those guilty of killing our father
    he warned me my heart's blood would harden and freeze.
    By not taking their lives my own would be taken
    but not before tasting great torture and torments.
    He detailed disease, malignant malaises
    the unappeased dead demand as appeasement –
    skin-canker, skin-scabs, flaying the flesh raw,
    crusted with fungus sprouting white bristles,

the perpetual prowling of the black pack of Furies
whose dark nightly saltlick 's the blood of my father,
darts from deep darkness, shafts shot from below
for the killing of bloodkin who bay for their bloodgrudge.
Frenzy and mania, phantoms at midnight,
venomous shadows that slink into his sleeptime.
He blinks, rubs his eyes. They're still at his bedside.

Harried and hounded out of his homeland,
a palsied pariah, scarred over by scourges,
flayed by brass flail-rods, a leprosied carcase.
Such scapegoats share in no wine-bowl libations.
No one spares him bed, bread, or broth-bowl.
All godstones are barred him, and, gobbled alive
by bubos and fleshblight, he perishes friendless.

When that god says *do it* no one says no.

Without any god-goad I've still got my grudges,
Still got my grief for Agamemnon, my father.
Dispossessed, I need no spurs to my spirit.
And these men of Argos, whose glory is greatest
who braved long war boldly and battered down Troy,
now sheepish and slave-like to a woman and she-man
who queens it beside the real clanchief, his consort.
This weapon I wield will unmask the woman.

CHORUS.
   She-gods of life-lot
   ZEUS   high he-god

   only gods can stop the rot
   drag good up out of bad

   Bloodflow for bloodflow
   deathblow for deathblow

   blood-debt for blood-debt
   keeping the blades wet

   bloodshed for bloodshed
   keeping the blades red

   What you do gets done back
   you/him   him/you

   hack   slash   slash   hack
   three generations through

She-gods of life-lot
ZEUS   high he-god

ORESTES.
Father, father doused in doom
kept immovable by death
what can grope through your grave-gloom
unbreachable by light or breath?

What words can worm their way
through the sour soil of sorrow
what beacon of bright day
burrow your dark barrow?

From all the bloodclan's grave-rites
they barred and blocked your bones,
never-budging, held by night's
death-heavy anchorstones.

CHORUS.
The gnashing jaws of fire gnaw
only the corpse's rotten flesh.
His bloodgrudge goes on craving gore
and doesn't crumble into ash.

When bloodkin keen the killer feels
their dirges haunt him like halloos.
The hounds of grief bay at his heels,
the dead demanding their blood-dues.

A bloodkin's dirge is a keening net
its trammels trawl for guilt
mourning spreads its mesh to get
guilt netted   gaffed   and killed.

ELECTRA.
Now it's Electra your she-child
who mourns and beats her breast.
The wailing comes out rushed and wild
long cooped up and repressed.

Now listen to your she-child's dirge
he-child, she-child both in turn,
both exiles, outcasts urge
your spirit from its urn.

bout one   bout two we lost to fate
the same fate that threw you
unless your spirit lends its weight
bout three will be lost too.

CHORUS.
Gods can make a gravedirge glad
dragging good up from the bad.

Instead of dirges we might sing

Welcome home, new clanchief, King!

ORESTES.
I wish that you had lost your life
to a Trojan in the War
not netted by a treacherous wife
your bathtrough grimed with gore.

Then hero's honour you'd bequeath.
We could have borne it if your bones
were still in Asia and beneath
a tomb of towering stones.

CHORUS.
A hero in a hero's grave!
A tombcairn like a tower!
The comfort of the clanchief's stave
still wielding its old power!

A monument, a glorious mound
Dignity   no shame
Agamemnon underground
with still unblemished name!

ELECTRA.
No hero's cairn, not killed, not dead!
No mass-grave by Scamander.
I want fate standing on its head
the goose hacked by the gander!

As your killers hacked you, hack,
hack down your killers first.
I want time to be turned back
my father's fate reversed.

CHORUS.
    North of the North Wind lives a clan
    spared the mortal lot of man

    but this is South, a man cannot
    turn back the tide of his life-lot.

    Gold comes cheaper than new blood
    but you are young and dream of good.

    When you two drum your palms together
    the pulse gets passed down to your father.

    If those with bloodguilt beat the ground
    their gloves of blood will dull the sound

    but the dead respond to you
    the guiltless tone of your tattoo

    underground the dead decide
    Agamemnon's on your side.

ORESTES.
    The bloodgrudge! ZEUS! It's been asleep.
    Drag it up from its earthen bed.
    The bloodgrudge bond that I've to keep
    's to strike my mother dead.

CHORUS.
    Aegisthus, Clytemnestra killed
    I'll shout a joyful shout.
    My heart's been bursting ages, filled
    with all the hate I now let out.

ELECTRA.
    ZEUS   your great steel fists   one   two
    crunch their skulls with all your might.
    Our country needs new trust in you
    bloodwrong to yield a new bloodright.

CHORUS.
    The law's the law: when blood gets spilled
    there's no rest till the killer's killed.

    Bloodflow for bloodflow the doomsong goes –
    blood shrieks for the Fury as it flows

    The Fury forges the long bloodchain –
    the slain that link the slain that link the slain . . .

ORESTES.
> Grudges of the dead below
> look we're the dregs of a royal race,
> the bloodclan of Atreus brought so low.
>
> ZEUS! Which way leads us from disgrace?

CHORUS.
> My heart-strings snap, my heart goes black
> it darkens if you weaken,
> but when I see your strength come back
> hope blazes like a beacon.

ELECTRA.
> *Our* strength's that we've survived the trials
> the one who bore us brought us.
> I'll bare my wolf-fangs when she smiles.
> Wolf mothers breed wolf daughters.

CHORUS.
> As in Persia both fists pound
> a dervish-like delirium,
> till the skull's blood-pulses sound
> like a battered battle-drum.

ELECTRA.
> Wolf mother murdering your man!
> Agamemnon got no graveside
> lamentation from his clan,
> dumped in a ditch you dug dry-eyed.

ORESTES.
> A ditch! The wolf-bitch dug his shame
> I'll hack my mother down to save
> Agamemnon's blood-grimed name
> then gladly go to my own grave.

CHORUS.
> To stop his bloodgrudge in its tracks
> she hacked off his cock, his hands, his feet,
> cleavered the king with her man-axe
> and jointed him like butcher's meat.

ELECTRA.
> And I imprisoned in a poky pen,
> cooped and kennelled like a rabid cur.

Let all the grief I poured out then
become the rage you pour on her.

CHORUS.
Yes, let it fire the rage you feel.
Two bouts are lost. The bout to be
depends upon your fire and steel,
hot heart, cool head to win bout three.

(*All addressing Agamemnon's tomb.*)

ORESTES. Be in my corner, help me win.

ELECTRA. Father all my tears say fight!

CHORUS. All as one cry: back your bloodkin,
              come up, come up into the light.

ORESTES. Bloodright versus bloodright! Ours or theirs?

ELECTRA. Gods, make it ours the juster cause.

ORESTES. It scalds my skull to know your prayers
              unlock doom's long-barred doors.

CHORUS.
This clan's got ruin in its veins,
its blood-strung lyre's cacophonous.
The chords it strums are death-black strains.
Its wounds don't scab. They spurt out pus.

The only way such sores get better
's keep the cure within the clan.
The clan's its own leech, own blood-letter,
its medicament's: man murder man.

Groundgods down below it's you
all our prayers are going to.
Back Agamemnon's child-bloodkin
and will with god-wills that they win.

ORESTES.
You, the great clanchief, were killed like a cur.
I pray for your help to be lord of your bloodclan.

ELECTRA.
I pray for escape from the bondage I've suffered
but not before shedding the blood of Aegisthus.

ORESTES.
> Then only then, in accord with clan custom,
> can a fitting funeral be offered with feasting,
> or, when fate and gore on the sacrifice crackle
> Agamemnon alone gets no goat to his glory.

ELECTRA.
> And, from what you bequeath me, your burial barrow
> will be overflowing with bridal libations.
> On the day that I marry your mound will mean most.

ORESTES. Earth, she-god, let my father back me.

ELECTRA. Persephassa, she-ground-god, grant victory.

ORESTES. Remember the bathtrough where you were struck dead!

ELECTRA. Remember the net-thing cast over your head.

ORESTES. In silk stuff not steelware you spewed out your blood.

ELECTRA. Humbled and hacked down under a hood.

ORESTES. Don't taunts such as these torment you down there?

ELECTRA. Shove your head through the earth to show us you care!

ORESTES. (*To Agamemnon's grave.*)
> Bloodright! I want it to back me in the bout that's to be.
> I want the headlock on them that they got on you,
> flatten them to the floor as they flattened you.
> They outwrestled you, but I'll best them this bout.

ELECTRA.
> This last, then no more. Eagle Agamemnon
> your egrets call you from your grave-eyrie,
> fledglings and fatherless, he-child and she-child.

ORESTES.
> Don't let the seed of Pelops perish for ever.
> Death's no death when the blood-kinder flourish,
> blood-kinder, cork-floats that keep the net buoyant,
> when the flax-strings get sodden they keep it from sinking.
> For the sake of your spirit we've spent this time pleading
> Grant us your grace and your ghost's the first gainer.

CHORUS.
> Since his grave has been given no clan lamentation
> the length of your mourning was right and becoming.

Now you've gorged on your grave-dirge, go into action,
and find out where fate and your life-lot will lead you.

ORESTES.
So I will but before I do battle I want to be told
why she sent out this crowd of you carrying cups,
libations so late for a crime past all curing.
Neither the honey, the milk, the wine nor the water
have savour or solace for skulls without senses.
What you pour may be precious but paltry as godsops.
The grave-gifts so meagre, the crime so immense.
A man can daub tombs with all his hives' honey,
swill all his winestores over the stones,
empty his flocks' and herds' udders daily,
waste all his water, and still smell of murder,
so what do they mean Clytemnestra's libations?

CHORUS.
I know what they mean. Clytemnestra had nightmares.
Shaken by shadows that slunk into her sleeptime.
Now, though she's godless, she sends gifts to his gravestone.

1. OR. Is there more to the dream you can tell me about?   ]
    CH. She opened her legs and a serpent crawled out.

2. OR. Tell me the rest if you know how it goes.   ]
    CH. She swathed her snake-baby in swaddling clothes.

3. OR. This baby, this snake-thing how did she feed it?   ]
    CH. She says that it sucked at her very own tit.

4. OR. And did it not pain her to give a snake suck?   ]
    CH. Bloodclots came out with each mouthful it took.
    OR. No dream, mother, here's your snake-baby. Look!

CHORUS.
She shrieked out in her sleep and woke with a start.
All the doused torchlights made eyeless for night-time
blazed out of their blindness to comfort the queen.
At dawn she despatched us with the dead man's libations
to lance the pus-bloated source of her sorrows.

ORESTES.
Then by the earth and the grave of my father
I pray I'm this vision's fleshly fulfiller.
The snake came out of the same womb as I did
swathed in the same swaddling clothes as myself,

sucked at the same breast I sucked as a baby,
got bloodclots mixed in, as it sucked the sweet milk out,
so that she who gave suck screamed out in a panic.
Same womb, same swaddling clothes, same breast to suck on,
blood and milk, all point to me, and to murder!
the son in the snake-scales sent as her slayer.

CHORUS.
My reason tells me that you read the dream rightly.

Now give your instructions to those on your side,
who should work with you, who should be watchers.

ORESTES.
Simple.   My sister must stay in the palace
keeping the bond struck between us a secret.
By cunning they killed.   By cunning they'll die
caught in the same net they caught Agamemnon.
Apollo commands it and Apollo's a prophet
whose habit has never been falsehood before.

I, like a stranger with backpack and bundles,
will come in this guise to the gates of the courtyard,
with Pylades here, son of Strophius of Phocis
bound to our bloodclan by handclasp and spearbond.
We'll both of us speak like they do in Parnassus
assuming the accent of the folk back in Phocis.
If the gateman's ungracious and treats us with gruffness
on the grounds that this house is afflicted by fate
we'll stay so that passers-by stop and start saying:
'Aegisthus goes against all god-ordained guestright
by keeping these wanderers waiting unwelcomed.'
But once past the gatelodge and into the palace
if I find that creature on the throne of my father
before he gets chance for looking me over
and asking 'Where does the stranger hail from?' I'll strike.
My answer to him will be straight to the point,
straight to the swordpoint, guts on my skewer.
The Fury that squats in this clan's never famished,
never gone short of its gore-shots to guzzle.
This third and last cup's to quaff undiluted.

ORESTES.
Electra, keep watch on what happens within
so that the details all dovetail in neatly.

(*To Chorus.*)
Keep quiet where you can, or take care when talking.

(*To Pylades.*)
And Pylades, my companion, keep close to me.
See I wield my sword well in the fight that's to follow.

Exeunt ORESTES, PYLADES, ELECTRA.

CHORUS.
What Earth breeds is appalling.
monsters rock in the arms of the sea.
Fearful sky-flames flare and fall
through terrible void territory.

Monsters, meteors, sea, soil, space,
things that fly, creep, crawl,
of all these horrors the human race
is the terror that tops them all.

Male boasting, pride in being HE
only one thing's got that beat
bursting the bedbond bestially
the female bitch on heat!

1.   When Althaia was brought to bed
with Meleager, fate
prophesied he'd soon be dead
if a log burnt in the grate.

Plucked from flames, under lock and key,
the half-burnt brand's the boy's life-charm.
Safe with his mother, except that she
will be the one who does him harm.

Her son killed two of her bloodkin
and murderous mother Althaia
flung the half-burnt log back in
the life-devouring fire.

2.   King of Megara, Nisos,
his life-charm was on his head,
one strangely purple lock whose loss
would mean he would be dead.

She knew this, she-child Skylla,
another bitch on heat,
she lopped the lock, foul father-killer
for the sake of the king of Crete.

The king of Crete had dangled gold
before her greedy eye.
For a paltry chain she sold
Megara and watched her father die.

Megara burnt, her people slain,
Minos keel-hauled her by her feet,
dragged her from his anchor chain
the whole way back to Crete.

This bloodclan too. A bedbond void
of love by which a man's destroyed.

The plot against your manlord's life,
you the cunning killer wife.

Against a man his enemies revered
and all his spear-foes justly feared.

You prized a fireless hearth instead
a spearless she-man in your bed.

3.   LEMNOS! Its very name is vile
Clytemnestra should have been
of that murderous and manless isle
the killer queen.

Queen of women who wield knives
or slaughtered husband's sword.
The Lemnos husband-killing wives.
LEMNOS – name to be abhorred.

The swordpoint pricks against the skin
ready to be driven in.

Bloodright pushes at the hilt
to broach the gory springs of guilt.

The transgressors, those who trod
down the laws of ZEUS, high he-god.

Bloodright's the whetstone where fate whets
the blades demanding old blood-debts.

Bloodgrudge leads the son at last
to purge the bloodspill of the past.

Enter ORESTES *and* PYLADES *as Phocians.*

ORESTES.
>Gateman! Gateman! Can't you hear all this knocking?
>Anyone there? Gateman! Gateman! Is there no one on duty?
>This is the third time of knocking. Is nobody there?
>Are the good laws of guestright ignored by Aegisthus?

GATEMAN.
>I hear you. I hear you. Where you from, stranger?

ORESTES.
>Go tell your masters there's someone with tidings.
>And quick. The warcar of night drives on the darkness.
>Time travellers were thinking about dropping anchor
>in a place that makes all wayfarers welcome.
>Fetch someone out in authority here.
>Fetch the mistress. No, maybe the man would be fitter.
>With women words have to be guarded and careful.
>But man to man I can say what I mean and no hedging.

Enter CLYTEMNESTRA.

CLYTEMNESTRA.
>Stranger, all you've to do is declare what your need is.
>Such a house can supply every kindness and comfort –
>warm baths, beds that are balm to limbs worn by travel,
>honest eyes that watch over your wishes and wants.
>But if what you've come for is weightier counsel
>that's work for the menfolk, and I'll see that you meet.

ORESTES.
>I'm not from these parts but from Daulis in Phocis.
>I was trekking to Argos, my gear in this backpack
>when I meet with a stranger who asks where I'm off to.
>I tell him Argos, and, when he hears that, this stranger,
>Strophius a Phocian (that's who the man turned out to be)
>says to me: 'Since you're, in any case, going to Argos
>you could save me a journey and take me a message,
>a message concerning a man called Orestes.
>Announce to the parents in Argos the death of Orestes.
>Then ask if they want him fetched home, his ashes,
>or if he's to lie here in Phocis for ever an exile.
>A good bronze urn guards his ashes at present.
>His ashes got tears shed. The man got some mourning.'
>
>I pass on his words as he spoke them, not knowing
>if whom I'm addressing 's directly related.
>It seems proper to speak to a parent in person.

CLYTEMNESTRA.

> Your news brings the whole house down on our heads.
> Ungrappleable bloodgrudge that bullies this bloodclan,
> possessing the piercing sharp eye of the preybird
> takes aim from safe ambush to send its sharp shafts home.
> You strip me of near ones, leaving me naked.
> And now Orestes . . . who seemed to tread surely,
> who kept clear of the clay this bloodclan gets stuck in.
> He was the one hope we still held for this household,
> the balm we all banked on for the bloodgrudge's orgies.
> Orestes, our hope, must be crossed off the rollcall.

ORESTES.

> With hosts such as you here so favoured by fortune
> I'd more gladly be a guest whose tidings were good ones.
> Between host and guest there's no goodwill greater.
> But the bonds that I've given both bind me to truth,
> my bond to Strophius, my guest-bond as stranger.

CLYTEMNESTRA.

> Your words won't make you the less warmly welcomed.
> If you hadn't brought them someone was bound to.
> It's time now that travellers who've spent the day trekking
> should cease feeling footsore and seek out their comforts.

> (*To attendants.*)
> Take them to where the man-guests get quartered,
> him and the man who's his travelling companion.
> Supply them with comforts this palace is famed for.
> Serve them in all things or answer to me.
> Meanwhile I'll convey your news to the clanchief
> and along with all our true loyal supporters
> we'll hold a clan council and consider the case.

Exeunt CLYTEMNESTRA, ORESTES, PYLADES.

CHORUS.

> Loyal supporters of the true bloodkin
> when can we let our pent feelings out,
> when snatch out the galling gag of grief
> and give Orestes the victory shout?

> Earth she-god, high gravemound
> dumped on the lord of the seas
> send help up from underground
> prosper these prayers and pleas.

Word-guile, word-guile gets things done
and ground-god Hermes who can throw
dust in the eyes of everyone
pushes the blade in from below.

It seems our fake Phocian is working already.
I see the old nurse of Orestes walking here weeping.
Cilissa! Where are you going to through the gateyard
with woe the unwanted one walking beside you.

Enter NURSE.

NURSE.
Queen Clytemnestra says 'Quick fetch Aegisthus!'
to meet man to man with some strangers who've come,
confront them in person and hear the new tidings . . .
In front of the serfs she faked grief on her features
but her eyes through the mask wore nothing like mourning.
Nay they blazed like joy beacons at what had befallen.
The news that's been brought's a great bane for this bloodclan
but for Aegisthus a just cause for rejoicing.
This household's caused me perpetual heartache.
No bane to this bloodclan ever beat this one.
Death shook the house and I shrugged – but now it's Orestes,
my little Orestes, who I wore out my life for.
Came straight off his mother and got clapped to my paps.
Got these very breasts as a baby, Orestes!
Trouble! That lad gave me trouble in tonloads!
Led me a dance he did, demanding, demanding,
getting me up from my couch with his crying,
and when I was with him there was nothing he wanted.
They're like puppies, aren't they though, babies?
Still in their nappies what can they do? Nothing!
While they lack language they just keep you guessing –
is it hunger or thirst pangs or wanting to piddle,
their little bellies just do it regardless.
You have to read minds, keep one jump ahead
or else you get caught with their crap to clean out.
Wet nurse and washerwoman I was to Orestes.
Had him entrusted by King Agamemnon.
Now I hear that he's dead, my dear little baby.
I'm off to Aegisthus, the bane of this bloodclan.
When he hears of the death, he'll be glad and delighted.

1. CH.   How is he to come? Does she say how, the queen?   ⎤
    NU.   How? Don't get you. Don't know what you mean.   ⎦

2. CH.   I mean does she tell him to come armed or not?   ⎤
    NU.   O armed and attended! His spearmen! The lot!   ⎦

CHORUS.
        Then tell him there's no need of his combatant gear.
        Tell Aegisthus there's joy in what he's to hear.
        Tell him come quickly the man we all hate.
        'The messenger's mouth sets a twisted tale straight'.

3. NU.   Are you trying to tell me this news makes you glad? ⎤
    CH.   Why not? If ZEUS will make good out of bad.   ⎦

4. NU.   But Orestes, our one hope, he's gone as you know.   ⎤
    CH.   Only a blind seer would say that was so.   ⎦

5. NU.   What are you saying? Is there more to be known?   ⎤
    CH.   The gods will do their work. You do your own.   ⎦

NURSE.
        I will. I'm off with my message. I've no doubt
        the gods in their wisdom will sort it all out.

CHORUS.
        Chief of the godclans, ZEUS, now send
        this house a balanced end.

        Let the lovers of good law
        get the bloodright they've longed for.

        Let the man who's gone within
        meet with his enemies and win.

        If you help him your godstone
        will get more goats than it's ever known.

        The colt of one dear to your heart.
        's coupled to disaster's cart.

        Now that he's nearly won his race
        see he keeps up his winning pace.

        Don't let him slacken off so late
        and falter half-way down the straight.

        Gods of this clan's rich stores
        the feelings that we have are yours.

Let fresh bloodflow now wash clean
all the bloodflow that has been.

Dry old murder's loins make barren
the teeming womb of this blood-warren.

APOLLO, healer, whose light even
makes the deep dark cave a haven.

Let this bloodclan's latest one
lift his eyes up to the sun.

Let the beacon of bright freedom blaze
through the veils of murk and haze.

HERMES, guile-god, if you choose,
those you champion can't lose.

You blind their opponents so
they can't see the coming blow.

Those you help see through the dark
and shoot their weapons at the mark.

Their targets can't see. All they feel
's their hearts pierced suddenly by steel.

Then sing this bloodclan brought to land
out of the wild sea, beached on sand.

Like the women of fishermen who wail
until they glimpse the first white sail.

The wind drops, the dark sky clears
the women's wailing turns to cheers.

Cheers as the laden ships reach shore
and loved one suffer storm no more.

And when the deed is to be done
courage when she calls you SON

Shout back MY FATHER'S, call his name
do the blood-deed with no blame.

Be like Perseus, one who slew
a monster woman as will you.

Those below the earth and those above
want their bloodgrudge not son's love.

Plunge your sword up to the hilt
in the cause of this bloodguilt.

Enter AEGISTHUS.

AEGISTHUS.
      Here I am as the messenger summoned.
      I'm told certain strangers have brought baleful tidings,
      news most unwelcome, the death of Orestes.
      The beast's back's already rubbed raw by its burdens
      and now it gets plagued by another sore pack-gall.
      Am I to take this as fact and as proven
      or is it mere women's talk starting a panic,
      words flying and burning themselves out for nothing?
      Who knows anymore to make it all plainer?

CHORUS.
      We heard the same story as you, but we're only women!
      You don't need to listen to second-hand hearsay,
      go inside straightaway and question the strangers.

AEGISTHUS.
      Yes, I want to have the messenger questioned
      if he himself witnessed the death of Orestes
      or whether he's simply passing on rumours.
      I'm too open-eyed to be gulled or outsmarted.

Exit AEGISTHUS.

CHORUS.
      Both bloodblades are now drawn out
      for the final killing bout.

      Either Clytemnestra's cleaver
      finishes the clan for ever

      or Agamemnon's son can light
      the beacon, freedom, in black night.

      In the blood-bout two to one,
      back up Agamemnon's son.

A cry from the palace. Should be identical to cry of Agamemnon.

AEGISTHUS.
      Aaaaggghhh!

CHORUS.
      Listen! Whose was that cry? The clan's in the balance.
      But better we women withdraw till it's settled.
      Whatever the outcome we must seem to be blameless.

One way or another the battle's decided.

Enter SERVANT.

SERVANT.
He's killed. The master! He's killed. The master. Aegisthus.
Open the door to the women's apartments . . .
A strong arm's needed, though he's past help, Aegisthus.

Help! Help! Everyone's deaf there's no point in shouting.
Deaf or asleep. But where's Clytemnestra?
Her head's the next one due for the hackblock.
The axeshaft's poised in the clenched fist of bloodright.

Enter CLYTEMNESTRA.

CLYTEMNESTRA.
Who's that shouting for help in the palace?

SERVANT.
The dead, the dead are hacking the living down.

CLYTEMNESTRA.
Ah, your riddle's by no means baffling to me.
We're to be killed by the same guile we killed by.
Get me my man-axe, my king-cleaver. Quick!

Exit SERVANT.

We'll put to the test who's victor, who's vanquished.

Enter ORESTES *and* PYLADES.

ORESTES.
It's you I'm after. He's had enough the one inside.

CLYTEMNESTRA.
Ah, dead, dead! My shield, dear Aegisthus.

ORESTES.
Your *dear* Aegisthus? Then into his grave-bed.
Continue your coupling as cold stiffened corpses,
carry on tupping under your tombcairn.

CLYTEMNESTRA.
Orestes! Have pity! These breasts you nestled on
and nuzzled the nipples for their nourishing milk.

ORESTES. (*To Pylades.*)
    Pylades! What shall I do? Shame, pity, awe,
    all make me shrink from killing my mother

PYLADES.
    Remember Apollo and all that you swore
    Give grudge to mankind but not the godclan

ORESTES.
    I remember. You were right to remind me

    (*To Clytemnestra.*)
    Inside! I want to kill you on top of his body.
    Since you preferred him (when alive!) to my father.
    Aegisthus greater than King Agamemnon!
    The one you should have showered love on not hatred.

    Sleep beside your dear one even in death.

1.   CLYT.   I want to grow old with the son these breasts fed!
      OR.   My father's murderess eating my bread!

2.   CLYT.   The she-god of Fate, son, she played her part.
      OR.   The same she-god then drives my sword through your
                                  heart.

3.   CLYT.   Your mother's bloodgrudges, don't they make you
                                  scared?
      OR.   Would a mother throw her son out if she had cared?

4.   CLYT.   Not thrown out, sent to an ally when Argos got hot.
      OR.   *Sold!* A chief's son, a free man, and sold for what?

5.   CLYT.   Yes, if I sold you, what was my pay?
      OR.   Too shameful to think of, let alone say.

6.   CLYT.   What of your father? What of his shame?
      OR.   He suffered. You sat here. Spare him your blame.

7.   CLYT.   A woman suffers with her man at the wars.
      OR.   But his toil supports her while she sits indoors.

8.   CLYT.   So you'll condemn me, your mother, to die.
      OR.   Your own actions condemn you, mother, not I.

9.   CLYT.   Your mother's bloodgrudges like dogs will hunt you.
      OR.   I'm hunted by my father's so what can I do?

10. CLYT.   Deaf as the gravehole my son pays no heed.
      OR.   When my father was murdered *you* started to bleed.

11. CLYT.   You! You were the snake crawled out of my womb.]
     OR.   Your nightmare was true. It showed you your tomb.]

            You killed my father. I kill my mother.
            One blood-wrong gives birth to another.

ORESTES *and* PYLADES *take* CLYTEMNESTRA *off.*

CHORUS.
        I spare some pity for this fallen couple,
        but better Orestes surfs over this bloodcrest
        than the eye of the bloodclan is shuttered for ever.

        Time brings bloodright to blast Troy.
        Agamemnon's house next call.
        Two lions enter and destroy
        the house, and now the lions fall.

        Orestes, guided by Apollo
        comes home and hacks them dead.
        The distant exile has to follow
        the god-goad in his head.

        At last this house is freed,
        restored to its old health.
        Dead the ones who let it bleed
        away its wealth.

        The killer had to be concealed.
        He counterfeited then attacked.
        Bloodright, Zeus's she-child, steeled
        his right hand as he hacked.

        At last this house is freed
        restored to its old health
        dead the ones who let it bleed
        away its wealth.

        APOLLO cries from deep cleftshrine
        guile crushes guile, deceit deceit!
        We've got to trust whatever divine
        power helps us to our feet.

        The beacon's relit
        light's in the halls
        harsh chain and bit
        cause no more galls

House of Atreus stand
get up off the ground.

Time brings it all about,
scrubs the blood off the bricks,
drives the bloodgrudge squatters out.
Now all three dice say six!

The beacon's relit
light's in the halls
harsh chain and bit
cause no more galls

House of Atreus stand
get up off the ground.

Palace doors open. ORESTES *with bodies of* CLYTEMNESTRA *and*
AEGISTHUS. *The tableau repeats the stance of* CLYTEMNESTRA *over*
AGAMEMNON *and* CASSANDRA.

ORESTES.
 Here they are, the two tyrants who crushed you.
 They killed my father and blasted the bloodclan.
 Puffed up with pride they were, up on their thronestools,
 and still in love, look, still clinging so closely,
 carrying their bedbond into the grave-hole.
 The pledges they gave have both been accomplished –
 kill my father together, together to fall.

 (*Shows robe.*)

 Now look again, you who are here to bear witness.
 This contrivance they fangled to fetter my father
 both his hands and feet held fast and hobbled.
 Spread the thing out. Gather round in a circle,
 display the great cloak-shroud so that the father (not mine
 but the sun who sees all things I mean by the father)
 can see the crime of my mother in all its true grimness,
 so when I stand trial the Sun will bear witness
 that Orestes was right to go through with this killing.
 Right to kill his mother. As for Aegisthus –
 he got the just death all adulterers deserve.
 What of her who hatched this horror up for her husband,
 whose children she carried under her girdle,
 a burden apparently loved but really abhorrent,
 what about her? If she'd been shark-hag or viper

just the mere feel of her, without any fang-marks
would turn her poor victim purple with poison,
make him all stiff and all swollen with blood.
Her spirit alone spurts out putrefaction.

(*Shows robe again.*)

What shall I call it? What name gives it status?
Net to snare animals, shroud for a corpse,
drape for a bath-trough. No, net's the best name.
Call it a hunting net, trip-rope, a trap-robe,
an ideal device for roadside desperadoes
who lurk by the highway waylaying wayfarers.
With one of these they'd snare them in thousands.

Rather than end up with a wife like my mother
I'd rather die without heir, without he-child.

CHORUS.
In that net you bled to death
a butchered carcase bathed in blood.
For the one who still draws breath
suffering bursts into bud.

ORESTES.
Did she do the deed or not? This is my witness,
the cloth all becrimsoned by the sword of Aegisthus.
The embroidery rotted by time and by bloodstains.
Wailing over this web gives my father this gravedirge.
My dirge is for all the deeds done by this bloodclan.
I've won this bout but the laurels are blood-smirched

CHORUS.
No man's life-lot ever goes
painless till the post is passed
Man gets preyed on by his woes
from his first day to his last.

ORESTES.
I've got to tell you. The whole thing's unending.
My chariot races. I rein my team in as they're charging.
The uncontrolled horses crash into the trackrails.
They gallop my mind off, dragging behind them.
Fear squats in my mind, plays music for scaring.
But while I still have some grip I say to the Argives,
I was right to kill Clytemnestra, my mother,

daubed in my father's blood, hated by he-gods.
Apollo's voice was my chief provocation:
Do what you have to, and go away guiltless.
Don't do it and . . . The pains that he promised
were out of all range of man's usual troubles.
Look at me now with this olive, this garland.
I go as a suppliant to Apollo's great godstone
where purifying fires are forever kept burning,
exiled for shedding the blood of my bloodkin.
Apollo said I should only seek help from this godstone.
I beg men of Argos now and in future
to bear witness as to how these horrors happened
I go as a wanderer, exiled from my bloodright.
Living or dead, I leave you my memory.

CHORUS.
The memory will be of a man who did well.
Don't burden your mouth with any bad-omens.
You've brought freedom back to the city of Argos
by lopping the heads off two serpents at once.

1.   OR.   Ah! Look! Coming! Gorgons. Garb black, entwined
            with snakes for hair. I've got to run.
     CH.   It's nothing, Orestes. It's all in your mind.
            Fear nothing. Your father's pleased with his loyal son.

2.   OR.   These aren't in the mind. They're real and they're near.
            My mother's grudge-dogs close at my heels.
     CH.   Orestes, it's fresh blood on your hands makes you fear.
            It's only blood-frenzy your spirit feels.

3.   OR.   Apollo! Look at them. More! More! More!
            Through black blood-ooze their eyes stare straight at me.
     CH.   Apollo's the one god to cleanse you of gore.
            The touch of Apollo will set you free.

ORESTES.
You can't see them. I can though.
They're baying for my blood. I've got to go.

Exit ORESTES *pursued by* FURIES.

CHORUS.
Then let the god you go to, give
you sustenance and help you live.

This, the third stormblast to buffet this bloodclan.

One: the banquet of babes, the bane of Thyestes.

Two: the Achaean warlord hacked down in his bath-trough.

Three: the deliverer . . .

                              or new doom in disguise?

When will the blood-grudge be weaned
off blood,

          when will it sleep,

                         the fiend?

END OF PART II

THREE
EUMENIDES

Temple of Apollo at Delphi.

PRIESTESS.

First in my prayers, Earth, Gaia, great she-god,
primeval prophetess and eldest diviner.
Then after her mother came Earth's she-child Themis
who handed it on to the Titaness Phoebe,
who bestowed it in turn on Apollo as birthgift.
Leaving rocks and bog on the island of Delos
Apollo made landfall on Attica's shoreline
where Pallas has harbours bristling with ships' masts
and then pushed on upwards as far as Parnassus
escorted by offspring of Hephaistos the smithgod
who laid roads for Apollo to lead him to Delphi.
Those Athenians made the whole wilderness docile.
When Apollo arrived, the people and Delphos,
Delphos of Delphi, state-pilot and steersman
greeted the young god with all welcome and worship.
Zeus gave Apollo divine inspiration,
made him fourth prophet here, and here he still is.
Apollo's the mouth of Zeus, the high he-god.

These prophet gods take first place in my prelude.

Next Pallas Athene who stands before god-shrines.
I honour the nymphs in the Corycian caverns,
hollow, where birds swoop, patrol place of spirits.
Dionysus too has a presence in Delphi
since the god headed his horde of Bacchantes
and got Pentheus hunted and trapped like a hare.
The spring of Pleistos, the power of Poseidon
and Zeus the Fulfiller, the highest of he-gods!

Now on the shrinestool, inspired and prophetic
I hope that my powers are as strong or are stronger.
Any Greeks here, come forward. Draw lots and enter.
I'll give you the answers the god sends in trances . . .

PRIESTESS *enters the shrine. Silence. Then a scream.*
Then PRIESTESS *comes out again on all fours like a dog.*

PRIESTESS.

Terrible things to clap mortal eyes on
have made me bolt out of the house of Apollo.
Sapped of all strength my feet can't support me.
I scrabble on all fours. My legs have gone liquid.

A scared old woman crawling, worse than a baby.

Entering the innermost shrine with its garlands
I set eyes on a man at the shrine's central stone,
an abomination to gods in the suppliant's seat.
His hands dripped blood. He had his drawn sword out.
He held an olive-branch tipped with white wool tufts.
In front of this person, a strange group of she-hags
sighing and snorting, asleep on the thronestools.
Not women really, but more like the Gorgons.
I call them Gorgons but they weren't that exactly.
I once saw a picture of Harpiae, Graspers,
unflaggingly swooping on Phineus the Thracian,
keeping the blind king in perpetual tension,
filched his food off him or left it beshitten,
splattered their bat-bowels over his platters
and kept him terror-stricken and starving.
These were black like Harpiae but they were wingless.
The snorts from their nostrils would keep you a mile off.
Their eye-sockets glued with sickening ooze-clots.
Their grave-garb's all wrong for the statues of godheads
nor would it seem right in the houses of mortals.
Don't know what brute-clan this brood belongs to,
what region would want to boast that it bred them
and didn't wish now that their birth had aborted.
What happens now depends on the master of Delphi,
Doxias Apollo, sign reader, all powerful, healer.

He purifies others' homes, let him cleanse his.

Exit PRIESTESS.
The inner shrine revealed with APOLLO *and* ORESTES.

APOLLO.
No, I'll never desert you. I'll guard you for ever,
either close by you, or if not, at a distance.
Towards all your enemies, like those pursuers,
I'll never show mildness, nor ever mellow.
I've put them to sleep, these creatures men spit on,
blood-battening bat hags, shrivelled but virgin,
crone-kinder no kind caresses, covers or couples.
Who'd tup these terrors? No god, man nor brute beast!
They're born to brew bale. They're evil for ever.
Their abode's the bottomless void black abyss,

abominations both to men and Olympian he-gods.

But still you must run. Don't flag and don't slacken.
They'll hound you through the whole length of the landmass,
tracking you over the well-beaten foot routes
then across seas, through cities lapped by the ocean.
Don't surrender. Don't let your step falter
by brooding on all the pain that you'll suffer.
When you come to the city of Pallas Athene
sit down in safety, embracing her image.
There we'll find judges and words of appeasement
and means to release you from this burden for ever.

I moved you, I, to murder your mother!

ORESTES.
Lord Apollo, you know about justice none better,
and since you know don't forget how to use it.
Apollo's potency goes without question.

APOLLO.
Remember that then! Don't give way to panic.

Invokes Hermes.

And Hermes, my brother, kin through one father
(and what bloodkin exists any closer than that?)
watch over Orestes, be Hermes Escorter.
Shepherd my suppliant. Guide him to Athens.
Zeus ever respects the rights of the outlawed.

Exeunt APOLLO, ORESTES.

Enter GHOST OF CLYTEMNESTRA *who speaks to the still unseen*
CHORUS OF FURIES *within.*

CLYTEMNESTRA.
You're supposed to be Furies and I find you sleeping!
When Furies need naps they're no longer Furies.
Dishonoured, defamed by the dead that I dwell with,
I walk underground through a gauntlet of ghost-cries,
catcalls that brand my phantom with blood-guilt.
Slaughtered though I was by the hand of my he-child
not one spirit's incensed at the sore fate I've suffered.
Look here at my heart with hackmarks all over.
Remember too all those midnight libations,
not winebowls, but liquor much redder and thicker,

poured at the hour when there's only you stirring
while mortals are sleeping, gods in god-spaces.
But you trample and spurn all my spendthrift libations.
He's given you the slip the quarry you're hunting
like a nimble deer clearing the spread of your net-mesh
belling his beast-taunts as he bounds off for freedom.
Listen! It's for my after-life that I'm pleading.
Wake up, she-gods of underneath spaces.
The Clytemnestra you're dreaming calls you from sleep.

FURIES *are heard within, moaning in their sleep.*

O make your cow noises! Your quarry's escaped.
He's lucky in *his* friends. At least they aren't Furies.

FURIES *are heard again moaning.*

Snoring and sleeping! Does my pain stir no pity?
Mother-killer Orestes got out of your clutches.

More FURY *noises.*

Sleeping and whining! Whining and sleeping! Wake up!
Aren't Furies supposed to make people suffer?

More FURY *noises from within.*

Fagged out by fatigue it sleeps off its labours
the she-snake, whose fangs have been syphoned of venom.

FURIES *whine louder and higher.*

CHORUS OF FURIES.
Get him! Get him! There he goes!

CLYTEMNESTRA.
Dreaming of hunting, like dogs, but not doing!
Baying like bloodhounds that track in their slumbers.
Dreaming not *doing*! Get up and get going.
Sleep only blunts your rage at my bloodwrong.
My bloodgrudge should boost you back into action.
Bloodgrudge is a goad to upholders of bloodright.
Let your breath billow round him its gore-reeking gases.
Shrivel his flesh with hot blasts from your bowels,
fart fire through your flues till he flops like a fruitrind.
Hound him and hunt him till he sags like a skin-bag.

Exit GHOST OF CLYTEMNESTRA. *Enter* CHORUS OF FURIES *one by one.*

CHORUS.
Wake up! Wake up your she-kin as I woke you.
Still asleep? Then shake off your stupor.
Make certain the chase here wasn't for nothing.

CHORUS *searches for* ORESTES.

All for nothing! Pointless, pointless pursuit!
Running till we dropped. A little nap.
All for nothing. The blood-guilty brute
still wide-awake leaps out of our trap.

(*Calling into Apollo's sanctum.*)

Apollo, Apollo, thief of a he-god!
we she-gods have the ancientest rights,
that you, a young he-god ride over roughshod.
Strutting young upstart! We spit on such slights.

You pamper this suppliant you hide,
and he's a mother-killing son.
a god condoning matricide!
who'd see right in what you've done?

Grudge gored my gut like a goad in a'racehorse.
Felt on my flesh like the flail of a flogger
sharp, vicious, whistling like pliable ice.
They do things like that the new era he-gods,
get their way only by forcing the feeble.

Look at his thronestool sticky with bloodspill.
His navelstone's only a blood-sodden hackblock.
Prophet Apollo pollutes his own godstone.
Of his own accord gets his stone caked with bloodclots.
He's breached all the godbonds to bolster up mortals,
poaching the preserves of she-fate and life-lot.
That abomination Apollo's protecting Orestes!

Has he crawled into the ground? Let him.
Wherever he is the FURIES will get him.

He brings his blood-guilt. Next in the chain's
the bloodgrudge-fulfiller who beats in *his* brains.

Enter APOLLO.

APOLLO.

>Get out! Get out! Out you go! Out you go!
>Leave the prophet's earthcleft free of pollution
>or a serpent with wings on and venomous fangbane
>shot from gold bowstrings will go through your gutbag!
>You'll spew up black slavver of gobbled up goreswill,
>gore-clots your crones' gobs sucked out of corpses.
>Not a finger of yours should befoul my own hearth-fane.
>You belong where heads go splat off the hackblock,
>eyes get gouged out and lugged from their sockets,
>where bloodright's castrations, boys' ballocks battered,
>men spitted on stakespikes screaming for mercy.
>Your bat-snouts go snorting in society's bloodtroughs.
>It's the food you get fat on makes you hated by he-gods.
>All your appearance says blood food and filth baths.
>You hags should live in the beast dens in jungles.
>dark lairs all larded with shit and chewed gristle,
>not here, contagious to all you come close to.
>Get out! Out you go! You goats with no goatherd!

CHORUS.

>Thank you, Apollo! Now may we reply?
>Apollo, how can you pose as a simple abettor
>when you and you only bear all the bloodguilt?

1. AP.   How? At least explain that charge. But then you must go. ⎤
    CH.   He killed his mother, because you said so.   ⎦

2. AP.   To avenge his dead father as any son should.   ⎤
    CH.   You harboured him here with his hands red with blood. ⎦

3. AP.   I told him to come here to be purged of bloodstains.   ⎤
    CH.   And *we* drove him here, but get abuse for our pains.   ⎦

4. AP.   You're not fit to set foot here, such hags as you.   ⎤
    CH.   We did only the work that we're destined to do.   ⎦

5. AP.   And what "special mission" have you ever had?   ⎤
    CH.   The mission of driving matricides mad!   ⎦

6. AP.   And if it's her manlord a woman has killed?   ⎤
    CH.   That wouldn't be bloodkin's blood that has been spilled! ⎦

APOLLO.

>So you'd scorn bondright, the man/woman bedbond?
>Hera, high she-god and Zeus, the high he-god,
>they even swore vows and were coupled in bondright.

So you'd dishonour and cast on the midden
the she-god of love, Aphrodite of Cyprus,
she with whose help men form bonds of the closest?
That bedbond's sanctified by the she-gods of life-lot
and needs no other oath if the guardian's justice.
So if one murders her mate in the bedbond
and you slacken your rigid rule against slaughter
then it's unjust your pursuit of Orestes.
One crime you come down on, the other pass over.

Athena must judge between bloodright and bondright.

7.   CH.   He'll never escape. I'll go on pursuing.   ⎤
     AP.   Do, by all means, it's your own bale you'll be brewing. ⎦

8.   CH.   You can't belittle our rights for all your abuse.   ⎤
     AP.   I wouldn't take them, for nothing, even from Zeus! ⎦

9.   CH.   Yes, we've heard you're well in with the throne!   ⎤
           But with shed mother-blood blazing the trail
           I'll keep on pursuing till the end of the hunt.
     AP.   You do your "duties". I'll do my own –
           which is protecting my suppliant. If I fail
           his rage will cause men and gods great affront. ⎦

Exit APOLLO.

Exeunt CHORUS *sniffing for the trail.*

Scene changes to Athens. Before the image of Athena. ORESTES
clasps the image.

ORESTES.
     Athena, high she-god, I was sent by Apollo.
     Look on me kindly. I'm cursed and an outcast.
     Though still a cursed outcast there's no need of more cleansing.
     My bloodguilt's been blunted enough by my contact
     with places and peoples who helped my purgation
     All this was decreed by Apollo at Delphi.
     I've crossed land and sea to your house and your statue.
     Until the issue's decided I stay beside you.

Enter CHORUS, *one by one, still sniffing the bloodtrail.*

CHORUS.
     Here! He's left a very clear track behind him.
     We don't need his cries but only these bloodclues.
     Like hounds tracking down a deer that's been bleeding

we bound between blood-drips till our quarry's cornered.
This manhunt's a killer. I pant with exhaustion.
We've combed the whole land, the coastline, the ocean,
swift flotilla of Furies, wingless sea-eagles.
My nostrils say here he's cornered and cowering.
The glad smell of gore smiles its warm welcome.

seek   seek   scour the ground
the mother-killer's got to be found

Sniff at the trail. The blood's still wet.
Don't let him flee from paying his debt.

He's there! And once again, look, begging protection,
this time his arms are wound round a she-god.
He won't pay his blood-dues. He wants to "stand trial".
What rubbish *trials* are when the blood shed's a mother's!

A mother's blood has run away
into the earth it goes to stay

The blood that trickles on the ground
's not balls of thread to be rewound.

Trial! This is the trial your trackers intend:
first suck red libations from limbs while they're living,
browse on your blood, all over your body,
broach you all bloodless, haul your husk off below,
a morsel of torment for your own mother's murder.
Down there you'll see all those who've offended
a god or a guest or the parents who got them,
get the blood-doom their deeds have duly deserved.

Hades, death-god holds assize
on a man's deeds when he dies

death-god Hades won't forget
the deed of blood and the blood-debt.

ORESTES.
I've been through them all, the forms of purgation,
rites which used speech, rites which used silence.
Here my wise mentor says words are in order.
The blood on my hands has already grown drowsy;
it lowers its eyelids. The stains have stopped staring.
It was washed off with pig's blood by Phoebus Apollo.
My hosts came to no harm by giving me housing.

So the mouth's unpolluted that pleads with Athena,
god-queen of the country, to come to my rescue.
She won't need her spear to make long-lasting allies
of me and my country, and the people of Argos.
Whether she's now in the Libyan deserts,
or by Lake Tritonis, her Libyan birthplace,
seated and skirted to receive men's obeisance,
or booted for battle, as brave as a he-god,
siding with her friends on the Phlegrean flatlands –

As a she-god she'll hear me over great spaces.
Come, Athena, come now to my rescue!

CHORUS.
Neither the power of Apollo, nor the power of Athena
can save you from perishing spurned and abandoned,
even forgetting that joy had a meaning,
broached of blood, banquetted on, flesh pod, shadow,
a shrivelled up fruitrind squeezed dry of its juices.

Won't answer! Spits what we say back in our faces!
Our little sacrifice all ready for slicing!
No need of godstones, we'll eat you still living.
It will swaddle you helpless, our "lullaby", listen –

She-kin, show our force. Join hands!
Dance the doom-dance steps, display
through our grim music that our band's
a power over men that gets its way:

Our mission's bloodright, we're not sent
ever to harm the innocent

Show us your hands. If they're not red
you'll sleep soundly in your bed.

Show us you hands. Left. Right.
You'll live unhunted if they're white.

Show us *your* hands. There's one we know
whose hands are red and daren't show.

With men like him whose hands are red
we are the bloodgrudge of the dead.

Our band of witnesses pursues
the bloodkin-killer for blood-dues.

NIGHT, Night, Mother Night
who bore us to uphold bloodright,
Leto's he-child takes away
the rights you gave us to our prey,
this cringing beast, his cowering whelp
evades us with that he-god's help.
Apollo's foiled us of the hide
of our allotted matricide.

Victim! Victim!
Listen! Our song!

The Furies' lyreless lullaby's
music maddening men's mind

Victim! Victim!
Listen! Our song!

it binds man's brain and dries
man's fruity flesh to rind.

The she-god of life-lot gave us these powers,
ours, ours, for ever ours.

Those who kill their kin I hound
until I've got them underground.

Even dead they don't go free,
I torment them endlessly . . .

Victim! Victim!
Listen! Our song!

The Furies' lyreless lullaby's
music maddening men's mind

Victim! Victim!
Listen! Our song!

it binds man's brain and dries
man's fruity flesh to rind.

When we came into being, they were marked out, the confines.
We and the Olympians have no intimate contacts.
Food's offered to either but not both together.
We don't wear white robes, they don't wear black ones.

Family strife, domestic pet
born in the wild and won't forget

When bloodkin kills bloodkin
that lets the Furies in

into the household keen-scented hound
blasting the building back into the ground

After the victim; hot on his trail
tracker Furies that never fail

He tries running. O let him try
a bloodkin's blood will never dry

He tries running. Fresh wet gore
keeps the Furies hot on his spoor.

We'll snatch back our prey from this she-god's protection.
There should be no question of such gods interfering
or muddying issues by setting up "sessions".
Zeus, the high he-god finds murderers hateful,
he bars that blood-dripping breed from his precincts.

Family strife, domestic pet
born in the wild and won't forget

When bloodkin kills bloodkin
that lets the Furies in

into the household keen-scented hound
blasting the building back into the ground

After the victim, hot on his trail
tracker Furies that never fail

He tries running. O let him try
a bloodkin's blood will never dry

He tries running. Fresh wet gore
keeps the Furies hot on his spoor.

The pomp and proud carriage a man's puffed up with above
moulders to nothing when he's dragged off below.
He sees the drab black we're draped with to dance in,
hears the feet pounding the pulse of the bloodgrudge.

Down, Down, down I dive from a great height
and fall on him with all my weight

Down, Down, down I dive, my leaden tread
cracks the bloodkin-killer's head

Down, Down, down he goes with sickening thud
slipping in his bloodkin's blood.

Down he falls, and falling knows nothing, nothing.
A smother of madness clouds round the victim.
The groans of old murders thicken the bloodsmog
that billows all round and blacks out his household.

Down, down, down I dive from a great height
and fall on him with all my weight

Down, down, down I dive, my leaden tread
cracks the bloodkin killer's head

Down, down, down he goes with sickening thud
slipping in his bloodkin's blood.

That's how it is, and that's how it's staying.
We've got all the skills. We get things accomplished.
We memorise murders. We're never forgetful.

We terrify mortals. We spit on their pleadings.
We relish our office, though spurned by the he-gods.

We're despised, we're rejected. The light we work by
is nothing like sunshine. Sharp and sheer-sided
our tracks are a peril to blind and to sighted.

So show us the man who can stop himself shaking
when he hears me lay claim to my titles
ratified by fate, and never, *never* rescinded.
My honours are ancient and in no way diminished
though I work underground, in the earth where it's sunless.

Enter ATHENA.

ATHENA.
I heard far away someone crying: ATHENA!
I was on the banks of the Trojan Scamander
taking possession of my portion of spearspoil,
land won by the Achaeans, then awarded to me
and offered by me to the children of Theseus.

And summoned I sped here, the scales of my aegis
whipped by the winds as my feet raced me onwards.

Sees CHORUS.

I see a strange breed here, new to my country.
This breed doesn't scare me but causes me wonder.

(*To Chorus.*)
Who are you? You and you, all here assembled?
the stranger prostrated before my own image,
and you, like nothing engendered by means that are normal,

neither like the she-gods that consort with the he-gods
nor like the humans in shape and appearance.

But since we've been made to share the same earthspace
it's wrong to abuse you as monstrous and shapeless.

CHORUS.
She-child of Zeus, we'll tell you all briefly.
We are the children of Night, and we're ageless.
Below ground where we live we're known as the Grudges.

1. ATH.   So now I know your mother and what to call you.
    CH.   And soon you'll know also the work that we do.

2. ATH.   I will, provided it's clear what you say.
    CH.   Kin-killers, we hunt them. They are our prey.

3. ATH.   Where do you land him when you've netted your fish?'
    CH.   Where all words for joy sound like gibberish

4. ATH.   Are *his* deeds the reason that you're in full cry?
    CH.   He murdered his mother in cold blood, that's why!

5. ATH.   Was he goaded or forced to against his own will?
    CH.   Forced! It was his *mother* this man dared to kill!

6. ATH.   There are two parties present. I must hear them both.
    CH.   He won't let us swear ours, nor swear his own oath.

7. ATH.   It's not justice you want but the mere outward show.
    CH.   How? You're the she-god of wisdom, say why that is so.

8. ATH.   Sworn oaths would unfairly favour your cause.
    CH.   You question him then. the decision is yours.

9. ATH.   The decision is mine. You'll give me you trust?
    CH.   Knowing your father it seems that we must.

ATHENA. (*Addressing Orestes.*)
Stranger, now it's your turn to speak and make answer.
Tell me your country, your bloodkin, what's happened
then make reply to the charges they've levelled.
Belief in your case brought you here to my godstone
clasping my image like the suppliant Ixion,

first man to kill, first cleansed of his killing.
Answer my questions and answer them clearly.

ORESTES.
       She-chief Athena, let me remove the misgivings
       implied in the last words you addressed me.
       Unlike Ixion, *I* need *no* blood-absolution.
       My undefiled hands cause no smirch to your image.
       And this is the proof I can give of my cleansing:
       the law is that one who's been guilty of bloodshed's
       debarred from all speech until sprinkled with pig's blood
       by one who's empowered to perform the purgation.
       Long since and elsewhere I was purged in that manner
       by sucklings with throats slit, streams with their currents.
       So dismiss your alarm at likely pollution.
       As for my bloodkin that's also told quickly –
       I'm Argive, and when you ask me who is my father
       I'm proud to reply that he *was* Agamemnon,
       commander of all Achaia's great ship-force
       with whose help you crushed Troy into nothing,
       one of those clanchiefs who won you your spearspoil.
       After Troy he returned to a death most unworthy.
       My black-hearted mother, she killed my father.
       She swaddled him first in a devious dragnet –
       its red eyes still stare at the blood in the bath-trough.
       Coming home after exile I killed my mother.
       I killed her because she killed my dear father.
       In all this Apollo was my god-accomplice.
       Apollo jabbed sharp spurs into my spirit
       and promised great pains if their guilt went unpunished.
       Just or unjust? You must give judgement.
       Whatever your verdict I'll take it as binding.

ATHENA.
       A hard matter, this, to judge for a mortal,
       and even for me it's too hard to pass judgement
       when retribution runs so close behind bloodguilt.
       It's made all the harder since you've come to my godstone
       a suppliant cleansed by all rites and procedures.
       Still blood-stained I'd have you barred from my city.

       (*Indicating Chorus.*)
       But these too have a cause which must be considered.
       They have certain duties it's pointless dismissing

and if the verdict frustrates them of victory
they'll disgorge their grudge-venom into the ground
and blight all the land with eternal diseases.
I let them stay or I drive them away –
That's the dilemma, my desperate decision.

I'll swear in a tribunal to be judges of murder
a tribunal for this case and all such for ever.

(*To Orestes and Chorus.*)
Gather your witnesses, gather your evidence,
your sworn support in the cause of true justice,
I'll pick and bring back the best men of Athens
to judge the facts fairly without any falsehood.

Exit ATHENA. ORESTES *and* CHORUS *remain.*
Scene changes to Acropolis.

CHORUS.
All right's destroyed by this new dispensation
if the wrong cause of this killer's allowed to succeed.
One murderer's freedom gives licence to all,
makes murder the norm not merely the nightmare
that gnaws at the sleeptime of fathers and mothers.
They'll be wide awake now when the wounds get inflicted.

We Furies were once mankind's sleepless watchdogs
inflicting transgressors with vehement madness.
Our anger and grudge have been put out to grass now
and all forms of death have the run of the world.
When he sees trouble looming over his neighbour
a man starts to wonder when his own turn will come
and asks someone else how to stop the contagion
and he offers philtres for safety. All futile!
And don't let someone smitten cry out the old cry
on bloodright or bloodgrudge or us, the *deaf* Furies.
Some father, some mother, their pain new upon them
might weep and might wail with such piteous appeals.
Bloodright! Like Troy it's all rubble and ashes.

Fear's a good gateman to stand guard of the passions.
Often men suffer to win some small wisdom.
Those men and those cities where fear has no franchise
will never show justice the slightest respect.
A life with no rules, a life of repression
anarchy, tyranny, you must respect neither.

Somewhere between's where the god plants his banner.
Out of two forces he makes a new fusion.
Going beyond bounds, overstepping the limits
that comes about where the gods get degraded.
The mind that is balanced, and keeps within confines
gets the happiness men struggle and pray for.
Above all respect the godstone of Bloodright.
Don't besmirch or befoul it with impious bootsoles
just because loot looms in front of your goldlust.
Blemishing bloodright makes catastrophe certain.
Honour mother and father, and welcome guest-strangers.
And the man who does right without fear's compulsion
he's the one who won't find his life-lot unlucky
or himself and his bloodkin blasted entirely.
But the man who scorns all and does what he wants to
and caring for no one heaps up his wealth-spoil
and believes his snatched freight's assured a safe voyage,
will be forced to strike sail when the stormwaves start swelling,
his prow and his spars all pulped into splinters.
He shouts as he feels himself tugged by the tide-race.
He shouts to deaf ears. The gods' laughter mocks him,
the hothead who boasted that this couldn't happen,
helpless, aghast, as he's hurled at the headland,
and leaves on Right's reef the wreck of his life-lot,
and is lost, and unwept for, wiped out, forgotten.

Enter ATHENA, JURY *of* 12 ATHENIANS, *and a* HERALD.

ATHENA.

Sound the trumpet, keep the people in order.
Let the shrill battle-horn the Etruscans invented
change mortal breath into blares from its metal.

Sound of trumpets.

This is a court now, and crowded with people.
We must have strict silence and closest attention
so the laws I lay down can be learnt by the city
and these hear their case decided on merit.

Sound of trumpets.

Now hear the laws I lay down, my Athenian people,
brought together to try the first case of bloodshed.
For the children of Aegeus, father of Theseus,
this council of judges will sit here for ever,

on this hill of Ares, the Amazons' camp-site
when they came to make war through their grudge against
                                                    Theseus.
They erected great turrets to overlook Athens
and sacrificed cattle to Ares the War God,
hence the name: Areopagus, rock-hill of Ares.
The people's reverence and the fear that they're born with
will restrain them day and night from acts of injustice
as long as they don't foul their own laws with defilement.
No one should piss in the well they draw drink from.
Anarchy! Tyranny! Let both be avoided
nor banish fear from your city entirely.
A man without fear abides by no law-forms.
If you justly cherish this new institution
you'll have a bulwark known to no other humans
from Scythia down to the Peloponnesus.
This established tribunal will be totally bribe-proof.
The watchdog stays wakeful to let you sleep soundly.
This long address I intend for you and the future.

Enter APOLLO.

ATHENA.
Lord Apollo, you are out of your precincts.
Explain your presence here at this meeting.

APOLLO.
I come as a witness. The man they're accusing
came as a suppliant and I gave him shelter.
I also purged him of the blood he had shed.
I'm his advocate too as well as a witness.
I share the blame for the death of his mother.

Begin the proceedings, that you preside over.
And make use of your wisdom to help us to judgement.

ATHENA. (*To Chorus.*)
The trial is now open. First, prosecution.
Speak, and put before us complete information.

CHORUS.
We may be many, but on this we're united.

(*To Orestes.*)
Answer the question each one of us asks you . . .

1. CH. You killed your mother. Say yes or no. ⎤
   OR. Yes, I can't deny it was so.

2. CH. First fall to us! We win with two more. ⎤
   OR. Don't crow too soon. I'm not on the floor.

3. CH. Now *how* did you kill her? (Judges take note!) ⎤
   OR. I drew my sword and gashed open her throat.

4. CH. Who was it drove you to dare such an act? ⎤
   OR. Apollo, and Apollo will witness that fact.

5. CH. You killed your mother at Apollo's behest? ⎤
   OR. I did, and still think it done for the best.

6. CH. I doubt if you'll think so once pinned by your doom. ⎤
   OR. I have faith in my father's help from the tomb.

7. CH. Your mother's among them so don't trust the dead. ⎤
   OR. My mother, she had two guilts on her head.

8. CH. Explain to the judges how you make two. ⎤
   OR. Her husband, my father, that's two men she slew.

9. CH. She paid by her death. You still have to pay. ⎤
   OR. When she was alive did you make her your prey?

10. CH. He wasn't her bloodkin, the man that she killed. ⎤
    OR. And you say that it's bloodkin's blood that I've spilled? ⎦

CHORUS.
        How could it not be? How else could the mother
        you murdered have fed you inside her body?
        Dare you disown the bloodbond that's closest?

ORESTES. (*To Apollo.*)
        Now be my witness. Explain to the judges
        whether I killed my mother with justice.
        That I did the deed there's no point denying
        but done rightly or wrongly, Apollo decide
        and help me to state my case with the judges.

APOLLO.
        To you the high tribunal sworn in by Athena,
        I, Apollo, the prophet, who can't utter falsehood
        say that Orestes here acted with justice.
        Whenever I speak to man, woman or city
        from the oracle shrine-throne I sit on at Delphi
        it's always as mouthpiece of Zeus, the high he-god,

so if I plea for justice, I speak for the Father,
Zeus, the high he-god, whose will you must bend to.
No oath has more power than the oath of the Father.

CHORUS.
So Zeus, you say, was behind your instruction
that Orestes avenge the death of his father?
Does Zeus disregard the rights of his mother?

APOLLO.
It's not the same thing the death of a man, though,
a man also honoured with Zeus-given chief-stave,
a *man*, moreover, killed by a *woman*
and not by war weapons, an Amazon's arrows,
but in a manner you'll hear, you, Pallas Athena,
and you sitting here to vote on this issue –
The man came home after ten years' campaigning
(and a fair judge would say that he'd gained himself glory)
came home from the wars to a "womanly welcome"!
And as he was stepping up out of his bathtrough
she pitched her dark doom-tent over his body,
she hacked down her husband while he was helpless,
fastened and feeble in the maze of its meshes.
A fine death for a man, clanchief, commander!
I show you the woman just as she was
to goad you to just grudge when weighing this issue.

CHORUS.
So Zeus thinks a father's death more important?
Yet Zeus was the one bound Kronos, *his* father!
Doesn't this act show a slight contradiction?

(*To Judges.*)
Consider this fact when reaching your verdict!

APOLLO.
Animals! Beast-hags hated by he-gods!
Chains, fetters, locks can all be unloosened.
There are many means to burst bonds and shackles,
but once a man's dead and earth's lapped his blood up,
the blood drains away and never returns.
Though Zeus can reverse all other conditions
he's never come up with a charm against dying.

CHORUS.
> So then supposing this man *is* acquitted,
> will the man who has shed the blood of his mother
> live in the house of his father at Argos?
> Who will want *his* hands griming the godstones?
> What clans will want *him* at their ritual cleansing?

APOLLO.
> I'll answer that, and this answer's decisive! . . .
>
> The mother of what's called her offspring's no parent
> but only the nurse to the seed that's implanted.
> The mounter, the male's the only true parent.
> She harbours the bloodshoot, unless some god blasts it.
> The womb of the woman's a convenient transit.
> I've got proof here at hand to back up my statement
> that the male can father with no help from the female.
> Here is the she-child of Zeus, the high he-god,
> who was nurtured in no womb's watery shadows.
> Such an offspring no she-god could bear on her own.
> (*To Athena.*)
> And I, Pallas, will do all that Apollo is able
> to make them both great, your city, your people.
> I sent him a suppliant hère to your godstone
> so that you'd have him as a true friend for ever,
> a spear-friend and ally, his people, your people,
> loyally bound in a bond that is lasting.

ATHENA.
> So, as both sides have spoken, I order
> the judges to come to the justest decision.

1. CH. All the shafts in our quiver, they're all of them shot.
         We need only your vote to make our word law.
    AP. You've heard what you've heard. Let each cast his lot.
         Remember the god-bond that each of you swore.

2. CH. Beware that in no way you dishonour our band.
         If we're dishonoured we'll poison your grass.
    AP. Fear the oracles, that's my command.
         My oracles, Zeus's, they must come to pass.

3. CH. Your oracles will never be free of the blot
         from dabbling in blood-deeds more than you should.
    AP. So you say Zeus the father was wrong or was not
         to purge Ixion first man to shed blood?

4.   CH.   Words! Words! But if I don't get the bloodright that's due
             I'll come down on this country with all of my force.
      AP.   What young god or old god cares about you?
             The case will be mine as a matter of course.

5.   CH.   You cheated old she-gods, the Fates, once before
             when you saved Admetus from a funeral pyre.
      AP.   We have to help suppliants, and all the more
             when he comes at a time when his need is most dire.

6.   CH.   You befuddled the ancient she-gods with wine!
             You made the old dispensation mere jest.
      AP.   And that's all you'll be when the victory's mine.
             You can spew all your venom. We won't be impressed.

CHORUS.
      You new he-gods trample the she-gods of old.
      When I hear the verdict then I'll decide
      whether or not this country gets blasted.

ATHENA.
      It's my duty to come to a final pronouncement.

      I add my own vote to those for Orestes!

      I myself was given birth by no mother.
      I put the male first, although I'm unmarried,
      and I am the wholehearted child of my father,
      so I can't count the death of a woman
      of greater importance than that of her manlord.

      If your votes turn out equal Orestes still wins

      Now turn the urns over and reckon the ballots,
      those of the judges assigned to this duty.

1.   OR.   O Phoebus Apollo, what will it be?
      CH.   O Night, our dark Mother, are you here to see?

2.   OR.   Now for the end, a noose or new day.
      CH.   Either honour, or ruin, if he gets away.

ATHENA.
      Count the pebbles you've shaken out of the vote-pots.
      Make sure there are no mistakes in your tally.
      The slightest error could lead to disaster.
      One vote could renew the strength of a bloodclan.

The votes are counted.

This man stands acquitted of the charges of murder.
The votes on each side turn out to be equal.

ORESTES.

Pallas Athena, you give my clan back its lifeblood!
You've given me back the fatherland barred me.
Once more Greece can say: Orestes of Argos,
restored to his bloodright by Pallas Athena,
by Apollo and by Zeus the Preserver.
Zeus saw my father's death in all its true grimness.
Zeus saw clearly that I needed preserving
from these terrible grudges who champion my mother.

Before I go to my country, I give you this god-bond –
this land and its people, now and for ever,
no clan-chief of Argos will ever attack you,
or I'll come as a ghost if they've broken my god-bond,
and mar all their marches, make journeys joyless,
until they repent their rash expeditions.
But so long as they honour this city of Pallas,
stay loyal in peace, and in war keep their spear-bond,
then I'll come as a ghost more gracious and kindly.

Farewell Athena, and people of Athens.
Get a good headlock on whoever you wrestle.
Come from all bouts with the victory laurels.

Exit ORESTES.

CHORUS.

You upstart gods
you've ridden down
the ancient laws
snatched my honours
out of my hands.

My rancour's roused,
my heart will ooze
black venom out
over the land
until it's waste.

Bloodright! Bloodright!

Womb-blight, crop-blight,
the earth all scorched,
the people starving.

The people mock me,
my wrongs are too much!
Daughters of Night
degraded and crushed.

ATHENA.

Listen to reason. Don't take things so badly.
You're not defeated. The votes came out equal.
There was no dishonour to you in the verdict.
Luminous proof came from Zeus the high he-god
and he who had spoken the oracle witnessed
that Orestes should not be condemned for his action.
So why do you ravage the land with your rancour?
Don't let your rage scorch all our fields cropless,
your dewfalls of acid shrivel the seedpods,
and I will make you the solemnest promise
that you shall be given a cavern for refuge
with glittering thronestools next to your godstones
held in great honour by all here assembled.

CHORUS.

You upstart gods
you've ridden down
the ancient laws,
snatched my honours
out of my hands.

My rancour's roused,
my heart will ooze
black venom out
over the land
until it's waste.

Bloodright! Bloodright!

Womb-blight, crop-blight,
the earth all scorched,
the people starving.

The people mock me.
My wrongs are too much.

Daughters of Night
degraded and crushed.

ATHENA.
>You're *not* dishonoured, so don't use your godhead
>to blast this country of mortals with earthblight.
>That would abuse your position as she-gods.
>I have access to Zeus, and what's more have access
>alone of all gods, to Zeus's munitions,
>the mighty high he-god's missiles of thunder!
>But this isn't a case for desperate deterrents.
>I'd rather you yielded to gentler persuasion.
>Take back your threats, don't spit spiteful poisons
>over the fruitcrops, so that harvests don't happen.
>Lull the black swell of your billowing bloodgrudge
>and have half of my honours here, half of my worship.
>The land's a broad land. It has people in plenty.
>As the Furies you'll be favoured with sacrificed firstfruits,
>propitiations preceding childbirth or bedbond.
>You'll only have praise then for my persuasions.

CHORUS.
>The ancient conscience
>pushed underground.
>The ancient conscience
>dishonoured, despised!
>
>My nostrils snort
>with rage at my shame.
>
>Terrible anguish
>bores under my ribs.
>
>Night! Mother!
>Listen! My cry!
>
>The new he-gods
>with their fouls in the ring
>have robbed me of honour
>making me nothing.

ATHENA.
>I'll allow you your anger since you are older.
>Your years in the world have given you wisdom
>and though yours may be greater, Zeus gave me insights.
>If you leave this land for an alien bloodclan's
>I tell you that you will learn to love this one.
>Time in its passage will honour my people,
>and you, enthroned by the shrine of Erechtheus,
>will get more in the way of rites and processions

from my men and women than from the rest of mankind.
On this land, my land, goad no one to bloodshed,
or let them strop their grudge on your whetstones,
our youth up in arms and drunk with aggression
battling like bantams in the strife between bloodkin.
Let them battle abroad if they need to gain glory.
I want no cocks fighting in my country's farmyard,
birds of a feather I forbid to do battle.

Such, if you'll have them, are the honours I offer.
For the good *you* do, good returns and good god-gifts,
a share in this country the gods above cherish.

CHORUS.
    The ancient conscience
    pushed underground.
    The ancient conscience
    dishonoured, despised.

    My nostrils snort
    with rage at my shame

    Terrible anguish
    bores under my ribs.

    Night! Mother!
    Listen! My cry!

    The new he-gods
    with their fouls in the ring
    have robbed me of honours
    making me nothing.

ATHENA.
    I'm making you offers which I'll go on repeating
    so that you'll never have any grounds for complaining
    that you, an old she-god, were spurned and dishonoured
    by me a young she-god, nor cast out by my people.
    But if you have any respect for Persuasion
    and feel its soothing charm as I'm speaking,
    and the linctus of language can placate you and lull you,
    you'll decide to remain. But if you don't want to
    it wouldn't be right to bring down on this city
    your grudge or your anger, or harm to the people,
    when you've been offered a share in the land here
    with a full portion of honour now and for ever.

1. CH. What kind of shrine did you say I'd possess?   ]
    ATH. One free from suffering. Will you say yes?

2. CH. And if I say yes what powers will I wield?   ]
    ATH. *You'll* make them flourish, flock, family and field.

3. CH. Would you entrust such powers to *me*?   ]
    ATH. Yes, and prosper the fortunes of each devotee.

4. CH. These powers, will you pledge they'll endure?   ]
    ATH. I'd make no offers if I weren't sure.

5. CH. You're beginning to charm me. My anger subsides.   ]
    ATH. Live in this land and win more friends besides.

6. CH. What charm for this land would you like me to chant?]
    ATH. Nothing where darkness is dominant.

ATHENA.
     Bring blessings from earth, sea-billows and sky.
     Let the wind warm the land as sun-filled sou'westers,
     let farm-fields and flocks always be fruitful
     and never fail folk who will farm them in future,
     and as the land prospers so will the people,
     especially those who give gifts to your godstones.
     Like a green-fingered gardener tending his garden
     I let the good grow, and nip the bad as it's budding.
     I see that the good's wants get well enough watered,
     protect their green life-lot from all blight and croprot.

     Your part's to prosper my people in peace-time,
     and mine, when the time comes for war-cries and weapons,
     is to make certain my city's triumphant.

CHORUS.
     I'll share in the homeland of Pallas Athena
     and not degrade a city
     that all powerful Zeus and Ares the War God
     make guardians of godstones,
     Greece's great glory.
     I pray the golden sun
     make the earth burst open,
     the ground gush with good life-gifts
     harvest after harvest.

ATHENA.
     I act on behalf of a people I cherish
     and instal among them these implacable spirits

whose province has been and is to manage mankind.
A man feels their onslaught but not where it comes from.
Crimes from the past get him hauled up before them.
And though he bursts his lungs with loud shouting
their silent grudge grinds him down into nothing.

CHORUS.

And no searing winds strip bare the orchards,
no scorching heat burn the new buds dry.
May Pan prosper the sheepfolds
doubling the increase at lambing
and Hermes of windfalls and godsends
disclose the rich streaks of silver

ATHENA.

Listen to what the Furies, the *Furies*, are pledging.
The Fury's a force both with the high he-gods
and with the powers beneath the earth's crust.
Anyone can see how they work among mortals –
one man's life-lot's as bright as a ballad,
another's life is one blinded with tears.

CHORUS.

I ban the death that descends too early
and cuts down a man who's barely reached manhood.

Grant good bed-bonds to girls that are graceful,
you she-gods of life-lot, sisters and she-kin,
both beings the offspring of one mother, Night.
You are present in every household,
at the family's feast-rites for death and delivery,
at the birth, and the death and the bedbond.
You are the most rightfully honoured of she-gods.

ATHENA.

These she-gods of all gods willing such good things!

How grateful I am that Persuasion was guiding
my tongue and my lips when they were resistant.
The Zeus of debates and assemblies presided
turning a battle to a debate about blessings,
the rivalry now only vying to bless best.

CHORUS.

May faction, sedition
for ever flesh-hungry,

civil disturbance,
cycles of slaying,
never bray in this city,
its dust never gulp
the blood of its people,
the state get ripped open
by the rages of bloodgrudge,
a chainlink of murder.
Let the linking be love-bonds,
common likes, common hatreds,
a group bond against
the troubles men suffer.

ATHENA.
   Listen!   They're learning to bless, groping for goodness.
   I foresee great future good in these fearful faces.
   If you show them the kindness they show you,
   your city's set fair on the straight road of justice.

CHORUS.
   Fare well, fare well, grow wealthy, grow great,
   fare well, citizens so close to Zeus,
   favourites of his favourite she-child.
   Under the wings of Athena grow wise
   with her father looking on you with favour.

ATHENA.
   Fare well to you too.   Now I'll lead the way
   to show you the chambers in the deep cavern
   by the light of the torches of those who'll escort you.
   Now, sped on your way by the savour of godsops
   go to your underground shrines in the rock hill
   and there keep what will harm Athens imprisoned
   and set free only what will help her to victory.
   Children of Cranaus, who reside on the rock-hill
   escort on their way these welcome guest-strangers,
   and give them the good will that they'll give to you.

CHORUS.
   Fare well, fare well, mortals, immortals,
   all of you here in the city of Pallas.
   Only give grace to your new guest-strangers
   and you'll never lack any luck in your life-lot.

ATHENA.
> I endorse all you pray for on behalf of my city.
> And now by the light of the blazing torch-beacons,
> I'll escort you to your underground chambers
> along with those who tend to my godstone,
> the flowers of Athens, once land of Theseus,
> the women of Athens, girls, mothers, old women,
> will come as a glorious group in procession.
> Drape our honoured guest-strangers in robes of deep sea-red
> and lead then with torchlight held up before you,
> so that these Furies, who turned out so kindly,
> will reside and show love, and bless Athens for ever.

PROCESSION OF WOMEN.
> Go to your home, children of Night,
> honoured with music and torchlight.

> *Silence while the Kind Ones pass.*

> Go to your home, underground and primeval
> honoured by sacrifice and libation.

> *Silence while the Kind Ones pass*

> Grave powers, gracious and kindly,
> attended by torches, follow us home.

> *Now echo our chorus, raise your own cry!*

> Peace between the Kind Ones and Athens!
> ZEUS/FATE, high he-god and she-god
> together helped all this to happen.

> *Now echo our chorus, raise your own cry!*

THE END

YAN TAN TETHERA (1983)

A Mechanical Pastoral

MUSIC: Harrison Birtwistle

YAN TAN TETHERA

Yan Tan Tethera was commissioned by BBC Television. It has the following characters:

SHEPHERD ALAN (bass/baritone)
HANNAH, his wife (soprano)
DAVIE & RAB, their twin sons (treble)
CALEB RAVEN (bass/baritone)
THE PIPER/THE BAD'UN (tenor)
JACK & DICK, the dark-haired twins (treble)

12 WOMEN & 1 MAN:
CHORUS of black-faced CHEVIOT SHEEP (Shepherd Alan's)
CHORUS of horned WILTSHIRE SHEEP (Caleb Raven's)
THE 'MUSIC' OF THE HILL

Total darkness. We hear the MUSIC *of the hill, which is composed of voices (12 female, 1 male). Slowly we see something like a sunrise but without the light. The hill rises slowly like a black sun over the horizon. We should feel it is actually a sunrise until half way over the horizon it stops, a round, unnatural looking hill, an ancient burial mound, such as one sees everywhere in the landscape of Wiltshire. From behind the round hill we should then see the "real" sunrise, and the scene is slowly revealed as the traditional "Arcadian" pastoral, green hill, bright blue sky, yellow sun. As the light increases the* MUSIC *of the hill becomes less audible, goes "underground". There are flecks of white on the green of the hill, chalk and flints, and occasional pieces of flint and chalk on the grass. At the foot of the hill is seated* SHEPHERD ALAN *with a Cheviot* RAM *and* EWE. *If the hill is to be imagined as a painted flat, or a decorative clock-face background, then it should be painted spring on one side and winter on the other, and its turning should show the passage of the seasons in a stylised fashion, like the mechanism of an intricate clock. In the distance we should see another mound on which stands the motionless silhouette of* CALEB RAVEN *and his herd of horned* WILTSHIRE SHEEP. *The two choruses of* SHEEP *can be doubled by using masks based on the features of the black-faced Cheviot sheep, and on the horned Wiltshire sheep respectively.*

When the seasons change, and the hill (or hills) turn the only constant should be the MUSIC *of the hill, which is the same voices as the two choruses of sheep.*

Each shepherd, ALAN *and* CALEB RAVEN, *has his "liberty", or his allotted portion of pasture, in this case the area of the respective burial mounds. When* SHEPHERD ALAN *is in the foreground we see* CALEB RAVEN *in the distance. When* CALEB RAVEN *is in the foreground, we see* SHEPHERD ALAN *in the distance. The distant figures should suggest silhouettes, or wooden figures. The effect of the two hills revolving with the figures of the shepherds and their distinctive sheep should be that of "weather men" figures in a peopled barometer, or like figures in an intricate clockpiece or those carved wooden figures from those moving German tableaux driven by small windmills and candle heat.*

The sheep could revolve with the hills as they turn, and change masks behind the hill and emerge as either the Cheviot sheep of ALAN *or the horned Wiltshire sheep of* CALEB RAVEN, *or remain behind the hill and be its* MUSIC. *The* MUSIC *of the hill should suggest its ancientness and mystery as a place of burial for the men who raised the*

*enormous sarsen stones. There should be one or two sarsen stones on
the scene.*

ALAN *is a newly arrived stranger from the North. He has arrived in
the downs with one* RAM *and one* EWE, *and they are having their firs
season on the downs.*

He indicates CALEB RAVEN *on the mound in the background.*

ALAN.
>I wave
>He never waves back.
>
>I wave
>He never waves back.
>He stands and looks black
>on that mound, Adam's grave.
>
>I came from t'North with one ewe and one ram
>and I don't care much for this place where I am,
>but the ram tupped the ewe and she's likely to lamb,
>likely to lamb any day,
>and though I long to go back
>along the old drovers' track
>back on the Pennine Way,
>away from these chalk downs and towering stones,
>back to rough crags and the Northern fells
>where the rocks are steep and the moor wind moans
>and sheep don't go round wearing bells . . .

*The hill begins to turn, and the figures freeze and revolve with the hill
like a clock mechanism.* SHEPHERD ALAN *and his* CHEVIOT EWE &
RAM *are now in the background as silhouettes on their mound. Now*
CALEB RAVEN *is in the foreground with his* CHORUS *of horned*
WILTSHIRE SHEEP, *where even the ewes have horns.*

CALEB RAVEN.
>He waves
>I never wave back.
>I stand and look black
>on this mound, Adam's grave.
>
>His sheep have black faces.
>For the chalk downs they're queer.
>His sheep have black faces.
>They don't belong here.

His sheep don't have bells.
All mine have bells.

The voices of the masked WILTSHIRE SHEEP *are like sheep-bells hung round their necks, so that the voice is like something loose from the body, but which is activated by bodily movement as a sheep-bell would be, so that each voice might have a characteristic rhythm or number of syllables. What the* CHORUS *utters here is in units of 13, the "unlucky number", which means that if we have 12 female voices (12* EWES) *and one male voice (*RAM) *there is one syllable per voice in each statement. The syllables could be broken down into smaller units, but probably not units of 3 (tethera) or 7 (lethera), the "lucky" or magic numbers. There should be a marked difference in vocal style, even if the voices are the same, between this* CHORUS, CALEB RAVEN's *herd of horned* WILTSHIRE SHEEP, *and* ALAN's CHORUS OF CHEVIOT SHEEP, *corresponding to the given fact that one set of sheep wears sheep-bells and the other doesn't.*

CHORUS OF HORNED WILTSHIRE SHEEP.
This is the sound of the bells folk hear in the valley . . .

SHEEP 1.
When I run with a dry throat to drink from the dewpond.

CHORUS.
This is the sound of the bells folk hear in the valley . . .

SHEEP 2.
When the thick grass of the downs is flooded with sunshine.

CHORUS.
This is the sound of the bells folk hear in the valley . . .

SHEEP 3.
When my hooves go slith'ring over the slipp'ry chalk slopes.

CHORUS.
This is the sound of the bells folk hear in the valley . . .

SHEEP 4. *(Ram.)*
When another ram's here and I jab my sharp horn in.

CHORUS.
This is the sound of the bells folk hear in the valley . . .

SHEEP 5. *(Ram.)*
When I've picked on a fine ewe that I fancy for tupping.

CHORUS.
>This is the sound of the bells folk hear in the valley . . .

SHEEP 6.
>When the ewe that the ram tupped 's later in labour.

CHORUS.
>This is the sound of the bells folk hear in the valley . . .

SHEEP 7.
>When the flock senses something or somebody scary.

CHORUS.
>This is the sound of the bells folk hear in the valley . . .

SHEEP 8.
>When I'm stopped in my tracks when I run with his leg-crook.

CHORUS.
>This is the sound of the bells folk hear in the valley . . .

SHEEP 9.
>When the flock all gets penned for the sheep-fair or shearing.

CHORUS.
>This is the sound of the bells folk hear in the valley . . .

SHEEP 10.
>When the buzzards tear the guts of a newly dropped lamb out.

CHORUS.
>This is the sound of the bells folk hear in the valley . . .

SHEEP 11.
>When they come in a pile on a cart back from market!

Pause in which SHEEP *register the fact of their death.*

CHORUS.
>This is the sound of the bells folk hear in the valley . . .

SHEEP 12.
>When Caleb Raven, our shepherd, trysts with the Bad'un.

CHORUS.
>This is the sound of the bells folk hear in the valley . . .

SHEEP 13.
>When our greedy shepherd sticks his crook in the gravemound.

The sound of the bells here should remind us of the MUSIC *of the hill.*

CALEB RAVEN. (*To audience.*)
> I'll tell you a secret that you'd better keep –
> I stole the church bell from the village steeple
> and melted it down for the bells on my sheep.
> I like sheep better than people.
>
> The other secret's one I won't share,
> that's the reason I'm poking this mound,
> here on the chalkdowns everywhere,
> there's graves full of gold underground.

CALEB RAVEN *pokes with his crook into three places in the mound. These are the three places, where with the help of the* BAD'UN, *he will later find gold artefacts. But now he finds nothing.*

CHORUS OF HORNED WILTSHIRE SHEEP.
> This is the sound of the bells folk hear in the valley
> when our greedy shepherd sticks his crook in the gravemound.

CALEB RAVEN *pokes in the ground with his crook. His probes and thrusts become like a dance.*

The figures freeze once more and the hills revolve like a clock mechanism. CALEB RAVEN *becomes a silhouette on his mound in the distance,* SHEPHERD ALAN *is in the foreground, this time with two sheep more than his original* RAM *and* EWE.

ALAN.
> My sheep have no bells.
> All his have bells.
>
> The music I hear 's a Northern air
> some piper plays to remind me
> of how I'm not happy and how my heart's
> not very content in these foreign parts.
>
> I know there's a piper but don't know where,
> the tune always comes from behind me.

We see THE PIPER *in a hat, and hear him play a Northern air.* ALAN *turns and* THE PIPER *vanishes.*

ALAN.
> I know there's a piper but don't know where,
> the tune always comes from behind me.
>
> And when I hear that piper play,
> I think of the North, and don't want to stay,

though my flock's growing bigger each day . . .

ALAN *begins to count his sheep. We need not see the sheep he counts.*

ALAN.

>   Yan, Tan, Tethera,
>   Methera,
>   Pimp,
>   Sethera, Lethera,
>   Hovera,
>   Dovera,
>   Dik!

>   I think of the North, and I don't want to stay,
>   though my flock's growing bigger each day.

(*Counts again.*)	CHORUS OF CHEVIOT SHEEP.
Yan Dik, Tan Dik,	(*Counting themselves off*
Tethera Dik,	*in units of 3 or 7.*)
Methera Dik,	Yan, Tan, Tethera . . .
Bumfit,	Yan, Tan, Tethera . . .
Yan a Bumfit,	Yan, Tan, Tethera . . .
Tan a Bumfit,	*or*
Tethera Bumfit,	Yan, Tan, Tethera,
Methera Bumfit,	Methera,
Jiggit!	Pimp, Sethera, Lethera . . .
	etc.

>   *Yan, Tan, Tethera,*
>   1-2-3
>   *Sweet Trinity*
>   *Keep*
>   *Me and my sheep.*

>   Stuff my ears with earth and clay
>   so I can't hear the piper play.

We hear THE PIPER *play the Northern air, and* ALAN *begins to follow the sound.*

ALAN.

>   I know there's a piper but don't know where,
>   the tune always comes from behind me.

>   When I hear that piper play
>   I think of the North, and I don't want to stay,
>   though my flock's growing bigger each day.

And I've taken a wife as my flock grew
to all these I've got now from one ram and one ewe,
and to that wife I shall have to stay true.

My flock and my wife are my reasons for staying
though the phantom piper never stops playing.

And my wife's about to lamb,
so I'm staying where I am.

THE PIPER *plays the air, and against the tune of the piper that draws*
ALAN *away, he sings the Northern Shepherds' charm again.*

ALAN.
Yan, Tan, Tethera,
1-2-3
Sweet Trinity
Keep
Us and our sheep.

Stuff my ears with earth and clay
so I can't hear the piper play.

Enter HANNAH, *clearly pregnant, with bread and a jug of cider.*

HANNAH.
Bread, bread, bread,
cider and bread,
bread and cider,
I feared, I feared, I feared that you'd fled,
fled from your wife with twins inside her,
fled to the North with that tune in your head.

Where will you be when I'm brought to bed
far from your wife, or beside her?
I feared, I feared, I feared that you'd fled.

The more my belly began to swell
the more I began to take fright
at shadows in the grass
that seem as you pass
to want to clutch you tight,
at things that prowl about at night
like the Bad'un who stole our church bell
like the Bad'un who stole our church bell
and carried it off to clang in hell.

When I'm nearer my time
I won't be able to climb
up the downs to be with you
or bring you your cider and your bread –
and where will you be when I'm brought to bed?

You'd wait all night with your ewes while they lamb
but about your own babies you don't give a damn.
If you don't care for the sons that I carry
you shouldn't have been in a hurry to marry.
You'd care for me more if I were a ewe
and I *would* be a sheep if it made you care
but I tell you that there are two in there,
but I tell you that I'm carrying two.

And it's harder to climb up here with two
and when I get nearer my time
I won't be able to climb
up the downs to be with you
or bring you your cider and your bread –
O where will you be when I'm brought to bed?
When the time comes round to give birth to these two
how can I run through the night to you?

And the sun goes down behind the mound,
the sun burrows back deep under the ground
and then the night comes and the slightest sound
makes me shiver and quiver with fright
at shadows in the grass
that seem as you pass
to want to clutch you tight,
at things that prowl about the night
like the Bad'un who stole the church bell
like the Bad'un who stole the church bell
and carried it off to clang in hell.

ALAN.
Bread and cider, cider and bread
won't seem so tasty when we're dead.

Bread and cider can't refresh
a corpse's decomposing flesh.

The church here's fallen into decay
since the Bad'un stole the bell away.
How can you toll the faithful to pray?

How can you bury the dead with no bell?
All we have now to keep the Bad'un away
is the old Northern shepherds' spell,
a spell any child could learn to say,
a charm any child could chant to keep
the darkness, the demons, the devil at bay,
away from us, our farm, and our sheep,
if we would always pray:

Yan, Tan, Tethera,
1-2-3
Sweet Trinity
Keep
Us and our sheep.

HANNAH. (*Following and singing as she learns.*)
Yan, Tan, Tethera,
1-2-3
Sweet Trinity
Keep
Us and our sheep.

ALAN & HANNAH.
Yan, Tan, Tethera,
1-2-3
Sweet Trinity
Keep
Us and our sheep.

Exit the pregnant HANNAH *with empty basket and cider jug. As she departs* ALAN *sings again the Shepherds' Charm and it is picked up like an echo by the receding voice of* HANNAH.

ALAN.
Yan, Tan, Tethera,
1-2-3
Sweet Trinity
Keep
Us and our sheep.

Bread and cider, cider and bread
won't seem so tasty when we're dead.

Bread and cider can't refresh
a corpse's decomposing flesh.

ALAN *begins to count sheep again.*
CALEB RAVEN *watches him unobserved.*

<table>
<tr><td>

ALAN.

Yan, Tan, Tethera,
Methera,
Pimp,
Sethera, Lethera,
Hovera,
Dovera,
DIK!
(*Pause.*)
Yan Dik, Tan Dik,
Tethera Dik,
Methera Dik,
Bumfit,
Yan a Bumfit,
Tethera Bumfit,
Methera Bumfit,
Jiggit.

Yan, Tan, Tethera,
1-2-3
Sweet Trinity
Keep
Us and our sheep.

</td><td>

CHORUS OF CHEVIOT SHEEP.

(*Counting themselves off*
in 3s and 7s.)
Yan, Tan, Tethera . . .
Yan, Tan, Tethera . . .
Yan, Tan, Tethera . . .
or
Yan, Tan, Tethera,
Methera,
Pimp,
Sethera, Lethera . . .
etc.

</td></tr>
</table>

On 1-2-3 of this refrain we begin to hear CALEB RAVEN *starting to count his own flock in conventional numerals. As* ALAN *sings the refrain he takes a piece of chalk or flint from the left pocket of his smock and puts it into his right, to mark the first score.*

CALEB RAVEN *counts quickly and competitively. The conflict of the two sets of numerals becomes a duet between* ALAN *and* CALEB RAVEN, *though neither one addresses the other. Both mounds might begin to revolve at this point, the mound of* ALAN *turning clockwise and the mound of* CALEB RAVEN *turning anticlockwise. The figures of the respective sheep,* CHEVIOT *and* WILTSHIRE *should go round with the revolving mound in a continuous procession. The turning of the mounds might also pass through the changing seasons, and the whole have the movement and immobility of a mechanical device.* CALEB'S *counting should stress the number 13 and its multiples: 13, 26, 39. If possible musically* ALAN'S *numerals might break up into 3s and 7s.*

CALEB RAVEN.
    1-2-3-4-5-6-
    7-8-9-10-11-12-
    THIRTEEN-
    14-15-16-17-18-19-
    20-21-22-23-24-25-
    TWENTY-SIX . . .

ALAN.	CALEB RAVEN.
Yan, Tan, Tethera,	(*Gloating at each unit of 13.*)
Methera,	27-28-29-30-31-32-
Pimp,	33-34-35-36-37-38-
Sethera, Lethera,	THIRTY-NINE . . .
Hovera, Dovera,	
DIK!	

ALAN.	CALEB RAVEN.
Yan Dik, Tan Dik,	40-41-42-43-44-45-
Tethera Dik,	46-47-48-49-50-51-
Methera Dik,	FIFTY-TWO . . .
Bumfit,	(*etc.*)
Yan a Bumfit,	
Tan a Bumfit,	
Tethera Bumfit,	
Methera Bumfit,	
Jiggit . . .	

Finally the duet should end with ALAN *having more sheep than* CALEB
RAVEN. CALEB RAVEN'*s counting could almost be like a Gilbert and
Sullivan "patter song" until he is left breathless and finally over-
taken by* ALAN. *We might also, during the turning of the mounds
through the seasons, only hear the* MUSIC *of the hill, with the
counting interrupted and only resumed when we actually can see the
two shepherds.* ALAN'*s scoring finally becomes dominant and in the
end we only see and hear him and his sheep. His* CHORUS *of* CHEVIOT
SHEEP *support his scoring by counting themselves off in units of 3
(Yan, Tan, Tethera, etc).*

ALAN.
    I think of the North and I don't want to stay
    though my flock's growing bigger each day.
    Stuff my ears with earth and clay
    so I can't hear the piper play.

We see and hear the mysterious PIPER.

> I know there's a piper but don't know where
> the tune always comes from behind me.

PIPER *disappears.*

ALAN.
> Men say that his pipe's made of finger bones
> that come from the dead who lie under these stones,
> these enormous, enormous sarsen stones.
>
> Some of 'em must weigh nigh on fifty ton,
> you'd need a 100 yoke of oxen just to drag one –
>
> His pipe is made of their finger bones.
> I know there's a piper but don't know where.
> His tune always comes from behind me.

ALAN'*s mound begins to recede into the background and* CALEB'*s to come into the foreground.*

CALEB RAVEN.
> The Northman who pastures the opposite hill,
> his stock increases and mine stands still.
>
> The way he counts is some sort of spell.
> Maybe he's got help from the Bad'un as well.

Exit CALEB RAVEN.

CHORUS OF HORNED WILTSHIRE SHEEP.
> This is the sound of the bells folk hear in the valley
> when Caleb Raven, our shepherd, trysts with the Bad'un.

We hear the sound of THE PIPER *playing his air, and we see* ALAN *following the sound.* THE PIPER *lures* ALAN *away.* THE PIPER *disappears. Enter* THE PIPER *playing a different air, perhaps related to the* MUSIC *of the hill.*

Enter CALEB RAVEN.

CALEB RAVEN. (*To the Piper.*)
> So why do you let this Northman succeed,
> let my ewes sicken and his flock breed?
>
> He chants some spell, and his flock grows.
> I suppose you taught him it. It goes:
>
> *Yan, Tan, Tethera . . .*

As soon as CALEB RAVEN *says these words,* THE PIPER *begins to spin round and round on the spot, and his hat falls off revealing a pair of horns.* THE PIPER *is the* BAD'UN. *He spins round giddily and disappears.* CALEB RAVEN *is left alone, puzzled, with the* MUSIC *of the hill.* THE BAD'UN *returns breathless, dizzy and annoyed.*

THE BAD'UN.
Tethera, Tan, Yan, 3 add 10
don't ever sing that song again!

Thirteen! Thirteen! 2 and 11
keep me safe from the power of Heaven.

CALEB RAVEN.
He's taken the woman I wanted to wed,
that's why I want the Northman dead.
I want his Hannah for my bed.

THE BAD'UN.
As I helped you steal the church bell
I'll rid you of the Northman as well.
My pipe will spirit your rival away
and the twins his Hannah will bear
will likewise vanish into thin air.
Then you can swoop down on your prey.

CALEB RAVEN.
Once I have the Northman's sheep and wife
all I need to complete my life
is the red gold that decks the bones
stretched out beneath these sarsen stones.
If I had the gold that's under our feet
then I could say that my life's complete.

THE BAD'UN. (*Pointing to a spot in the mound.*)
Thirteen! Thirteen! You're in luck!
Poke the mound there with your shepherd's crook!

CALEB RAVEN *pokes his crook into the mound and finds a bracelet, or some other artefact of gold.*

THE BAD'UN. (*Pointing to another spot in the mound.*)
Thirteen! Thirteen! You're in luck!
Poke that mound there with your shepherd's crook.

CALEB RAVEN *pokes his crook into the mound and finds a gold brooch.*

THE BAD'UN. (*Pointing to another spot in the mound.*)
>   Thirteen! Thirteen! You're in luck!
>   Poke that mound there with your shepherd's crook.

CALEB RAVEN *pokes his crook into the mound and finds a gold ring.*

CALEB RAVEN & THE BAD'UN.
>   Thirteen! Thirteen!
>   Eleven and two . . .

CALEB RAVEN.
>   This ring from the grave
>   weds the ram to the ewe.

CALEB RAVEN & THE BAD'UN.
>   Thirteen! Thirteen!
>   Ten and three . . .

CALEB RAVEN.
>   With this ring from the grave
>   she'll marry me.

CALEB RAVEN & THE BAD'UN.
>   Thirteen! Thirteen!
>   Four and nine . . .

CALEB RAVEN.
>   With this ring from the grave
>   the plump ewe's all mine.

CALEB RAVEN & THE BAD'UN.
>   Thirteen! Thirteen!
>   Three and ten . . .

CALEB RAVEN.
>   With this ring from the grave
>   she'll grow fat in my pen.

CALEB RAVEN & THE BAD'UN.
>   Thirteen! Thirteen!
>   Thirteen and nought . . .

CALEB RAVEN.
>   With this ring from the grave
>   my catch will be caught.

The BAD'UN *replaces his hat and as* THE PIPER *begins to play the Northern air,* CALEB RAVEN *leaves.*

Enter ALAN *following the air on the pipe.*

ALAN.
>*Yan, Tan, Tethera*
>*1-2-3*
>*Sweet Trinity*
>*Keep*
>*Us and our sheep.*

Now THE PIPER *begins to spin on the spot as* ALAN *sings the Shepherds' Charm. The movement and figures should once more suggest the changeable tableau of an intricate clock mechanism. Whenever* ALAN *stops singing* THE PIPER *plays. When* ALAN *sings,* THE PIPER *spins on the spot, his posture frozen in one position. We see* THE PIPER *and* ALAN *alternately until finally* THE PIPER*'s air proves too much for* ALAN, *and* ALAN *disappears.*

Re-enter THE PIPER/BAD'UN *triumphant. He plays the Northern air until it gradually changes into the* MUSIC *of the hill (to which* ALAN*'s voice now belongs). The hill revolves and the* MUSIC *of the hill becomes louder and louder, then quieter and quieter, as the scene darkens.*

As the light grows again we see HANNAH, *now in a very advanced stage of pregnancy, staring at* ALAN*'s crook sticking out of the mound. (The shepherd crooks of* CALEB RAVEN *and* ALAN *should be distinctive so that we could recognise the shadow of either by the bend of his crook.)*

HANNAH *searches for* ALAN, *following the patterns of his disappearance but always returning to the crook sticking out of the mound. The movement again is like a figure in a mechanism until she returns to the crook. She takes the crook out of the ground, and as she does so we hear the* MUSIC *of the hill.*

HANNAH.
>*Yan, Tan, Tethera,*
>*1-2-3*
>*Sweet Trinity*
>*Keep*
>*Me and my sheep.*

HANNAH*'s labour pains begin. She takes off the shawl she is wearing and performs the old country charm for lessening labour pains, by passing the shawl through the hole in the sarsen stone.*

HANNAH.
> Sarsen stone, sarsen stone over the dead
> lessen my labour when I'm brought to bed.
> Sarsen stone, sarsen stone, old Adam's tomb,
> lessen my labour when I empty my womb.

As HANNAH's *labour pains increase we hear the air of* THE PIPER/ BAD'UN, *and* HANNAH *becomes frightened of bearing her twins alone on the darkening downs.*

HANNAH.
> *Yan, Tan, Tethera,*
> 1-2-3
> *Sweet Trinity*
> *Keep*
> *Me and my sheep.*

As she sings the above, broken by labour pains, the sound of THE PIPER/BAD'UN *stops and starts. First the 'Yan, Tan, Tethera' Shepherds' Charm, then* THE PIPER/BAD'UN's *air becomes dominant. Then we see* THE PIPER/BAD'UN *emerge from behind the sarsen stone carrying two small bundles. Darkness grows and the* MUSIC *of the hill becomes louder and louder, then subsides.*

As the light grows we see CALEB RAVEN's *silhouette with his* CHORUS *of* HORNED WILTSHIRE SHEEP.

CHORUS OF WILTSHIRE SHEEP.
> This is the sound of the bells folk hear in the valley
> when the flock senses something or somebody scary.

CALEB RAVEN *deposits at the foot of the mound, where* ALAN & HANNAH *stand to look after the sheep, the three artefacts of gold he discovered with the aid of* THE BAD'UN. *They are gifts of gold to impress* HANNAH. *He wants his gifts discovered and accepted. He is about to hide when his* CHORUS OF WILTSHIRE SHEEP *scatter.*

CHORUS OF WILTSHIRE SHEEP.
> This is the sound of the bells folk hear in the valley
> when the flock senses something or somebody scary.

CALEB RAVEN *pursues his sheep, leaving bracelet, brooch and ring at the foot of the mound for* HANNAH *to find.*

As the CHORUS OF WILTSHIRE SHEEP *exit they change masks and become* HANNAH's CHORUS OF CHEVIOT SHEEP. *Enter* CHEVIOT SHEEP *followed by* HANNAH *now her normal size. She adopts the attitude of* ALAN *watching over the sheep. We see* CALEB RAVEN *in the distance, a silhouette on his mound.*

HANNAH. (*Indicating Caleb.*)
    He waves.
    I never wave back.
    He waves.
    I never wave back.
    (*Looks at brooch, bracelet, and ring at the foot of the mound.*)
    He sends me these things,
    these brooches and pins,
    these twisted gold rings –
    I grieve for my twins
    ONE year gone away.

CHEVIOT SHEEP. (*Echoing ONE.*)
    YAN!

HANNAH.
    Each day
    I pray:
    Yan, Tan, Tethera,
    1-2-3
    Sweet Trinity
    Keep
    Me and my sheep.

At this refrain we see CALEB RAVEN *spin on his mound.*

HANNAH.
    He pokes with his crook
    into each ancient mound.
    I won't even look
    at the stuff that he's found –
    I mourn my ill-luck
    and my loves underground
    TWO years underground.

CHEVIOT SHEEP. (*Echoing TWO.*)
    YAN! TAN!

HANNAH.
>I grieve for my twins
>THREE years underground!

CHEVIOT SHEEP. (*Echoing THREE.*)
>YAN! TAN! TETHERA!

HANNAH.
>*Yan, Tan, Tethera,*
>*1-2-3*
>*Sweet Trinity*
>*Keep*
>*Me and my sheep.*
>
>I grieve for my twins
>FOUR years gone away.

CHEVIOT SHEEP. (*Echoing FOUR.*)
>YAN, TAN, TETHERA,
>METHERA!

HANNAH.
>I grieve for my twins
>FIVE years gone away.

CHEVIOT SHEEP. (*Echoing FIVE.*)
>YAN, TAN, TETHERA!
>METHERA!
>PIMP!

HANNAH.
>I grieve for my twins
>SIX years gone away.

CHEVIOT SHEEP. (*Echoing SIX.*)
>YAN! TAN! TETHERA!
>METHERA!
>PIMP!
>SETHERA!

HANNAH.
>I grieve for my man
>SEVEN years underground.
>
>I grieve for my twins
>SEVEN years gone away.

CHEVIOT SHEEP. (*Echoing SEVEN.*)
   YAN! TAN! TETHERA!
   METHERA!
   PIMP!
   SETHERA! LETHERA! . . . LETHERA . . . LETHERA . . .

HANNAH.	CHEVIOT SHEEP.
Yan, Tan, Tethera	YAN, TAN, TETHERA
1-2-3	METHERA!
Sweet Trinity	PIMP!
Keep	SETHERA! LETHERA!
Me and my sheep.	

   Will we ever be
   together a-
   gain?
   (*Indicating Caleb Raven who is beginning to draw near.*)
   He waves.
   I never wave back.

Enter CALEB RAVEN *who picks up the artefacts* HANNAH *has ignored, and puts them away except for the ring which he brandishes at* HANNAH.

CALEB RAVEN. (*To audience.*)
   Thirteen! Thirteen!
   13 and nought,
   with this ring from the grave
   my catch will be caught.
   (*To Hannah, approaching her.*)
   Thirteen! Thirteen!
   13 and none,
   take this ring from the grave.
   Your husband has gone.

As CALEB RAVEN *approaches* HANNAH, *she and the* CHEVIOT SHEEP *begin lto sing the Northern Shepherds' Charm.*

HANNAH.	CHEVIOT SHEEP.
Yan, Tan, Tethera,	YAN! TAN! TETHERA!
1-2-3	METHERA!
Sweet Trinity	PIMP!
Keep	SETHERA! LETHERA! . . .
Me and my sheep.	

As they sing CALEB RAVEN *begins to spin and exits twisting round and round.*

When HANNAH *and the* CHEVIOT SHEEP *stop singing,* CALEB RAVEN *hesitantly re-enters and tries again.*

CALEB RAVEN.
>   Thirteen! Thirteen!
>   13 and none,
>   take this ring from the grave.
>   Your husband has gone.

HANNAH.
>   *Yan, Tan, Tethera,*
>   1-2-3
>   *Sweet Trinity*
>   *Keep*
>   *Me and my sheep.*

CHEVIOT SHEEP.
>   YAN! TAN! TETHERA!
>   METHERA!
>   PIMP!
>   SETHERA! LETHERA!

>   I grieve for my twins
>   SEVEN years gone away.

CALEB RAVEN *once more exits spinning. When* HANNAH *and* CHEVIOT SHEEP *stop singing,* CALEB RAVEN *enters again, but this time he has with him two twin boys with dark hair,* JACK & DICK. *He has clearly ill-treated them.* HANNAH *is about to sing 'Yan, Tan, Tethera' at him, when she pauses, struck with pity for the boys, although she has already realised they are not her own. Her instinct is to protect them.*

CALEB RAVEN.
>   Thirteen! Thirteen!
>   THIRTEEN and nought,
>   these are your twins
>   that you have long sought.

HANNAH.
>   The locks of those two
>   have too dark a hue.
>   My twins had hair
>   that was very fair,
>   but I'll take them in care
>   to save them from you.
>   I'll take them in care
>   to save them from you.

As soon as JACK & DICK *realise that* HANNAH *has accepted them, they rush to her side, take a hand each, then sing defiantly at* CALEB RAVEN:

JACK & DICK. (*Singing together as twins.*)
> 13! 13! minus ten
> now we are 1-2-3
> *yan, tan, tethera*
> which makes us free
> of such evil men,
> and makes us together a
> force to flout thee!

HANNAH/JACK & DICK. (*Counting themselves.*)
> *Yan, Tan, Tethera,*
> 1-2-3
> *Sweet Trinity*
> *Keep*
> *Us and our sheep.*

Exit CALEB RAVEN *spinning wildly.*

JACK & DICK.
> We will be seven tomorrow.

HANNAH.
> My twins would be seven tomorrow.

JACK & DICK.
> You'll have them back tomorrow at dawn
> seven years to the minute that they were born.

HANNAH/JACK & DICK.
> *Yan, Tan, Tethera,*
> 1-2-3
> *Sweet Trinity*
> *Keep*
> *Us and our sheep.*

CHEVIOT SHEEP.
> YAN! TAN! TETHERA!
> METHERA!
> PIMP!
> SETHERA! LETHERA . . .

Night falls, and when the new day is not very far from dawning we see JACK & DICK *hand in hand before the mound.* HANNAH *stands apart watching.* JACK & DICK *kneel and make the sign of the cross, then begin to walk/dance round the mound. The sheep are now behind the hill and are its* MUSIC. JACK & DICK *go round the mound seven times clockwise, counting as they go. At each turn the* MUSIC *of the hill grows louder and louder.*

JACK & DICK. (*Counting each turn.*)
> YAN! TAN! TETHERA!
> METHERA!
> PIMP!
> SETHERA! LETHERA!

On LETHERA *the* MUSIC *of the hill is at its loudest, and the hill opens and out come two fair-haired boys,* HANNAH's *twins,* DAVIE & RAB. *Along with them comes the* RAM *and the* EWE *that* ALAN *first brought with him from the North.*

HANNAH.
> My twins! My twins! Yes, those are they
> and they are exactly *seven* today.

RAM & EWE.
> (*Counting Hannah, Jack & Dick, Davie & Rab and themselves.*)
> Yan, Tan, Tethera, Methera, Pimp, Sethera, Lethera!

HANNAH.
> But where is their father who was stolen away?

RAM & EWE.
> Yan, Tan, Tethera, Methera, Pimp, Sethera, Lethera!

JACK & DICK.
> Lethera! Lethera! Keeps us from ill.

DAVIE & RAB. (*Also singing together as twins.*)
> Our father, our father's shut fast in the hill.
> Our father, our father's shut away still.
> Our father's been with us all these seven years.

RAM & EWE.
> Yan, Tan, Tethera, Methera, Pimp, Sethera, Lethera!

HANNAH.
> Your father's been gone from me seven whole years.

JACK & DICK.
> Tomorrow will bring an end to your tears.

Exit JACK & DICK, HANNAH *and* DAVIE & RAB. *Exit* RAM & EWE. *Enter* CHORUS OF WILTSHIRE SHEEP *followed by* CALEB RAVEN.

WILTSHIRE SHEEP.
> This is the sound of the bells folk hear in the valley
> when Caleb Raven, our shepherd, trysts with the Bad'un.

Exit CHORUS OF WILTSHIRE SHEEP *to become the* MUSIC *of the hill.*

CALEB RAVEN.
>   I know these ancient gravemounds hold
>   untold fortunes in silver and gold.
>   Once I've got 'em I can go away
>   and leave the Bad'un behind me
>   and go where he'll never find me.

Enter JACK & DICK. CALEB RAVEN *hides, and watches to find out the secret of opening the mound.* JACK & DICK *make the sign of the cross. They go round the mound 3 times clockwise. The* MUSIC *of the hill is louder still, and grows louder with each turn.*

JACK & DICK. (*Counting as they go on each turn.*)
>   Yan! Tan! Tethera!

On TETHERA *the hill opens and out comes* ALAN *carrying the church bell, which is now coated in gold. The "mechanism" is now at its most elaborate, and the clockpiece works with mechanical intricacy.* ALAN *holds the bell out and one by one the voices that were the* MUSIC *of the hill enter as* CHEVIOT SHEEP. *They come to greet their long lost shepherd, in formal procession of groups of 3. They strike the gilded church bell as they pass. The chimes come in groups of threes and* JACK & DICK *count them as they occur 1-2-3.*

JACK & DICK. (*Counting each set of chimes.*)
>   Yan! Tan! Tethera!

Exit CHEVIOT SHEEP *followed by* ALAN *and* JACK & DICK. CALEB RAVEN *who has watched all this from the shadows now emerges.*

CALEB RAVEN.
>   Now for the red gold that decks the bones
>   stretched out beneath these sarsen stones.

He begins to imitate the ritual of JACK & DICK *for opening the mound. But he does not remember to make the sign of the cross, and he goes round the mound widdershins (anti-clockwise). He goes round the mound THIRTEEN times counting with some difficulty each time he goes round.*

CALEB RAVEN.
>   Yan . . . Tan . . . Tethera . . .
>   (*Pause. Nothing happens. He continues.*)
>   . . . Methera . . . Pimp . . . Sethera . . . Lethera . . .
>   (*Pause. Nothing happens. He continues.*)

Hovera . . . Dovera . . . Dik . . . Yan Dik . . . Tan Dik . . .
TETHERA DIK!

The MUSIC *of the hill grows louder and louder, almost deafening, and on* TETHERA DIK *the hill opens,* CALEB RAVEN *rushes inside, and the hill closes on him with a snap. We hear* CALEB RAVEN *calling and falling, the voice growing fainter and fainter but not inaudible, and we hear it from this point to the end of the piece.*

VOICE OF CALEB RAVEN.
    Tethera Dik . . . Tethera Dik . . . Tethera Dik . . . Tethera Dik
    Tethera Dik . . . Tethera Dik . . . Tethera Dik . . . Tethera Dik

We go on hearing this until the end of the piece, louder or softer. CALEB RAVEN'*s voice is now the only one providing the* MUSIC *of the hill. Enter* ALAN, HANNAH, JACK & DICK, DAVIE & RAB *and* CHEVIOT SHEEP. *They see* CALEB RAVEN'*s crook sticking out of the same spot as* ALAN'*s crook previously.*

ALAN/HANNAH/JACK & DICK/ DAVIE & RAB.	CHEVIOT SHEEP.
Yan, Tan, Tethera,	YAN! TAN! TETHERA!
1-2-3	YAN! TAN! TETHERA!
Sweet Trinity	YAN! TAN! TETHERA!
Keep	YAN! TAN! TETHERA!
Us and our sheep.	YAN! TAN! TETHERA!

VOICE OF CALEB RAVEN.
    Tethera Dik . . . Tethera Dik . . .
    Tethera Dik . . . Tethera Dik . . .

ALAN/HANNAH/JACK & DICK/ DAVIE & RAB.	CHEVIOT SHEEP.
Yan, Tan, Tethera	YAN! TAN! TETHERA!
1-2-3	YAN! TAN! TETHERA!
Sweet Trinity	YAN! TAN! TETHERA!
Keep	YAN! TAN! TETHERA!
Us and our sheep.	YAN! TAN! TETHERA!

VOICE OF CALEB RAVEN.
    Tethera Dik . . . Tethera Dik . . . Tethera Dik . . . Tethera Dik . . .
    Tethera Dik . . . Tethera Dik . . . Tethera Dik . . .

An elaborate tableau formed with the hills turning from summer to winter and back, etc.

ALAN.

When you're out on the downs alone	HANNAH ET AL.
and low clouds blacken the sky	Yan, Tan, Tethera
you can hear beneath that mound a moan	Yan, Tan, Tethera
like a damned soul's tortured cry.	Yan, Tan, Tethera
	Yan, Tan, Tethera

You may shelter behind a sarsen stone	Yan, Tan, Tethera
to keep out of the wind and the rain	Yan, Tan, Tethera
and the wind drops and you hear the sound	Yan, Tan, Tethera
like a man being tortured under the ground	Yan, Tan, Tethera
and you hear the eternally repeated pain	Yan, Tan, Tethera
of his eternally repeated refrain . . .	Yan, Tan, Tethera

VOICE OF CALEB RAVEN.
  Tethera Dik!

ALAN.
  These Wiltshire mounds are the mammoth muck-heaps
  of a maddened man-mole who never sleeps . . .

  There comes from the depths a muffled voice
  the weight of the earth makes hoarse and thick,
  you hear from the depths an agonised voice
  for ever stuck at . . .

ALAN/HANNAH/JACK & DICK/DAVIE & RAB/CHEVIOT SHEEP.
  Yan, Tan, Tethera, Methera, Pimp,
  Sethera, Lethera, Hovera, Dovera, DIK,
  Yan Dik, Tan Dik . . .

ALAN.
  For ever stuck at . . .

ALL.
  TETHERA DIK!

VOICE OF CALEB RAVEN.
  (*From under the ground like an echo.*)
  TETHERA DIK!

ALL.
  He goes on falling . . .
  He goes on calling . . .

VOICE OF CALEB RAVEN.
  TETHERA DIK!

*The voice begins to grow fainter. Darkness grows. We hear the
newly restored church bell chime 3 times.*

CHEVIOT SHEEP.
    This is the sound
    folk hear in the valley
    when the church has its bell
    and the Bad'un that plagued them's
    been packed back to hell . . .

Bell chimes once.

ALL.
    YAN!

Bell chimes a second time.

ALL.
    TAN!

Bell chimes a third time.

ALL.
    TETHERA!

VOICE OF CALEB RAVEN.
    (*From under the ground.*)
    (TETHERA) DIK!

Darkness.

THE BIG H (1984)
A Music Drama

MUSIC: Dominic Muldowney

'*What a strain it is to be evil*' – BERTOLT BRECHT

THE BIG H

The Big H was first performed on BBC 2 Television on 26 December 1984 with the following cast:

MATHS TEACHER	Barrie Rutter
HISTORY TEACHER	June Watson
GEOGRAPHY TEACHER	James Carter

and from Woodkirk High School, Tingley, Yorkshire:

THE BOYS	THE GIRLS
Michael Day	Andrea Cholmondeley
Simon Smith	Paula Yeoman
Timothy McArdle	Cheryl Green
Damon Evans	Amanda Waugh
Jason Fountain	Julie Cliffe
Martin West	Joanne Hall
Philip Grimes	Sarah Squire
Neil Hargreaves	Amanda Trowsdale
Dennis Pinchen	Gillian Curtin
Michael Dunn	Lisa Jarvis
Mark Tyson	Andrea Shales
Simon Goodson	Joanne Madarasz
Matthew Haslam	Lara Thompson
Jason Nowell	Louise Close

MUSICAL DIRECTOR	Dominic Muldowney
SAXOPHONES	John Harle
	Tim Payne
	Dave Roach
	Glen Martin
PERCUSSIN	John Harrod
	Tony Wagstaff
ORGAN	Mark Hamlyn
PRODUCER	Andree Molyneux
DIRECTORS	Bill Hayes
	Jeremy Ancock
DESIGNERS	Stuart Walker
	Raymond Cusick
MAKE-UP DESIGNER	Elaine Smith
COSTUME DESIGNER	Nicholas Rocker

PRODUCTION MANAGER	Vivien Rosenz
PRODUCTION ASSISTANTS	Marissa Cowell
	Thelma Helsby
ASSISTANT FLOOR MANAGER	Dermot Boyd
FILM CAMERAMAN	Fintan Sheehan
FILM RECORDIST	Ron Brown
FILM EDITOR	Alistair Mackay
STILLS PHOTOGRAPHY	Peter Lane
GRAPHIC DESIGNERS	Graham McCallum
	Peter Wane
PROP BUYERS	Monica Boggust
	Paul Schrader
TECHNICAL CO-ORDINATOR	Alan Arbuthnott
VISION MIXER	John Barclay
CAMERA SUPERVISOR	Geoff Feld
VIDEO EFFECTS	Roger Francis
VIDEOTAPE EDITOR	Phil Southby
SOUND SUPERVISOR	Chick Anthony
LIGHTING DIRECTOR	John Summers

Overture.

Establishing shots of Leeds.
Children on their way to school.

Shots of the Leeds coat-of-arms on some of the following locations:
1. *Leeds Town Hall, front facade beneath the clock.*
2. *Stone carving above the offices of Metro Leeds.*
3. *Cockburn High School, Dewsbury Road. Stained glass coat-of-arms above school entrance.*
4. *Old Midland Bank in City Square across road from Queens Hotel.*
5. *Leeds Civic Hall. Front facade. PRO REGE ET LEGE carved on the facade in large latters.*
6. *Leeds Civic Hall. Side entrance above door. The arms are in blue, red, gold and therefore have a "medieval" look appropriate for Herod.*
7. *City Library, Headrow entrance. Wrought iron coat-of-arms gilded.*
8. *Cross Flatts Park, old entrance gateposts, Dewsbury Road end. Blackened sandstone.*
9. *Metropole Hotel, Wellington Street entrance.*
The whole effect should establish the rule of Herod in every nook and cranny of life.

In the activity of Leeds people going to work and their children to school, we follow 12 BOYS *who are making their way to school. In groups of 3, making 4 groups.*

We notice signs indicating the way to places in and around Leeds beginning with H: HEADINGLEY, HOLBECK, HUNSLET, HAREHILLS, HORSFORTH, HOLMFIRTH, HALIFAX, HECKMONDWIKE, HUDDERS-FIELD, HULL, HEBDEN BRIDGE, HEPTONSTALL, HARROGATE, HAREWOOD, HOO HOLE, HOG HOLES, HANGING HEATON, *etc.*

The children and the 3 TEACHERS *arrive at school.* BOY 12 *is seen running, late. Classroom.*

We hear the voices of RACHEL *(the leader of the chorus of* MAMS*) and the* 11 MAMS *calling the names of their sons over the* TEACHER *giving register call.*

ALL MAMS. (*Voice over.*)
    He were a lovely lad

Each of the MAMS *fits in the name of her massacred son.*

MAM 1. Our Roger!

MAM 2. Our Johnny!

MAM 3. Our Frank!

MAM 4. Our Malcolm!

Boys start softly singing 'We Three Kings' and fade out under MAMS.

MAM 5. Our David!

MAM 6. Our Jason!

MAM 7. Our Ronnie!

MAM 8. Our Michael!

MAM 9. Our Peter!

MAM 10. Our Tony!

MAM 11. Our Mark!

MAM 12. Our 'arry!

Register still being called.

RACHEL.
He were a lovely lad.
And God alone knows why
my baby had to die!

BOY 12.
We were bonny babies so say our mams
but we all got murdered in our cots and prams!

I.   THE MATHEMATICAL HEROD.

On the blank blackness of the blackboard a hand writes TEST.

Then we are in a classroom of 28 kids, the 14 BOYS *we have already seen and the* 14 GIRLS *some of whose voices we have heard as* RACHEL *and the* 11 MAMS. *The* TEACHER *is one of the faces we saw in the playground.*

The kids protest against the word TEST *written on the blackboard.*

KIDS.
Aw, sir, it's Christmas!

TEACHER.   No, it isn't, yet!
We're going to have that maths test I promised you I'd set.

INNER VOICE OF HEROD.
> Make way for ranting Herod, The Anti Christ Kid King
> who cringes every Christmas when the Noels start to ring.
> Make room for me king Herod your Inner Mr Hyde
> who'd rid himself of Jesus by unleashing genocide,
> searching for that Christ Kid through all Leeds cots and prams
> leaving blood stained bundles to be blubbed at by their Mams.

TEACHER.
> I want to do more work on parallelograms,
> and tonight . . .

BOY 2.   Aw, Sir!

TEACHER.   For homework you'll revise trapeziums.

BOY 3. Sir . . .
GIRL 2.   It's Christmas!
GIRL 3.   'omework!
BOY 4.   Crumbs!

BOY 12. (*Raising his hand for attention.*)
> I 'ave to 'elp mi mam to 'ang the 'olly . . .

TEACHER. (*Emphasising the dropped aitches.*)
> Have to Help your mother Hang the Holly!
> Try to find some aitches on your Christmas tree.
> Ask Santa to leave some in the toe-end of your stocking.

INNER VOICE.
> Ok, Dr Jekyll, that's enough of being jolly.
> Time for sceptre shaking and shouting something shocking.
> Give me room to rant and rage, and leave the rest to me.
> Make way for horrid Herod your inner Mr Hyde
> who's been revving up all morning hatching homicide.
> The Homicide I'm Hatching is Hardly against Hommes –
> it's boy babies under two I'm after with my bombs!

> There should have been a Herod with his heavy mob in Halifax.

KIDS.
> a 'erod with 'is eavy mob in 'alifax!

TEACHER. (*Emphasising H's.*)
> There should have been a Herod with his heavy mob in Halifax
> descending on he-children with head cracking hatchet hacks!
> and terminating toddlers with his lethal axe-attacks.
> There should have been a Herod who kinged it hereabouts.

KIDS.
'ereabouts.

TEACHER.
Hereabouts.

INNER VOICE.
There should have been a Herod who kinged it hereabouts,
clobbering the kids before they grew up lazy louts.

BOTH.
Yes.

INNER VOICE.
There ought to be Herod now in Hunslet or in Hull . . .

KIDS.
In 'unslet or in 'ull!

TEACHER.
In Hunslet or in Hull! In Hunslet or in Hull!

INNER VOICE & TEACHER.
Yes.

INNER VOICE.
There ought to be a Herod now in Hunslet or in Hull
hammering kids' heads in till the morgue slabs are all full!

BOTH.
Yes.

INNER VOICE.
There ought to be a Herod alive and well and here . . .

BOYS.
'ere! 'ere! 'ere! 'ere! 'ere! 'ere!

TEACHER.
Here! Here!

INNER VOICE.
There ought be a Herod alive and well and Here
in full infanticidal flow in full KILL-ALL KIDS career . . .

TEACHER.
Before they grow up squirting aerosols graffitiing our garages,
rip open the upholstery in cup-excursion carriages
and end up with some lass like these in monstrous fertile
                                                              marriages.

Before they grow up to squirt aerosols and start to spray
the few words they can spell right or UNITED RULES OK,
then get some fertile female in the family way . . .
Best batter 'em while they're still brats, yes, batter 'em *before*
they come and squirt four letter words all over your front door.
Before they start percussion bands with your street's dustbin
                                                                                                    lids,
Before they bump on purpose into supermarket soupcan
                                                                                            pyramids,
then, still kids themselves, start producing their own kids!
Wives traipsing for their ciggies still in their curling pins,
starting boozing first with *Babychams* then graduate to gins,
slopping in worn slippers fringed with orange nylon fur
shopping for their *babies* . . .

VOICES OF RACHEL & THE 11 MAMS. (*Interrupting very ter derly.*)
                                        Gold, frankincense and myrrh!
Shopping for their babies, gold, frankincense and myrrh!

BOYS 1-12.
Myrrh myrrh myrrh myrrh myrrh myrrh myrrh
myrrh myrrh myrrh myrrh myrrh myrrh myrrh

TEACHER. (*His anger escalating.*)
STOP that myrrhmyrrhing!

TEACHER.
I see her in the future a shapeless shambling cow
with kids I'll end up teaching twenty years from now,
when happiness is crappy nappies lurching round the
                                                                                            laundromat
and a belly bulging big again with one more bawling brat
and in Herod's world of weeping women the last thing we need
                                                                                            is THAT.

VOICES OF RACHEL & THE 11 MAMS.
A word that's wiped the worn-out WELCOME off the front
                                                                                            door mat.

BOY 1.
Sir, mi mam says babies are all bonny.

BOY 7.
. . . and mi aunty, sir, says every baby's worth gold,
                                        frankincense and myrrh . . .

BOYS 1-12.
>   myrrh myrrh myrrh myrrh myrrh myrrh
>   myrrh myrrh myrrh myrrh myrrh myrrh.

TEACHER. (*Loud, at explosion point.*)
>   Stop that bloody myrrhmyrrhing!

The TEACHER OF MATHEMATICS *is transformed into* KING HEROD, *and launches himself in the 'Rant of Herod'.*

The TEACHER *is on the classroom dais. Behind him chalked, on the blackboard is the Leeds coat-of-arms with its prominent PRO REGE ET LEGE.*

The classroom is now bare of chairs and tables and desks and is the performance area for the PREL, HEROD'*s death-squad (played by the* 12 BOYS) *and for* RACHEL *and the* 11 MAMS *(played by the* 12 GIRLS).

HEROD/TEACHER.
>   And now I am a Herod in my proper Herod gear
>   I'll kick off my campaign by clouting this lad's ear!
>   Let every so-called innocent be designated X
>   and let this ruler be the axe that swipes off their 'sweet' necks!
>
>   And now I am a Herod, a true-blue HERODES REX
>   a REX whose every little word's interpreted as LEX,
>   your first maths assignment is the measuring of necks!
>   Now calculate the necessary length of noose
>   if the gibbet in Judaea has a 6 ft. hypotenuse!

We now see the 12 BOYS *transformed into the* PREL, *the deadly death-squad of* HEROD.

The PREL *with arms raised simultaneously as if in competitive eagerness to give an answer to* HEROD'*s question, but giving the effect of a long drilled Sieg Heil!*

THE PREL.
>   SSSSSSSSSSSSSSSSSSSSSSSSSSSSSSSSir!

HEROD. (*Warming to the subject.*)
>   If a gallows set in Galilee is .95 metres high
>   and a toddler 30 centimetres takes .31 secs to die
>   how long a length of rope does Herod's hangman have to buy?

A pause while the PREL *consider the problem.*

The PREL *raising their arms simultaneously to answer the question and again giving the effect of a drilled Sieg Heil!*

THE PREL.
    SSSSSSSSSSSSSSSSSSSSSSSSSSSSSSSSir!

HEROD.
    Now this is a hard one: how many furlongs, yards and chains
    would a toddler have to toddle before the Prel beat out his
                                                        brains?

The PREL *raising arms again with effect of drilled Sieg Heil.*

THE PREL.
    SSSSSSSSSSSSSSSSSSSSSSSSSSSSSSSSir!

HEROD.
    If 4 mph's the speed at which an infant fled
    and the PREL pursued at 60 how soon was that kid dead?

THE PREL.
    SSSSSSSSSSSSSSSSSSSSSSSSSSSSSSSSir!

HEROD.
    If the PREL pursue their little prey on speedy roller skates
    and the innocents are toddling as 2 year toddlers do
    one's going at 40, the other a mere 2,
    calculate the seconds before they meet their fates.
    Then tot up the tonnage of TNT
    to liquidate all toddlers from Tynemouth to Torquay,
    then the whole kid population from North to Irish Sea!

The PREL, *with arms raised simultaneously again.*

THE PREL.
    SSSSSSSSSSSSSSSSSSSSSSSSSSSSSSSSir!

HEROD. (*Holding up his jewelled orb which is a disguised aerosol.*)
    If I press this little ruby on my shining regal orb
    HEROD RULES OK, ok, is what my orb'll daub.

PRELS 1-11.
    Herod rules OK.

PREL 12.
    'erod rules OK.

PRELS 1-11.
    (*Turning on* PREL 12, *shocked at his lapse, his dropped H.*)
    HEROD, HEROD, HEROD, RULES OK.

HEROD.
>With my ruby-studded orb I'll daub HEROD RULES OK
>or eliminate this horrid kid by aerosolling X
>wherever lives a little lad my PREL platoons should slay,
>for I am HEROD, the regal REX and legal LEX.

The PREL, *now worked up for their "prowl", begin to chant.*

THE PREL.
>REX! LEX REX! LEX!

HEROD. (*Over the chant of the Prel.*)
>Go out and gut the lot, my goodly ghoulish geezers,
>wherever I have squirted X might be the home of Jesus . . .

The PREL *beginning to form up for the "prowl" of the* PREL.

THE PREL.
>*PRO REGE ET LEGE.*

HEROD. (*Over chant of Prel and pointing to Leeds coat-of-arms with its owls.*)
>*PRO REGE* (that's me, folks) *ET LEGE* (me too).
>*I'm* the king and the Law, the tu-whit and tu-wu!

THE PREL.
>*PRO REGE ET LEGE!*

Then the PREL *"number off" in Latin and proceed on "the prowl" to massacre the innocents.*

PREL 1. *Unus!*
PREL 2. *Duo!*
PREL 3. *Tres!*
PREL 4. *Quattuor!*
PREL 5. *Quinque!*
PREL 6. *Sex!*
PREL 7. *Septem!*
PREL 8. *Octo!*

>(*4 beats.*)

PREL 9. *Novem!*
PREL 10. *Decem!*
PREL 11. *Undecim*
PREL 12. *Er* . . .

The PREL *all turn towards him.*

PREL 1-11. *Duodecim!*
PREL 12. *Duodecim!*

The PREL, *beginning "the prowl" of the* PREL.

THE PREL.
>PRO REGE ET LEGE! P.R.E.L.
>PRO REGE ET LEGE! P.R.E.L.

PREL 1. When the PREL is after prey.
PREL 2. When the PREL is on the prowl.
BOY 1. You'll hear foreboding hootings.
BOY 2. From the left and right Leeds owl.

THE PREL.
>PRO REGE ET LEGE!
>THE MEN FROM THE PREL!

BOY 1.
>What guarantees a nation
>will be free from unrest?

BOY 2.
>It's swift elimination
>of all boys at the breast.

THE PREL.
>PRO REGE ET LEGE,
>THE MEN FROM THE PREL.

BOY 3.
>Our corps goes kid-coshing
>and zapping the prams.

BOY 4.
>We've nabbèd some still noshing
>the milk from their mams.

THE PREL.
>PRO REGE ET LEGE
>THE MEN FROM THE PREL!

BOY 5.
>To stop rabble rousers
>and rockers of boats

BOY 6.
>We mow them with mausers
>and slit their wee throats.

THE PREL.
>   *PRO REGE ET LEGE*
>   *THE MEN FROM THE PREL!*

BOY 11.
>   Hacking   slashing
>   slitting babes' throats

BOY 8.
>   Keeps the blood splashing
>   our black leather coats.

THE PREL.
>   *PRO REGE ET LEGE,*
>   *THE MEN FROM THE PREL.*

BOY 9.
>   I dropped one off the top floor
>   of a high-rise hotel.

THE PREL.
>   Bang! Bang! on the door,
>   the PREL.

BOY 10.
>   One mailed fist to the jaw
>   can toll a nipper's knell.

THE PREL.
>   Bang! Bang! on the door,
>   the PREL.

ALL.
>   *Pro rege et lege*
>   the men from the PREL!

BOY 11.
>   One day I killed a score
>   went the baby hunt went well.

THE PREL.
>   Bang! Bang! on the door,
>   the PREL.
>   *BANG! BANG!* on the door,
>   the PREL!

The members of the PREL *reappear in the classroom and number off in Latin as before.*

PREL 1. *Unus!*
PREL 2. *Duo!*
PREL 3. *Tres!*
PREL 4. *Quattuor!*
PREL 5. *Quinque!*
PREL 6. *Sex!*
PREL 7. *Septem!*
PREL 8. *Octo!*
PREL 9. *Novem!*
PREL 10. *Decem!*
PREL 11. *Undecim!*
PREL 12. *Er!*

PREL 1-11 *turn towards* PREL 12.

PREL 1-11. *Duodecim!*
PREL 12. *Duodecim!*

HEROD. (*Inspecting his men.*)
>   Well, leader of group 1, step forward and report
>   how many lives of little ones your platoon's cut short.

PREL 1.
>   All Hail, Herodes Rex
>   we have done to death this day.

BOYS 1-4. CCVIX.

HEROD *writes* CCVIX *on the blackboard.*

HEROD. (*Solemnly.*)
>   The title I hereby bestow upon thee
>   is Grand Child Eliminator – G.C.E.

>   Well, leader of group 2, step forward and report
>   how many lives of little ones your platoon's cut short.

PREL 8.
>   All Hail, Herodes Rex
>   we have done to death this day.

BOYS 5-8. CCCIX.

HEROD *writes* CCCIX *on the blackboard.*

HEROD. (*Solemnly.*)
>   The title I hereby bestow upon thee
>   is Grand Child Eliminator – G.C.E.

Well, leader of group 3, step forward and report
how many lives of little ones your platoon's cut short . . .

PREL 12.
    All 'ail . . .!

Shocked silence at the dropped aitch.

PREL 12. (*Thinking Herod hasn't heard his greeting.*)
    All 'ail . . .!

Deeper shocked silence.

    All 'ail, 'erod . . .

HEROD.
    Take him to the H-block. Let.him cool his heels.
    Feed him Preparation H and then see how he feels.
    H as in block, H as in bomb,
    feel the aitches in your lungs where the air comes from.
    The proles may drop their aitches but yours must never slip
    H-defaulters lose their fan-club membership
    which includes the toffeenoses but not your tongue-tied Tyke
    who utters 'eck – instead of Heckmondwike . . . *Harrogate.*

  BOYS. *Hunslet.*
  HEROD. *Holmfirth.*
    BOYS. *Hull*
  HEROD. *Huddersfield.*
    BOYS. *Holbeck.*
     ALL. HHHHHHeckmondwike!

Again HEROD *points to the ladder built of H's.*

HEROD.
    The ladder of aspiration, the more you aspire
    the more your aspiration will take you higher.
    Those who drop their aitches fall and break their necks.
    But those with proper aspirations end up REX and LEX!

    End to end laid aitches are a ladder to the top,
    so never never let me hear your aitches drop.

THE PREL.
    ALL HAIL HEROD.

HEROD.
    Now to reward you for your kills
    and honour your kid-killing skills . . .

PREL 1 *steps forward to receive his medal. With pomp and solemnity.*

HEROD.
> For blasting the Red
> still a babe in his bed
> and stopping the Trot
> stone-dead in his cot,
> for niftily netting
> the nippers you nab,
> and liberally letting
> with slash and with stab
> of hatchet and sword a
> lot of lads' blood
> I hereby award a
> star of Herod class 1.
> *Pro Rege et Lege*

THE PREL.
> *Pro Rege et Lege.*

HEROD.
> Well done!
> Well done.

HEROD *attempts to pluck the top centre star from the Leeds coat-of-arms but finds it stuck. It will later be the Star of Bethlehem.*

HEROD. *PRO REGE ET LEGE!*
  BOY 1. *PRO REGE ET LEGE!*
HEROD. Well done! Well done!

HEROD *plucks the left star from the coat-of-arms and pins it on the diligent* PREL 1. PREL 1 *steps back and* PREL 8 *steps forward.*

HEROD. (*With pomp and solemnity.*)
> For blasting the Red
> still a babe in his bed
> and stopping the Trot
> stone-dead in his cot.
> for niftily netting
> the nippers you nab,
> and liberally letting
> with slash and with stab
> of hatchet and sword a
> lot of lads' blood

I hereby award a
star of Herod Class 1
Pro Rege et Lege.

THE PREL.
Pro Rege et Lege

HEROD.
Well done!
Well done!

HEROD *attempts to pluck the top centre star from the Leeds coat-of-arms but finds it stuck. So he plucks the right hand star from the coat-of-arms and pins it on the diligent* PREL 8. PREL 8 *steps back into line.*

HEROD.   *PRO REGE ET LEGE!*
BOY 8.   *PRO REGE ET LEGE!*
HEROD.   Well done! Well done!

Those are the diligent, those who worked well
and now let us turn to the delinquent PREL.
Fetch back the sacked DUODECIM
and let's find a punishment suitable for him.

THE PREL *march away to fetch* PREL 12 *from the H-Block.*

HEROD.   (*Considering Boy 12.*)
What good's a ratter
who catches no rats?
What good's a bratter
who catches no brats?

PREL 1.   What good's a ratter
THE PREL. Who catches no rats?
PREL 1.   What good's a bratter
THE PREL. Who catches no brats?

HEROD.   (*To Boy 12.*)
For not doing well
as a member of PREL
with all those who fail
you'll weep and you'll wail,
and, tormented you'll yell and howl like HELL!

HEROD *with a teacher's blackboard pointer, points to the left-hand owl on the Leeds coat-of-arms.*

HEROD. Howl!
BOY 12. Owl!
HEROD. Howl!
BOY 12. Owl!
HEROD. Howl! Howl! Howl!
BOY 12. Owl! Owl! Owl!

HEROD.
>   If you don't get it right,
>   nobody'll leave
>   if we have to stop all night
>   or till Christmas bloody eve.
>   Howl!

BOY 12. Owl!
HEROD. Howl!
BOY 12. Owl!

HEROD.
>   H as in Bomb, H as in Block
>   We're stopping here tonight till 12 o' bloody clock
>   Howl!

BOY 12. Owl!
HEROD. Howl!
BOY 12. Owl!

HEROD.
>   H as in Rachel, lamenting sons I slew
>   and the next dead son is going to be you.

HEROD. HOWL!
BOY 12. Owl!

This goes on being repeated and repeated as though indeed they were being kept in until 12 on 'Christmas Bloody Eve'. We hear Herod with his 3 howls and the boy following with his owls over the montage of Leeds coat-of-arms in various locations but focussed successively on the 3 owls on each.

RACHEL & 11 MAMS. (*Sung.*)
>   Heu! quia memores
>   nostroque levare dolores
>   Gaudia non possunt
>   nam dulcia pignora desunt.

RACHEL & THE 11 MAMS *lament their massacred sons. We see also the* 13TH MAM.

RACHEL. *(To the 13th Mam.)*
    Your lad did for my lad.

13TH MAM.
    My lad?

RACHEL & THE 11 MAMS.
    Your lad!

RACHEL.
    Your lad did for every little lamb
    and you ought to be ashamed to be his Mam!
    It must be awful to 'ave given birth
    to one of the worst monsters ever on the earth.

MAMS *hum.*

13TH MAM.
    Some poor woman gave 'im birth
    and dandled on 'er knee
    one of the scourges of the earth
    and that poor soul were me.

    Somebody put 'im to 'er breast
    and taught 'im ABC.
    In case you 'aven't already guessed
    that somebody were me.

RACHEL.
    She wishes she'd never given birth
    to one of the worst monsters ever on the earth.

13TH MAM.
    Me and 'is dad we chose 'is name
    before our lad's nativity
    but when I see what 'e became
    I wished 'e'd died in me.

MAM 6.
    The causers of all cruel wars,
    this unjust Judaean king
    don't seem so scary when their jaws
    gnaw on a teething ring.

MAM 9.
> A mam's 'eart is the soonest broke!
> What mother wants to dream 'er
> little boy will be the bloke
> who A-bombs 'iroshima?

RACHEL.
> Your lad did for every little lamb.

13TH MAM.
> And I'm ashamed, to be 'is mam.

ALL. (*Sung.*)
> And God alone knows why
> My baby 'ad to die!

We see the TEACHER *with class register as we hear the voices of* RACHEL *and the* MAMS.

MAM 1.   You can cross our lads off your list –
MAM 2.   It's not like other days they've missed.

We see the TEACHER *with the class register as we hear the voices of* RACHEL *and the* 11 MAMS.

MAM 1.   You can cross our lads off your list –
MAM 2.   It's not like other days they've missed.
MAM 4.   It's not the croup or chicken pox.
MAM 5.   It's not a bad case of the runs.
MAM 6.   The *Rex* did for our sons.
MAM 7.   'erod has put 'em in a box.
MAM 8.   Mowed down by men with guns.
MAM 9.   And they won't come to school no more . . .
MAM 10. And they won't come to school no more.
MAM 11. And they won't come to school no more.
MAM 3.   And they won't come to school no more.

We see the pen of the TEACHER *cross out the names of* 12 BOYS.

Blackboard. Blackness. Blackout.

Silence.

Then we see another hand write TEST on the blackboard.

II.   THE HISTORY HEROD.

Again we are in an identical classroom, this time devoted to history, and the decorations and wallcharts are appropriate to the subject.

The TEACHER OF HISTORY *is a woman.*

It is her hand that has written TEST on the blackboard behind her.

KIDS.   Aw, miss, it's Christmas!
BOY 1.   and 'ist'ry's boring!

TEACHER.   (*Quite pleasantly, correcting the dropped aitch.*)
       History, Michael, History's boring. Why's it such a bore?

BOY 8.   You've only got to say the word and everyone starts snoring.
GIRL 1.   It's just king after king, War then War then War,

BOY 2.   First World, Second World, White Rose and Red.
GIRL 2.   It's all boring 'cos it's all about the dead.
BOY 3.   Can't we do somebody living for a change instead?

TEACHER.   (*Being calm and reasonable.*)
       Well, tell me what else can history be about!

There is a general cacophony of suggestions, including pop-groups, popular individuals, footballers and football teams, etc.

TEACHER.
       Come on, hands up, please don't shout.

The hands are raised, not as with the PREL *simultaneously like a Sieg Heil, but in a bored ragged wave.*

INNER VOICE OF HEROD.
       Please is the first word a king can do without!

TEACHER, *as though not hearing her inner voice picks one hand out of the 24.*

GIRL 3.
       'air! miss!

TEACHER.
       Aviation, yes, we could give that a try.

INNER VOICE.
       Actually it's me that's about to bloody fly
       into the loudest rage ever heard in any Anno Domini.

GIRL 3.

No *'air*, miss, *'air*, like we 'ave on our 'ead!
Instead of all this boring stuff about the boring dead.

INNER VOICE.

The Bethlehem barber Herod employs
cuts off heads as well as hair when he barbers boys.
He's a boring barber with a boring skill
of boring babies' bonces with a Black and Decker drill.

TEACHER. (*Finding it harder to keep control.*)
What other things in history can we study?

Arms up.

INNER VOICE.

Something about babies, beastly, black and bloody!

TEACHER *points to a* BOY.

BOY 5.

Murder, miss, and weapons, and how the bomb gets bigger.

INNER VOICE.

And how my finger itches on my sten gun trigger!

GIRL 4.

Miss, can you tell us, who got it in 'is 'ead
that stuff about the olden days can give some folk a thrill.

TEACHER.

Herodotus, an ancient Greek, or so it's sometimes said.

BOY 8.

Well, your ancient Greek, what's 'is name makes me feel ill.

TEACHER.

Herodotus.

GIRL 5.   'erodotus?

BOY 12.   Who the 'ell's 'e?

TEACHER. (*Wearily resigned and stressing the aitches.*)
He when He's at Home invented History!
His name's a hard one. He's an ancient Greek.
You've forgotten him already, though I mentioned him last
                                                            week.

GIRL 5.
      Last week's ancient 'ist'ry by now though, innit, miss?

TEACHER.
      Better get your notebooks out and make a note of this.

TEACHER *begins to write down the name of Herodotus very slowly separating the letters to make it easier to remember.*

The class begin to copy it out laboriously saying it to themselves mechanically as the elements come out.

TEACHER *writes* HE —

BOYS. (*Writing.*) 'e — !

TEACHER *turning from the blackboard automatically to correct the permanently dropped 'H'.*

TEACHER. *He* — !

TEACHER *writes* HER —

GIRLS. (*Writing.*) 'er — !
TEACHER. (*Correcting.*) *Her*!

TEACHER *writes* HERO —

CLASS. (*Writing.*) 'ero — !
TEACHER. (*Correcting.*) *HERO*!

TEACHER *writes* HEROD —

CLASS. (*Writing.*) 'erod — !

The TEACHER OF HISTORY *is transformed into* KING HEROD *as the* TEACHER OF MATHS *before her.*

The GIRLS *have disappeared and the* BOYS 1-12 *have been transformed into* THE PREL *once more, ready for the prowl.*

THE PREL. (*Chanting.*)
      HE — HER — HERO — HHHHHHHHEROD!
      HEROD the HE/HER HERO
      all HAIL, HEROD, THE REX and the LEX.

HEROD/TEACHER OF HISTORY.
      These days of full equality he comes in either sex!

      And now I am a Herod in my proper Herod gear
      let's say, historically speaking, that equality is here.
      SSSSSSSSSSSSSSSSSSSSSSSSSSSSSir!

In these days of freedom the flogger and flesh-render
can also be a Herod of the feminine gender.
If you think mass-murder is monoplised by men
watch how this King Herod does it, then think again.
HIStory is HERstory, girls, now mark this well
you too might be recruited into Herod's PREL.

PREL BOY 1.
Lasses in our legions?
BOY 2.   Like bloody 'ell!

HEROD.
A lass can be a foremost and famous infant slayer
like that jealous, jilted wife, the babe-murdering Medea . . .

Who was who?

PREL 1-12. (*Raising their arms to answer like a drilled Sieg Heil.*)
SSSSSSSSSSSSSSSSSSSSSSSSSSSSSSSIR!

PREL BOY 3.
Don't be bloody barmy this Herod is a Her!

HEROD.
Tomorrow's Mussolini needn't be a muscleman –
A Jill can kill as jollily as Jack the Genghis Khan.
So, great macho masters, give us girls a year or two
and we'll turn out our Herods horrider than you!

BOY 12.
'erod's 'orrider.

Pause.

HEROD.
Who's that dropping aitches.
I'll put you in the corridor.

Those who drop their aitches like those types who down their
                                                                    tools
never had an H-block in their infants schools.
O yes, great macho masters, just wait a year or two
and we'll turn out our Herods horrider than you.
Tougher than tormentor and tongue-twister Torquemada . . .

Who was who . . . ?

PREL. (*Raising their arms simultaneously like a drilled Sieg Heil.*)
SSSSSSSSSSSSSSSSSSSSSSSSSSSSSSSir!

HEROD.
>   O all right SIR . . .
>   tougher than tormentor and tongue-twister Torquemada
>   like a HErod but a SHErod horrider and harder.
>   Though I might wear slinky numbers, I still know how to slay
>   and for the massacres I mistress-mind I'm asking equal pay.
>   If Herods can be feminine I wonder if that means
>   that Jesuses in future could be Janets, Janes and Jeans.
>   By my tormentor's twinset and my persecutor's pearls
>   does that mean our massacre must murder baby girls.

THE PREL.
>   Yes sir! Yes sir! Yes sir!

HEROD.
>   And now before I send you into town on cot attacks
>   I want to check what each of you have in your "terror packs".

BOY 1.
>   A bomb, airgun, axe, ammonia,
>   aerosols of acid and an Anaconda, sir,
>   Arsenic-laced apples and an assegai.

BOY 2.
>   Blackjack, belladonna, bacilli,
>   blowpipe, boomerang, bicycle chains,
>   and a blood-stained battleaxe for bludgeoning brains.

BOY 3.
>   Catapult, cutlass, Cruise missile, cosh.
>   Cannonades of cowclap, caustic squash.

BOY 4.
>   Depth charger, dagger. D.D.T.
BOY 5.
>   Enfields and other guns starting with an E.

BOY 6.
>   A flask full of infected farts . . .

BOY 7.
>   . . . gooly grinders, gas —

PREL 12. (*Engineered into wrong place.*)
>   'arpoon, 'owitzer.

Shock. Horror.

HEROD.
> HHHHarpoon and HHHHowitzer and what else!

PREL 12.
> 'arpoon and 'owitzer, MISS!

HEROD. (*Mad.*)
> HHHHarpoon and HHHHowitzer and . . .?

PREL 12.
> 'arpoon and 'owitzer, SIR?

HEROD. (*Threateningly.*)
> HHHHarpoon and HHHHowitzer and . .

Silence.

HEROD.
> Harpoon and Howitzer and H-bomb, OK?

PREL 12.
> But H-bomb, miss, begins with an A!

Shock. Horror.

HEROD, *in the solemn voice reserved for rewards and punishment.*

HEROD.
> For saying that H-bomb begins with an A
> you'll stay behind and Howl while the PREL go out to play!

HEROD *stands beside the Leeds coat-of-arms with his/her blackboard pointer about to start the punishment of* PREL 12.

HEROD 1 *suddenly appears.*

HEROD 1.
> I also am a Herod in my proper Herod·gear.
> I thought I'd help you punish him, King Herod, dear!

HEROD 2. (*Offended.*)
> I think I can manage quite well on my own;
> but think how many kids I'd kill if I had a clone.

HEROD 1.
> Your Herodship is great alone, but Herod's twice as gruesome
> when the solo slayer's cloned and turns up as a twosum!

HEROD 1. *UNUS.*
HEROD 2. *DUO.*

The TWO HERODS *begin the punishment of* BOY 12.

They begin to point to the owls on the Leeds coat-of-arms, HEROD 2
to the left owl, and HEROD 1 *to the right owl and both together to the
owl in the centre.*

HEROD 1. Howl!
BOY 12.   owl!
HEROD 2. Howl!
BOY 12.   owl!
HEROD.   Howl!
BOY 12.   owl!

During this "punishment" the PREL *have left to go on the prowl. We
hear the* PREL *and the howl/owl together as we see the montage of the
Leeds coat-of-arms with the focus on the owls.*

As before the howl of the HERODS *and the 'owl' of the* BOY 12 *bring in
the genuine tragic howl of* RACHEL *and the* 11 MAMS.

The MAMS *huddle together.*

MAM 1. Your lad did for my little Lamb.
MAM 2. And you ought to be ashamed to be 'is Mam.
MAM 3. It must be awful to 'ave given birth
MAM 4. to one of the worst monsters ever on the earth.

MAM 13. (*Sung.*)
          A nice lad an so sweet to me
          a dear when 'e were littler
          'ow could I know 'e'd grow up to be
          an Adolf bloody 'itler!

MAM 9.
          She doesn't see Attila —
          or that more recent 'un —
          or any kind of killer —
          when she gazes on 'er son. —

MAM 6.
          All swaddled in warm baby clothes
          'is mother's little darling.
          Who'd know 'e'd grow mustachios
          and end up Joseph Stalin.

RACHEL & From boils on bum to H bomb blast
13TH MAM.

13TH MAM. I'd shield 'im from disaster
RACHEL.   she'd shield 'im from disaster

13TH MAM. but 'ow I groan and stand aghast
RACHEL.   but 'ow she groans and stands aghast

13TH MAM. when my boy is the blaster.
RACHEL.   when 'er boy is the blaster.

MAM 8.   It's not their throats that are sore.
MAM 9.   It's not the boils on their backside. –
MAM 10.   They won't come to school no more. –
MAM 1.   They've been killed in your Herod's kiddicide.
MAM 11.   They won't come to school no more. –

ALL MAMS. (*Sung.*)
      It's 'erod's mam who mourns the most –
      who wails at the world's news –
      when she reads in t'Yorkshire Post
      'er lad, 'erod's on the loose.

13TH MAM.
      A mam loves 'er Baby bad or not
      even 'erod was to 'er
      still summat special in his cot
      and worth Gold, Frankincense and Myrrh.

12 MAMS.
      Gold, Frankincense and Myrrh.

General myrrhmyrrhing.

TEACHER. (*Tears in her eyes.*)
      Stop that myrrhmyrrhing.

III.   THE GEOGRAPHY HEROD.

Again, an identical classroom, this time devoted to geography, and the decorations and wall chart are appropriate to the subject being taught.

The TEACHER OF GEOGRAPHY *is a man. He has a slightly "religious" air. Pedantic and a bit prim.*

It is his hand we have seen write TEST on the blackboard.

KIDS.
 Aw, sir it's Christmas!

TEACHER.   No, it isn't, yet!
 We're going to have that test I promised you I'd set.
 And, Ronnie, I'm aware it's near the birthday of God's son.
 But now it's geography. Ready! Question 1!

BOY 1. Aw, sir.

Having another try.

BOY 2.   It's Christmas!

TEACHER.   The fact that Jesus Christ was born's
 as relevant just now to what we're going to do
 as that He ended his life on a cross crowned with thorns.

INNER VOICE OF HEROD.
 And that's the sort of school-cap I'd fit on most of you!
 Babies' bonnets should come with thorns or made of briar
 their little heads be bound with the rustiest barbed wire.

The TEACHER OF GEOGRAPHY *is the first of the teachers to acknowledge the presence of the inner voice of* HEROD, *which he does with slight facial winces of a rather prim kind, as if afflicted with twinges of indigestion.*

BOY 3.
 Aw, SIR, it's Christmas!

TEACHER. (*Insisting.*)
        The fact our Lord was born's
 got nothing whatever to do with our immediate task
 namely the questions that I'm going to ask.
 So no more about Christmas and

 (*As if to the inner voice.*)   No more about thorns.

BOY 12. (*Quoting a sweet ad.*)
 'Thornes gives Leeds the lead in toffees.'

TEACHER. (*Looking round the class.*)
 Alright! Who?

The TEACHER *searches the faces and lights upon that of* BOY 12.

 I might have known. How come it's always you?
 Well that earns you, 10,000 lines OK?
 Write 10,000 times: Christ is born today!

It'll take you until Christmas before you've done.
That might teach you to blaspheme against God's Son.
Right, Geography, question one.
The river Mississippi, name its source.

BOY 12. (*Quoting Yorkshire Relish ad.*)
'The sauce that takes the name of Leeds to the ends of the earth.'

TEACHER.
TWENTY thousand lines! (*Loud, angry.*) – is that understood?
(*Quietens himself.*)
I don't want any mockery about our Lord, who gave his blood.

INNER VOICE.
Well, I wish he'd gone and given it thirty years before
instead of 3 decades spent flouting King and Law.

TEACHER. (*To Inner Voice.*)
Whatever devil that you are, you won't take over me.
I'm a Christian, a Pacifist. I belong to CND.

INNER VOICE. (*Bored and cynical.*)
I don't know why you bother. You'd do better with the bomb.

TEACHER *with some difficulty getting on with the lesson.*

TEACHER.
Right, where does the Mississippi start flowing from?

BOY 8, *suppressing a giggle, hoping to get* TEACHER *on to a pet subject
and off geography.*

BOY 8.
When we pray at dinners sir
what's that language that you speak?
It sounds that funny, sir,
I bet it's Ancient Greek.

TEACHER.
I know it's just my test you're trying to avoid.

INNER VOICE.
Go on, get the whole damn lot of 'em destroyed!

Smugly but having trouble keeping the HEROD *down.*

TEACHER.
But I'll tell you, Walshaw, just so we can proceed
that the language is Latin, that I once learned to read.

KIDS 10/5/6/7.
    Go on, sir.

KIDS ALL.   Go on, sir.

BOY 7.   Let's 'ear you 'ave a go.

TEACHER *seeing the trap but knowing no way to avoid it.*

TEACHER.
    There are some Latin words that all of you should know
    and that's the motto of your city which is: *Pro
    Rege et Lege* for King and Law.
    How many have never heard those Latin words before.

He finishes writing PRO REGE ET LEGE on the board. The KIDS
have begun saying it to themselves as if trying to memorise it.

TEACHER. PRO
    CLASS. PRO
TEACHER. REGE
    CLASS. REGE
TEACHER. ET
    CLASS. ET
TEACHER. LEGE
    CLASS. LEGE
TEACHER. PRO
    CLASS. PRO
TEACHER. REGE
    CLASS. REGE
TEACHER. ET
    CLASS. ET
TEACHER. LEGE
    CLASS. LEGE
            PRO REGE ET LEGE
            PRO REGE ET LEGE
            PRO REGE ET LEGE

THE PREL. HEROD!
            HEROD!
            HEROD!
            HEROD!
            HEROD!

    All hail, Herod, the Rex and the Lex.

The TEACHER *cowers in fear behind his desk and resists being taken over by* HEROD *(like Jekyll resisting Hyde) but at the insistence of the chanting by the* PREL, *flash! He finally becomes* HEROD.

HEROD 3.
>How I become a Herod in my proper Herod gear
>is something of a mystery, and not at all too clear,
>but I might as well let rip and rant, seeing as I'm here!
>
>Liquefy all lousy lads and have their liquids poured
>drop by nauseating drop in Norway's deepest fjord.
>Which is. Where?

The PREL *arms raised to answer like a drilled Sieg Heil.*

THE PREL.
>SSSSSSSSSSSSSSSSSSSSSSSSSSSSSSSIR!

HEROD.
>Or weathered and eroded and denuded down to bone
>and powder the remainder and dissolve it in the Rhône . . .
>Which is where . . .?

THE PREL. (*Arms raised etc.*)
>SSSSSSSSSSSSSSSSSSSSSSSSSSSSSSSIR!

HEROD.
>The Rhône's good for drowning but maybe all you need 's
>to tip your lorry load of toddlers in the River Aire at Leeds.
>Far or near, near or far, there's all the water that you'll need
>whether Lake Tanganyika or the rivers Tyne and Tweed.
>Which are where?

THE PREL. (*Arms raised.*)
>SSSSSSSSSSSSSSSSSSSSSSSSSSSSSSSIR!

HEROD.
>Every mam's sweet darling, every daddy's little pride
>whirled in person-processors and Irrawaddyfied.
>Every nipper Mississipified and splurted down a sewer
>the Volga's volume growing as the solid kids get fewer.
>Where's the Volga . . .?

THE PREL. (*Arms raised.*)
>SSSSSSSSSSSSSSSSSSSSSSSSSSSSSSSIR!

HEROD.
>   All the infants that you find two years old and younger
>   drag 'em up and drop 'em down K2 or Kangchenjunga,
>   Which is higher? Hands up those who know!

THE PREL. (*Arms raised etc.*)
>   SSSSSSSSSSSSSSSSSSSSSSSSSSSSSSIR!

HEROD. (*Aside.*)
>   I think my little death-squad's all revved up to go!
>   Drown 'em in any water but the Okhotsk Sea (*Pause.*) Why?
>   because there's no damned rhyme for it, you go ahead and try.
>   All the hidden babies, each ferreted out lad
>   chain 'em all together and chuck 'em in Lake Chad . . .
>   What's its area . . .?

THE PREL. (*Arms raised etc.*)
>   SSSSSSSSSSSSSSSSSSSSSSSSSSSSSSIR!

HEROD 1 *appears.*

HEROD 1.
>   I also am a Herod in my proper Herod gear –

HEROD 2 *appears.*

HEROD 2.
>   I also am a Herod just as good as these two here.

HEROD 1 & 3.   Off we go then, Herod

HEROD 2.   After you then dear.

HEROD 1. UNUS!
HEROD 2. DUO!
HEROD 3. TRES!

And all the THREE HERODS *launch themselves off onto a final trio rant.*

HEROD 1.
>   I'll get that rabble-rouser Jesus jelly-babified by Jiminy!

HEROD 2.
>   Destroy all babies born between year dot and 2 Anno Domini.

HEROD 3.
>   Teeny-weenies under two, all tots still at their mothers' tits.

HEROD 1.
>Cherished chubby little cherubs, choke and chop to little bits,

HEROD 2.
>Bazooka all bambinos that are newly born in Bethlehem.

HEROD 3.
>If you have to murder millions then go ahead and murder 'em.

HEROD 1.
>Millions of bloody babes I'll butcher and I'll barbecue,

HEROD 2.
>Boil the buggers down to bones and bubbly barley sugargoo.

HEROD 3.
>You get Herod's kingly go-ahead to gun the kindergartens
>   down

HEROD 1.
>Massacring all manikins from China up to Chapeltown,

HEROD 2.
>Annihilate each nursery, carnageizing creche and cribs,

HEROD 3.
>Pour petrol into diapers and benzine over bibs,

HEROD 1.
>Napalm nippers still in nappies from New York to
>   Northumberland

HEROD 2.
>Sling the swaddled sucklings into never-ending
>   slumberland.

HEROD 3.
>Daub their dummies and their teats with diptheria bacteria

HEROD 1.
>and when the children all get killed

ALL 3 HERODS.   King Herod will be cheerier.

THE PREL *leave to go on the prowl.*

The Massacre of the Innocents takes place to percussion.

THE PREL *return from the prowl.*

HEROD 3.
>Step forward, 1, and tell me all the once infested spots
>you've made entirely free, for me, of toddlers and tots.

PREL 1. (*Stepping forward.*)
         Hiroshima, Hanoi, Hamburg . . .

HEROD 1. And how many?
PREL 1. Thousands and thousands!

HERODS *write on the board the thousands in roman numerals:*
MMMMMMMMMM etc.

HEROD 3.
         The title I hereby award to thee
         is Grand Child Eliminator G.C.E.

PREL 1 *steps back into line.*

         Step forward, 8, and tell me the once infested spots
         you've made entirely free, for me, of toddlers and tots.

PREL 8. Hong Kong, Hungary, Holland –
         Hawaii, Houston and Harlem –
         Honduras, Haiti, Hyderabad –
         Helsinki and the whole of the Hague –
PREL 5. Heidelberg, Hanover, Hilversum
PREL 6. Hove, Hastings, Havant
PREL 5. Harpenden, Hull, Harlow
PREL 6. The Hebrides, Haddington, Hamilton
PREL 8. Holyhead, Harlech, Halewood
PREL 5. Holborn and Hillingdon High Street
PREL 6. Hemel Hempstead, Hatfield, Harwich
PREL 7. Haywards Heath, Habberly and Hallow.
PREL 8. Harrogate, Haywood, Headingley
         the whole of Humberside,
         Horsforth and Holbeck
         Heckmondwike, Helmsley and Haxby,
         and Halifax, Hunslet and Hull.
HEROD. . . . and how many!?
PREL 8. Hundreds and hundreds!

The THREE HERODS *write hundreds and hundreds on the board in*
roman numerals: CCCCCCCCCCCCCCCCCCCCCCCCCCC.

HEROD 3.
         The title I hereby award to thee
         is Grand Child Eliminator G.C.E.!

PREL 8 *steps back into line.*

HEROD 3 *is about to call* PREL 12 *forward, but* PREL 12 *with a resolve we have so far not seen in him steps forward of his own accord much to the shock of all assembled.*

PREL 12.
>Sir!
>It's 'orrible, sir! I'm sick of all this 'orror!'
>(*Pause.*)

The rest of the PREL *are shocked.*

HEROD 3. (*With the manner of Teacher 3.*)
>THIRTY thousand lines! AND by first thing tomorrer!
>Now, 12, tell me all the once-infested spots
>you've made entirely free, for me, of toddlers and tots.

PREL 12.
>None! It's Christmas, sir, women shouldn't weep
>and the lion shouldn't lurk to kill the little sheep.
>We've run about killing and we're all that out of breath,
>can't we 'ave an 'oliday? from all this blood and death.
>(*Pause.*)

HEROD 1. (*Correcting Boy 12's perennially dropped H.*)
>It's Holiday!

HEROD 2.   Holiday!
3 HERODS.   Holiday!
PREL 1.   Thank you sir.
3 HERODS.   Holiday!
PREL 2.   Thank you sir.
3 HERODS.   Holiday!
PREL 3.   Thank you sir.
3 HERODS.   Holiday!
PREL 4.   Thank you sir.
3 HERODS.   Holiday!
PREL 5.   Thank you sir.
3 HERODS.   Holiday!
PREL 6.   Thank you sir.
3 HERODS.   Holiday!
PREL 7.   Thank you sir.

HEROD 1.
>Hey, who said you could go away?

3 HERODS.   Holiday!
PREL 8.   Thank you sir.

3 HERODS. Holiday!
PREL 9.   Thank you sir.
3 HERODS. Holiday!
PREL 10.   Thank you sir.
3 HERODS. Holiday!
PREL 11.   Thank you sir.

HEROD 1.

> You drop all your aitches so you'll have to stay
> behind & howl while the rest break up for holiday!
> Howl!

HEROD 2. Howl!
HEROD 3. Howl!

*Again we go through the montage of the Leeds coat-of-arms in
various locations.*

*The montage comes to rest on the arms of the front facade of Leeds
Town Hall clock.*

BOY 12.

> I know that to you kings the owl's a bird of prey
> but to me it means wisdom, at least for today!
> owl! owl! owl!
> The owls are for wisdom not for pain.

We hear the lamentation of the MAMS *slowly stop and then their
voices take up a new song but still very far away.*

RACHEL & 11 MAMS., (*Sung under boy 12's speech.*)

> in terra pax
> hominibus bonae voluntatis
> alleluia! alleluia!

BOY 12.

> The owls are for wisdom not for pain
> and being evil must be such a strain
> and I tell you by that flashing star

*The flashing star is the one left in the centre (top) of the Leeds coat-
of-arms.*

BOY 12.

> and I tell you by that flashing star
> you're going to follow near and far
> you're no longer Herods, now you are
> UNUS! DUO! TRES

The THREE HERODS *become* THREE WISE MEN.

BOY 12.

> UNUS! DUO! TRES!

> (*Speaking to the tune of the Christmas carol 'We Three Kings'.*)

> The Rex that men of peace are all pro
> isn't a 'erod

HEROD 1. ˙   No!

HEROD 2.   No!

HEROD 3.   No!

BOY 12. (*Still speaking to the tune of 'We Three Kings'.*)
> Where the fleece is the King of Peace is
> and that's where we all must go.

> 1, 2, 3, all stand in a line
> let's check you over, you'll do fine
> with your crowns on, Wisemen's gowns on,
> go follow the Big H sign.

ALL.

> Ooooo Big H sign in white and blue
> H for 'ope depends on you
> From tomorrer H for 'orror's
> banned with 'erods 'ellish crew.

We see road signs, the H in white and blue for Hospital, with arrows going forward, left, right, forward again, until we reach Leeds Maternity Hospital. Town Hall clock starts striking midnight. Stills of BOYS 1-12 *mixing with their baby pictures.*

BOY 1. One
GIRL 1. Our Roger.

As if counting the dead in some distant past.

BOYS 1 & 2. Two!
GIRLS 1 & 2. Our Johnny.

After the second stroke of 12 we should be aware that the second lion on the steps of Leeds Town Hall has left its place near the sign reading Police and gone about walking as the Leeds legend insists that it does.

Town Hall Clock: Bong 3!

BOY 3. Three!
GIRL 3. Our Frank.
BOY 4. Four!
GIRL 4. Our Malcolm.
BOY 5. Five!
GIRL 5. Our David.

Between each bong we should see the THREE WISE MEN *making their way to the nativity followed by the class of children, who walk towards the Leeds Maternity Hospital outside of which is a big H sign in white and blue.*

BOY 6. Six!
GIRL 6. Our Jason.
BOY 7. Seven!
GIRL 7. Our Ronnie.
BOY 8. Eight!
GIRL 8. Our Michael.
BOY 9. Nine!
GIRL 9. Our Peter.
BOY 10. Ten!
GIRL 10. Our Tony.

The road signs we should see are those we saw at the beginning, signs pointing to places round and suburbs of Leeds: HEADINGLEY: HOLBECK: HUNSLET: HAREHILLS: HORSFORTH: HUD-DERSFIELD etc except that now they are aitchless and read: EADINGLEY: OL:BECK: UNSLET: ARE ILLS: UDDERSFIELD.

BOY 11. Eleven!
GIRL 11. Our Mark.

Voices of 12 MAMS *coming closer: ALLELUIA etc.*

Town Hall clock: Bong 12!

ALL. Twelve!
GIRLS. Our 'arry!

Procession. Girls sing under BOY 12's *speech.*

BOY 12.
    The white Town Hall lions came to life
    as midnight chimes on Christmas Eve
    and they look for the joiner Joe and his wife
    and you'll see them walking if you'll only believe . . .

The lions that stirred when the first stroke was struck
they stroll down the 'eadrow to take a look
at the baby of Mary and the Joiner Joe
and the cops have problems with the traffic flow
as loads of folk come to Leeds to see
the North's most noted Nativity,
and the lions lay down with the lamb,
and the lions lay down with the lamb!
They lick the 'ands of 'is dad and mam
and the lions, the lions lay down with the lamb,
and they lovingly lick the lad in his pram,
and the lions, the lions lay down with the lamb,
and the lions lay down in Leeds with the lamb,
and the lions lay down with the lamb.
And the roaring lions pipe down to a purr
and there's a midnight feeling over the earth
and a sense of somebody special's birth,
a sense of somebody special who's worth . . .

ALL.

GOLD!

FRANKINCENSE!

and MYRRH!

We see the CLASS *and the* THREE TEACHERS *singing a carol ('We Three Kings') round a Christmas tree in the Leeds Maternity Ward. We see a sequence of babies in incubators.*

ALL.

Every babe's worth . . .
GOLD . . . FRANKINCENSE . . . and MYRRH!

Classroom. BOY 12 *is alone writing his 30,000 lines: 'Christ is Born Today.' The classroom is decorated for Christmas. The blackboard now reads Merry Christmas made from an M and a C from the Roman numerals of Herod's score of dead innocents.*

BOY 12.

And he'll grow up to be a teacher!

The End.

MEDEA: a sex-war opera (1985)

MUSIC: Jacob Druckman

'We define the myth as consisting of all its versions.'

CLAUDE LÉVI-STRAUSS,
'The Structural Study of Myth',
Structural Anthropology (1958).

'A myth is a polyphonic fugue for many voices.'

WILLIAM IRWIN THOMPSON,
The Time Falling Bodies Take to Light (1981).

MEDEA: *A SEX-WAR OPERA*

Medea: a sex-war opera was commissioned by the New York Metropolitan Opera.

ACT ONE

The OVERTURE *spills over on to the stage where we see a circle of threatening* MEN, *chanting their hostility to a murderer of children as yet unidentified. They express their horror and hostility in words culled from the world's drama and opera on the subject of* MEDEA, *the murderer of her own children.*

CHORUS [M].

παιδολέτορ [Euripides, *Medea* 1393]

παιδοφόνου [Euripides, *Medea* 1407]

nefanda liberorum carnifex [Buchanan 515]

natorum caede cruenta [Buchanan 516]

exécrable tigresse [Corneille V.vi]

furie exécrable [Corneille V.vii]

mrzká, hnusná, zhubitelko dêti!
    [*Euripidova Medeia* tr. Dr Petr Durdik (Prague, 1878)]

tu, tu, malorum machinatrix facinorum [Seneca 226]

O madre iniqua e perfida! [Mayr]

Crudel! Feroce! Barbara! [Cherubini]

Hechizera! [Calderón, *Los Tres Mayores Prodigios*]

This bedlem Wight, and divelysh despret dame
    [John Studeley/Seneca, 1566]

O vile malitious mynded wretch [*ibid*]

'The murd'rous witch . . ' [*Medea; or the Best of Mothers*, 1856]

As the CHORUS [M] *chant their multi-lingual hatred, which becomes more and more intense, a vast female figure rises from the stage and this becomes the focus of male hatred. It is a vast effigy of the murderous* MEDEA *and as it becomes more gigantic we see that in its hand is a knife and hidden in its skirts frightened children. When the chant of the* CHORUS [M] *reaches a climax of hatred the knife plunges down, and the hostile circle of chanting men is dispersed and scattered in fear and panic, and the giant effigy collapses like a deflated blimp.*

Out of the confusion two processions form. The CHORUS [M] *are seen leading* WOMAN 1 [MEDEA] *to an electric chair. They are still chanting a fragmentary version of the chant of hate for the child-killer.*

WOMAN 1[MEDEA] *is accompanied by a female warder,* WOMAN 2 [NURSE, QUEEN ARETE OF MACRIS] *in the uniform of a female prison officer. She escorts* WOMAN 1 [MEDEA] *as far as the electric chair, then stands back to allow the executioner* [JASON], *who will pull the switch, to strap her into the chair. There is a simultaneous procession of* CHORUS [W] *as wedding attendants leading* WOMAN 3 [CREUSA, HYPSIPYLE] *to a golden throne. The throne is a mirror image of the electric chair.* WOMAN 3 *has the 'gifts of Medea', the golden robe and crown. The poisoned, flame-impregnated crown should mirror in some detail the "cap" used in the electrocution.* CHORUS [W] *sing quietly the* WEDDING HYMN *we shall hear in various forms throughout the piece.*

CHORUS (*Wedding Hymn.*)
    O digno coniuncta viro, dotabere virgo.
    Ferte facis propere, thalamo deducere adorti.
    Ore favete omnes et cingite tempora ramis.
           [Hosidius Geta (2nd century A.D.), *Medea*]

The two processions reflect one another, one the solemn processional of execution, which, in this case, is a male wish-fulfilment, the other a wedding preliminary. One music is a black version of the other. As the electrocution cap is placed on the head of WOMAN 1 [MEDEA], WOMAN 3 [CREUSA] *places the crown impregnated with invisible fire on her head. We hear the hostile chants of* CHORUS [M] *become dominant. The* EXECUTIONER, *the "State Official"* [JASON] *prepares to pull the switch that will pump the huge voltage through the body of* WOMAN 1 [MEDEA]. *The switch is a handle more out of dream than reality and it could probably "double" as the tiller of the Argo later, as the bars of the prison we see behind the electric chair could "double" as the oars of the Argo. The electrocution cap will later become the bowl which* MEDEA *uses to mix the poisons and philtres with which she drugs the Dragon guarding the Golden Fleece, prepares a charm for* JASON *against the fire-breathing bulls, and especially mixes the poison of invisible fire with which she impregnates the crown and robe which consume* CREUSA.

CHORUS [M]. (*Gloating, mocking.*)
    A woman sits in the electric chair
    like waiting for the drier to dry her hair
    in the beauty parlour.

    Soon the State Official will come and pull
    the switch and energy will fill her skull
    like the violins of Mahler.

The STATE OFFICIAL [JASON] *moves towards the switch.*

> Monsters like this one ought to be fried.
> It's rising the graph of infanticide.
> Severity's long overdue.
>
> Statistics kept at the FBI
> predict more kids are going to die
> before women get through,
>
> get through showing womanhood
> better than manhood or as good –
> damn woman's lib!
>
> FATHER, in whom *men* believe,
> Thou shouldst have left that evil Eve
> as Adam's rib!

The multi-lingual chant, the echo chamber of male mythologising, and patriarchal history continues, and reaches a crescendo.

CHORUS [M].
> State Official, throw the switch
> on MEDEA, the child-killing witch.
> Burn her like she burned CREUSA.

The STATE OFFICIAL [JASON] *takes hold of the lever and seems about to pull it and send the voltage through* WOMAN 1 [MEDEA]. CHORUS [M] *increases the venomous intensity of their chant towards the murderess. It ceases suddenly as if in hushed anticipation of the long-awaited wish-fulfilment of electrocution. At the same time, in the stillness that immediately precedes the throwing of the switch, we see* WOMAN 3 [CREUSA] *raise the fire-impregnated crown above her head ready to wear it for the wedding.*

CHORUS [M].
> State Official, throw the switch,
> on MEDEA, boy-butchering bitch –
> burn her like she burned CREUSA . . .

The STATE OFFICIAL *is on the point of throwing the switch, when* CHORUS [W] [DSW] *interjects:*

CHORUS [W] [DOWNSTAGE WOMAN].
> Remember when you hear her screams
> that a woman goes to such extremes
> when men abuse her . . .

Remember when you hear her cries
and the MEDEA you see before you fries
a man's the cause,
though women in their last death-throes
have always drawn male fans' bravos
and fags' applause!

Ah, yes, you say, she cut their throats
but what you wait for are high notes
she's got to reach.
When the mother's pain's the maximum
you want pure, pear-shaped tones to come
and not a screech.

No matter if she's got TB
so long as air for the high C
gets through one lung.
She dies of stabwounds, fever, pox
and all *you* care, up in your box,
is how it's sung.

Tosca, Carmen, Butterfly,
it seems all women do is die
in music drama.
A woman is what men desert;
in opera (as in life!) men hurt
and harm her.

CHORUS [M] [DOWNSTAGE MAN].
We don't put in a hard day's work
and pay good dough to hear some jerk
preach women's rights.
Politics are not the thing
we pay to hear sopranos sing
on gala nights.

The CHORUS [M] *once more invoke the* STATE OFFICIAL [JASON] *to pull the switch. This time more rapidly and urgently.*

CHORUS [M].
State Official, pull the switch
on MEDEA, the child-killing witch.
Burn her like she burned CREUSA . . .

Once more we are poised on the brink of electrocution. The STATE
OFFICIAL [JASON] *makes ready to pull the switch.* CREUSA *is on the
point of placing the golden, fire-impregnated crown on her head.
Again, at the very point of action, the scene is interrupted:*

CHORUS [W] [DSW].
Listen! All of you! Before
you hear tonight's new score
what strikes your ears?

*She pauses, and in that brief pause, we hear, as if from outside in
Broadway or somewhere in the vicinity of the Lincoln Center, the
urgent sound of a hurrying ambulance.*

CHORUS [W] [DSW]
Not strings, an ambulance that skids
round other traffic, carrying kids
killed like MEDEA's.

Some mother, some deserted wife
kills her kids with a kitchen knife,
here, today!
When you read the press reviews
of what you're seeing she'll be news
and not a play.

MOM KILLS KIDS reads *New York Post*
and that "Mom" 's MEDEA's ghost
still unfulfilled.
As long as things go on like this
without a sex-war armistice
kids will be killed.

Not costumes and old myths of Greece;
the Argonauts and Golden Fleece –
Manhattan!
Infanticide appears to grow
and in the female crime bureaux
files fatten.

As the sex war's still being fought,
which sex does a myth support?
you should be asking.
What male propaganda lurks
behind most operatic works
that Music's masking?

> Beneath *all* Greek mythology
> are struggles between HE and SHE
> that we re still waging.
> In every quiet suburban wife
> dissatisfied with married life
> is MEDEA, raging!

*The anti-*MEDEA *multi-lingual chant grows predominant and silences the feminist critique of* CHORUS [W].

CHORUS [M].
> State Official throw the switch
> on MEDEA, boy-butchering bitch.
> Burn her as she burned CREUSA . . .

The STATE OFFICIAL [JASON] *once more is poised, ready to pull the lever that will electrocute* WOMAN 1 [MEDEA] *seated strapped in the electric chair. Once more we see* CREUSA *on her golden throne, which is a mirror image of the electric chair, poised to place the crown impregnated by invisible fire, on her head.*

CHORUS [M].
> State official, throw the switch
> on MEDEA, the boy-butchering bitch.
> Burn her as she burned CREUSA.

This time the STATE OFFICIAL [JASON] *pulls the lever (that will later become the tiller of the Argo). But instead of the expected electrocution of* WOMAN 1 [MEDEA], *our attention is transferred by a great cry to the extreme agony of* WOMAN 3 [CREUSA] *who is now wearing the robe and crown impregnated with poisonous, invisible fire.* WOMAN 3 [CREUSA] *is in the extremest agony. The music is electrocution, every brain cell alive with electrical pain, an "Aureole" whose dynamic is agony. We should also feel that what we see is taking place in the brain of* WOMAN 1 [MEDEA], *a brain like* WOMAN 3 [CREUSA]*'s fragmented by high-voltage and momentous shock.*

As the agony of CREUSA *attracts all attention,* WOMAN 1 [MEDEA], *strapped in the electric chair, sinks into the pit, leaving a hole in the stage, which for the moment is to be a well but will serve also as the entrance for the* GODDESS *when she emerges as the image of the ancient 3 in 1* GREAT MOTHER. *The Pit will also be the pool in which* HYLAS *is drowned, dragged below by the voices of water nymphs. It will also be the place, the underground cave where the Golden Fleece is guarded by the Dragon. It is also a place of burial, and* JASON *will*

*be buried in it at the end of the piece. The Pit now serves as what is
called in the site of ancient Corinth 'the well or fountain of Glauce',
another name for Creusa. Into this well the agonised* WOMAN 3
[CREUSA], *in unbearable agony from the poisoned robe and crown,
leaps, hoping that the water in it will cool the flesh that is on fire. She
jumps into the Pit and disappears. There is a great hiss, as of fire
meeting water, and slowly a great cloud of smoky steam arises from
the Pit. We hear an extraordinary voice of incredible vocal range
coming from the steam, and as the smoke clears we see the* GODDESS,
*the triple goddess, called many things in the ancient world, the oldest
of all goddesses, and female images, here the* VIRGIN, MOTHER,
CRONE *who are* WOMAN 3 [CREUSA, HYPSIPYLE], WOMAN 1 [MEDEA]
and WOMAN 2 [NURSE, OLD WOMAN OF LEMNOS and QUEEN ARETE OF
MACRIS]. *The* GODDESS *emerges on a revolving platform, and sings as
though the three had one voice as some of their ancient names were
Nete, Mese, and Hypate which signify the low, middle, and high
tones of the Greek system of scales. The three should be soprano,
mezzo-soprano and contralto, and sometimes take alternate notes in
their lowest or highest ranges so that the* GODDESS *seems to embody
the total resource of the female voice, and by extension the total
range of the female. Diva triformis* [Ovid.7.177]. *The* GODDESS *rotates
on the platform. They sing in round and in three different languages.*
[v. Valerius Flaccus, *cantuque trilingui* vii.184]. **There are many different
representations of the** GODDESS [3 in 1] **and in all one figure carries a
knife in each hand, one a torch in each hand, and the third figure
something like a sickle or sheep hook. In this case** WOMAN 1 [MEDEA]
carries the two knives, WOMAN 2 [NURSE etc] **the hook, and** WOMAN 3
[CREUSA] **the torches. When the** GODDESS **is fully risen and rotating on
her platform, singing as one voice, we see the 14 children beneath the**
GODDESS **rotating in the opposite direction. This forms what is
virtually a tableau of death and regeneration, the children being
killed and restored to life.**

GODDESS 3/1.

ἄνω ποταμῶν ἱερῶν χωροῦσι παγαί,
καὶ δίκα καὶ πάντα πάλιν στρέφεται.
ἀνδράσι μὲν δόλιαι βουλαί, θεῶν δ'
οὐκέτι πίστις ἄραρε·
τὰν δ' ἐμὰν εὔκλειαν ἔχειν βιοτὰν στρέψουσι φᾶμαι·
ἔρχεται τιμὰ γυναικείῳ γένει·
οὐκέτι δυσκέλαδος φάμα γυναῖκας ἕξει.

μοῦσαι δὲ παλαιγενέων λήξουσ' ἀοιδῶν
τὰν ἐμὰν ὑμνεῦσαι ἀπιστοσύναν.
οὐ γὰρ ἐν ἁμετέρᾳ γνώμᾳ λύρας
ὤπασε θέσπιν ἀοιδὰν
Φοῖβος, ἁγήτωρ μελέων· ἐπεὶ ἀντάχησ' ἂν ὕμνον
ἀρσένων γέννᾳ. μακρὸς δ' αἰὼν ἔχει
πολλὰ μὲν ἁμετέραν ἀνδρῶν τε μοῖραν εἰπεῖν.

[Euripides, *Medea* 410-430]

Retro ad fontes sacra feruntur
Flumina, ius et fas vertuntur
Hominum plena dolis consilia,
Nec pacta fides diis sed certa est.
Audiet ex hoc muliebre bene
Genus: *accrescet gloria nobis.*
Non iam deinceps fama sinistra
Traducet foemineum sexum.
Ex hoc mutabit Musa modos
Vatum priscorum, qui canta
Muliebrem celebrant perfidiam:

[George Buchanan (1506-1582), Latin translation of Euripides' *Medea*]

O Chant! que n'avons-nous, fileuses que nous sommes,
La lyre en main au lieu de la quenouille, pour
    Faire enfin, c'est bien notre tour –
    Des poèmes contre les hommes.

[Catulle Mendès (1841-1909), *Médée* (1898)]

On the platform of the GODDESS, WOMAN 1 [MEDEA] *gives one of her knives to* WOMAN 3 [CREUSA, HYPSIPYLE] *and* WOMAN 2 [NURSE, OLD WOMAN OF LEMNOS, QUEEN ARETE OF MACRIS]. WOMAN 3 *and* WOMAN 2 *also take a torch each and* WOMAN 1 [MEDEA] *is left with the other implements, the hooks.* WOMAN 3 *is now* HYPSIPYLE, *the Queen of Lemnos, and* WOMAN 2 *an Old Woman of Lemnos. They descend from the platform, which now contains only* WOMAN 1 [MEDEA] *who watches the other two depart each bearing a knife and a torch. They are joined by* CHORUS [W] *who also each bear a knife and torch.* WOMAN 3 [QUEEN HYPSIPYLE] *sits in the throne, where she sat as* CREUSA. *She is crowned Queen and hailed as Queen, then the women depart in sinister and stealthy procession (in actual fact to kill all the men in the island of Lemnos). They each bear a torch, and hold a knife, ready to use it at any minute. They go off stage to kill their menfolk.*

The DOWNSTAGE MAN [DSM] *comes forward:*

DOWNSTAGE MAN.

> Those are the loathsome women of Lemnos isle;
> of all the world's women considered most vile,
> whose name stinks to Heaven
> because they were driven
> to kill fathers, husbands, sons,
> yes, even, like Medea, all their little ones.
> All their *male* little ones.

DOWNSTAGE WOMAN [DSW] *steps forward to respond:*

DOWNSTAGE WOMAN.

> The men started sleeping with slave girls from Thrace.
> They said their wives stank and they spat in their face,
> and set male gods up in the MOTHER's place.
>
> If that was *my* husband with his concubine
> snoring from swinish coupling and wine
> I too would mash in his head with a rock,
> I too would hack off his wandering cock
> and hang it up in the EARTH MOTHER's shrine
> where it would wither into final decline.

The DSM *goes over the Pit into which the remaining* WOMAN 1 *descended and looks cautiously into it, and then finding it is indeed empty, he is emboldened to say:*

DOWNSTAGE MAN.

> That EARTH MOTHER, that Goddess whore
> goads the female sex to war
> with men, and undermine
> with tactics, sneaky, serpentine,
> our natural male supremacy,
> even denying God's a HE!
> Ridiculous! Men overthrew
> the Goddess, women, you,
> ages ago, beyond recall.
> Men became masters of it all.
> Men built vessels to explore
> the wrinkled body of your whore,
> the Great Mother, 3 in 1.
> She's finished, burned out, done!

Your Andrews Sisters deified
couldn't change things if she tried.
Your Goddess had her chance and failed.
The world moved on. The ARGO sailed.
Look JASON, the chief Argonaut . . .

Enter JASON, *bearing in his hand what will become in the construct-ion to follow, the tiller of the Argo, but which is recognisably the lever he pulled as* STATE OFFICIAL.

DOWNSTAGE MAN.
Look, JASON the chief Argonaut,
handsome, bold, the man who brought
the Mother's precious Golden Fleece
back to the He-god's shrine in Greece.
The Argonauts made Earth belong
to men, the upper dogs, the strong . . .

Enter THE ARGONAUTS *following* JASON. *They begin to build the Argo from everything left on stage. They man the oars of the completed vessel and set sail, to a strong rhythmic pace.*

ARGONAUTS.
There's nowhere a man feels any more free
than the wide open sea
with no land to the North, no land to the South,
no land to the East or West,
and the spray leaves a salt-taste in the mouth
and the men's hearts are one on an heroic quest
for the Golden Fleece,
the Golden Fleece.

We love the brine and the boiling foam
and the steady beat of the heavy oars
and the sweat that comes oozing out of our pores,
and we're glad to be away from the women at home,
away from women's incessant demands
into the sort of heroic life
a man couldn't share with any wife,
and only a man understands:
the open sea, adventures, and strange lands,
the truly manly heroic life
a man couldn't share with any wife
and only a man understands:
the open sea, adventures and strange lands.

We are the pick of the whole of Greece
crossing the sea for the Golden Fleece,
the Golden Fleece.

The chorus fades down and comes back up to denote the passage of time.

ARGONAUTS.
    The Golden Fleece!

JASON.
    The Golden Fleece!
    The Fleece will bring me fame
    The Fleece will spread my name
    all over Greece.

    I'll have me a kingdom by a peaceful shore
    and I'll have all the pleasures of peace.
    And I won't need to go to sea any more
    and women will want me because I won the Fleece.

    The Golden Fleece!

ARGONAUTS.
    JASON! King Jason, and long may you reign!
    (*Quietly, confidentially.*)
    Sometimes he uses those masculine charms
    to further ambition without force of arms.
    Jason, our leader, has women on the brain!

    The Golden Fleece!

HERCULES.
    The Golden Fleece!
    The Dragon, I mean Dragon*ness*
    that guards the Fleece I'm told
    I'll club and batter to a bloody mess –
    my club will knock Her out cold!
    I'll chop the Serpent piece by piece
    into a cauldron of bubbling stew
    and the Dragon*ness* guard of the Golden Fleece
    will make a year's meat for the crew.

ARGONAUTS.
    Hercules!

    The strongest man in the whole of Greece
    and we'll need his strength to win the Fleece –

Dropping their voices to a very discreet low tone, aware as they are of the thin skin and easily provoked violence of HERCULES.

> BUT he's a bit stupid and he never thinks
> and he gets very violent when he drinks
> which can be for weeks on end.
> Then he slobbers over his 'little friend'.
> He's a brute and a braggart, a boozer and a boor,
> his behaviour's crude and crass.
> He brands every woman as a wicked whore
> and his other little weakness is . . .
> (*Dropping their voices even lower.*)
> > > > . . . ASS!

HERCULES *turns round angrily, reaching for his club.*

HERCULES.

> What was that that I just heard?
> Did somebody say a dirty word?
> Or was it just the voices in my head?
>
> The next man to say it 's dead. Dead!

ARGONAUTS.

> Hercules!
>
> The strongest man in the whole of Greece
> and we need his strength to win the Fleece,
> the Golden Fleece!

BUTES.

> (*Sadly unconvinced by the general atmosphere of male heroics.*)
> The Golden Fleece!
> I'd sooner have stayed at home in peace!

ARGONAUTS.

> BUTES! Though he's old we brought
> along Butes as an Argonaut,
> not because he can row or fight
> and he's not much use with a spear,
> but he knows by heart the stars of the night
> that helps us all to steer
> the Argo straight and keep her right
> on course for the Golden Fleece,
> the Golden Fleece!

BUTES.

>The Golden Fleece!
>I'd sooner have stayed at home in peace!

ARGONAUTS.

>Butes! But even more Butes has a nose
>for honey, and everywhere he goes
>he scents out the bees and their full hives
>and he brings a little sweetness into our lives
>and takes the bitterness out of our beer.
>(*Softer, more confidential.*)
>He's the only one of us loves his wife,
>and she died on him, and he's sick of life.

HERCULES. (*Butting in with typical tactlessness.*)

>Lucky for some folk! So say I!
>I wish my wife would go and die!

ARGONAUTS.

>Hercules!

Suddenly the watchman, LYNCEUS, *the man with telescopic eyesight, cries out that there is land ahead.*

LYNCEUS.

>Land! Land! There's a fine, green island ahead!

This unexpected news is greeted with a chorus of various cries of expectation from the ARGONAUTS, *each fantasising about the thing he has missed most during the gruelling voyage.*

ARGONAUTS.

>Land!

>Fresh water!
>Wine!
>Fruit!
>Meat!
>Honey [*Butes.*]
>Women!
>Women!
>Women!
>Women!

>WOMEN!

The reiteration of 'Women! Women!' possile here propels JASON
into his first quotation: 'Delizie Contenti' from Cavalli's Il Giasone.
This provokes a fulminating reaction from HERCULES.

HERCULES.

>You've scarcely been at sea a month and a day
>and I thought we were all glad to be far, far away
>from womenfolk who make hell of our lives
>but you're already drooling for the next damned lay!
>The next thing I'll hear is a bloody great sigh
>with that far away look in each lustful eye –
>'We don't need the Fleece we need our wives!'
>
>The Golden Fleece is the Argo's goal
>and we are only landing a short time for stores,
>several skins of wine for me, some pigs for my meat.
>But I'll club the next man that I hear bleat
>like a bloody horny ram for a bloody ewe,
>and, if I were in command, I'm telling you
>we don't have time to play with whores!
>They're bad for the body, and bad for the soul –
>
>The Golden Fleece is the Argo's goal!

JASON. (*Quoting Cavalli's opera.*)
>*Delizie Contenti!*

LYNCEUS.

>Land! Land! There's a fine, green island ahead.

The ARGONAUTS *row the Argo to the shore of an island which is
Lemnos. They throw themselves, exhausted and in a state of near
nakedness, on to the beach. They are all, even* HERCULES, *glad to be
on terra firma. They stretch themselves out, rub their muscles with
oil, luxuriate in the solidity of the ground. They unwind.*
Suddenly from behind there appears a group of heavily armed
SOLDIERS. *The* ARGONAUTS, *defenceless, almost naked, are frozen
with horror.*

JASON.

>We're trapped, and not a sword in reach!

HERCULES *makes a slight forward move but* JASON *arrests him.*

>Don't move! Keep still! Let me try speech!

He moves like a Herald towards the SOLDIERS *who now form a solid
threatening phalanx.*

JASON.
    I am JASON, these the ARGONAUTS
    may we land and take on drinking water?

BUTES. (*Unaware of the seriousness of the confrontation.*)
    And maybe a little honey from your hives?

HERCULES.
    And maybe a goatroast cooked by your wives?

Silence from the armed soldiers. Forbidding silence.

JASON *tries again.*

JASON.
    I am JASON, these the ARGONAUTS
    may we land and gather fruit?

BUTES.
    And a little honey, maybe, from your combs?

HERCULES.
    And perhaps you keep good wine back in your homes?

Again a stony silence from the armed phalanx of SOLDIERS. JASON
tries once more.

JASON.
    I am JASON, these the ARGONAUTS,
    may we land to rest and sleep?

BUTES.
    And a little honey, maybe, from your bees?

HERCULES *is about to add something else, when a voice, loud enough
to be heard, comes from the band of* ARGONAUTS.

VOICE OF ARGONAUT.
    And maybe a spare whore or two, PLEASE!

HERCULES *turns round on the voice, and threatens towards where he
thinks it came from.*

HERCULES. (*Threatening the Argonauts.*)
    What was that that I just heard?
    Did somebody say a dirty word?
    Or was it just the voices in my head?
    The next man to say it's dead. Dead!

*At the same time there is a marked rustle of weapons from the solid
phalanx of armed* SOLDIERS. *There is a moment of tension when it
seems that battle may commence.*
JASON *steps forward once more, and in the confidential tone of a man
sure that he is addressing men of like minds and interests says:*

JASON. (*Apologetically, "man to man".*)
    You have to understand they're a horny crew.
    If you had been at sea for a month and a day
    and this was your first sight of land
    then I think you men would understand
    and I think that you'd be pretty horny too.
    You know how it is when a man needs a lay
    when a man 's in want of a screw?

HERCULES.
    But me I'd prefer we were on our way
    and that we left you men in peace.
    Go home to your wives
    and your daily lives
    and let us do what *we* have to do –
    cross the sea for the Golden Fleece.

ARGONAUTS. (*Reprising what they sung on board the Argo.*)
    The Golden Fleece!

*The moment of tension and silence from the phalanx of soldiers, and
then with one movement the* SOLDIERS *push back their helmets and
reveal* THE WOMEN OF LEMNOS *led by* QUEEN HYPSIPYLE.

QUEEN HYPSIPYLE & WOMEN OF LEMNOS.
    Welcome, Argonauts, yes, come ashore,
    you may have water, fruit and sleep, but not before
    you've given us what we need, and more!
    (*Turning to Butes but with eye on Jason, admiringly.*)

HYPSIPYLE. (*To Butes.*)
    Have all the freedom of our hives
    and all the sweetness of our . . . wives

General laughter, and final release of tension.
Then again to BUTES, *but with an eye still on* JASON *who returns her
look.*

HYPSIPYLE. (*To Butes ostensibly, but a general invitation.*)
    Our mountain flowers are open to blue skies
    and stay open when the sun goes into cloud.

The bees make free with them, and you're allowed
to make free with all their sweetness, and make free
with all you've hungered for at sea
and with the sweetness that you find between our thighs.

There is general jubilation and a general pairing off of man and woman, ARGONAUT *and* WOMAN OF LEMNOS, JASON *with* HYPSIPYLE. JASON *is still musing on 'Delizie Contenti'. There might at this point be some sort of mating "dance". The pairing off is resisted only by* BUTES, *the old Bee Man, still faithful to the memory of his dead wife, and, of course, by* HERCULES. *The 'little friend' of* HERCULES, HYLAS, *tries to get himself paired off with a* WOMAN OF LEMNOS *but* HERCULES *pursues him, threatening, and drags him off by the ear back up the gangplank of the Argo.* BUTES *follows* HERCULES & HYLAS, *sadly and slowly.*
Once HERCULES *is back on board he begins to harangue the* ARGONAUTS *joyfully becoming acquainted with their respective women.*
During the following HYLAS *keeps trying to creep back off the ship and find himself the* GIRL *who keeps calling from various places:* HYLAS! *Whenever he responds to the call,* HERCULES *grabs him and hauls him back.*

HERCULES. (*To Argonauts.*)
    I'm not setting foot on an isle with no males.
    I'm suspicious that there are none in sight.
    I'm staying on board till the Argo sails.
    I don't care for women equipped for a fight.

BUTES.
    And I'm staying here to watch the night

VOICE OF THE GIRL OF LEMNOS.
    Hylas!

HERCULES. (*Hauling back Hylas by the scruff of the neck.*)
    I don't like fighting women; I deplore
    women carrying swords and shields,
    women dressed like real men for war.
    A woman's a woman, and she yields!

BUTES.
    O how I miss my own small flowery fields!

VOICE OF THE GIRL OF LEMNOS.
    Hylas!

HERCULES. (*Hauling back Hylas by the scruff of the neck.*)
    O when I was younger, yes, I whored
    along with the rest from shore to shore
    but I tell you I didn't like a whore
    who came to bed with a sword!

BUTES.
    O the sound of my bees' honey as it poured!

VOICE OF THE GIRL OF LEMNOS.
    Hylas!

HERCULES. (*Hauling back Hylas by the scruff of the neck.*)
    Women are never to be trusted
    and women with weapons much less.
    And a woman who wants to be lusted
    should wear a woman's dress.

BUTES.
    O since she died, the loneliness!

VOICE OF THE GIRL OF LEMNOS.
    Hylas!

HERCULES. (*Hauling back Hylas by the scruff of the neck.*)
    Are you all staying here in Lemnos
    to end up pushing a plough
    or are you all coming with me
    to plough the Argo through the sea
    and go on with our journey NOW?

BUTES.
    O I wish I were in Hades with her now!

VOICE OF THE GIRL OF LEMNOS.
    Hylas!

And through this we hear JASON's *'Delizie Contenti' and it is those quoted sentiments that win the day with the* ARGONAUTS *who are in no mood, with a woman at their side, to take notice of* HERCULES's *misogyny.* THE ARGONAUTS *troop off with the* WOMEN OF LEMNOS *to a grand orgy of coupling.*

THE ARGONAUTS.
    Between her waist
    and plump round knees
    there's a sweet taste
    beats that of bees.

FIRST ARGONAUT.
> Let epicures who've sucked them boast
> of fat fig and lush litchee
> but the juicy fruit that tastes the best
> lies nine inches from her knee.

CHORUS OF ARGONAUTS.
> Between her waist
> and plump round knees
> there's a sweet taste
> beats that of bees!

SECOND ARGONAUT.
> Let men hymn the mangosteen
> and praise the plump papaya
> they're nothing to the fruit I mean –
> that's formed of flesh and fire!

CHORUS OF ARGONAUTS.
> Between her waist
> and plump round knees
> there's a sweet taste
> beats that of bees!

THIRD ARGONAUT.
> Let men go mad for mango juice
> and for guavas pink and white
> but me I'd fill the Argo's jars
> with the juice I'll sip tonight!

CHORUS OF ARGONAUTS.
> Tonight!

> Between her waist
> and plump round knees
> there's a sweet taste
> beats that of bees!

> Tonight!

The ARGONAUTS *exit laughing with the* WOMEN OF LEMNOS, *leaving on the Argo,* HERCULES, HYLAS, *and the moping* BUTES. HERCULES *drags* HYLAS *off into the stern, leaving* BUTES *alone, as the sound of the festive* ARGONAUTS *dies away, and the night begins to fall slowly.* BUTES *leans over the Argo, looking at the night and the stars.*

BUTES. (*Alone with the night.*)
>   O moon, whose bees are stars
>   send out your swarms tonight
>   and on this sea that scarcely stirs
>   ooze your honied light.
>
>   O moon, whose stars fly out to cull
>   the pollen from the flowering dark
>   let no rough current crush our keel
>   no waves crash on our bark.
>
>   O moon, O distant golden hive
>   where all Earth's light is stored
>   don't let the tranquil ocean heave
>   the huge sea-beasts on board.
>
>   The sea that lies so calm and flat
>   I could scoop out the Pleiades.
>   O nebulae of silver bees
>   how glad I am to see you flit.
>
>   When a man gets to the age I am
>   Death seasons every day
>   as honey might taste of marjoram
>   or my dead wife's soup of bay.
>
>   Death gives the brightest day its flavour
>   when a man has reached my age.
>   Days are spiced with death's own savour
>   as her potroasts were of sage.
>
>   The wine of life's down to the lees
>   and death is its bouquet
>   I won't see my beloved bees
>   before I'm laid in clay.
>
>   When a man gets to the age I am
>   Death seasons every day
>   as honey might taste of marjoram
>   or my dead wife's soup of bay.
>
>   Who wants to voyage for a Fleece
>   and leave his pines and orange trees
>   when he could live and die in peace
>   among his flowers and his bees.

> Who wants to voyage for a Fleece
> and cross these empty seas
> when he could live and die in peace
> among his flowers and his bees.
>
> All these wide waters never yield
> one blossom for a browsing bee.
> Give me the flowers of one small field
> for all this blank and bloomless sea.

Re-enter HERCULES *and* HYLAS *from the stern of the* Argo. *They break into the quiet reveries of* BUTES.

BUTES.

> Since the day my loved one died
> who was for fifty years my wife
> I've been glad to feel my life
> ebbing on that same black tide.
>
> I don't care for the beeless deep
> or for the treeless sea,
> the fleeces on my few lean sheep
> are gold enough for me.

HYLAS. (*To Hercules.*)

> Please! Please! Please! Please!
> Let me go ashore now, Hercules!
> The water you mix your wine with's low
> and you'll soon need more, so let me go,
> let me go ashore now, Hercules.

HERCULES.

> You must, think, boy, that my mind's slow
> if I can't see why you want to go.
> But for your own good my answer's no!
> No! No! No! No!

HYLAS.

> Please! Please! Please! Please!
> Let me go ashore now, Hercules!
> There are no springs and wells at sea
> so when you need water don't blame me
> and let me go ashore now, Hercules!

HERCULES.

> You must think, boy, that my mind's slow
> if I can't see why you want to go,

but for your own good the answer's no!
No! No! No! No!

HYLAS.

Please! Please! Please! Please!
Let me go ashore now, Hercules.
When supplies run out in a day or two
and you're raging for water what will you do?
Please let me go ashore now, Hercules!

HERCULES.

No! No! No! No!
We'll get our water at the next landfall
and now I'm going to make them *all*
get back on their benches and row,
get off their women and row,
get back on their benches and ROW.

BUTES.

Who wants to voyage for a Fleece
and cross these empty seas
when he could live and die in peace
among his flowers and his bees.

HERCULES.

Bees! Bees! Bees! Bees!
Never thinks of anything else but *he*'s
not mooning after amazon shes.

BUTES.

I wonder if, I wonder if maybe . . .

HERCULES.

Maybe's a bee that breeds in May!

BUTES.

Maybe this island's a gynocracy
and the Queen here is a gynocrat.

HERCULES.

Gynocrat! What the hell is that?

BUTES.

A woman who controls the state!

HERCULES.

Zeus save us from that dreadful fate!
Control the state! Do you suppose

that this island's a . . . one of those.
If that's so we may be too late.
Those what do you call 'ems make me sick.
The Argonauts better get back quick
or they might discover death's their date.

BUTES.
They say in the older times of Greece
in the golden ages which knew peace
the female ruled and not the male . . .

HERCULES. (*Roaring in panic.*)
All aboard the Argo! We're setting sail!
How can you even think such a thought
Women rule men! And you an Argonaut!
All aboard the Argo! We're setting sail!

BUTES.
All I'm sure of is I'm not your sort!

HERCULES.
All aboard the Argo! We're setting sail

HERCULES *makes such a commotion that slowly, one by one, or in bedraggled groups the love-worn* ARGONAUTS *appear. As they appear* HERCULES *bullies them back to their benches.*

JASON *alone remains standing still wrapped in thoughts of "delights".* HERCULES *stands by him silently, sullenly, with a sense of threat, and superior physical power.* HYPSIPYLE *is seen running to the shore.* JASON *doesn't want to leave but* HERCULES's *glowering presence makes him finally speak.*

JASON.   We have to set sail while the sky is clear.
HYPSIPYLE.   Was it only the weather that drove you here?
JASON.   A sailor has needs he must satisfy.
HYPSIPYLE.   You came for food and water, is that why?
JASON.   Those needs led us to more delights.
HYPSIPYLE.   Not delightful enough for another few nights?
JASON.   Delightful for years. But we must set sail.
HYPSIPYLE.   Then I pray that the winds blow up a gale.
JASON.   They have things to do this chosen crew.
HYPSIPYLE.   More interesting than what I do for you?
JASON.   The ARGO has a solemn mission.
HYPSIPYLE.   Love always lags behind a man's ambition.
                It was only the weather drove the ARGO here.
JASON.   We have to set sail while the sky is clear . . .

The ARGONAUTS, *urged by* HERCULES *with his club, reluctantly prepare to set sail, and wearily take up their oars.*

HYPSIPYLE.
> So quickly at the first clear sky
> you unfurl the Argo's sails and say goodbye.
>
> And the sailor's heart is lifted by blue skies
> and he sniffs the sea-breezes and he's ready to depart
> and he doesn't give a fig for the girl's
> broken heart
> or the tears that start welling in her eyes
> as the Argo's sail unfurls.

HERCULES. (*His eye, not to mention his club, restraining Jason.*)
> Don't let her fool you. It's all women's lies!

HERCULES *turns his attention to the* ARGONAUTS *and begins to set a murderous pace with the rowing, knowing that the crew are exhausted from their excursion with the Lemnian women.*

HERCULES. (*Setting the murderous rowing pace.*)
> Instead of the thrills of voyage and battle
> you could be farmers and fatten up cattle
> or kneel in wet fields to plant and sow
> then stand around waiting for your wheat to grow –
>
> but you chose to be heroes
> so ROW!
>
> Instead of crossing over dangerous seas
> you could be like Butes here and keep bees
> busying your lives with buzzing hives
> and be like those bees, bossed by your wives –
>
> but you chose to be heroes
> so ROW!
>
> Instead of gaining glory with the Golden Fleece
> you could have stayed at home in Greece
> (and most of you should have done so)
> but you're the Argonauts now so row –
>
> you chose to be heroes, so ROW!
>
> When you're complaining that your bodies are sore
> remember what you did with them just now on shore.

Remember that only an hour or so ago
you were more than happy with the same to and fro –

but now you are heroes,
so ROW!

The ARGONAUTS *row reluctantly and wearily under pressure from the menacing* HERCULES. *With a weary resignation they reprise an earlier "rowing chorus".*

ARGONAUTS.
We love the brine and the boiling foam
and the steady beat of the heavy oars
and the sweat that comes oozing out of our pores
and we're glad to be away from the women at home,
away from the woman's incessant demands
into the sort of heroic life
a man couldn't share with any wife,
and only a man understands:
the open sea, adventures, and strange lands.

This is punctuated with sneering, ironic grunts from HERCULES *who is continually forcing the pressure in the rowing.*

HERCULES.
Instead of gaining glory with the Golden Fleece
you could have stayed at home in Greece
(and most of you should have done so)
but you're the Argonauts now, so ROW –

you chose to be heroes so ROW!

When you're complaining that your bodies are sore
remember what you did with them just now on shore.
Remember that only an hour or so
you were more than happy with the same to and fro –

but now you are heroes
so ROW!

This continues and the ARGONAUTS *row under threats from* HERCULES *and one by one they drop out exhausted until there is only* JASON *and* HERCULES *left rowing together.* JASON *too begins to flag. Then the watchman cries out that there's land ahead.*

LYNCEUS.
Land!   Land!   There's a fine green island ahead!

ARGONAUTS.
>Land! Land! Sleep! Sleep! Rest! Bed! Bed!

Once more the ARGONAUTS *land, utterly exhausted. They settle themselves down at once to sleep.* HERCULES *regards them contemptuously.*

HERCULES.
>Call yourselves men, you effeminate lot.
>I'm going to kill something for the pot!

HERCULES *kicks the sleeping, weary* HYLAS *with his foot and wakes him.*

HERCULES.
>Hylas! I know how eager you were before
>to do me a service and go ashore,
>so NOW go and find a fresh spring.
>I've a flagon of wine needs watering!

HYLAS *is exhausted like the other* ARGONAUTS, *but has little choice but to obey* HERCULES, *and slowly he gets up out of his sleep, lights a brand from the camp-fire, as the evening approaches, and goes off reluctantly, still half asleep, in search of fresh water. He protests meekly, and* HERCULES *relishes denying him his sleep.*

HYLAS. (*Reprising earlier duet.*)
>Please! Please! Please! Please!
>please let me sleep now, Hercules!
>I'll go tomorrow at the break of day
>I'll need the daylight to find my way!
>Please, let me sleep now, Hercules!

HERCULES.
>No! No! No! No!

HYLAS, *with his torch lit to find his way, reluctantly departs.* HERCULES *watches him leave, then shoulders his weapons and goes hunting. We see the torch of* HYLAS *wandering to and fro in the distance. Then from the "hole", the "pit" in the stage from which the* GODDESS *made her appearance we hear a voice singing* HYLAS. *It is the voice of the* YOUNG GIRL OF LEMNOS. *Gradually other female voices are added to the solo voice and the calling of* HYLAS *becomes a rich, complex chorus, luring the torch nearer and nearer to the hole until we see it dragged into the hole and extinguished.*

CHORUS OF WOMEN.
>Hylas! Hylas! Hylas! Hylas! Hylas! Hylas!

The torch wanders then stops and the CHORUS *becomes louder and louder and the torch of* HYLAS *is extinguished. Night thickens. Dawn breaks. Enter* HERCULES *bearing his "catch", animals to cook in the pot. He flings them down noisily, waking some of the sleeping* ARGONAUTS. *He shouts for* HYLAS, *gradually waking up the whole crew.*

HERCULES.

Hylas!	Why's everybody sleeping? I'm wide awake!
Hylas!	I've been hunting all night for these weaklings' sake!
Hylas!	Come and rub my muscles. They ache.
Hylas!	Come and see the beasts that I've caught.
Hylas!	Let's have some of the water you brought.
Hylas!	Bring me a drink, boy, my throat's so dry.
Hylas!	I need a cup of wine now or I'll die!
Hylas!	Come here quick, or you'll get a black eye.
Hylas!	my little friend, please don't tease!
Hylas!	my dear one, come to me, *please*!

Silence follows each of his cries for HYLAS.
Finally a weary JASON *approaches* HERCULES.

JASON.
Do you need to be so noisy, Hercules?

Look your bawling's gone and woken all *my* men
They needed their sleep for the voyage ahead.
In a few minutes we have to put to sea again!

HERCULES.
To find my Hylas, I'd wake up the dead!
I can't believe the boy is still in his bed!

JASON.
Hylas hasn't come back, I'm sorry to say.
He's tired of your bullying. He's gone his own way.

HERCULES.
Don't joke with me. I'm dangerous.

JASON. (*Summoning the Argonauts to his side.*)
We know you're dangerous, *all* of us!
But what I'm telling you is true
your 'little friend' has run out on you.

HERCULES *drops everything and begins to run about searching for* HYLAS *while the* ARGONAUTS *begin to prepare to leave.*

ARGONAUTS. (*Mockingly after Hercules.*)
> Do you think the Golden Fleece
> will fly here of its own accord?
> Was this the reason why we crossed the seas?
> Come on!   Get moving!
>> Hercules!

JASON *now sees his way clear to being the undisputed leader of the expedition, and begins to hasten the preparations, with a view to leaving* HERCULES *on the island.*

JASON.
> Come on! Get moving! Back on board!

ARGONAUTS. (*Calling after Hercules.*)

HERCULES. (*In the distance.*)
> Hylas!   Hylas!   Hylas!   Hylas!

We hear the echo of the VOICES OF THE NYMPHS *who dragged* HYLAS *to his death, mocking* HERCULES.

VOICES OF THE NYMPHS.
> -ass!   -ass!   -ass!   -ass!   -ass!

ARGONAUTS. (*Taking up the echo with gusto.*)
> -ass!   -ass!   -ass!   -ass!   -ass!

The ARGONAUTS *board the Argo and, as they do, reprise their former words about their comrade.*

ARGONAUTS.
> He's a brute and a braggart, a boozer and a boor,
> his behaviour's crude and crass.
> He brands every woman as a wicked whore
> and his other little weakness is . . .

HERCULES. (*In distance, growing fainter.*)
> Hylas!   Hylas!   Hylas!   Hylas!

VOICES OF THE NYMPHS. (*As echo, mocking.*)
> -ass!   -ass!   -ass!   -ass!

ARGONAUTS.
> -ass!   -ass!   -ass!   -ass!

HERCULES. (*Ever fainter, panicking.*)
> Don't leave me behind!

VOICES OF THE NYMPHS. (*As echo, mocking.*)
    behind!   behind!   behind!   behind!

ARGONAUTS.
    behind!   behind!   behind!   behind!

HERCULES.
    Hylas!   Hylas!   Hylas!   Hylas!

VOICES OF THE NYMPHS.
    -ass!   -ass!   -ass!   -ass!

The ARGONAUTS' *refrain gets louder the further away from the island they row.*

ARGONAUTS.
    -ass!   -ass!   -ass!   -ass!

    Hercules who wouldn't come ashore
    to find a girl to enjoy
    now deserts his place at the oar
    to go chasing after a BOY!

HERCULES. (*Faintest.*)
    Hylas!   Hylas!   Hylas!   Hylas!

VOICES OF THE NYMPHS.
    -ass!   -ass!   -ass!   -ass!

ARGONAUTS. (*Speeding the rhythm of their rowing to the echo.*)
    -ass!   -ass!   -ass!   -ass!

Once the ARGONAUTS *have established the rhythm of their rowing they reprise.*

ARGONAUTS.
    There's nowhere a man feels any more free
    than the wide open sea
    with no land to the North, no land to the South,
    no land to the East or West,
    and the spray leaves a salt-taste in the mouth
    and the men's hearts are one on an heroic quest
    for the Golden Fleece,
    the Golden Fleece!

The ARGONAUTS *exit and fade away gradually on the Argo. The voyage is taking place over a number of weeks, and meanwhile we are transferred to the court of Colchis.*

It is hard, metallic, male, rigid. A barbaric splendour, severe and menacing.

KING AEETES, *the father of* MEDEA, *sits among a group of armed men. At high level behind a kind of zenana grille are* MEDEA *and attendant girls.*

JASON *and the* ARGONAUTS *are brought in under armed guard. Formalities are cautiously exchanged. Many people come looking for the Golden Fleece but none has passed the tests prescribed by* AEETES, *which he does now for the benefit of the new hopeful,* JASON.

AEETES.
    Colchis is littered with Fleece-seekers' skulls.
    They didn't pass the first test: fiery bulls.
    So far all those who've tried
    lasted a minute before they died.
    The bulls whose breath is searing flame
    have to be harnessed and made tame.
    Get the bulls into harness, then
    face the fury of the earth-sown men.
    After the bulls with the flaming breath
    you next have to fight these to the death,
    men who when the Dragon teeth are sown
    leap armed from the earth, fully grown.
    and anyone wanting to possess
    the guarded Golden Fleece
    first must fight the Dragoness
    who devours those who break her sleep.

    And sleep is what I now suggest.
    Tomorrow at dawn you face your test.

The GUARDS *escort the* ARGONAUTS *and* JASON *out. Then with barbaric ceremony the court of* AEETES *parade out with their king. The upper grille (which might reflect the bars of the first prison scene) now descends and we see the girls in a huddle discussing the pronouncement of* AEETES *and* JASON's *reaction, and their mistress* MEDEA's *reaction to* JASON. MEDEA *is apart, deep in thought.*

GIRLS A.   Did you see how pale he turned?
GIRLS B.   Did you see how her cheeks burned?
GIRLS A.   Did you see his eyes on fire?
GIRLS B.   Did you see her eyes on fire?
GIRLS A.   With fear!
GIRLS B.   With love!
GIRLS A.   Medea?
GIRLS B.   In love!

GIRLS A.   Did you see how his men grieved?
GIRLS B.   Did you see how her breasts heaved?
GIRLS A.   Did you see the panic in his eyes?
GIRLS B.   Did you see the passion in her eyes?
GIRLS A.   Did you see him shake, did you see . . .?
GIRLS B.   Did you see her shake in sympathy?

GIRLS A.   I think he saw himself already dead!
GIRLS B.   I think she saw herself in Jason's bed!
GIRLS A.   His fear!
GIRLS B.   Her love!
GIRLS A.   Medea?
GIRLS B.   In love!

Exit the attendants of MEDEA, *leaving* MEDEA *alone.*
As they leave we see on the opposite side of the stage JASON *alone in his "quarters".*

JASON. (*Alone.*)
        I'd sooner have his muscles than my masculine charms.
        Now we could do with his beef and his brawn.
        Although he's a braggart, a boozer and a boor
        his strength not his brains are what we chose him for,
        his iron fists, his tree-trunk arms
        and I wish we hadn't left him on that distant shore
        and that tomorrow he stood by my side
        when I'm put to the test at dawn.

        That was a terrible trick that we played.
        Only a god can come to my aid.
        I could do with his beef and brawn
        not to mention his blundering bravery
        when I'm put to the test at dawn
        and the bulls start breathing their fire at me.

MEDEA. (*Alone.*)
        The herbs I cull from hidden vales
        can't cure my desperate case.
        Every magic potion fails
        to make me forget his face . . .

As she sings the NURSE [WOMAN 2] *enters and joins in* MEDEA's *words half reminding us that we have seen them as "components" of the Goddess.*

The herbs I cull from hidden vales
can't cure my desperate case.
Every magic potion fails
to make me forget his face.

MEDEA. (*To Nurse.*)
Say to him:

The bulls whose flaming nostrils snort
with fierce flesh-withering fire
my magic soon can set at naught
but can't harness my desire.

The Dragoness you will defeat
I can drug into a doze
but something of far fiercer heat
has robbed me of repose.

NURSE *leaves with the message and crosses the stage to* JASON's
"*quarters*". *As she crosses we hear* JASON *still regretting the absence
of Hercules and wishing he had never come to Colchis.*

JASON.
I wish that I could still hear the trees
we cut down for oars to cross the seas
still swaying and sighing in the breeze
and hear them creak in the wind and continue to grow
not creak in our hands as we row, row, row,
through the clashing Symplegades.
Better that the Argo's boards still grew
on Pelion and drank up the dew,
and were not sodden with the salt of the sea
and I wish each part of our ship were a tree
as it was on some mountain near our own shores
where the people were friendly, were in Greece
rather than what they are now, oars
that shipped us here for the Golden Fleece
and now we're trapped here with no hope of release . . .

The weakness I'm feeling in my knees
reminds me I'm not Hercules.

Enter Medea's NURSE.
*She immediately without formalities of explanation tells him her
urgent message:*

NURSE.

> Go at the dead of night and stand alone,
> dig a pit, kill a lamb, and sacrifice
> to the Goddess, call her once, twice, thrice,
> call the Virgin, call the Mother, call the Crone,
> and you'll see the Goddess begin to rise
> from the earth in her threeform guise,
> the Virgin, the Mother, the Crone!

> Medea, my mistress also told me to say:

> The herbs I cull from hidden vales
> can't cure my desperate case.
> Every magic potion fails
> to make me forget his face.

> The bulls whose flaming nostrils snort
> with fierce flesh-withering fire
> my magic soon can set at naught
> but can't harness my desire.

> The Dragoness you will defeat
> I can drug into a doze
> but something of far fiercer heat
> has robbed me of repose.

The NURSE *then adds stanzas of her own, thus showing the continuity of the* VIRGIN *and* CRONE, *and that somewhere they are part of the same triple Goddess.*

NURSE.

> I can help you win this fight
> and drug the Dragoness
> but love is quite beyond my might
> with love I am powerless

> Why if I can make you like Hercules
> is there one thing I can't do.
> Though I can help you conquer these
> I can't help loving you.

> Go at the dead of night and stand alone
> Call the Virgin, call the Mother, call the Crone!

Exit NURSE. JASON *alone. Darkness.*

Dawn. The ARGONAUTS *and* COLCHIANS *are ranged, like rival foot-ball supporters, on each side of the stage, facing out into the audience, where the contest is to be imagined taking place.*
MEDEA *is seated, alone among men, next to her father,* KING AEETES. *She appears, for once on these occasions, nervous and apprehensive about seeing yet another victim of her father's court mutilated and killed.* AEETES *notices, with some surprise, the unusual squeamish-ness of his favourite daughter.*

AEETES.
      Medea, you've always been your father's daughter,
      a daughter after my own iron heart,
      appealed to often by those that I condemn
      who thought that a girl would take their part,
      appealed to with an awful groan,
      appealed to with a dreadful cry
      but your heart, like your father's, was a stone.
      Like me you have a stony, icy heart,
      and you said *no* and watched them die.
      You looked unflinchingly on *them*
      and offered *them* no quarter
      and because you're your father's stony daughter
      you didn't bat an eye
      as you watched those victims die
      but now you seem nervous, why, Medea, why?

      You've seen men trampled by bulls before,
      you've seen them trampled into bones and gore
      and the bulls' breath flaying their flesh raw
      so what's made that icy heart of yours thaw?

      You've watched often and I never saw you wince
      when reckless foreign prince after prince
      drawn to Colchis for the Golden Fleece
      but never leaving Colchis in one piece,
      was impaled or castrated or boiled in oil
      and never did I see you once recoil,
      so what is this Jason that you should shy
      from seeing *him* tormented and die?

      Your mother had a certain squeamish streak
      which I'd hoped I'd eradicate in you.
      I hope that in the end you won't turn out weak
      and identify with victims as your mother used to do.

You've seen the victims I've had garrotted
or chained to the rocks until they rotted,
you've watched with me many hundreds die
but now you seem squeamish, why, Medea, why?

I didn't know *my* daughter knew how to cry!

You've watched unflinching while the flogger flogs
men's flesh off their backs in bloody strips.
I've seen you beat time to the whistling whips
and you've watched while men's still beating hearts
as well as their other even fouler parts
get torn out, torn off and flung to the dogs,
but now you seem squeamish, why, Medea, why?
But now you seem squeamish, why?
I didn't think my daughter knew how to cry.

MEDEA.
The seawind's blown some grit into my eye!

ARGONAUTS. (*On their side of the "arena", fearfully.*)
The bulls! They're breathing fire! He's going to die!

COLCHIANS. (*On their side of the "arena", triumphantly.*)
The bulls! They're breathing fire! He's going to die!

Music of struggle. The ARGONAUTS *and* COLCHIANS *react in their respective ways to the contest of* JASON *with the fire-breathing bulls taking place in the audience space.* MEDEA *alone of the* COLCHIANS *reacts like the* ARGONAUTS. *The* ARGONAUTS *on one side and the* COLCHIANS *on the other behave like team-supporters at a football match.*

ARGONAUTS.
He's beaten them. He's yoked the bulls somehow.
He's making those monsters pull the plough!

COLCHIANS.
But now he has to fight the Dragon men.
He has to fight the Dragon men now.
He can't be so lucky again.
He doesn't stand a chance against these!

ARGONAUTS.
Maybe Jason's become a Hercules!

Now the two groups react to the second struggle between JASON *and the* DRAGON MEN. *At first things appear to go badly for* JASON, *being outnumbered.*

ARGONAUTS.
>But even Hercules couldn't succeed
>against so many of the Dragon breed.

COLCHIANS.
>Jason is wounded. He's starting to bleed!

Then, through the magic of MEDEA, *whose reactions among the* COLCHIANS *are singularly different,* JASON *begins to win. The change is registered on the faces of the* ARGONAUTS *and* COLCHIANS.

ARGONAUTS.
>Look! The monsters are leaving Jason alone!
>They are murdering each other instead.

>Someone started it by throwing a stone.
>Look, all the Dragonmen are dead!

COLCHIANS.
>How could it happen. I don't understand.
>Some god or goddess had a hand.

AEETES.
>More like the work of my daughter, MEDEA!

MEDEA *is nowhere to be seen, she has vanished.* COLCHIANS *scatter.*

COLCHIANS.
>Kill him!   Kill her!   Slay him!   Slay her!

General confusion and alarm. ARGONAUTS *flee in one direction,* COLCHIANS *in another, leaving the stage bare but for the presence of the Pit. The Golden Fleece is in the pit, the hole into which we saw* CREUSA *leap, and the* GODDESS *emerge from, and into which* HYLAS *was dragged by the nymphs. The same voices form the "voice" of the* DRAGONESS, *which we never see, but which we hear singing in the Pit. The voice is 20 voices* 1/2/3/4/5/6/7/8/9/10/11/12/13/14/15/16/17/18/19/20. *The 20 female voices of the* CHORUS [W] *sound like a serpentine link, a vast "round" which both suggests the smooth sinuous, gliding motion of the snake and also the internal jointed, more angular motion of its skeletal vertebrae, all 20. Nevertheless it forms one continuous serpentine voice. The text for the* DRAGONESS *uses the Greek, Latin and French texts set out on page 373 but given a more "snake-like" setting. Another ancient aspect of the "female" like the* GODDESS, *and should have some musical connection with those linked 3 voices. The 20 voices are one continuous voice, writhing, squirming, fierce, fiery, threatening, ever-wakeful, coiling, and unwinding, making sudden darts with its head. The* DRAGONESS *uses as her text the words from European languages for snake: Schlange [German], serpent [French], reptile, snake, cobra, python, anguis [Latin], ophis [Greek], sierpe, serpiente, culebra [Spanish], colubro, serpe [Italian], etc etc. The separate words could be considered its "vertebrae", the total sound its continuous glide.*

Wisps of smoke come out of the Pit, thickening. JASON *enters and approaches the Pit which smokes even more as he draws near. The voice of the* DRAGONESS *becomes ever more threatening.* JASON *backs away. Enter* MEDEA *as if pursued.*

MEDEA.
> I can help you in this fight
> and drug the Dragoness
> but love is quite beyond my might
> with love I am powerless,
> and Jason I love you.

JASON.
> Only help me in this fight
> and drug the Dragoness
> and you and I will know tonight
> the joys of tenderness . . .

MEDEA *produces from her robes the electrocution cap/bowl in which she mixes a potion, which she sprinkles slowly and solemnly into the Pit. The smoke begins to reduce, the voices of the* DRAGONESS *drop out 3 by 3 (or 1 by 1) as the monster becomes drowsy. There should be some connection between the way the* DRAGONESS *voices drop out and the way the voices of the stoned 14 children drop as they die in Act 2, and a similar charm song against evil.*

JASON *descends into the Pit and emerges with the Golden Fleece.*

MEDEA.
> You have the fleece, now flee.
> They're following. Take me.
> Take me with you and the Fleece.
> Carry us both away to Greece.

JASON *takes hold of* MEDEA *and they flee.*

The Argo meanwhile has been prepared in haste. The ARGONAUTS *are in place ready to make a quick getaway. They sing their rowing song darkened with foreboding at having a woman on board a ship.*

ARGONAUTS.
> We love the brine and the boiling foam
> and the steady beat of the heavy oars
> and the sweat that comes oozing from our pores
> and we're glad to be away from the women at home
> away from the women's incessant demands . . .

ARGONAUT 1.
> But now we've got a woman on our hands!

ARGONAUT 2.
> *Jason's* got a woman on his hands!

ARGONAUT 3.
> Jason's got a woman. If the choice were mine
> I'd pitch the damned woman into the brine.

ARGONAUT 4.
> Jason's got a woman. If I were him
> I'd drop her in the ocean and let her swim!

ARGONAUT 5.
> Jason's got a woman. If it were me
> I'd fling the foreign bitch into the sea!

ARGONAUT 6.
> It's nothing but bad luck, a woman on board!
> Jason should run her through with his sword!

ARGONAUT 7.
> We all know how Jason will run her through.
> You're jealous, all of you, *you* haven't a screw!

ARGONAUT 8.
> Well, if Jason were to share her around.
> I'd vote for one that she shouldn't be drowned!

ARGONAUT 9.
> If Hercules were here Jason wouldn't dare
> gaze at the woman and stroke her dark hair!

ARGONAUT 10.
> Hercules would have wrung her neck
> before she set her dainty foot on deck.

ARGONAUT 11.
>   Hercules wouldn't allow on the Argo's decks
>   any member of that unlucky sex!

ARGONAUT 8. (*Again.*)
>   Well, if Jason would only share her around,
>   I'd vote for one that she shouldn't be drowned!

ARGONAUT 12.
>   Well not until we'd all had a go.
>   I wouldn't want her after Jason though!

BUTES. (*Interrupting.*)
>   She seems a fine, noble woman, don't be crude!

LYNCEUS. (*The watchman.*)
>   Row faster! Row faster! We're being pursued!

BUTES.
>   She seems a fine noble woman, there's no need to be crude!
>
>   She even seems a little shy,
>   and as we left her homeland shore
>   I saw a tear fall from one eye
>   and her fear for what lies in store,
>
>   I saw the fear on her face,
>   fear she'll be shunned, or fear she'll be cursed
>   as a stranger in a foreign place
>   and wish fate could be reversed.
>
>   Medea might make Jason an excellent wife
>   to keep him stable for the rest of his life!

ARGONAUT 12.
>   For the rest of the year maybe she'll do
>   but he'll want a change before the year is through!

BUTES.
>   On a small farm bounded with olives and pine
>   I lived over fifty years with mine,
>   from when she was a virgin, straight and slim
>   when we marched together to the wedding hymn
>   to when she was big-bellied with our boys,
>   and to when she was old and bent and lame
>   and my golden-haired girl was grey
>   and every age was a source of new joys
>   and I loved my woman till her dying day

and for those fifty years my love stayed the same,
and the fire of my first love never lost its flame.

And the torch that guided us first to bed
when, almost still children, we two were wed
I relit again when I found my love dead
and with the same brand that had lit our way
to our first embrace on our wedding day
I guided my dear one to her bed of clay,
and for fifty years our love stayed the same.
The fire of our first love never lost its flame . . .

ARGONAUT 3.
    Well, I still think Medea ought to be drowned!

LYNCEUS.
    Careful down there! Or we'll run aground!

The Argo runs aground on the island of Macris. The ARGONAUTS *are at once welcomed by the people of Macris, which is everything that Colchis wasn't, friendly, warm, hospitable, Greek.*
The court here is presided over by an old King and Queen, King ALCINOUS *and Queen* ARETE, *who appear to have the kind of long-established loving relationship described by* BUTES *the bee man in his last words.*
There is feasting, displaying of the Fleece, celebration, wine, food.
It is all interrupted by the entry of a breathless MESSENGER.

MESSENGER.
    A fleet from Colchis has entered our water.
    King Aeetes demands the return of his daughter.
    The king has sent a herald ashore.
    He claims his daughter by the Fathers' law.

All celebration ceases.
MEDEA *begins to appeal first to* ARETE [WOMAN 2] *then* JASON, *then* ALCINOUS.

MEDEA.
    Arete, you're a Mother, I appeal to you!
    Once my father gets me back
    he'll close the last chink in his armoured heart
    and the daughter he loved once
    he certainly loved once
    will have her body stretched on the rack
    and be slowly torn apart.

I daren't speak of the things he'll do.

Jason, I helped you, I appeal to you!
Arete, you're a mother, I appeal to you.

Alcinous, kind king, I appeal to you!

ALCINOUS. (*Gravely.*)
Give me the night to think what to do.
A father has a paramount right.
I promise you are safe here for the night,
But give me the night hours to think it through.

The Court clears, the festivity and celebration by now totally subdued.
We see the private bedroom of ALCINOUS *and* ARETE.
ARETE *is in bed.* ALCINOUS *paces in thought, burdened by decision. There is a deep tenderness between the two.*

ALCINOUS.
Her father has the gods' law on his side!

ARETE.
But not if Medea is Jason's bride!

ALCINOUS.
She may be still a virgin. We don't know.

ARETE. (*Gesturing him to bed.*)
Decide in the morning. The morning will show.

ALCINOUS.
If Medea still has her maidenhead,
it's to her father she must belong.

ARETE.
You're tired. Let me sing you a song.
Come and rest in my arms. Come to bed.
I'll sing to you, and stroke your troubled head.

ALCINOUS.
Her father has the gods' law on his side.

ARETE.
Yes, yes! In the morning you can decide.
(*Aside.*)
The *gods'* law, maybe, but the GODDESS says no!
I heard the Goddess say Medea shan't go.

ALCINOUS
  What was that you muttered just then?

ARETE.
  Nothing, my darling. Come to bed! (*Aside.*) Men!

ALCINOUS *comes to bed and* ARETE *takes him in her arms and soothes him to sleep with a song that should echo the last song of* BUTES *the bee man, and might even contain the "seeds" of the* WEDDING HYMN *which will conclude this act and start Act 2.*

ARETE.
  For fifty years you've come to my bed
  with an anxious heart or a troubled head
  and you've lain your weary head on my breast,
  my once full but now withered breast
  and the feel of my body gave you rest
  and does still,
  and will, and will,
  and for fifty years our love's stayed the same
  and the fire of our first love never lost its flame.

  Dream, dream of when you took me first to bed
  dream of when you took my maidenhead!

Already this might be an early cue for the Wedding Hymn to follow. As soon as ARETE *perceives that, as usual,* ALCINOUS *has fallen into a deep contented sleep she goes to the door and summons a* WOMAN, *and whispers:*

ARETE.
  Jason must bed Medea by dawn!

Now there is a long line of identical waiting WOMEN *stretching from the palace bedroom to a place offstage where we presume the* ARGONAUTS *to be sleeping. The first* WOMAN *passes the message to the second* WOMAN *who passes to the third and so on until the message reaches the other side.*

WOMEN 1/2/3/4/5/6/7/8/ . . .
  Jason must bed Medea by dawn!

Also the relay begin to pass lit torches from the palace along the line to where the ARGONAUTS *will finally emerge as a* WEDDING PROCESSION *singing the Wedding Hymn and bearing each a marriage-torch.*

CHORUS. (*Wedding Hymn.*)
> O digno coniuncta viro, dotabere virgo.
> Ferte facis propere, thalamo deducere adorti.
> Ora favete omnes et cingite tempora ramis.
>> [Hosidius Geta (2nd century A.D.) *Medea*]

MEDEA *and* JASON, *bride and groom, precede the* WEDDING
PROCESSION. *We see a slow, solemn procession, quiet because of the
circumstances and whenever a natural need for celebration makes
the Wedding Hymn too loud, a hissed message is passed along the
relay of* WOMEN *from the palace bedroom door, where* ARETE
watches the sleeping ALCINOUS.

WOMEN (*In relay.*)
> Not so loud! You'll wake the king!

*And accordingly the natural celebration of the Wedding Hymn is
suppressed so that* ALCINOUS *doesn't discover it taking place.
A line of torches also, in the hands of the* WOMEN *stretches from
palace to procession. The king stirs in his sleep.
The new message that is passed along is:*

WOMEN.
> Douse the torches! Douse the torches!

*And one by one the line of torches which stretches from palace to the
door of the wedding chamber for* MEDEA *and* JASON *which is a bed
over which the Golden Fleece has been thrown, are extinguished by
those who carry them, either* WOMEN *from the palace or* ARGONAUTS
*who stand in a line that leads to the bed chamber. All the torches go
out except the one held by* BUTES *who is the last to extinguish his,
then only* JASON *is left holding a torch to illuminate the bed spread
with the Golden Fleece.*

BUTES. (*Holding up the last torch.*)
> And the torch that guided us first to bed
> when, almost still children, we two were wed
> I relit again when I found my love dead
> and with the same brand that had lit our way
> to our first embrace on our wedding day
> I guided my dear one to her bed of clay,
> and for fifty years our love stayed the same
> and the fire of our first love never lost its flame.

JASON/MEDEA.

> O love, my love, before
> the last torch darkens at the door
> and the bright love-brand grows cold,
> hold the last flame up to shine
> on the Fleece's flashing gold
> where I shall make you mine,
> the Golden Fleece that has been spread
> to furnish us a marriage bed,
> the Golden Fleece all night will shed
> its truest light on you and me
> and sanctify our unity
> and sanctify our unity.

JASON's torch is extinguished and in the glow of gold they enter.

From the shadows at either side of the stage enter the DOWNSTAGE MAN *and* DOWNSTAGE WOMAN, *who move as if influenced by the air of solemn union to be reconciled and follow* JASON *and* MEDEA, *but before they meet in the centre there is a loud discordant sound from the orchestra which stops them dead in their tracks.*

END OF ACT ONE

ACT TWO

*The Wedding Hymn is heard, loud, clear, joyful, where the Wedding
Hymn of the marriage of* JASON *and* MEDEA *was quiet, subdued,
secretive. Where we heard only the male voices of the* ARGONAUTS *in
the previous Wedding Hymn, we now hear a rich, harmonious
complement of male and female voices, hymning the true, potentially
peaceful, union between man and woman. As the curtain rises we see
the* WEDDING PROCESSION *grouped as before, with the addition of
women, but as near as possible to the concluding spectacles of Act
One. Whereas on Macris the procession was conducted in the dark
with torches that had to be doused, this procession is in the full light
of day. The elements of the ritual are identical and we should feel we
are watching a continuation of the same procession we saw at the
end of Act One. Once more we see the bridegroom* JASON *come into
view with his bride, only this time the bride is not* MEDEA *but* CREUSA,
daughter of CREON, *King of Corinth.*
The WEDDING PROCESSION *should begin to establish itself both as
"real" and as in the mind of the raging* MEDEA *we now see with the*
NURSE.

MEDEA. (*With the hymn still audible, to Nurse.*)
 I wish now my father had got me back!
 The terrors of torture, the pains of the rack,
 the scars of the whip and the *scourge,*
 the flesh stripped bare to the bloodied bone,
 the gamut of agonies and cruel hurts
 are nothing to the pains that sear and *surge*
 through the heart of a woman a man deserts
 for another, leaving her alone
 in a hostile land, with her children, *alone,*
 for the mad mob who hate her to stab and to *stone.*

NURSE.
 Call the Virgin! Call the Mother! Call the Crone!

MEDEA.
 In Colchis at least I'd have died before I knew
 that a man who loved you could be untrue.
 Though love took me wholly by surprise
 I'm more surprised now that his love dies
 and his faithless heart is a nest of lies.
 It's taken ten years for the truth to eme*rge:*
 he doesn't want his children or their *mother*

he wants to bind himself to another
and all to possess a paltry *throne.*

NURSE.

Call the Virgin! Call the Mother! Call the Crone!

The sounds of the Wedding Hymn continue to return.

MEDEA. (*To Nurse.*)
I should have let him be burnt to death,
his flesh set aflame by the bull's fierce breath,
I should have let them trample him dead
cracking his bones and crushing his head
I should have let the men hack him piece by piece,
I should have let him die, but instead,
deceived by love my magic can't check
I put a noose round my own neck
and let him win the Golden Fleece,
and all for these ten years in his bed,
wandering with him from place to place
being abused for my foreign face,
only to be thrown aside
once he found himself a "better" bride!

I'll turn their wedding hymn into a *dirge.*
I'll *smother* the torches in the smoke of death,
and change their joy-chants to a dismal *drone.*

NURSE.

Call the *Virg*in! Call the *Mother*! Call the *Crone*!

MEDEA.
I'll turn their wedding hymn into a *dirge.*
I'll *smother* their torches in the smoke of death,
and change their joy-chants to a dismal *drone.*

NURSE.

Call the *Virg*in! Call the *Mother*! Call the *Crone*!

This leads the two women into an invocation of the GODDESS, *one of
the "quotations" from a previous opera, the* Medea *of Cherubini.
The Invocation is heard against the sound of the Wedding Hymn as
the* WEDDING PROCESSION *re-enters. The* WEDDING PROCESSION
*should be felt as a continuous presence, a perpetual goad to the rage
of* MEDEA, *and present on stage, either as "real" or still tormentingly*

imagined by MEDEA, *stung that* JASON *and* CREUSA *are marrying to the same ritual by which he married her on Macris 10 years ago, a ritual hurried, hushed and suppressed. Its musical presence should also be continuous, giving us a hymn to the potential union of man and woman and something which continually enrages the mind and heart of* MEDEA.

The WEDDING PROCESSION *in all its glory "delivers"* JASON *to* MEDEA *and possibly continues and then re-emerges to "pick up"* JASON *after his confrontation with* MEDEA, *or stays in a "freeze" which is reanimated each time* JASON *rejoins his bride.*

M.   Your marriage torch will be a funeral brand.
J.   You are meddling in things you don't understand.
M.   Deceit and fraud I don't understand, no!
J.   Don't cause trouble. Creon wants you to go.
M.   I don't want to stay here. We'll go away!
J.   Creon may allow the children to stay.
M.   Our sons will go where their mother goes.
J.   They'll stone you, you witch in barbaric clothes.
M.   I have my magic! I can get by!
J.   Corinth doesn't want you, nor do I!
M.   Once you couldn't wait to drag me to bed.
J.   That part of me will never be dead.
M.   Then why take some little virgin instead?
J.   To be able to wear a crown on my head.
     King Creon's daughter gives me power in this land.
M.   Your marriage torch will be a funeral brand.

As if to prove her wrong JASON *raises his wedding torch and rejoins the* WEDDING PROCESSION *which resumes, the* Wedding Hymn *loud and dominant.*

MEDEA.
        I'll turn their wedding hymn into a *dirge*.
        I'll *smother* their torches in the smoke of death
        and change their joy-chants to a dismal *drone*.

NURSE.
        Call the *Vir*gin! Call the *Mother*! Call the *Crone*!

MEDEA & NURSE. (*Invocation*.)

From the Pit comes the sound of many women's voices.

The Invocation and the Wedding Hymn struggle together.
The WEDDING PROCESSION *"delivers"* JASON *again to* MEDEA *(and*

either continues, or pauses in freeze).
JASON *comes towards* MEDEA, *one hand carrying the wedding torch and the other raised to forestall the new torrent of hatred from* MEDEA.

J. No more! Pack what you need, and go!
M. Can one who loved me once turn out so low?
J. Creon wanted you to die. I changed his mind.
    I shed a few tears, or you'd be dead.
M. Thank you, Jason, you are very kind.
    I'm glad to hear you still have tears to shed.
J. Creon has agreed to safeguard our sons.
M. 'Our' sons are mine. Have other ones!
J. I couldn't give them up. I gave them life.
M. Give life to new ones then by your new wife!

J. My feelings run too deep. They stay with me! ⎤
M. My feelings run too deep. They stay with me! ⎦

Out of this tension and conflict, at this point, they explode into a quoted hostile confrontation from Cherubini. Then:

M. You speak about your feelings. Think of mine.
J. You're not a Greek. You feelings aren't so fine!
    Barbarians are all passion and no mind!
    Barbarian *women* are even coarser bred!

M. You never scorned those passions in our bed
    or wished your woman then were more refined.
    You'll miss your Colchian when Creusa's slow.

J. No more! Pack what you need, and go! Go! Go!

JASON *is "picked up" again by the* WEDDING PROCESSION *which here-enters. The Wedding Hymn continues even more maddening to* MEDEA.

MEDEA. (*To Nurse.*)
    If I'd been childless I'd understand
    that he wanted now to seek another's hand.
    If I'd never been a mother
    I'd understand him taking another
    woman for his bed
    someone not barren in my stead.

    My body is a thoroughfare
    for life to return to earth.

It would have been my joy to bear
Jason more than two, and go on giving birth . . .

Though I'd prefer to face ten men with spears
or a phalanx of bowmen in war, yet I *would*
have gone through the pain, have gone through the fears
and endured all the birthpangs and blood.

I would have suffered everything for you.
I would have born you seven times two . . .

I would have born you seven times two.

NURSE. (*Quoting Seneca.*)
                    . . . . *bisque septenos parens*
natos tulissem!

MEDEA.
          I would have born you seven times two!

NURSE. (*Quoting John Studeley's translation of the above.*)
                    . . . . O that the fates of heaven
          A fruitful mother had me made of children seven and seven.

MEDEA.
          If I'd been childless I'd understand
          that you wanted to seek another's hand,
          but I've born you two sons you adore,
          two sons who are your pride.
          I would have born you many more.
          I would have born you seven times two,
          but if you feel that now you need more,
          'give them life' inside your new whore,
          squirt your seed into your new young bride
          and let her feel the pangs and moan,
          let her feel the pangs and moan!

NURSE.
          Call the Mother! Call the Crone!

MEDEA.
          Call Jason. Tell him I will leave alone.

Exit NURSE *to follow procession and give the message to* JASON *who,
in due course, is once more "delivered" by the* WEDDING
PROCESSION. JASON *approaches* MEDEA *this time without the same
apprehension, relieved by the* NURSE's *message that* MEDEA *agrees to
leave Corinth without the sons. He tries, from relief, to address*

MEDEA *somewhat brightly, and* MEDEA *replies in a flat monotone, continually looking past* JASON *for signs of the approach of* NURSE *and two* SONS OF MEDEA.

J.   I'm told that you've now had a change of heart.
M.   No, *you* have, but it's true I'm ready to depart.
J.   I'm glad to hear you've decided to comply.
M.   My mind's made up. That I don't deny.
J.   Our sons will be safe here and will want for naught.
M.   Only a mother! Safety dearly bought!
J.   So, in their interests, you will stand aside?

MEDEA.
     Yes, and I'll send a gift to your bride.
     I'll send them to her, my little ones,
     with gifts so she'll love them, our, no *your* sons!

During this the NURSE *has arrived with the two* SONS OF MEDEA. *The* NURSE *is carrying a casket which contains a golden cloak and coronet which* MEDEA *intends to send to* CREUSA.

J.   Do you suppose this palace has no gold in store.
M.   But no one here has seen these things before.

MEDEA *with a flourish produces the cloak and coronet of gold from the casket. We should recognise them immediately as the garments worn by* MEDEA *at her secret wedding to* JASON *on the island of Macris.* MEDEA *clearly also expects* JASON *to recognise the garments that his bride wore, but there is no reaction from him. Either he doesn't, in fact, recognise the crown and cloak that* MEDEA *wore ten years before or he is indifferent.*
MEDEA, *though, is shocked.*
MEDEA *holds the cloak and coronet towards* JASON.

MEDEA.
     Don't you remember?

JASON. (*Seemingly puzzled.*)
                              No! No!

MEDEA.
     Our wedding! These clothes were what I wore.

JASON.
     I don't remember that night any more.
     It was dark and secretive, and ten years ago!

MEDEA. (*Shakes the crown and cloak before him.*)
You don't remember, but I do! I do!

JASON.
I don't remember and I don't want to!

MEDEA.
For me it's all still strong and clear:
the way *your* garments clung to you
because the night was hot . . .

JASON.
I don't remember, and I'd rather not!

MEDEA. (*Continuing relentlessly.*)
The wedding hymn we could scarcely hear,
the bed with the glowing Golden Fleece,
the ocean sucking at my ear
as passion ebbed back to peace . . .

For me it's all still strong and clear:
when this garment you now don't recall
slid off my body and fell to the ground
your eyes were afire with what they found?

Both bodies seemed moulded out of gold,
a gold to embrace to touch and to hold,
soft and warm to the wandering fingertips.
Gold light seemed to gush out of every pore
as your lips, glowing, met my glowing lips
and gold flesh fused back to its glowing ore,
and for all the dense darkness of that night
the flesh of our bodies was fused into one,
first as gold, then intensest light,
then we glowed in the night like the rising sun.

The glow from the Fleece was so strong and bright,
my whole body was bathed in its golden light,
gold face, gold breasts, gold belly, gold thighs,
and their gold flashed back from your eyes.
The glow from our flesh on the Fleece was so strong,
it was so strong and bright the glow,
and you gazed on me so lovingly and long
that I thought you would be blinded . . .

JASON *is drawn closer to* MEDEA, *impelled by the erotic passion of her recollections, but at this point he suddenly draws back away from temptation.*

JASON.
>
> I don't want to be reminded!
> I don't want to be reminded!
> I don't want to be reminded!
>
> All I want is that you go! Go! Go!

Once more JASON *is "picked up" by the* WEDDING PROCESSION *which continues its celebratory journey.*

MEDEA. (*After Jason.*)
>
> But this time watch your bride with open eyes!
> She'll be the centre of attention . . .
>
> > as she fries!

As the WEDDING PROCESSION *exits once more, the* NURSE *comes forward with the* SONS OF MEDEA. *They find* MEDEA *half embracing the robe of gold. Now she holds out the cloak and coronet to the* SONS.

MEDEA.
>
> I was saving these things for *your* brides to wear.
> They're very old. They're from far away,
> from the land of my fathers far over there
> and I'd saved them for your wedding day . . .
>
> When your father married me
> these were the things I wore
> and we walked in the night by a silent shore.
> It was night and no one could sing.
>
> All we could hear was the sound of the sea,
> and the sea-birds and wild beasts and whispering
> of women afraid of their king.
>
> No one could sing us the wedding hymn,
> no one made glad music or caroused.
> It was done in the dark and the night was grim
> and all the torches had to be doused.
>
> But at least I wore this golden crown
> the Sun made out of his rays,
> and I wore this woven bridal gown,
> though no torches were ablaze,
> and I'd saved them for your wedding days
> I'd saved them them for your wedding days.

As she sings MEDEA *begins to impregnate the gown and crown with a potion from her bowl, the electrocution cap worn in the first scene of all. Then she puts the cloak and the coronet back into the casket which she hands to the* SONS, *who are to take these "gifts" to* CREUSA, *their father's new bride.*

MEDEA.
>   Take them now to the woman who'll care
>   for you when your mother's gone.
>   Tell her they're from you, for her to wear
>   but don't wait for her to put them on.

The SONS OF MEDEA *take the casket.* MEDEA *kisses them, and the* NURSE *leads them away. We still can hear the Wedding Hymn for* JASON *and* CREUSA *which is identical to that of* JASON *and* MEDEA *before.*

The SONS *and the* NURSE *begin what is to be an interrupted walk towards* CREUSA *who is seated on a throne surrounded by* WOMEN ATTENDANTS *as we saw her at the beginning of Act One.*

MEDEA *watches her sons depart, pained, full of anguish, and oscillating between what she feels is justified jealousy and revenge and terror, at the fearful knowledge that she has decided to kill her* SONS *as the ultimate means of revenging herself on* JASON.
She seem to fluctuate between thoughts of never seeing her SONS *as men and gloating over the truly dreadful demise she has devised for* CREUSA.

MEDEA. (*Thinking of sons.*)
>   I'll never see how tall you've grown
>   and see you grow taller than me.
>   I'll never see you with sons of your own
>   or take them on my knee . . .

The sounds of the Wedding Hymn grow audible again and MEDEA *sings in the direction of where* CREUSA *is seated.*

>   And none of this *you*'ll see!
>   (*Thinking of Creusa.*)
>   She'll don the destroying diadem
>   and the dress of woven fire,
>   venomous flame from neck to hem,
>   a fitted funeral pyre!
>
>   Fire's the glow that's deep within
>   Creusa's lethal wreath,

fire that eats through hair and skin
to the scalded skull beneath.

MEDEA *as rapidly reverts to thinking again of her* SONS.

MEDEA. (*Thinking of sons.*)
I'll never know that moment when
though every day I've watched them grow
I'll see that my boys have turned into men
though mere babes not long ago.
None of this I'll know . . .

The sounds of the Wedding Hymn grow audible again and MEDEA *turns her mind to gloating on her coming revenge, any moment imminent.*

MEDEA. (*Thinking of Creusa.*)
And none of this *you*'ll see!

The canker in the coronet
she can't shake loose, can't pull
bathes her hair in acid sweat
corroding her whole skull.

The love for Jason that she stores
in a deep place in her heart
gushes hissing through her pores •
as her body falls apart!

MEDEA *once more rapidly reverts to regretful, tender thoughts of her* SONS, *then in a blaze of fury continues to gloat over the imminent combustion of* CREUSA.

MEDEA.
She can't shake off the coronet
and silks that flay her skin,
the incandescent marionette,
the molten mannequin.

Kiss the cheeks the fire charred,
the breasts burned brittle, black,
the smoked thighs that are roasted hard
and taste like a chimney stack!

The bride's sweet body's all ablaze.
Her flesh is like mashed fruit.
The raiment with the broiling rays,
clothes that electrocute!

Her rage and fury almost spent, MEDEA *thinks once more of the occasions in her* SONS' *lives that will never happen because they will be soon murdered by their mother.*

MEDEA.
> I'll never make your marriage beds
> or place the garlands on your heads
> or walk behind you with my torch ablaze.
>
> I'll never know your wedding days!
> I'll never know your wedding days!
>
> I'll never make your marriage beds
> or place the garlands on your heads
> or walk behind you with my torch ablaze . . .
>
> I'll never know your wedding days!
> I'll never know your wedding days . . .
>
> I'll never make your marriage beds
> or place the garlands on your heads
> or walk behind you with my torch ablaze . . .
>
> I'll never know your wedding days!
> I'll never know your wedding days . . .

MEDEA *keeps repeating this and fades out. It is like a thought that will not leave the mind. We hear also in the distance the Wedding Hymn. As* MEDEA *fades obsessively away, we again focus on the* SONS OF MEDEA *with the* NURSE *walking slowly and solemnly towards* CREUSA *seated in the far distance on her throne, exactly as in the Act One tableau.*

The words of MEDEA *gloating over what is to happen to* CREUSA *have already started something in the music which is sinister and foreboding, like a "black" version of the Wedding Hymn thus fulfilling* MEDEA's *threat to turn the hymn into a dirge, the wedding torch into a funeral brand.*

Enter HERCULES *drunk, looking for the wedding. He stops the* NURSE *and the* SONS OF MEDEA *to ask them where the wedding is. He is totally unaware who they are, since after being marooned on the island when looking for* HYLAS *he has been doing more labours and he has only heard the story of* MEDEA *and* JASON *and the Golden Fleece by hearsay. The* SONS OF MEDEA *are amused and giggle at this drunken giant, but their amusement alternates with fear at his size and occasional dangerous rage. The* NURSE *knows that their errand is urgent and wants to get away from the importunate stranger looking*

for the wedding of an old comrade who deserted him. HERCULES
*becomes maudlin drunk every time he has occasion to remember his
dead friend* HYLAS.

HERCULES *carries an enormous club and a monstrous jar of wine.*

He staggers towards the SONS OF MEDEA *and the* NURSE. *The* SONS OF
MEDEA *huddle, scared of* HERCULES, *into the skirts of* NURSE.

HERCULES.
> Here, don't huddle into your mother's skirt!
> Come out of there, now, you won't get hurt.

SONS OF MEDEA.
> O sir you scare us with that big club.

HERCULES.
> This big club of mine's all stained
> with many a monster's blood.
> There's many a beast I've brained
> with this knotted lump of wood.
> Many's the monster savage and wild,
> the fiercest that could be found
> whose blood I've spattered on the ground,
> but I'd never harm a child . . .
>
> I have two boys very like you!

NURSE. (*Trying to steer Sons towards their uncompleted errand.*)
> The boys have an errand that they must do!

HERCULES. (*To Sons of Medea.*)
> Running errands for your mother then?
> That's not the way you'll grow up to be men!

SONS OF MEDEA.
> O sir, you frighten us with your size!

HERCULES. (*Appalled at their lack of manliness.*)
> Take that scared look out of your eyes!
>
> Cut yourself loose from the apron strings,
> start learning to do really manly things
> like wielding a sword or spear,
> running to battle in metal gear
> and getting away from your mother here.
>
> Come with me!
> learn to make a good fist,

break a man's neck with a twist of the wrist,
throw a man on his back with a flip of the hip,
throttle a serpent with an iron grip.
Learn to shatter the teeth from a monster's jaw,
learn to keep good time with an oar
and get to know what a *man*'s muscles are for . . .

speaking of muscles, have a feel of these
the enormous muscles of Hercules!

Learn to spear a bull right between the eyes
and after six months of my training
you'll soon be up to braining
monsters twice your size . . .

Here have a feel of these iron thighs!

SONS OF MEDEA *shrink from the drunken giant.*

HERCULES.
And take that scared look out of your eyes!

I was the strongest Argonaut
and if Jason, out of petty jealousy,
hadn't left me behind and put to sea
he wouldn't in Cochis have had to resort
to the help of that witch to win
the Golden Fleece from the Dragoness.
I would have done the Dragoness in!
I would have ground it beneath my heel.
All that was needed was these muscles – feel!

The SONS OF MEDEA *back away from the drunken* HERCULES *flexing his muscles.*

I would have tamed the fire-breathing bulls,
and those men that sprang from the Colchian ground
I'd take this club here and bash in their skulls . . .

HERCULES *suddenly breaks off, with a memory of why he wasn't, in fact, at Colchis doing all the things he is boasting of. He remembers* HYLAS *and becomes maudlin. He lurches from one mood to another in a dangerous way.*

HERCULES.
But Hylas, poor Hylas was drowned!
Hylas!   Hylas!   Hylas!

HERCULES *pauses threateningly to catch the mocking echo -ass -ass -ass -ass that he heard on the island when searching for Hylas and abandoned by the* ARGONAUTS. *But the mocking echo doesn't come. In the pause of silence, though, we begin to hear again both the Wedding Hymn and the sinister "black" version of the hymn.*

HERCULES. (*As if challenging the echo to mock him back.*)
　　Hylas!　Hylas!　Hylas!

He listens for the echo. It doesn't come. He, nevertheless, is nervous enough to issue a threatening warning to the SONS OF MEDEA *who again look timid and frightened.*

HERCULES.
　　What was that that I just heard.
　　Did someody say a dirty word?

HERCULES *then switches to the muscular braggart again.*

　　I was the Argonaut for muscle and brawn.

　　(*To Sons.*)
　　All this happened before you were born!
　　but they left me abandoned, alone and forlorn,
　　howling for my Hylas who was never found.
　　Hylas!

He listens for the echo. It doesn't come. But we hear after the pause the Wedding Hymn and the sinister "black" version of it directed towards the fate of CREUSA. HERCULES *is holding the proceedings!* HERCULES *leans forward to confide in the* SONS *and excludes the* NURSE *from the confidence.*

HERCULES.
　　There are sisters of the Mother Hag,
　　women who live in water who drag
　　young men down into their wet hole.
　　I was left with an emptiness in my soul
　　when my poor Hylas was drowned.
　　Hylas!

He listens threateningly for the echo. It doesn't come.
In the pause of silence we hear the Wedding Hymn and the sinister "black" version of it.

HERCULES *once more is transformed from the maudlin drunk to the drunken braggart.*

HERCULES.
> I would have tamed the fire-breathing bulls
> and the soldiers who sprang from the Colchian ground
> I'd take this club here and bash in their skulls . . .
>
> And instead of relying on Hercules
> and the mighty strength of my mighty arms . . .

HERCULES *flexes his muscles.*

> Here, boys, have a feel of these!

SONS OF MEDEA *back away.*

HERCULES.
> And instead of relying on Hercules
> Jason resorted to a witch's charms.
> He left the strongest Argonaut
> and then later in Colchis had to resort
> to some barbarian witch's black magic charms
>
> I've come to forgive,
> live and let live.
>
> (*Hears the Wedding Hymn in the distance.*)
> Is that the Wedding Hymn that I hear?
> Is that the procession drawing near?
> I'm going to stand behind him and cheer!
>
> If Jason's witch is dead
> and he's bringing a new wife to his bed
> that's fine.
> No business of mine.
> I've come to see the bastard wed
> and I've brought my own bottle of wine . . .

He swings the enormous wine-jar towards the SONS.

> Time to move on from mother's milk to wine
> (Here whydontya have a little swig of mine?)
>
> Time to learn to drink a little wine,
> wine from Chios, Thasos and Cos,
> wine with the flavour of Mt Pelion's pine
> (Here whydontya have a little swig of mine!)
> wine from Chios, Thasos and Cos
> but not wine from Lemnos where a woman's boss.
> An unnatural island peopled only with SHES.

I'd sooner quaff gallons of the bitterest lees
than the wine of that vile isle!

You need to be men not timid little mites,
you need to grow up to cope with the frights
of sudden ambush and skirmish at night
and keep a cool head in the fight . . .

Time to move on from mother's milk to wine.
(Here whydontya have a little swig of mine?)

Time to cut through the apron strings,
time to cut the umbilical cord,
time to make a start on manly things
like wielding a spear or a sword!

Time to move on from mother's milk to wine!
(Here whydontya have a little swig of mine?)

HERCULES *brandishes the giant wine-jar.*

I brought this jar of Chian for this special day
and just had a little taste of it on the way!
Only wanted a little bit to celebrate
Jason getting matched to his new little mate.
What did he do with the old one, the barbarian bitch?
or did he just murder the foreign witch?

He takes the wine-jar.

Watch me lift it.

He lifts it to his lips. It's empty. He shakes it, puzzled.

HERCULES.
The sun's made all the wine evaporate!
(*To Sons.*)
Now you try!

SONS OF MEDEA *try to lift it, and can't even budge it, either singly, in
turn, or both hoisting together.*

HERCULES.
Shall I throw it up into the sky?
and let it fall down with a mighty crash.
Let's throw it up and let it smash.

*He is about to do just that, when he notices the casket for the first
time.*

HERCULES. (*Confidentially again to Sons.*)
>Whatya got in your little casket, then?
>There shouldn't be secrets between us *men*!

NURSE. (*Anxious.*)
>The boys have an errand that they must do.
>They don't have time to play the fool with you.

HERCULES. (*Offended.*)
>But I have two boys of my own like them!

He lifts the lid of the casket a little.

>Here, what a fine robe and gold diadem

HERCULES *is about to open the casket when he hears, somewhat louder, the Wedding Hymn and the sinister "black" version, the "black" version hovering predominantly as* HERCULES *investigates the casket.* HERCULES *cocks his ear.*

HERCULES.
>Is that the Wedding Hymn I can hear?
>Is that the procession drawing near?

He forgets about the casket.

>I'm going to stand behind him and cheer!

>Maybe it's not too late
>to give Jason some advice:
>Anyone who's tried the married state
>is a fool to try it twice!

>But if Jason's witch is dead
>and he's bringing a new wife to his bed
>that's fine!
>No business of mine!
>I've come to see the bastard wed
>but I seem to have run out of wine . . .

Starts to stagger off. We begin to hear MEDEA *again off-stage.*

HERCULES.
>(*Chuntering to himself as he staggers off to the Wedding.*)
>Don't have Hylas to fetch water from springs,
>to water my wine, and do all those things,
>so now I drink it neat, al*as*!

He turns round suddenly to catch the mocking echo then lurches off.

As HERCULES *lurches off the voice of* MEDEA *comes back into focus exactly at the place we last left her, then she enters. The* SONS OF MEDEA *and the* NURSE *resume their interrupted journey towards the throne where* CREUSA *is seated as if waiting. We see them present the casket in dumbshow and begin to return.*

MEDEA.

     I'll never make your marriage beds
     or place the garlands on your heads
     or walk behind you with my torch ablaze . . .

     I'll never know your wedding days.
     I'll never know your wedding days . . .

     I'll never know your wedding days.
     I'll never know your wedding days . . .

This reiterated regret of the mother MEDEA *generates in her imagination two* WEDDING PROCESSIONS *(which are made up of the* WEDDING PROCESSION *which we have seen and heard intermittently throughout the act). Each procession takes one of the* SONS OF MEDEA *accompanied by his "bride" who is a grown woman though the* SONS *remain their childish selves. The two brides are dressed in exactly the same robe and crown in which we saw* MEDEA *and which have now been given to* CREUSA *impregnated with a poisonous invisible fire. The two processions are accompanied by the members of the* WEDDING PROCESSION *begun at the beginning of the act. They bear the wedding torches and sing the Wedding Hymn. They make two solemn processions in different directions back to* MEDEA, *where they will "deliver" her* SONS *from the imagination back to reality.* CREUSA *meanwhile is sitting on the throne about to put on the robe and crown. Over her hovers the sinister "black" version of the Wedding Hymn.*

As the processions proceed towards the place where MEDEA *is racked by the thoughts of her* SONS *never growing up because she is to kill them,* BUTES, *the bee-man Argonaut, enters also looking for the wedding. As this scene takes place in* MEDEA's *imagination* BUTES *could have the appearance of a drowned man, the ghost of* BUTES, *who leaped overboard to swim towards the* SIRENS *(which we shall later witness).* BUTES *carries two bee-hives which he presents, one each, to the* SONS OF MEDEA.

BUTES.

     I liked your mother. I give you these,
     a hive each of my best honey bees.

May all your days from now distil
as much sweetness as these bees will.
May both your hearts, yours and your wives'
cull a blessed sweetness from your lives.

BUTES *exits (or as a ghost simply vanishes)*.

The processions continue towards MEDEA, *each of the* SONS *bearing a bee-hive. The processions "deliver" back the* SONS OF MEDEA *from "imagination" to "reality".* MEDEA, *now grimly resolute, leads her* SONS *off to their deaths, into the doors of a palace or, at least, off-stage. As they leave we see the knife in* MEDEA'*s hand. It is as if the bees in the hives the* SONS *carry are hugely amplified in a foreboding buzz. At the moment when we expect the knife blows to fall there comes from* CREUSA *an unearthly, shrill electrifying cry.* CREUSA *is now wearing the crown and robe, the gifts of* MEDEA, *and the invisible fire with which they are impregnated is burning her alive. The* WOMEN ATTENDANTS *turn into* FURIES, *their wedding torches, as* MEDEA *promised, now funeral brands which they apply to the head and body of* CREUSA *as she writhes in agony and attempts to take off the lethal garments.*

FURIES.
 Creusa's body
 like a candle dripping wax
 Creusa's body
 as the venomous fire attacks
 Creusa's body
 as the tongues of fire scorch
 Creusa's body
 is one huge wedding torch
 Creusa's body
 The young girl fine in bridal lace
 Creusa's body
 dressed in flames that eat her face
 Creusa's body
 her molten heart burst through each pore
 Creusa's body
 a million bees of fire gnaw

Creusa's body
a fiery hive
where death's swarms eat her alive
Creusa's body.

FURY 1.   Torment is the girl's trousseau
that grips her flesh and won't let go.

FURY 2.   Flesh so heated eyes can't gaze
at the glowing girl ablaze!

FURY 3.   Flesh incandescent, and no eyes
dare watch the lit limbs liquidise!

FURY 4.   Not a lover's tongue but fire's
gluts its shameless hot desires.

FURY 5.   It's witch Medea's art that flays
flesh off her bones in one fierce blaze!

FURY 6.   And fair Creusa's crown of pain's
a skull that bubbles with boiled brains!

CREUSA, *again as in Act One, runs back and forth, and finally leaps into the Pit, now the well of Corinth, in the hope it will cool her anguished body. There is a great hiss and a cloud of steam. The stage is empty. Everyone has fled in terror. A great cloud of steam comes from the Pit. Once more we hear the music of the emerging triple* GODDESS. *But she doesn't rise. Pause. Again we hear the music of the triple* GODDESS. *But she doesn't rise. Pause. Again we hear the music of the triple* GODDESS *emerging from the Pit. But she doesn't rise. Pause.*

Empty stage. Smoke and steam subside.

Then we hear what seems to be the sound of millions of bees.

The SONS OF MEDEA *burst in from where they had been killed. We hear* MEDEA *repeating 'I would have born you 7 times 2'. Another pair of* SONS OF MEDEA *enter, then another, 1/2/3/4/5/6/7. They are being pursued by* CORINTHIAN MEN *who are going to stone them to death.*

The CHORUS *of* CORINTHIAN MEN *form a threatening circle round the* FOURTEEN SONS OF MEDEA, *a circle which recalls the circle of hostile male figures that we saw during the overture. The* CHORUS *"stone"*

the SONS OF MEDEA *with their voices.* TWO MEN *restrain* MEDEA, *who
helpless and pinioned, has to watch her sons die one by one.
She sings.*

MEDEA.

> I'll never make your marriage beds
> or place the garlands on your heads
> or walk behind you with my torch ablaze.
>
> I'll never know your wedding days!
> I'll never know your wedding days!
>
> I helped your father in his fight
> and drugged the Dragoness
> but saving you's beyond my might.
> Now, now I am powerless.
>
> I'll never make your marriage beds
> or place the garlands on your heads
> or walk behind you with my torch ablaze.
>
> I'll never know your wedding days!
> I'll never know your wedding days!

As she sings the CHORUS OF CORINTHIAN MEN *stone her* SONS *who cry
out to their mother for help. Their cry of 'MOTHER' is an ever-
diminishing 'tutti', as they each in turn are killed. Their death and
their cries bring on stage the* DOWNSTAGE WOMAN *and the*
DOWNSTAGE MAN, *seemingly for a moment united in the face of the
distress and doom of the children before them.*

FOURTEEN SONS OF MEDEA.

1. *MOTHER, MOTHER, MOTHER* on you we call
2. *MOTHER*, they're killing, killing us all.

DSW.   Is there nothing that we can do?
DSM.   I can't see that there is, can you?

3. *MOTHER*, why do you leave us alone?
4. *MOTHER*, why did you leave us for these men to stone?

DSW.   These are former times not ours.
DSM.   And past history's beyond our powers.

5. *MOTHER*, your children don't want to die.
6. *MOTHER*, you've gone away, why, why, why?

DSW.   **But it happens now to others.**
DSM.   **Yes, kids still get killed by their mothers.**

DSW. No, can't you see, it's MEN like you!
DSM. But this part of the play's not true.

7. *MOTHER,* so caring, so gentle, so kind.
8. *MOTHER,* why did they make you leave us behind?

DSM. This isn't true. It was the mother.
DSW. That's the male version. Now watch the other.
DSM. Why all these children? There were only two.
DSW. Only according to male pigs like you.
DSM. No, according to the stories, the *proper* ones.
DSW. NO, the true story is there were fourteen sons.

9. *MOTHER,* your children don't want to die.
10. *MOTHER,* you've gone away, why, why, why.

DSM. Euripides says there were only two
       and that it was the mother who slew.
DSW. Another male plot to demean
       woman's fertility. Fourteen! Fourteen!

       Euripides blackened her in his play
       These MEN bribed him. He was in their pay.

11. *MOTHER,* they're killing us what can we do?
12. *MOTHER,* our only hope is in you.

DSM. And we have to watch all fourteen die?
DSW. Truth needs repeating, fool, that's why.

13 & 14 (*Together.*)   *MOTHER, MOTHER,* on you we cry.
14. (*Alone.*)   *MOTHER,* I'm alone, I'm the last. I don't want to die.

Now all the FOURTEEN SONS OF MEDEA *lie in a heap, dead.*

DSW. Euripides blackened the woman in his play
       because these murderers bribed him. He was in their pay.

The CHORUS OF WOMEN *enter and "bury" the* SONS OF MEDEA *in the Pit. The sound of the* GODDESS *is heard from the Pit and the* CHORUS *with the texts as set out on page 373.*

The DOWNSTAGE WOMAN *begins to lecture the* DOWNSTAGE MAN *and the audience, as the* CHORUS *becomes increasingly more complex.*

DOWNSTAGE WOMAN [+ CHORUS OF WOMEN/GODDESS]
       As part of their hostile campaign
       against the old Earth Mother's reign
       men degrade her

in whatever form she takes
Goddess brandishing her snakes,
Helen, Leda . . .

Men's hatred had to undermine
MEDEA's status as divine
and to reduce her
to a half-crazed children-slayer
making a monster of MEDEA
like the Medusa.

The point of this projected role
is that it's the opposite pole
of Mother Earth,
and what was once the source of life
's degraded to a murderous wife
destroying birth.

By shedding her own children's blood
MEDEA negates all motherhood –
grist to the mill
of menfolk who attempt to drag
the All-Giving Goddess down to Hag
and source of ill.

That monstrous patriarchal fib
of Eve being made from Adam's rib
is just another
obviously childish sign
that poor men want to undermine
the primordial Mother.

Evil's all a woman's fault
if we believe the male assault
on poor Pandora
but when the horn of plenty poured
with all the good with which Earth's stored
she was the pourer.

Embattled men had to reply
with gods, male gods from the sky
and not the earth.
They longed to find another
more, say, 'male' way than the Mother
to give them birth,

a way where men could reproduce
like their patron Father Zeus
who bore Athena
bloodlessly, full-grown instead
of from his belly from his head
all so much cleaner!

They could dispense with Motherhood
and 9 month pregnancies and blood
and breast feeding.
Euripides makes Jason say
if only men could find a way
of wombless breeding,

and omit that childish phase
those far too formative first days
of nipple sucking
and, in fact, dispense with all desires,
find reproduction that requires
no fucking!

As the sex-war's still being fought
which sex does a myth support
you should be asking.
What male propaganda lurks
behind most operatic works
that music's masking?

During this diatribe, responding to the invocation from the CHORUS
OF WOMEN *the triple* GODDESS 3/1 *rises from the Pit now recognisably
consisting of* VIRGIN [CREUSA/HYPSYPILE], MOTHER [MEDEA] *and*
CRONE [NURSE/QUEEN ARETE].

DOWNSTAGE WOMAN
This is the Earth Mother, serve her,
your Destroyer, your Preserver,
3 in 1.
No man who ever lived on earth
ever bypassed human birth;
each is her son.

THE GODDESS! If you men can't learn
to live with women SHE'll return
while you are sleeping
and in the darkness of the night
show all her old EARTH MOTHER might
and leave you weeping.

Perpetual power no little boy
grown big and ballsy can destroy
for all his trying.
He's the MOTHER's all life long.
It's to HER all men belong,
living, loving, dying.

Once the woman had been hurt
the GODDESS had to reassert
her former power,
the power to deal out death and doom
the GODDESS in whose Earth womb
all men cower.

When she feels threatened she can win
as archetypal feminine
that fills men's dreams.
No longer the deserted wife
the GODDESS makes men beg for life
deaf to their screams.

GODDESS 3/1.
The Argo's "manly" ghosts I summon
to suffer at the hands of woman.

Enter HERCULES *at first in traditional garb of lion-skin carrying his club. The* CHORUS OF WOMEN *headed in procession by two sons (they are the same children we saw as the* TWO SONS OF MEDEA*) bring a set of women's clothes which* HERCULES *is made to put on. One of the* WOMEN *takes away his club and threatens the "female"* HERCULES *with his own weapon.*

HERCULES. (*Recognising the Goddess.*)
All the sundry monsters that I slew,
the bloody-jawed hounds and the beasts with scales,
the terrible dragons with fire in their tails,
the vicious creatures with torches for eyes,
all, ALL, were the MOTHER in disguise.
All the monsters that I ever slew
were only the great EARTH MOTHER, you!
The one in the end I couldn't subdue.
If I lopped off its head, it grew another.
I killed all the monsters, but can't kill the MOTHER!

They begin to taunt HERCULES.

GODDESS 3/1 [+ CHORUS & DOWNSTAGE WOMAN]
    First HERCULES, arch-macho, what
    is his appointed lot?

    He who fought us as the Dragoness
    has first to don a woman's dress.

    Instead of killing those branded 'bitches'
    he has to learn his sewing stitches.

    Instead of leading Argo's rowing
    he sits among the slave-girls, sewing.

    Not male comrades on the rowing benches
    but sewing with the serving wenches.

    He who scorned all female rule
    forced by a Queen to wind a spool.

    She lords it in his lion-skin
    while he sits in her skirts to spin.

    And palace sentries as they pass
    goose the spinning girl's big ass.

CHORUS OF WOMEN. (Mocking.)
    ASS!   ASS!   ASS!   ASS!   ASS!   ASS!

GODDESS [+ CHORUS & DOWNSTAGE WOMAN]
    And when they reach to feel *her* breast
    recoil from *his* rough hairy chest!

    A lifetime's famous labours, wars
    finishing with female chores,
    peeling carrots, mopping floors!

    Not cutting off the Hydra's head
    but struggling with sewing thread.

    Here is Hercules the Strong
    draped in Omphale's sarong.

    Arch-enemy of Hag and Bitch
    learning how to sew and stitch.

    Arch-enemy of Bitch and Hag
    ends up doing chores in drag.

    Arch-enemy of 'cunt' and 'cow'
    tell us who's the DRAG-ON now!

The CHORUS OF WOMEN, *who have been surrounding* HERCULES, *as if they were the other slave-girls of Queen Omphale, mock him and pick up the text of the* GODDESS *through repetition and vocal support, clearly differentiated into soprano, mezzo and contralto. Suddenly things become darker, the* CHORUS *turn again into* FURIES *and the two* SONS OF HERCULES [= TWO SONS OF MEDEA] *are left to face their father, maddened and humiliated by the taunts of the* GODDESS *and* CHORUS OF WOMEN.

The FURIES *pursue* HERCULES *who pursues his terrified* SONS *with the famous club (recognisable also as a piece of the Argo) left on the ground when the slave-girls turned into* FURIES.

GODDESS 3/1.
>   Then I drive him off his head
>   and he clubs his two sons dead.

HERCULES, *a little slowed down by the dress he is wearing, pursues his* SONS *along the same track of the stage taken by* MEDEA *when she escorted her sons off to be killed. The* SONS OF HERCULES *try to plead and reason with their crazed father.*

SONS OF HERCULES.
>   1. FATHER, your children don't want to die.
>   2. FATHER, I don't like that look in your eye.
>   1+2. FATHER, you're killing us! Why? Why? Why?
>
>   FATHER you promised to teach us how
>
>   1. to make a good fist
>   2.   to make a good fist.
>   1+2. to break a man's neck with a twist of the wrist.
>   1. to throw a man on his back with flip of the hip.
>   2. throttle a serpent with an iron grip.
>   1. shatter the teeth from a monster's jaw
>   2. keep good time with an oar, with an oar
>   like the Argonauts did in days of yore . . .
>   1+2. get to know what a *man*'s muscles are for.
>
>   Are a man's muscles for this, FATHER, this
>   killing the sons you once loved to kiss.

HERCULES *moves in for the kill, uncomprehending, mad.*

SONS OF HERCULES.
>   We're not serpents. We're your sons!
>   We're not monsters. We're your little ones!

HERCULES *begins to club them to death.*

SONS OF HERCULES. (*By this point, off-stage.*)
    1. FATHER, look who you're killing, it's your son, me!
    2. FATHER, look who you're killing, can't you see?

DOWNSTAGE WOMAN.
    He killed his children! I don't hear you
    give even a *sotto voce* boo.
    He killed his children. So where
    is Hercules's electric chair?
    A children slayer? Or is Medea
    the one child-murderer you fear.
    He killed his children. So where
    is Hercules's electric chair?

    In any case the macho brute
    gets clothes that will electrocute
    from his dear wife Deianeira
    clothes that will cremate the wearer . . .

Re-enter HERCULES *with bloody club and daubed dress. In the centre of the stage is a casket, identical to the one in which the* SONS OF MEDEA *took the poisoned wedding gown from* MEDEA *to* CREUSA. *He opens it and finds a robe, sent to him by his wife. The robe is made from the identical material to the wedding gown of* MEDEA, *which later, after magic impregnation with poison, became the death robe of* CREUSA. HERCULES *changes his blood-stained women's clothes for man's clothes again. He feels "clean", "himself". His feeling of relief is only momentary, however.* HERCULES *begins to burn in exactly the same way that* CREUSA *did. He goes through identical movements (dances?) of pain, mimicking as closely as possible the tormented motion of the scorched* CREUSA. *This could extend even to singing the same notes, in a shrill agonised falsetto.*

FURIES *repeat their gloating over* CREUSA *and applying their flaming torches to the body of* HERCULES.

FURIES.
    Hercules's body

    like a candle dripping wax

    Hercules's body

    as the venomous fire attacks

    Hercules's body

his molten heart bursts through each pore

Hercules's body

as the million bees of fire gnaw

Hercules's body

a fiery hive
where death's swarms eat him alive

Hercules's body

Supposing you jumped into a vat
of spitting, chicken-frying fat,
into its depths you took a dive
and the horror is you're still alive,
or into a pool of molten steel
and still be conscious and still feel –
that's how Hercules's body felt
as flesh and bones began to melt.

HERCULES.
I burn, and feel my flesh-smoke rise
away from women to the skies
which gods not goddesses control
and let the FATHER have my soul.

Death I've never feared at all.
What I feared most was burial,
back in that dark place I hate
from which all Mankind emanate.

At last in death I shall be free
of enfolding Femininity!

GODDESS 3/1 [+ CHORUS].
O Hercules, a little rain
will make your smoke the Earth's again.
O Hercules, the strongest man
ends up where he first began.
You started and you'll end up in
some form of the Feminine.
The flesh and bones that you thought free
of the MOTHER, free of me
will finally come back to earth
back to the place you had your birth.
As dust, as motes, as smoky specks
you'll still be subject to our sex.

HERCULES.
>Don't put my body into the ground.
>I want to be smoke in the sky.
>I don't want to be ashes to be left around
>for the MOTHER still to hold me by.

>Don't bury my body in the Earth's warm womb.
>I don't want to go back in there.
>Let a man that's a man get no earth-bound tomb
>but let me burn and rise into the air.

>I could become smoke and in that guise
>drift free of the female to the male skies
>and maybe the ashes that once were me
>are free of the MOTHER if flung in the sea.

>I'm finished with Earth. I don't want to stay.
>She can't hold me forever if I burn.
>I want to be smoke and fly far far away
>from the clutch of the MOTHER and never return.

GODDESS 3/1 [+ CHORUS].
>O Hercules, a little rain
>will make your smoke the Earth's again.
>O Hercules, the strongest man
>ends up where he first began.
>You started and you'll end up in
>some form of the Feminine.
>The flesh and bones that you thought free
>of the MOTHER, free of me
>will have to come back to the Earth
>back to the place you had your birth.
>As dust, as motes, as smoky specks
>you'll still be subject to our sex.

HERCULES.
>I hope that when you women inhale the smoke
>from my funeral pyre, you'll choke! You'll choke!

>Stronger men will come along
>stronger than Hercules the Strong,
>Argo armadas, iron-clads
>to flush the hills of Oreads,
>defoliate the Dryads' den
>and give world power back to *men*!

That's where it always should belong
with the male sex, with the strong.
And not the smallest rabbit hole
left in the Earth Mother's control.
In every sex-war that will be fought
you'll find Hercules the Argonaut.

DOWNSTAGE WOMAN.
He's nearly done, the evening roast
but listen to the buffoon boast!

GODDESS 3/1.
The MOTHER rules. The alternative
is very simple – NOT TO LIVE!

HERCULES *is dead and the* CHORUS *bury him in the Pit.*

The CHORUS OF WOMEN *then become* THE SIRENS. *Enter* BUTES *with a straggle of former* ARGONAUTS *who from the bits of bleached spar, the sticks they support themselves with, build a skeletal Argo.*

BUTES.
Since the day my loved one died
who was for fifty years my wife
I've been more than glad to feel my life
ebbing on that same black tide.

BUTES *hears a complex of* GODDESS 3/1 *and* CHORUS OF WOMEN [SIRENS] *clearly stratified into soprano, mezzo, contralto, a complex that recalls the sound of the* DRAGON *from the Pit and the nymphs calling* HYLAS. *The text they sing is that set out on page 373. There should, however, be an alluring sweetness, a suggestion of bees, about the sound they make.*
The stratification of the female voice into three, soprano, mezzo, contralto, reminds BUTES *of his wife's voices at the three stages of her life, the virgin, the mother, the dying old woman, or as represented in the triple* GODDESS 3/1: VIRGIN, MOTHER, CRONE.

BUTES.
I hear the voices of my wife
as if she were alive,
all the voices of her life
hum from one hive,
and all I need to do is dive . . .

The ARGONAUTS *miming the rowing of the skeletal Argo restrain* BUTES, *as he makes to dive into the ocean and swim to the sound.*

BUTES.

> I hear the voices of my wife
> as if she were alive,
> all the voices of her life
> hum from one hive
> and all I need to do is dive . . .

> The voice of the virgin, the voice of the mother,
> the voice of the old one who died in my embrace.
> I hear all her voices one after the other.
> I see all her faces in the one face.

> The face of the virgin with such beautiful skin,
> the face of the mother with the look of care,
> the face of the old one sunken in
> and framed by the wisps of grey hair.

> I hear the voices of my wife
> as if she were alive.
> All the voices of her life
> hum from one hive . . .
> and all I need to do is dive . . .

GODDESS 3/1 & BUTES.

B. For fifty years I've come to your bed
G. For fifty years you've come to my bed

> with an anxious heart or a troubled head

B. and I've lain my weary head on your breast
G. and you've lain your weary head on my breast
B. and the feel of your body gave me rest
G. and the feel of my body gave you rest

> and for fifty years our love's stayed the same
> and the fire of our first love never lost its flame.

GODDESS [VIRGIN].

> Dream, dream of when you first took me to bed.
> Dream of when you took my maidenhead.

GODDESS [MOTHER].

> Dream, dream when I was brought to bed
> and I opened my legs and you saw your son's head.

GODDESS [CRONE].

> Dream, dream of when I lay in our bed
> in the last and longest sleep of the dead.

BUTES.
>I dream of how I came to your bed
>for fifty years and now you are dead.

GODDESS 3/1 & BUTES.
B.   For fifty years I've come to your bed
G.   For fifty years you've come to my bed

>with an anxious heart or a troubled head

B.   and I've lain my weary head on your breast
G.   and you've lain your weary head on my breast

B.   and the feel of your body gave me rest
G.   and the feel of my body gave you rest

BUTES.
>I hear the voices of my wife
>as if she were alive.
>All the voices of her life
>hum from one hive,
>and all I need to do is dive . . .

>Dive . . . dive . . . dive . . . If I leap
>into the swollen surging sea's
>frenzy of white froth and foam
>and swim to her, there I'll sleep
>on my wife's breasts, with all my bees
>among my pines and orange trees
>among my pines and orange trees
>with my dear, dead wife at *home*.

BUTES *leaps from the skeletal spars of the Argo into the "sea"*

GODDESS 3/1. (*Suddenly darker.*)
>See all that honied sweetness sour
>as Butes enters the baited bower.
>Of the Argonauts he alone
>served the Sirens, as their drone.
>But I tell you he won't survive
>too long in the Sirens' hive.

>The bee hum turns to Furies' hymn
>and they tear him limb from limb . . .

The CHORUS OF WOMEN [SIRENS] *turn into* FURIES. *The* ARGONAUT *stragglers flee the menacing sound of the* FURIES, *leaving one man among the Argo's planks and spars. We now see that this man is the broken* JASON.

GODDESS. (*To the cowering figure.*)
　　So much for some of your famous crew
　　and now all that's left is you.

JASON *regards the* GODDESS 3/1 *who towers above him on her revolving pedestal. He "disembarks" the skeletal Argo and stares up at the* GODDESS 3/1 *revolving round and round, and as she sings* JASON *recognises in the now all-powerful figure* MEDEA, CREUSA, NURSE/ARETE *etc, all the women he has had dealings with so far. The three voices reprise moments from earlier scenes to remind* JASON *who they are.*

GODDESS [CRONE].
　　Go at the dead of night and stand alone,
　　dig a pit, kill a lamb, and sacrifice
　　to the GODDESS, call her once, twice, thrice
　　call the VIRGIN, call the MOTHER, call the CRONE
　　and you'll see the Goddess start to rise
　　from the earth in her threeform guise,
　　call the VIRGIN, call the MOTHER, call the CRONE.

　　Go at the dead of night and stand alone.
　　Call the VIRGIN, call the MOTHER, call the CRONE.

JASON *sings ('I feel such dread . . .') as part of the following quartet:*

GODDESS [NURSE].
　　Go at the dead of night and stand alone,
　　dig a pit, kill a lamb, and sacrifice
　　to the Goddess, call her once, twice, thrice,
　　call the Virgin, call the Mother, call the Crone
　　and you'll see the Goddess begin to rise
　　from the earth in her threeform guise,
　　the Virgin, the Mother, the Crone.

　　Go at the dead of night and stand alone
　　call the Virgin, call the Mother, call the Crone.

GODDESS 3/1 [MEDEA].
　　I'll turn their wedding hymn to a dirge.
　　I'll smother their torches in the smoke of death
　　and change their joy-chants to a dismal drone.

GODDESS 3/1 [CREUSA].
　　I was the virgin. You forced the mother
　　to make fire eat my flesh and bone.

JASON. (*Quartet.*)
    I feel such dread, such fright. I stand alone.
    there's the pit – I, I am the sacrifice
    to the Goddess. Call her once, twice, thrice,
    call the Virgin, call the Mother, call the Crone
    and I see the Goddess before my eyes
    grown from human to Goddess size,
    and with dreadful vengeance in her eyes,
    the Virgin, the Mother, the Crone.

    Now at the dead of night I stand alone
    before the Virgin, Mother, Crone,
    before three women I have known.

    The one I'm dreading 's not the virgin
    but the mother who scorched my Creusa to death
    and made fire eat her flesh and bone

    (*Appealing.*)
    Virgin!   Mother!   Crone
    Creusa!   Medea!
    Virgin!   Mother!   Crone!

JASON (*To the revolving Goddess.*)
    O love, my love before
    the last torch darkness at the door.

GODDESS 3/1.
    No more! No more! No more!
    The last torch darkens at the door.

We see the FURIES *with their torches approaching.*

GODDESS 3/1 [MEDEA]. (*With support from Goddess 2/3.*)
    The glow from our flesh on the Fleece was so strong
    It was so strong and bright the glow . . .

The Pit glows with a golden light as it did when JASON *went to take
the Fleece from the* DRAGONESS. *We hear again the complex "snake"
chorus of the* DRAGONESS.

    You gazed on me so lovingly and long
    that I thought you would be blinded . . .

JASON.
    I don't want to be reminded!
    I don't want to be reminded!
    I don't want to be reminded!

GODDESS.
    1. All *we* want is that you go!
    2. All *we* want is that you go!
    3. All we want is that you go!

    and go into the pit that lies beneath
    where the Dragoness devours
    and the rending teeth, the rending teeth,
    the rending teeth will be ours.

JASON.
    You're a murderess!

GODDESS 3/1.   No, I GIVE LIFE.

JASON.
    You're a murderess!

GODDESS 3/1.   No, I WAS YOUR WIFE.

    Medea's a murderess in the history
    of *men* who plotted against the great SHE
    and that's the version that's now most rife.
    The truth's much older: I GIVE LIFE
    and receive it back when life's done
    as yours soon will be . . .
                      Husband!
                        Son!

DOWNSTAGE WOMAN.
    Clear her name from all the smears
    heaped on her 2000 years,
    on poor Medea.
    Now time at last has to reverse
    the old male-concocted curse
    of infant-slayer.

    Know that life's primeval source
    when life has run its destined course
    has to refill
    itself so that it can
    renew life in some other man—
    that's not to kill.

    Like that wreck you're standing under
    once the ARGO, a world wonder
    look at it now,
    a skeleton of proud male boast,
    a pathetic, puny ghost
    with wilting prow.

We claim back Pelion's trees
that helped you once to cross the seas
and now's this wreck.
We make that prick, the ARGO's prow
wilt and fall on your head *now*
and break your neck!

The prow of the Argo falls on to the head of JASON *and the music here should remind us of the electrocution music for* CREUSA [p. 367] *as* JASON's *life and sensations are shattered apart by the blow.* JASON *summons up the last of his strength and hauls on the prow which we once saw as the lever for the electric chair. The revolving* GODDESS 3/1 *we now see are all 3 strapped to electric chairs which are gilded like thrones. The dying* JASON *pulls the lever, the "electrocution" music rises to a crescendo, and the 3 strapped* GODDESS *figures die in their gilded chairs. The electrocution "caps" are also of gold and seem like upturned versions of the bowl by which* MEDEA *poisoned the wedding gown for* CREUSA.

Enter the CHORUS OF WOMEN, *stripped of any mythological association, and members of an opera chorus dressed for going home after work, appropriately attired according to the season when the piece is played. Their own clothes, no stage make-up. They enter in ones and twos. They are singing a rich text from the Greek of Euripides. A group of them pick up the body of* JASON *and put it into the Pit and then the pedestal with the dead* GODDESS *figures descends on top and closes the hole.*
The CHORUS OF WOMEN *face the audience and sing, with the three ranges, soprano, mezzo, contralto, well stratified.*

CHORUS OF WOMEN.

ἄνω ποταμῶν ἱερῶν χωροῦσι παγαί,
καὶ δίκα καὶ πάντα πάλιν στρέφεται.
ἀνδράσι μὲν δόλιαι βουλαί, θεῶν δ'
οὐκέτι πίστις ἄραρε·
τὰν δ' ἐμὰν εὔκλειαν ἔχειν βιοτὰν στρέψουσι φᾶμαι·
ἔρχεται τιμὰ γυναικείῳ γένει·
οὐκέτι δυσκέλαδος φάμα γυναῖκας ἕξει.

μοῦσαι δὲ παλαιγενέων λήξουσ' ἀοιδῶν
τὰν ἐμὰν ὑμνεῦσαι ἀπιστοσύναν.
οὐ γὰρ ἐν ἀμετέρᾳ γνώμᾳ λύρας
ὤπασε θέσπιν ἀοιδὰν
Φοῖβος, ἁγήτωρ μελέων· ἐπεὶ ἀντάχησ' ἂν ὕμνον
ἀρσένων γέννᾳ. μακρὸς δ' αἰὼν ἔχει
πολλὰ μὲν ἀμετέραν ἀνδρῶν τε μοῖραν εἰπεῖν.

[Euripides, *Medea* 410-430]

Retro ad fontes sacra feruntur
Flumina, ius et fas vertuntur
Hominum plena dolis consilia
Nec pacta fides diis sed certa est.
Audiet ex hoc muliebre bene
Genus: *accrescet gloria nobis.*
Non iam deinceps fama sinistra
Traducet foemineum sexum.
Ex hoc mutabit Musa modos
Vatum priscorum, qui canta
Muliebrem celebrant perfidiam:

    [George Buchanan (150621582), Latin translation of Euripides' *Medea*]

O Chant! que n'avons-nous, fileuses que nous sommes,
La lyre en main au lieu de la quenouille, pour
    Faire enfin, – c'est bien notre tour –
    Des poèmes contre les hommes.

    [Catulle Mendès (1841-1909), *Médée* (1898)]

*The chorus composed out of these trilingual texts becomes rich and
complex.*
Over and through the chant the DOWNSTAGE WOMAN *addresses the
audience.*

DOWNSTAGE WOMAN.
    Did you know that what you hear
    is from Euripides *Medea*
    of 431
    that's 431 BC!
    The breaking of male monopoly
    has just begun!

    These words from a women's chorus
    at least 2000 years before us
    weren't much heeded,
    but since what they sung then
    should still be listened to by men
    a translation's needed . . .

*She translates into a prose English version as the choral chant soars
behind her.*

DOWNSTAGE WOMAN.
    'The waters of the hallowed streams flow upwards to their
sources, and justice and everything is reversed. The counsels of
men are treacherous, and no longer is the faith of heaven firm.

But fame changes, so that my sex may have the glory. Honour cometh to the female race; no longer shall opprobrious fame oppress the women.' [Oxford, 1837]

We hear the Greek chant become dominant.

DOWNSTAGE WOMAN.
These words form a woman's chorus
at least 2000 years before us
weren't much heeded,
but since what they sung of then
should still be listened to by men
a translation's needed . . .

'The waters of the hallowed streams flow upwards to their sources, and justice and everything is reversed. The counsels of men are treacherous, and no longer is the faith of heaven firm. But fame changes, so that my sex may have the glory. Honour cometh to the female race; no longer shall opprobrious fame oppress the women.' [Oxford, 1837]

As the DOWNSTAGE WOMAN *translates the* CHORUS *reaches a growing climax, and during this finale, projections appear on a screen behind this* CHORUS *of modern New York women. They are the projections of newspaper headlines, front-page reports of mothers murdering their children. They should be culled from the papers of New York, the United States, and the world's capitals. They flash on one after the other in merciless succession but in no way diminishing the triumphal swell of the* CHORUS OF WOMEN:

1. MOM KILLS KIDS

2. MOM DROWNS KIDS IN BOILING WATER

3. MOTHER DROWNED SON FOR INSURANCE

4. MOM SLAYS 2 KIDS, SELF [*New York Post*, 4 September 1982]

There are many that follow alternating the papers of New York and London with those of France, Germany, Italy etc. But the final projection which freezes the music and the CHORUS *is:*

A FATHER CUTS HIS 4 KIDS' THROATS [*The Sun*, 19 October 1983].

The 'FATHER' of the headline has been crudely underlined in red.

THE END

BLOODAXE BOOKS

POETRY WITH AN EDGE

HART CRANE
Complete Poems

One of America's most important poets. Lowell called Crane 'the Shelley of my age' and 'the great poet of that generation'. This new *Complete Poems*, based on Brom Weber's definitive 1966 edition, has 22 additional poems. *Sunday Times* Paperback of the Year.

JENI COUZYN (editor)
The Bloodaxe Book of Contemporary Women Poets*

Large selections – with essays on their work – by eleven leading British poets: Sylvia Plath, Stevie Smith, Kathleen Raine, Fleur Adcock, Anne Stevenson, Elaine Feinstein, Elizabeth Jennings, Jenny Joseph, Denise Levertov, Ruth Fainlight and Jeni Couzyn. Illustrated with photographs of the writers.

FRANCES HOROVITZ
Collected Poems*

'She has perfect rhythm, great delicacy and a rather Chinese yet very locally British sense of landscape . . . her poetry does seem to me to approach greatness' – PETER LEVI

MIROSLAV HOLUB
On the Contrary and Other Poems*
Translated by Ewald Osers

Miroslav Holub is Czechoslovakia's most important poet, and also one of her leading scientists. He was first introduced to English readers with a Penguin *Selected Poems* in 1967. This book presents a decade of new work. 'One of the half dozen most important poets writing anywhere' – TED HUGHES. 'One of the sanest voices of our time' – A. ALVAREZ

PETER DIDSBURY
The Butchers of Hull

'Peter Didsbury is a clever and original poet . . . He can be simultaneously knowing and naive, wittily deflationary yet alive to every leap of the post-Romantic eye . . . a soaring, playful imagination . . . I suspect that he is the best new poet that the excellent Bloodaxe Books have yet published' – William Scammell, TIMES LITERARY SUPPLEMENT

KEN SMITH
The Poet Reclining*

Ken Smith is a major British poet. *The Poet Reclining* was internationally acclaimed: 'A poet of formidable range and strength' (CHICAGO SUN-TIMES) . . . 'With Ken Smith we expect excellence . . . his achievement is remarkable' (SCOTSMAN) . . . 'Formidable, brilliant' (CITY LIMITS) . . . 'Compulsive, impressive' (LITERARY REVIEW) . . . 'Brilliant, impressive' (TLS).

SEAN O'BRIEN
The Indoor Park
Sean O'Brien won a Somerset Maugham Award and a Poetry Book Society Recommendation for *The Indoor Park*, his first collection of poems. 'I would back O'Brien as one of our brightest poetic hopes for the Eighties' – Peter Porter, OBSERVER

DAVID CONSTANTINE
Watching for Dolphins
Constantine's second book won him the Alice Hunt Bartlett Prize in 1984, and with it the judges' praise for 'a generous, self-aware sensuality which he can express in a dazzling variety of tones on a wide range of themes'. 'His imagination moves gracefully within the classical precincts of the pure lyric . . . There are some very beautiful poems in this collection' – George Szirtes, LITERARY REVIEW

PAUL HYLAND
The Stubborn Forest
'Paul Hyland has never written much like anyone else' (THE CUT). 'His is a rugged, hewn, earthbound poetry' (ENCOUNTER). 'Hyland's work has the character of primitive sculpture . . . an impressive, memorable and powerful talent' (NORTH). 'This is work of power and subtlety . . . *The Stubborn Forest* is a strikingly impressive achievement' (ANGLO-WELSH REVIEW). Winner of the 1985 Alice Hunt Bartlett Prize.

MARIN SORESCU
Selected Poems ·
Translated by Michael Hamburger
'Sorescu is already being tipped as a future Nobel prizewinner. His poems, however, have crowned him with the only distinction that matters. If you don't read any other new book of poetry this year, read this one' – William Scammell, SUNDAY TIMES

JOHN CASSIDY
Night Cries
'John Cassidy has produced a strong, delicate volume of nature poetry in *Night Cries*, sensitively alert to the mysterious unpredictability of natural things, lucid and tenaciously detailed . . . A kind of *Lyrical Ballads* of our time' – Terry Eagleton, STAND. Poetry Book Society Recommendation.

*Asterisked titles are available in hardback and paperback. Other books are in paperback only.

For a complete list of Bloodaxe publications, write to:
**Bloodaxe Books Ltd, P.O. Box 1SN,
Newcastle upon Tyne NE99 1SN.**